BRITISH & AMERICAN
ARTILLERY
OF WORLD WAR TWO

BRITISH & AMERICAN
ARTILLERY
OF WORLD WAR TWO

Ian V. Hogg

GREENHILL BOOKS, LONDON   STACKPOLE BOOKS, PENNSYLVANIA

This edition of *British and American Artillery of World War Two* first published 2002 by Greenhill Books, Lionel Leventhal Limited, Park House, 1 Russell Gardens, London NW11 9NN www.greenhillbooks.com and Stackpole Books, 5067 Ritter Road, Mechanicsburg, PA 17055, USA

British Library Cataloguing in Publication Data
Hogg, Ian V. (Ian Vernon), 1926–
British and American artillery of World War II. – Rev. ed.
1. Artillery – History – 20th century
2. World War, 1939–1945 – Artillery operations
I. Title
623.4'1'09044

ISBN 1-85367-478-8

Library of Congress Cataloging-in-Publication Data available

Publishing History
British and American Artillery of World War Two was first published in 1978 (London, Arms and Armour). The original edition is here reproduced, complete and unabridged.

Printed and bound in Singapore by Kyodo Printing Company

Illustrations on preceding pages: Half-title page, *top:* The 75mm RCL in use on Okinawa. Note that the jets were formed as slots in the breech ring, and did not protrude as in the Burney guns (data page 242). *Middle:* The first pilot model of the 105mm HMC M37, which used the M24 Light Tank chassis and retained the characteristic pulpit (data page 61). *Bottom:* Wanstone No. 1 firing at night (data page 201). **Overleaf:** Training with 105mm howitzers. Note the 37mm sub-calibre attachment in the foreground; this was the old 37mm Trench Gun M1916 on a special mounting that could be clamped on top of the barrel. It was then fired by a linkage from the 105mm firing lanyard, thus allowing practice at reduced range – and expense (data page 59). **This page:** Loading numbers at work, on the 9.2in howitzer. The shell driving band is being scrubbed with a wire brush to remove grit (data page 143).

Contents

Preface

When I joined the 21st RA Training Regiment at Doniford Camp, Watchet, Somerset, many years ago, my first parade was 'The Introduction to the 25-pounder' where I learned, among many other things, that this was the 25pdr Mark 2 and that the shell was fitted with either the Fuze No. 117 or 119. With the curiosity which only recruits can muster, I asked what happened to the Mark I and the No. 118 fuze. Common decency forbids the reproduction of the answer in these pages. In the event, it was to be several years before I managed to find the answer to both these questions, but in the process, I discovered a lot about the history of some of the weapons I saw every day. In later years I was fortunate enough to be in posts where I was able to ask questions and get more polite answers and to talk to the men who had actually been involved in the development of artillery weapons and ammunition. Curiosity feeds on itself, and I was never short of questions, though some of them have never been answered to this day.

The result of all this is in the pages which follow. Many people have expressed the opinion to me that there was little Allied development work in the artillery field during the war; I trust that these pages will refute that idea. The information presented here is as accurate as can be found; with the exception of some of the more obscure American weapons, such as coast artillery and railway guns, there are few weapons in these pages which I have not personally fired or handled at one time or another. The data and

Below: Anti-tank shooting with the 25pdr. (See data page 25.)

history have been derived from weapon handbooks, official development histories, and similar authoritative sources. Opinions as to the effectiveness, utility or handiness of the weapons are my own, based on my own experience or upon the study of reports of their employment in action.

It would be idle to suggest that I have been able to travel to the ends of the earth to discover information and I must acknowledge my indebtedness to many friends and acquaintances who have helped me in finding out odd pieces of information to fill in gaps. I would particularly like to thank Commander D. P. Kirchner, USN for his kindness in making available to me the results of his researches into American railway artillery, and for much background information on the development of US coast mortars. Also Dick Hunnicutt for providing me with photographs of the 105mm Gun T8 and information on that and on the American work on follow-through projectiles; to Geoff Tillotson for the loan of various informative books and papers; to Peter Chamberlain for providing some photographs; to the late Major Bartelot and the staff of the Royal Artillery Institution Library for access to their records and photographs; and, of course, to Lance-Serjeant Lambourne for that first 'Introduction to the 25-pounder' which started it all off so long ago.

Ian V. Hogg

Note on the Presentation of Data

The sections dealing with the various weapons have been laid out in a uniform manner; the following notes will explain the various entries.

Because of the complexities of nomenclature, the sections are headed by what might be called the 'common' title of the weapon or, in the case of complex groups, the group. It will be noted that British and American terminology separates the ordnance from the carriage or mounting, each being developed independently of the other to some extent, so that the Mark or model number of the gun is not necessarily the same as the Mark or model number of the carriage. It is this which precludes using a specific nomenclature for the section heading. British equipment Marks used Roman numerals until 1944, when Arabic numerals were introduced; in order to avoid confusion, Arabic numerals have been used throughout, whether or not the original nomenclature was in Roman or Arabic notation. American Navy nomenclature used Roman numerals and these have been retained since they are a useful indication of the origin of a design.

The sections begin with a summary of the development of the weapon and a brief description, together with notes on any important features. This is followed by a tabular list of any variant models or Marks, those of the gun first and those of the carriage following. The development of any self-propelled equipment is also detailed.

The data table which follows is identified by the particular model to which the figures apply, if there is any likelihood of confusion with a variant model. The following items are then tabulated.

Weight of gun and breech mechanism. This is a useful guide to the improvements from model to model, a comparison of weights and powers often indicating the degree of advance.

Total length. This is the length from the muzzle face to the rear face of the breech ring; it includes the muzzle brake if fitted, and includes the length of the venturi jets in recoilless guns. Its principal use is as a yardstick for gauging other dimensions from photographs or drawings.

Length of Bore. This is given both in inches and in calibres, and is a useful guide to the relative power of guns of otherwise similar characteristics.

Rifling. Indicates the type of rifling, either uniform twist or increasing twist, and the pitch, expressed as one turn in so many calibres, e.g. 1/25, one turn in 25 calibres length.

Breech mechanism. Brief description of the type of mechanism employed and the system of firing.

Elevation. The minimum and maximum limits of the gun barrel.

Traverse. The amount which the barrel can be trained to one side or the other without the carriage being moved.

Recoil system. Classified as to type, whether the length of recoil is constant or variable with elevation, and the length of recoil movement.

Weight in action. The weight in march order (US) or in draught (UK) is generally greater due to the addition of limbers, covers, stores, etc.

The performance of the gun using the standard projectile is then given. Where guns have variable charges, the figures given indicate performance at the highest charge. Finally, the ammunition is detailed in brief.

Note that in the above explanation the word 'gun' is used to denote the operative weapon; it covers, in this context, 'howitzer' or 'mortar' as well.

Note: the provenance of each piece of artillery described in this book is indicated by a miniature national flag symbol, which appears beside the entry heading.

Artillery Development by the Western Allies

The development of artillery in Britain and America during the Second World War was, at first sight, somewhat pedestrian and lacking in the spectacular, particularly when compared to German development in the same period. Here were no 1,250-ton railway guns, no Peenemunde Arrow Shells, no solenoid anti-aircraft guns, no ramjet shells. The research and experimental departments of the West appear to have devoted their time to such worthy, but unromantic, projects as determining the best twist of rifling, improving fire-control systems, developing methods of reducing wear in gun barrels, and so forth. To be sure, some remarkable inventions did make an appearance – the proximity fuze, discarding sabot shot, hypervelocity guns, Kromuskits – but in comparison with the profusion of German development, the overall level is so small that the casual onlooker is inclined to wonder how Woolwich Arsenal, Aberdeen Proving Ground, Fort Halstead, Shoeburyness, Fort Sill and similar establishments were passing their time.

Only when the once-confidential records are examined does it become apparent that they were, in fact, extremely busy; not only in the fundamental research problems exampled above, but on more exotic projects, some of which will be described in the following pages. But relatively few of these projects made an appearance in the field, and this is because both Britain and the USA had produced modern and efficient designs just before the outbreak of war, designs which had sufficient development potential to last through the war without requiring major replacement. As a result, most of the wartime Allied development was aimed at the day when such replacement would be needed, and was geared to begin getting weapons into the hands of troops in 1946–47, by which time the war's demands would have exceeded the potential of the existing designs. So the end of the war in 1945 found

a number of projects in an advanced state of development, but not yet ready for service adoption. And when the war ended, the inevitable reaction was to throw half of them out and then get down to some slower and more detailed research on those which were left, so that they eventually appeared in service in the 1950s.

Another reason for the lack of flamboyance in Allied development was that by 1939, armament design in both countries was firmly tied to Government establishments and under the overall supervision of single agencies. In Germany, gunmaking was in the hands of commercial companies; although guided to some extent by military requirements and specifications, they were entirely free to develop weapons in whatever manner they chose, to produce competing designs for a given specification, and to develop weapons on their own initiative in the hope that they might find favour with the military and be adopted. In addition to this system – which, on the whole, worked well – there were so many political and party agencies anxious to be seen to be assisting the war effort that it was relatively easy for any inventor or entrepreneur to find an influential ear and set forth on a development programme without military knowledge or approval.

This was scarcely possible in the West. Design and manufacture of weapons was controlled by central authorities, by virtue of the fact that gunmaking and weapon development was largely in the hands of Government establishments. There were a few commercial firms in the artillery business, but by the 1930s, these were much reduced from their former greatness, a process brought about by the events of the First World War. Prior to 1914 the British Army, requiring artillery, drew up a broad specification and circulated it among the gunmakers – Vickers, the Elswick Ordnance Company, Beardmore, the Coventry Ordnance Works – and to the Royal

Gun Factory and the Royal Carriage Department, both part of the great complex of Woolwich Arsenal. After this, the Army sat back to await results. Eventually, prototypes would appear, comparative tests would be made, a design would be selected, and contracts would be let for its manufacture, spreading the work about so that all the factories were kept in business. In those leisurely days this was all very well, since it brought out the best in the designers and made for employment in industry. It also allowed the gunmakers to maintain expensive machinery and large skilled staffs. But under the pressure of war it became necessary to speed up the process, and this led to the rise of Government research establishments, design offices and ordnance engineering factories. After the war was over, much of this specialized plant was retained, and so the commercial gunmakers found less and less work coming their way. The shrunken budgets meant less work all round, while the pacifist campaigns against the 'Merchants of Death' led numbers of companies to diversify into other activities, amalgamate with other firms in other fields, or simply fold up. By 1939, commercial gunmaking, in the West, was a dying art, the only major company remaining being Vickers-Armstrongs of Britain. In 1915 it had been possible for a British purchasing commission to go to the USA and place contracts for the manufacture of artillery with companies which had some experience in that line of work; in 1940 this was no longer possible.

With the expertise and manufacturing capability largely in Government hands, it was thus easy to control the research and development programme so as to avoid overlapping and the exploration of blind alleys. As the war progressed, more and more research agencies sprang up, and some of them took to tinkering with artillery, but they were still under central direction, they were required to report progress periodically, and, since the supply of raw materials was controlled, they were in no position to take the bit between their teeth and start producing something without the proper authority. And if, in the course of all this, the central authority decided that what they were doing was nonsense, then it was quietly knocked on the head and interred. The only exception to this general course of events was where an agency managed to develop some small device using non-critical material and capable of being made in a non-specialized workshop; for example, some of the more exotic and nervous types of hand-grenade and mine developed in Britain in 1940–41

came from this type of source. But the prospect of manufacturing artillery as a private venture was almost impossible except for an authorized establishment who could possibly manage to do 'a bit on the side' and play with a pet design, provided that it did not interfere with anything more vital.

The overall picture of artillery development during the war years reflects the changing tactical demands of the war and the changing strategic theories which held sway from time to time. In the 1930s, for example, much play was made of the potential capability of aircraft bombing to damage an enemy, bring him to his knees and thus determine the course of the war. As a result, and looking to obtain the maximum worth from what pitiful finance was available, and because the air forces of the world were top-heavy with people who actually believed this, and because it seemed to promise a short and relatively bloodless war, the idea was embraced with great enthusiasm, and development of heavy artillery came to a virtual standstill. Not until war was round the corner was it appreciated that air forces, equally short of money, had set their sights on strategic bombing, and were neither capable nor particularly willing to act in a tactical manner to assist the soldiers on the ground. This led to some very hurried development of heavy guns, much of which did not produce results until late in the war.

On the whole, though, Allied artillery development was highly successful because it progressed in logical fashion and because it was kept firmly under control. Moreover, the designers and researchers were granted a breathing space by the fact that the guns which Britain and the USA had on the stocks at the outbreak of war were good enough to run a few years without needing replacements, so the available expertise could be put to work on new material. This was in contrast with the German designers who were always trying to overhaul the current service weapon with one hand while attempting to design something fresh with the other.

This is not to say that wild ideas were ruthlessly stamped on in the West; they were not, but the proposer of the idea had to show how he proposed making it work. And in this connection it must be remembered that during the First World War, both Britain and the USA had Munitions Invention Departments which had been deluged with crackpot ideas; they had assessed them, initiated research on some of them, and had seen them fail in most cases. So that when the same ideas made their appearance in the Second World

War, they could be instantly refused without wasting further time; in many cases the appropriate authority could give chapter and verse for its refusal. For example; in 1940, an inventor proposed a shell embodying the 'Chilovsky Effect', in which a burning substance in the shell nose released gases which flowed over the shell body in flight and reduced skin friction and drag – a forerunner of what aviation people nowadays call the 'boundary layer effect'. In his refusal of the idea, the Superintendent of the Experimental Branch of Woolwich Arsenal wrote "The Chilovsky Effect was given some consideration in France at the end of the 1914–18 war. A British Mission witnessed firing trials in 1918 . . . but did not recommend further action . . . due to the loss of shell capacity and complication of design. The effect would be negligible at supersonic speeds . . . I recommended no further action . . ."

The basic demand was, of course, to keep artillery abreast of enemy developments, best exemplified by the constant improvement in anti-tank and anti-aircraft weapons needed to keep up with the improvement in their targets. Next came the improvement of existing guns' performance, generally by minor improvements in ammunition. Then came such fundamental questions as the relationship between the twist of rifling and gun accuracy; the question of reducing gun barrel wear so as to make barrels last longer and thus reduce the demand for high-grade steel and also relieve the transportation problems inherent in such a far-flung war; methods of reducing the bulk and weight of artillery and improving suspension and travelling arrangements to allow guns to move faster in a fast-moving war; investigations into muzzle brakes in order to extract more performance from the gun without increasing weight; and even such questions as 'Are gun-carriages governed by tradition or is there a better way to design them?'.

An interesting facet of Allied research policy was the diversity of the agencies involved. Inter-service collaboration was the rule, rather than the exception; much of the early work on methods of overcoming wear in gun barrels was done by the Royal Navy, the results being made available to all services. The development of the proximity fuze was similarly undertaken by the US Navy, to the great benefit of all army artillery. One British anti-tank gun project was carried through by the Petroleum Warfare Department, while much of the fundamental work on shell fragmentation was carried out by the Safety in Mines Research Station, and early work on continuously-adjustable electric shell fuzes was done in the Mond Laboratory of the Royal Physical Society.

Priorities in Allied development were determined largely by the tactical problems thrown up as the war progressed, and the most important of these were the problems of dealing with the tank and the bomber. In consequence, more work went into anti-tank and anti-aircraft gun development than into, for example, field artillery. Since the war was one of mobility, American expertise in automobile design and production was soon harnessed for the production of self-propelled guns, while the war in the Pacific and Far East, with its peculiar demands for light-weight fire-power, led to the recoilless gun.

The development history of particular weapons will be dealt with in the appropriate sections, but ammunition development, since it frequently spread across a variety of weapons, can be more conveniently discussed here.

In the anti-tank field, the outstanding development was that of the discarding sabot shot, carried out at the British Armaments Research Establishment by Permutter and Coppock, but it came as the culmination of a long and progressive development of a series of 'composite shot' projectiles. The basis of this class of projectile is the use of a core of tungsten carbide of less than gun calibre; this is then brought up to full calibre by being enclosed in a sheath of light metal – hence the expression 'composite'. This development was brought about by the gradual improvement of tank armour to the point at which it was no longer possible to penetrate it with conventional steel shot; stepping up the power of the gun so as to throw the shot at higher velocity merely meant that the shot failed to withstand the impact when it struck, and shattered on the outside of the armour. In order to overcome this 'shot shatter' problem, tungsten carbide was suggested, since it is much harder in compression than plain steel, and can withstand striking velocities well in excess of anything likely to be achieved by any form of gun. Unfortunately, its mass is about 1.5 times that of steel, which means that a full-calibre projectile made entirely of tungsten carbide would weigh so much that it would not be possible to attain a very great velocity at all. The only way out of the impasse was to build the composite shot, so that the overall weight was no more than that of a conventional shot; indeed, it was generally possible to have the weight rather less, so that a more powerful propelling charge could be used, and a higher velocity obtained. On reaching the target, the light metal sheath came to a stop, but the heavy tungsten core carried on and penetrated the target.

But this form of projectile – known in British service as 'Armour Piercing, Composite, Rigid' or 'APCR', and in US service as 'Hypervelocity Shot' or 'HVAP' – carries its own peculiar penalty. Although it leaves the gun at high speed, its combination of weight and size – which is best expressed as the ratio of weight to the cube of the diameter, or w/d^3 – gives it a poor ability to retain its high velocity in flight. At short ranges, therefore, the penetrative ability is formidable, but as the velocity rapidly drops off,

the penetrative ability drops off with it, and after about one thousand yards it falls off to such a degree that an ordinary steel shot can generally out-perform it. It can be appreciated that what is wanted is, in fact, a contradiction; a shot which is light in weight in the gun bore so as to develop a high velocity, but which is of a high w/d^3 ratio in flight so as to retain that velocity for a long way.

That such reasoning was not the prerogative of any one country is evidenced by the fact that Germany was the first country to produce a projectile which solved this problem. The Gerlich

taper-bore gun fired a shot with a tungsten core and a soft iron sheath formed with skirts; as this passed up the tapering gun barrel, the skirts were compressed until, at the muzzle, the w/d^3 ratio was favorable and the shot sustained its high velocity for considerable ranges. The same technique was used in the 'Littlejohn Adapter' developed by the Czech designer Janacek in conjunction with BSA Ltd in 1941 and applied to the 2pdr tank gun. This was a smooth-bore tapered extension which was screwed to the muzzle of the 2pdr gun; technically speaking, it was a success, but by the time it entered service,

the 2pdr was no longer a viable weapon and thus the adapter saw little practical application. But the principle was applied to a number of experimental weapons during the war years; among them were a 2.25/2.0in rifled gun, tapering from breech to muzzle; a 40/30mm based on the Naval 2pdr gun; and a 55mm/45mm smoothbore proposed by General A. G. L. McNaughton, the Canadian artillery expert. The 2.25in design was closed down after firing trials in May 1943 had shown that much fundamental research into the design of skirt driving bands was needed. The 40/30mm project continued throughout the war, but was finally abandoned in 1945 on the grounds that the 2pdr was, by then, an obsolete weapon and there was little profit to be found in basing a development project upon it, though the work continued for some time using the 40mm Bofors gun as a basis. The smoothbore project was abandoned in 1943 after the first firings showed that the projectiles invariably broke up as they left the muzzle.

But by late 1943, there was little to be gained in following up the taper-bore idea, for something better was at hand. In the 1930s, the French ordnance engineer Edgar Brandt had worked on 'sabot' projectiles, in which a sub-projectile of less than gun calibre was carried in a sleeve or 'sabot' of full calibre, the sabot being separated from the sub-projectile and discarded after leaving the gun muzzle. Brandt's object was to achieve greater range without having to overstress the gun; the sub-projectile for, say, a 105mm gun would be the standard 75mm gun shell made up to 105mm by a light metal sabot. This would have a total weight less than a conventional 105mm shell and would thus achieve a greater muzzle velocity. On leaving the muzzle and discarding the sabot, the smaller shell would continue to the target moving at a greater speed and on a better trajectory than either a 105mm shell from the same gun, or the 75mm shell fired from a 75mm gun.

In Britain, in 1940, the researchers Permutter and Coppock applied Brandt's idea to the object of developing high velocity in order to achieve penetration. By making the sub-projectile a tungsten slug, and building it up with light alloy, the complex problem could be easily solved, and a projectile having light weight in the bore, but good sectional density in flight was achieved. Early work with a 20mm gun showed the validity of their theory, and in 1942, a General Staff Specification was issued to cover their work. The

Left: A Scots Yeomanry Regiment at drill with the 6in howitzer. (See data page 50.)

result was the discarding sabot shot, first for the 6pdr anti-tank gun, and then for the 17pdr gun and, of course, these formed the basis for far-reaching post-war developments.

Taper-bore and sabot solutions were also canvassed for the anti-aircraft field, but in this case, the object was simply to reduce the time of flight to the target by improving the muzzle velocity of the gun and the carrying power of the projectile. By cutting down the time of flight, accuracy of fire could be improved, since the aircraft moved less distance in the time the shell spent in getting up to the aircraft's height. The 6pdr anti-aircraft gun was suggested as a taper-bore at one stage of its development, while the possibilities of developing both taper-bore and sabot solutions for the 3.7in and 5.25in AA guns was also investigated. However, at that stage of sabot development, it was one thing to produce a projectile which would perform accurately over the short ranges demanded by anti-tank shooting, but producing one which would maintain accuracy out to the extreme ranges demanded by AA firing involved long and difficult research, and it was not until well after the war that an AA gun using a sabot projectile got within measurable distance of service acceptance. And just as it entered the final straight, it was overtaken and beaten to the post by the guided missile.

Another problem facing the anti-aircraft gunner was that of bursting the shell at the correct point in the sky. The shell's burst was controlled by a time-fuze, and even if all the other calculations, of bearing, elevation, range, and so forth, were correct, any error in the setting of the time-fuze or of its operation, would result in the shell burst appearing in the wrong place. There were two aspects to this problem. The first was that the time to be set on the fuze was calculated relative to the time of flight from shell to target (or rather to the anticipated position of the target at the end of the shell's flight) and was then adjusted to allow for the time elapsing between the gunner actually setting the fuze with a hand implement, loading the shell and firing the gun. Known as the 'dead time', it was determined empirically, after holding a stopwatch on a variety of gun detachments as they performed the loading drills. But with the best will in the world, it could hardly be proof against Gunner Atkins' 'Monday-morning feeling', or, more seriously, against the gradual slowing down of a detachment during a long engagement. The answer to this was the invention of the combined fuze-setter and rammer; the shell was loaded into this device, after

which, the fuze was set and the shell loaded and fired at a constant 'dead time'. This produced a fixed and unvarying dead time which could be included in the fuze-length calculation and which, by improving the rate of fire as well as the putative accuracy, made anti-aircraft fire much more effective.

The second part of the problem lay in the fuze mechanism itself, whether the fuze relied on a train of burning gunpowder or a mechanical escapement. Either way, there was a degree of tolerance in manufacture and operation, since no mechanical device, turned out in the millions, could be expected to perform with absolute accuracy in every example.

An early attempt to kill both birds with the same stone was the British development of the 'continuously adjustable fuze', which could be loaded at any arbitrary setting and which could be adjusted to the most up-to-date value while in the gun chamber and immediately before firing. There were two lines of approach; the first, exemplified by the 'Grey-Midgeley Fuze' (Fuze, Time, Continuously Adjustable, No. 216) relied on an electrical connection running from the fuze through the shell and cartridge to a contact in the breech block of the gun. Electrical impulses fed through this contact caused the fuze-setting ring to be indexed round. Development of this fuze began in 1941 and continued throughout the war, but it was ended in 1945 after the death of the inventor, Major Grey, RM, and because other types of fuze were entering service which were well in advance of Grey's idea.

The other line of approach, which also attempted to solve the fuze inaccuracy problem, was to have the timing done electrically, by a resistor-condenser circuit which was charged to the correct value by a muzzle wire which swept across a contact ring on the fuze as the shell left the gun, and thus set the most recent time value. Work on this 'Fuze, Time, CA, No. 717' began in mid-1941 and was based on theories advanced by Dr. Schonberg, a television and electronics pioneer. Again, work continued throughout the war, but although some small production was done for naval use, the project was abandoned in 1945.

All these ideas were rendered obsolete by the perfection of the proximity fuze, which actually detected the proximity of the target and then set itself off when within lethal range. The idea for this fuze arose when scientists, working on the

Right: 12in howitzer Mk 4 in position in France, 1939. (See data page 144.)

early radar programme, began to interest themselves in the application of radar to gun control. Once exposed to this, they became aware of the problem of fuze accuracy and were somewhat dismayed to think that their best efforts were likely to be sabotaged by the performance of the fuze. Their first suggestion was to make the fuze into some sort of receiver which could detect the minute reflections of radar energy coming from the target as it was 'illuminated' by the gun-directing radar, but calculations soon showed this to be impracticable. At this stage of radar's development, a radar receiver required a sizeable caravan-load of equipment to detect the returning echo and transform it into a signal on a cathode-ray tube, and the chances of compressing this into the few cubic inches available inside a fuze were non-existent.

Precise authorship of ideas in this field at that time is hard to determine, but the names of Forman, Butement and Pollard in Britain and Tuve in the USA are certainly connected with the early work on proximity fuzes. Whose ever it was, the next idea was to place a complete radio transmitter and receiver inside the fuze, so that the shell sent out its own signal as it flew through the air and detonated on receiving an echo from a target.

The idea of a proximity fuze was proved to be feasible in 1940 when a photoelectrically-operated fuze was perfected and put into production for use with anti-aircraft rockets; this used the shadow cast by an aircraft to trigger the fuze by altering the amount of light falling on the photoelectric cells. Preliminary calculations showed that the self-contained radio idea was workable provided the necessary components could be made – tiny valves, minute condensers and resistors, and, above all, a powerful but small battery which could sit in an ammunition store for years if need be and yet deliver full power a second or two after firing. But in 1940, the development and production of such components was out of the question in Britain, since the British radio industry was already over-stretched trying to produce radar and radio material of all sorts. And so when the Tizard Mission went to America in August 1940 to enlist scientific aid, one of the projects they took with them was the proximity fuze, the theoretical work on which was virtually complete.

The US Navy, alert to the dangers of air attack, were interested in the idea and took responsibility for the development. Section 'V' of the Bureau of Ordnance was in charge of the programme, and they allotted it the code-letter 'T'

from whence the fuze came to be called the 'VT' fuze. The belief that these letters stood for 'Variable Time' is incorrect, but it was tacitly fostered as a suitably vague explanation of what was going on. In point of fact, the fuze is not a time fuze, nor is it variable; other names which graced it in those early days were 'Pozit', 'Peter' and 'Special'.

The US Navy placed a development contract with the Eastman Kodak Company, and they, in turn, sub-contracted various features to specialist companies; the valves to Sylvania, the battery to the National Carbon Company (Exide), and so on. Eventually, the first proximity fuze became a reality and in June 1943 the USS *Helena* shot down a Japanese aircraft, the first victim of the electronic fuze. From then on, it was merely a matter of perfecting designs to suit various guns, since the size of the shell and the rate of spin had their effect on the radio emissions. By 1944, the fuze was available for army AA guns and proved invaluable in the fight against the flying bombs over south-east England, and in December 1944 it was introduced for field artillery in the Battle of the Ardennes, providing accurate air-burst fire in poor visibility.

Parallel with the development of the fuze was the question of developing shells to go with it, or, more precisely, shell fillings. This was because the shank or body of the fuze was up to 8½in long, even though the nose, that part visible after the fuze had been fitted to a shell, was more or less the same size and shape as a normal fuze. But to accommodate the battery and other components, the long shank was necessary and this, of course, would not fit into shells which had been designed to accept the normal inch or two intrusion of conventional fuzes. The explosive filling had to have a large cavity bored out to take the proximity fuze; this, in turn, meant that a special supply of shells had to be made, suited only for use with the proximity fuze, and the supply organization had to be careful to send the right shell to the right place. To simplify matters, a 'universal' filling was designed in Britain, in which the explosive filling for all shells was bored out to take the proximity fuze and was then filled by inserting a removable 'supplementary charge' of explosive. With conventional fuzes, this supplementary charge was left in place; when a proximity fuze was to be fitted, the charge could be withdrawn, exposing the cavity for the longer fuze.

Another point which arose from this was, that the boring out of a large hole in the explosive filling meant that there was that much less explosive in the shell, thereby reducing its lethal performance, obviously a retrograde step. With the first fuzes, for the US Navy 5in guns, the small amount of explosive did not matter very much, but when the calibres crept down to, for example, the British 3.7in AA gun and the 25pdr field gun, the amount of explosive removed was a sizeable percentage of the shell's filling, and had to be compensated by introducing more powerful compositions, notably RDX/TNT and Pentolite mixtures in place of the old Amatol and TNT fillings.

One ammunition development which failed to have the impact on artillery that had been hoped for, was the hollow charge. Interest in this was sparked off by a demonstration in Switzerland in 1938 by two Swiss inventors, Matthias and Mohaupt. Whether they actually sold their ideas to anyone is in some doubt, but the experts of various nations who witnessed their demonstration realized that what they were seeing was a practical application of the old 'Monroe Effect', in which a hollowed-out charge of explosive could reproduce its own shape in a target plate. Spurred on by the Swiss display, ordnance engineers in many countries went on to develop hollow-charge projectiles. The basic layout of all of them was a charge of explosive with a cone-shaped hollow in the front end, lined with a metallic liner. On detonating the explosive from the rear end, the liner was deformed into a high-speed jet of metal vapour which would blast its way through quite remarkable thicknesses of armour. The idea was embraced with great enthusiasm, and hollow-charge shells were designed for several weapons. The design for the 25pdr gun, for example, occupied two or three years of work. But during the research and investigation into the hollow charge, it was found that a spinning shell tended to cause the jet to disperse through centrifugal action and thus lose a large proportion of its penetrative powers. As a result, British work on hollow charges was confined to unspun projectiles, and the only artillery hollow-charge shell to be developed was that for the 3.7in howitzer, a weapon of such low velocity that no other method of producing an anti-tank projectile was feasible. It was largely used in the Far East where even the lower performance of its hollow-charge shell was sufficient to deal with Japanese armour.

An interesting by-product of hollow charge which appeared in the later months of the war was the idea of fitting a hollow charge into the ballistic cap of a 9.2in armour-piercing shell; the theory being that the hollow charge would punch a hole into the plate which would then allow the hard tip of the 9.2in shell to take a grip and penetrate that much easier. Some experimental firings appeared to bear out the theory, but the project was one of many which were terminated when the war ended.

Another hollow-charge variation was the 'follow-through' projectile, development of which went on in both the USA and Britain. In essence, it consisted of a hollow-charge projectile which, in a lengthened body, also carried a small-calibre sub-projectile which could be loaded with explosive or, in some suggestions, tear-gas or incendiary material. The theory was that the hollow charge would blast a hole in the tank, and momentum would launch the sub-projectile through the hole to burst inside the tank. Experimental firings demonstrated that the idea did work, exactly as forecast, but the project never attained any popularity and was abandoned after the war. It seems probable that the reason for abandoning was simply that a well-placed hollow charge could do quite enough damage without going to any great lengths of engineering ingenuity to gild the lily.

To sum up. Allied artillery development was largely concerned with gradual improvement, with building a solid base of fundamental research upon which future weapons, when they were needed, could be designed with the minimum of wasted time. As a result of this policy, much of the wartime work showed little effect on the surface until several years had passed; the Korean War was fought with the same artillery that had fought in north-west Europe, and it was not until the middle 1950s that new artillery began to appear in British and American gunparks. And even then, there was little that was innovative or unusual. Cleverness for cleverness' sake is not a tendency to be found among gun designers, and there are very few ideas which can be called original; for example, in the early 1970s there was a great to-do over something called 'soft recoil', but on examination this turned out to be the same thing as the 'differential recoil' used on Austrian and French mountain howitzers in the days before the First World War. The only difference today, apparently, is the addition of electronics, something which is hardly likely to endear the idea to dyed-in-the-wool gunners. So the work of British and American designers during the Second World War was unspectacular, unsung and a long time coming to fruition. Nevertheless, the story is an interesting one which deserves to be told, if only to show that ingenuity and good mechanical design were not the sole prerogative of the Axis powers.

Field and Medium Artillery

The division of the guns, in this and the fourth section, into 'Field and Medium' and 'Heavy and Super-heavy' is somewhat arbitrary. For one thing, the US Army rarely spoke of 'medium' guns, and the British 'Medium Regiment RA' had no strict American equivalent. Calibre alone is no yardstick, since much depended upon what the weapon was expected to do. I have, therefore, put into this section those weapons which might reasonably be expected to be found in support of the infantry or armoured divisions, and under command. Weapons more usually found under the control of Corps, or higher formations, are classed as Heavy. Even this distinction gets a bit blurred round the edges, but it will suffice.

The field and medium guns (and howitzers) were, therefore, the weapons which the infantry-man had as his basic support, day in and day out, rain or shine. The basic unit of this support

was, of course, the divisional field gun; the 25pdr in British service and the 105mm howitzer in American. The lighter weapons were generally hangovers from the days when such weapons were thought to be sufficient, while the heavier weapons were there, available, but spent most of their working hours trying to attain some measure of superiority over their opposite numbers and keep them off the infantryman's back.

If there is one subject guaranteed to bring out the worst in artillerymen, it is that of the relative merits of their chosen field pieces. Infantrymen argue about the Lee-Enfield and the Garand rifles; aviators, about the Spitfire and the P38 Lightning; gunners, about the 25pdr and the 105mm howitzer. Since readers will be expecting some sort of conclusions to be drawn, I will stick my neck right out and say that I preferred the 25pdr. This is no mere chauvinism; I have fired

both and, what is a great deal more to the point, I have shoved both of them through mud. As shooting weapons there was little to choose between them; the greater range of the 25pdr was offset by the heavier shell of the 105mm. In anti-tank fire, the 25pdr was definitely the better weapon, being handier to swing from target to target, and having an AP shot which delivered a more punishing blow than did the 105mm hollow-charge shell. But as a practical gunner, I have to say that the 105mm was a vilely balanced contraption when it came to man-handling.

Readers may be a little surprised to find the Smith Gun in this section; so am I, but it is difficult to say where else it could have been put. And it does qualify as a field weapon, since it was officially adopted by both the Army and RAF for airfield defence. And anyway, perhaps a little light relief is no bad thing now and again.

4.13 tons in soft ground . . . Manhandling the 6in howitzer (see data page 50).

The Smith Gun

The Ordnance, Smooth Bore, 3in Mk 1 on Carriage, 3in Mk 1, or 'Smith Gun' was one of the many 'private enterprise' weapons which appeared in the dark days of 1940. The inventor, Mr. Smith, was the Chief Engineer of the Trianco Engineering Company, and his gun made its first appearance in Ordnance Board Proceeding 8033 of 14 August 1940.

A demonstration had been carried out on 31 July, and the Superintendent of Experiments reported that there were several features of the weapon which he considered unsafe. In the 'Remarks by the Board' the following comments appeared: 'The Smith Gun consists of a smooth-bore breech-loading mortar of 3 inch calibre, mounted on a carriage with a limber, both of light construction. On the journey to Shoeburyness they were both towed behind a 9 horsepower car.

'The limber consists of a pair of steel disc wheels with solid rubber tyres, about 3ft 6in in diameter, connected by an axle. At either end of the axle is a cylindrical ammunition holder, free to rotate, each designed to hold ten rounds.

'The carriage consists of two steel disc wheels on an axle, both dished the same way, the nearside wheel inwards and the offside wheel outwards. The piece is mounted on the axle and is free to rotate about it. A curved shield is fitted. On coming into action the whole carriage is turned over onto its nearside wheel, which thus becomes the platform of the gun and the axle, in effect, the pivot. The other wheel gives cover from view . . .

'The gun is capable of elevation up to 30° and all-round traverse. The shield traverses with the gun. Both traverse and elevation are free but can be clamped. A crude but reasonably effective sight is fitted. The breech mechanism is crude and somewhat complicated in operation.

'The bomb is apparently of cast iron, deeply segmented, cylindrical, and about 9lb in weight.

The cartridge consists of a tinned plate cylinder with a hole in the centre to take a .38in blank cartridge which acts as a primer. The front of the cartridge is designed to travel up the bore with the bomb and to act as a gas-check.

'This is an ingenious invention . . . The present design suffers, however, from a number of defects. To put these right would inevitably retard and reduce the production of the weapon . . . It is reasonably accurate . . . Will the Director of Artillery say whether it is intended to develop this weapon?'

The Director of Artillery replied on 17 August (three days later) to say that several of the defects had already been rectified and that development was proceeding. But on 20 September came a bombshell from Home Forces:

'It is a second-rate weapon and there are first-rate weapons which can do the job as well or better . . . it would be useless as an anti-tank weapon . . . as an anti-personnel weapon, heavy machine-guns are more suitable . . . .'

This opinion was based on a demonstration which had apparently taken place early in July, obviously of a very early stage in the gun's development, and it seems that in recommending other weapons as being more suited to the task in hand, the Home Forces spokesman had overlooked the basic fact that at that time there simply were no weapons of any sort available, which was the very reason that the Smith Gun was being offered. But faced with this weighty opinion, the Ordnance Board had no option but to 'recommend no further action with this weapon'.

At this point, the story becomes mysterious. The Smith Gun was never discussed by the Ordnance Board again until April 1941, when the subject was ammunition; during the interval, the Smith Gun had, by some unrecorded sleight of hand, been accepted into military service. Some differences

Above: The Smith Gun with its trailer, ready to move.

appear between the version described by the Ordnance Board and the issued model; the barrel now passed through a yoke in the axle and was provided with a primitive recoil absorber, and the breech mechanism had been simplified. Formal approval was given on 18 September 1941, but it was undoubtedly in service by June of that year. It was generally issued to Home Guard units, but a handful found their way into more formal hands when they were issued to Army and RAF units responsible for guarding airfields. The limber was graced with the formal title of 'Trailer Artillery No. 39'. The whole equipment survived until it was declared obsolete in December 1945.

Data
Total length: 54.0in.
Length of bore: 52.0in.
Rifling: None.
Breech mechanism: Vertical swinging block, percussion fired.
Elevation: $-10°$ $+40°$.
Traverse: 360°.
Recoil system: 11 rubber bands between barrel and axle.
Total weight in action: 605lb.

Performance firing standard 8lb HE shell
Muzzle velocity: 400ft/sec.
Maximum range: 500 yards.

Two views of the Smith Gun. **Top:** A side view of the Gun in firing position. **Right:** A rear view, showing the open sight with 'aim-off' notches above the muzzle.

Ammunition Fixed, cased charge.
Propelling Charge. This consisted of 20 grammes of chopped cordite in a tinplate case about $3\frac{1}{2}$in in diameter and $\frac{3}{4}$in deep. The case was attached to the tail of the projectile by a shear wire which broke on firing and allowed the bomb to separate from the case, though the front portion of the case went up the bore behind the bomb and fell some distance from the muzzle.

Shell, SB, HE, 3in Gun Mk 1. This was a cylinder of cast iron about 9in long, the ends being accurately turned to 3in diameter and the centre section left rough-cast. A percussion fuze No. 245 (an all-ways fuze, later used extensively with various hand grenades) was fitted into the nose, and a steel spigot extended from the base and formed the means of attaching the cartridge. The filling was a small charge of Amatol.

Bomb, SB, HEAT, 3in Gun Mk 1. This was a hollow-charge bomb for anti-tank shooting. The basis was the 3in Mortar cylindrical smoke-bomb body, complete with fins. The normal rounded nose was replaced by a flat cover plate held by a locking ring. Beneath this was a steel cone and the explosive filling of Pentolite or TNT. The base fuze No. 284 was fitted into the tail tube, and a short steel spigot closed the end of the tube and held the cartridge case in position. The bomb weighed 6lb and could penetrate approx $2\frac{1}{2}$in of plate at any range. A Mark 2 bomb was also approved, at the same time as the Mark 1; this had some changes in the internal

design which made it more reliable and effective, but it was externally the same as the Mark 1. It is perhaps worth recording that the Smith gun HEAT bomb was the first gun-fired hollow-charge shell ever to be used in British service; when the design was requested, in April 1941, the Ordnance Board was moved to comment that 'Neither the safety in the gun nor the efficiency of shell filled on the Hollow Charge principle . . . has yet been established.'

Early in 1942, a high-explosive round was developed by converting the standard 3in Mortar high-explosive streamlined bomb, removing the propelling and secondary cartridges and fitting a spigot and cartridge case into the tail unit. Development then began on the design of an alternative type of propellant system to fire the bomb to 1,500 yards, but the barrel of the Smith Gun could not withstand the increased pressure and the project was abandoned.

75mm Guns

The 75mm gun, in any form, has never been a standard British Army artillery weapon, though a number were obtained from France in 1915 and taken into use as anti-aircraft guns as the 'Ordnance QF 75mm Mk 1'. These were declared obsolete in April 1919.

In 1940, the severe shortage of field artillery led to the purchase of a quantity of obsolescent but still serviceable 75mm field-guns from the United States. Although given British nomenclature they were all of standard American military patterns, and to avoid unnecessary repetition, full details will be found in the American section on page 54. The relationship between British and American terminology is as follows:

Ord., QF, 75mm Mk 1 = US 75mm Gun M1897
Ord., QF, 75mm Converted Mk 1 = US 75mm Gun M1917
Ord., QF, 75mm Converted Mk 1* = US 75mm Gun M1917A1
Ord., QF, 75mm 'S' Mk 2 = US 75mm Gun M1916 (There were six slightly different models of the 'S' Mk 2, corresponding to the variants of the M1916.)
Ord., QF, 75mm 'S' Mk 2* = US 75mm M1916A1

Below: Winston Churchill watches a detachment drilling with the 'Ordnance QF 75mm Mk 1'.

All these equipments came on their standard field carriages, but a number of Mk 1 were removed from their original carriages and fitted to the 'Mounting 75mm Mk 1' in late 1940. The conversion consisted of removing the wheels, axle-tree and traversing gear, and cutting off most of the trail so as to be able to mount the weapon on a pedestal. In this configuration it became a 'Coast Artillery Equipment' according to the official announcement; more accurately, it became a Beach Defence weapon.

All these 75mm guns were declared obsolete on 8 March 1945, though for some obscure reason (probably somebody's oversight) the pedestal mounting was not disposed of until May 1946.

In addition to these field-artillery weapons, a 75mm AA gun, the 'Ordnance, QF, 75mm Mk 4' was approved by the Ordnance Board in July 1943. This was a Vickers-Armstrong design which had been supplied to Turkey, and so far as can be ascertained, the Ordnance Board's approval was merely a precautionary measure in case some disaster overtook the provision of other anti-aircraft guns. In the event, there was no supply problem and the 75mm Mk 4 was never formally introduced, nor were any of the guns ever taken into service.

18pdr Field Gun

The 18pdr was introduced in 1904, and was the backbone of British field artillery during and after the First World War. The original design was typical of its era, with pole trail, shield and wooden wheels, and more than ten thousand were made. In 1916, an improved design was begun, but it was not until 1918 that this reached production as the Mark 4 gun on Mark 3 Carriage. This was a considerable improvement insofar as it used a box trail allowing better elevation, an Asbury breech mechanism, and a hydropneumatic recoil system. It became the post-war standard equipment, and in the years which followed it was further improved by the adoption of a split-trail carriage and pneumatic tyres.

As detailed in the section on the 25pdr gun, the hunt for a replacement began in the 1920s, and when the 25pdr Mark 1 was introduced, it absorbed a number of 18pdr guns which were converted by simply changing barrels – not 'boring them out' as is frequently stated. But since the 25pdr was slow in coming into full production, the 18pdr remained in service for much of the war; strangely, it was the Mark 4 gun, the last to be introduced, which was the first to be made obsolete, in August 1940, when the last had been converted to a 25pdr. The other Marks lingered until 1944, having been used as training weapons and, in 1940–41, dispersed around the country as anti-invasion weapons and as the primary armament of several field regiments which had left their equipment in France. Numbers remained in various overseas stations and were employed on the Sudan-Eritrean border in 1940, and during the early part of the campaign in Burma.

Variants

Ordnance:

Mk 1: Original pattern; wire-wound, screw breech. 1904.

Mk 1*: Mk 1 repaired by insertion of a new 'A' Tube and wire, the jacket being tapered to approximate to Mk 2, and the gun assembled by hydraulic pressure.

Mk 2: Differed in construction so as to allow the gun to be assembled by hydraulic pressure instead of by heating and shrinking. 1906.

Mk 2*: Mk 2 gun converted for anti-aircraft mounting in 1915. Re-converted back to field use in 1920.

Mk 3: Developmental model, not adopted. 1917.

Mk 4: New design using Asbury breech mechanism. 1918.

Mk 4A: Mk 4A repaired by removal of 'A' tube and wire and insertion of an auto-frettaged loose liner. 1935.

Mk 4B: As Mk 4A, but of new manufacture. 1935.

Mk 5: Generally as Mk 4, but minor differences to

suit mounting in the Birch self-propelled gun. 1926.

Carriage:

Mk 1: Original type; pole trail, hydro-spring recoil system, elevation 16°. 1904.

Mk 1*: Mk 1 modified to a hydropneumatic recoil system. 1916.

Mk 1R: Mk 1 with solid rubber tyres.

Mk 1*R: Mk 1* with solid rubber tyres.

Mk 1**: Mk 1* with lengthened cradle.

Mk 1C: Mk 1 with extended cradle.

Mk 1D: Mk 1 with cradle of Mk 2 carriage.

Mk 2: Similar to Mk 1, but with hydropneumatic recoil system, longer cradle, and of new manufacture.

Mk 2*: Mk 1* with Mk 2 carriage cradle.

Mk 2PA: The 'Martin-Parry Conversion', using pneumatic tyres on light-weight steel disc wheels and a light-weight axletree to allow high-speed towing.

Mk 2R: Mk 2 with solid rubber tyres.

Mk 3: For Mk 4 gun; box trail, extended cradle, variable hydropneumatic recoil system. Elevation 30°.

Mk 3T: Mk 3 modified to approximate to Mk 4 standard by fitting new cross-axle traverse, shock absorbers, etc.

Mk 3*: As for Mk 3, but with 37½° elevation.

Mk 4: Generally as Mk 3, but with new trail and traversing gear with three-speed selection and with shock absorbers between trail and axletree. Elevation 37½°.

Mk 4R: Mk 4 with solid rubber tyres, and elevation 38°40′.

Mk 4P: Mk 4 with pneumatic tyres and elevation 37½°.

Mk 4TR: Mk 4, but with only 30° elevation.

Mk 5: Split trail, 50° traverse, 38°55′ elevation.

Mk 5R: Mk 5 with solid rubber wheels.

Mk 5P: Mk 5 with pneumatic tyres and 37½° elevation.

Data Gun Mk 4, on Carriage Mk 5P.

Weight of gun and breech mechanism: 952lb.

Total length: 96.96in.

Length of bore: 92.735in (28 cal).

Rifling: 18 grooves, uniform RH 1/30.

Breech mechanism: Asbury interrupted screw, percussion fired.

Elevation: −5° +37½°.

Traverse: 25° right and left.

Recoil system: Hydropneumatic, variable, 26in to 48in.

Weight in action: 3,507lb.

Performance firing standard 18lb HE shell

Muzzle velocity: 1,625ft/sec.

Maximum range: 11,100 yards.

Ammunition Fixed, cased charges.

The number of different designs of shell and cartridges approved for the 18pdr during its forty years of service is astronomical; most of them were First World War innovations and manufacturing expedients, but a vast number managed to stay in the Vocabulary until 1944. Since most of them are only of specialist interest, the details below show only one representative round of each type.

The propelling charge varied according to the projectile, and there was also a 'Reduced Charge' for use at practice and for service firing at short ranges in order to save wear on the gun.

Cartridge, QF, 18pdr HE Shell Mk 46. This consisted of the HE shell Mk 7, a non-streamlined shell filled with Amatol or TNT, and with the Percussion Fuze No. 106 or 106E. This was attached to the 11.6in brass cartridge case which contained a propelling charge of 1lb 7oz of Cordite and a Percussion Primer No. 1. The complete round weighed 23½lb and was 23.379in long.

Cartridge, QF, 18pdr HE Shell S/L Mk 13C. Similar to the previous round, but using the streamlined shell Mk 2C, filled with Amatol and fuzed Percussion No. 115, 117 or 119.

Cartridge, QF, HE Shell Reduced Mk 14. Similar to Mk 46 above, but with a propelling charge of only 5¼oz of Cordite.

Cartridge, QF, 18pdr Smoke Bursting S/L Mk 11C. Comprised a nose-fuzed streamlined shell filled with white phosphorus and with the Percussion Fuze No. 117. The propelling charge was 1lb 6¼oz of Cordite.

Cartridge, QF, 18pdr Shrapnel Mk 63. Consisted of a nose-ejection shrapnel shell Mk 17 containing 375 lead/antimony bullets, and with the Time & Percussion Fuze No. 80. The propelling charge was 1lb 7oz of Cordite and, because of the slightly different weight and balance of this shell, the maximum range was only 9,400 yards.

Cartridge, QF, 18pdr AP Shot Mk 3T. Consisted of a solid steel-piercing shot fitted with a tracer, and a propelling charge of 1lb 7oz of Cordite.

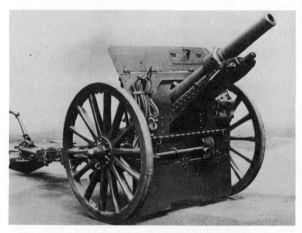

Above: The Mk 4 gun on (top) Mk 4 carriage, complete with all its accessories and stores; and (bottom) on the Mk 5 split-trail carriage.
Left: Rear of the 18pdr gun on Mk 4 carriage.

Opposite page: A 25pdr in Italy, with camouflage nets, drag ropes and other paraphenalia of war.

25pdr Field Gun

To some degree, the 25pdr can be said to have originated during the closing months of the First World War, when the Royal Artillery Committee began considering the next generation of guns and, in particular, a field-gun which would replace both the 18pdr and the 4.5in howitzer. This demand stemmed from a consideration of the projectiles – for it must always be remembered that it is the shell which is the weapon, the gun is merely a method of delivery. The 18pdr had been designed around a shrapnel shell, chosen because in 1904, troops in the open were the accepted standard target. The 4.5in howitzer, designed at much the same time, was intended to fire a high-explosive shell to deal with entrenchments and field fortifications, backing-up the anti-personnel activities of the 18pdr. But the Great War had put an end to the tactics of using masses of troops in the open, had turned the accent to the high-explosive shell, and had put an end to rigid demarcation of tasks between guns and howitzers; and the truth of the matter was that the high-explosive shell developed for the 18pdr wasn't big enough (nor, for that matter, well-enough designed) to be a worthwhile projectile. On the other hand, the 4.5in howitzer could not entirely replace the field-gun, since it had limited range, extremely limited traverse, and was entirely unsuitable for dealing with fast-moving targets.[1] What was needed was a sort of 'half-way house' between the two extremes, more nimble than the 4.5in, but firing a better weight of shell than the 18pdr.

After the Armistice, development began at a low priority, and in 1924, a 3.9in howitzer mounted on an 18pdr Mk 5 carriage was tested,[2] but it proved to be unsatisfactory, and in August 1924, the Ordnance Committee were asked by the Director of Artillery 'To examine the possibilities of obtaining a great increase of range for our next Field Artillery equipment . . . a range of 15,000 yards might be obtained with a super-charge', and went on to suggest a 3in gun firing a 16lb shell at 2,200ft/sec.[3] Preliminary studies indicated that a gun of the necessary power would far exceed the strength of the 18pdr carriage (which it had been hoped could be used) and the entire equipment would weigh $37\frac{1}{2}$cwt. As the shell would be lighter than that of the 18pdr, the additional range gained was insufficient to compensate for this, and so the idea was dropped, but it is noteworthy as being the origin of the demand for 15,000 yards range which became the almost-constant theme in every new design from then on.

The Director of Artillery's next proposal was for a 4.13in (i.e. 105mm) howitzer with a 33lb shell and a range of 12,000 yards,[4] and this appeared to promise a good solution. By March 1926, the design had become a BL (bagged charge) howitzer, and it was specified that mechanical draught would be used, thus easing the weight restriction.[5] (Thirty hundredweights (3,360lb) was considered to be the maximum weight that could be pulled by a six-horse team on service, and this was an important consideration in gun and carriage design.) Several designs were put forward, some with wire-wound and some with auto-frettaged barrels, with various grades of steel and factors of safety, some of 20 calibres length and some of 25. A firm specification was finally drawn up, for a

howitzer with 1,600ft/sec muzzle velocity, a 35lb shell, elevation of $-5°$ $+45°$, and traverse of 4° either side of zero, the total weight of which was not to exceed the magic 30cwt. A circular firing platform was to be provided upon which, the gun wheels could rest and allow the equipment to be swung round bodily through 360°, and 'attention must be directed in design to meeting the stresses imposed by mechanical traction at high speed.'[5]

Shortly after this, a QF (cartridge case) 3.9in (100mm) design was put forward on the grounds that it would weigh less, yet give but a small loss of performance. A comparative analysis[6] showed that the 3.9in would fire a 30lb shell at 1,600ft/sec to 11,900 yards and weigh 29¾cwt in action, while the 4.1in would weigh 31¼cwt, and range to 12,200 yards. This dilemma was solved by the War Office ruling that the range must not be less than 12,000 yards, so the 3.9in was dropped. Two 4.1in models were put in hand, one developed by Vickers and the other by the Royal Carriage Department of Woolwich Arsenal.

Meanwhile, another project had begun. In December 1926, the Director of Artillery minuted that 'a decision has now been obtained as to the main requirements of an experimental field gun' and went on to specify a 3.3in gun (the same calibre as the 18pdr) to range not less than 12,000 yards, be capable of anti-tank fire, and be towed by a motor vehicle.[7] This idea was mulled over for some considerable time, but eventually a conference held on 22 May 1928 settled the basic requirements[8] and eventually a request was sent to Vickers in June 1929 for them to produce a design.[9]

The BL 4.1in howitzer was produced 'in the flesh' in 1931, and trials were carried out on Salisbury Plain, but a decision was deferred until the 3.3in gun was ready. But by this time, the question of finance had arisen. It was possible that money might be found to provide the army with one field equipment, but it was highly improbable that two would be approved, particularly as the whole programme of development had been founded on the assumption that one weapon could be developed to replace two. In 1928, the concept of a combination weapon, a 'gun-howitzer' began to take hold, and after contemplating this, and considering the results of the trials of various experimental equipments, a proposal was put forward in October 1933 for a 3.7in gun-howitzer firing a 25lb shell.[10] This was followed by discussions with the General Staff in which this '25-pounder' was proposed as the sole field artillery equipment in place of both the BL 4.1in and QF 3.3in models.[11] Finally, in September 1934, the Director Royal Artillery, Major-General H. A. Lewis, ordered the construction of a pilot model.[12]

The difficulty lay in convincing the purse-holders, and the only way around this was to use as much existing equipment as possible. So the planned 3.7in calibre was reduced to 3.45in, since with this dimension it would be possible to make an auto-frettaged loose barrel which could be slipped into the jacket of the existing 18pdr guns, accept the 18pdr breech ring and mechanism, and thus provide a new equipment without the expense of a new carriage. At the same time, however, General Lewis had the designers push ahead with the development of a complete new 25pdr equipment, new from muzzle to trail-eye, against the day when finance would become available.

The 18pdr conversion was officially approved on 26 August 1936[13] as the 'Ordnance QF 3.45in Mk 1' 'To govern conversion of 18-pr Mark IV guns' and these were fitted either to the box trail Mark III or split trail Mark V carriages, as opportunity offered. In February 1938, the nomenclature was changed to 'Ordnance QF 25pr Mark I'[14] and rather more than 1,000 equipments were manufactured. They were, however, rarely called by their proper name, the term '18/25 pounder' rapidly acquiring currency since it seemed more accurately descriptive.

The design of the all-new equipment set the draughtsmen a great opportunity for exercises with clean sheets of paper, and some splendid ideas found their way on to the drawing-board, some even getting as far as the mock-up stage. Among these was a remarkable, three-legged mounting with retractable wheels which allowed the gun a 360° traverse; split, pole and box trail patterns with sprung and unsprung suspension; and an unusual idea, attributed to a Captain Wood of the Design Department, which had four wheels in place of the usual two. As the split trail was opened, a linkage coupled to the wheels pivoted them so that they turned inwards to provide a rotating base for the gun to allow a complete 360° of traverse by swinging the trails.

The final accepted designs were two split-trail mountings, one from Woolwich and one from Vickers, which, although highly regarded by their progenitors, did not meet with complete approval from the Regiment which was going to have to use them. The view of many officers was that both designs were unnecessarily cumbersome, too heavy, and awkward to manhandle as well as being inconvenient to operate. An approach was made to the Superintendent of Design, Major-General Macrae, asking if second thoughts might not be possible, but to go back to the beginning and start a fresh design was out of the question with the fact of Germany's re-armament staring everyone in the face. What General Macrae could, and did do, was to revive the carriage of the 4.1in BL howitzer, which had used a humped box trail with a circular firing platform beneath. This was rapidly modified to take the 25pdr barrel and cradle, and the result, among other advantages, was some 5½cwt lighter than either of the split trail types. Early in 1938, a comparative demonstration and test was held at the School of Artillery, Larkhill, witnessed by the most important figures in the military hierarchy. The DCIGS, DMT, DST, Dof A, I of A and similar luminaries were there, as were every CRA and many regimental and battery commanders. After the tests and demonstration –

Top: The 4.1in howitzer of 1931, the carriage of which was used for the 25pdr. **Top left:** Wooden mock-up of the Woolwich design for the 25pdr. **Lower left:** Another Woolwich mock-up, using a three-legged platform to give all-round traverse. **Top right:** The all-round traverse model ready for travelling. **Lower right:** Captain Wood's four-wheeled carriage adapted to the 18pdr Mk 5. **Bottom:** Ordnance 3.45in Mk 1 on Carriage 18/25pdr Mk SP.

which lasted no more than a day – the DCIGS, General Adam, held a post-mortem conference and called upon the audience for a show of hands. On this basis, the box-trail model was selected, and there can be no doubt that the choice was the right one.

The completely new design of ordnance – i.e. gun, jacket and new breech mechanism – was approved as the Ordnance QF 25pdr Mark II on 7 December 1937,[15] but the new design of carriage, the 'Carriage 25pdr Mark I' did not receive full approval until late in 1939.[16] Production of the complete new equipments began in the winter of 1939, and by the outbreak of the war, there were only 78 guns and no carriages. Hence the British Expeditionary Force went to France and fought there during 1939–40 with the 18/25pdr equipments. The first Mark II equipments were issued to the 8th Army Field Regiment, Royal Canadian Artillery, in April 1940. The Mark II was first used in action during the brief campaign in Norway in 1940.

Thereafter, the 25pdr served with few changes until it was retired from first-line service in 1967, being then retained as a training equipment until 1975. There were variant Marks and some abortive designs (see below) but the only significant change was the adoption of a two-port Solothurn muzzle brake in 1942.[17] This was done at the suggestion of the Chief Superintendent of Armament Design in order that Super charge could be used with the 20lb armour-piercing shot; originally this shot was only used with charge three, but the increasing thickness of German tanks led to the proposal to use charge

Super, whereupon it was found that the gun was unstable because of the high recoil stresses. First trials with a muzzle brake were carried out in April 1942, using a German brake adapted from the 105mm leFH18M design; this showed the equipment to be much steadier, but all the tracers in the shot were extinguished as they left the muzzle. It took some time for this to be tracked down and turned out to be a fault in the filling of the tracer and nothing to do with the muzzle brake at all. In July 1942, the Solothurn design was tried and recommended for issue, and in the following month, the Director of Artillery recommended equipping all guns with the brake. In spite of this, though, it was only applied to guns in those areas where the more dangerous tanks could be anticipated; it was rarely seen in the Far East, and even in post-war years the 25pdrs of the Australian and New Zealand armies never had brakes.

Variants

Ordnance:

Mk 1: Consisted of an auto-frettaged loose liner inserted into 18pdr Mk 4 guns by removal of the 18pdr 'A' tube and wire. It differed from subsequent Marks by its length, 96.725in.

Mk II: Standard pattern; see Data Table (p 32).

C Mk II: As for Mk II, but with minor dimensional changes to suit Canadian manufacturing techniques.

Mk III: Introduced 31 January 1944. Generally as Mk 2, except that the shot seating was reduced

This page, below: 25pdr Gun Mk 2 on Carriage Mk 1; and (right) the closed breech of the 25pdr. The large metal slab on top of the jacket is the counterweight to balance the muzzle brake.

Opposite page, right: Rear view of the 25pdr on Mk 1 carriage. Above left: The open breech of the 25pdr.

to 4° to prevent the shell slipping back after loading at high angles of elevation.

C Mk III: As for Mk III, but Canadian manufacture.

Mk 4: Introduced 17 October 1946. As for Mk III, but with the rear corners of the breech ring mortice cut to a radius of 0.15in in order to prevent cracking of the ring by set-back of the breech block on firing.

Mk 5: Number not allotted.

Mk 6: Introduced 17 November 1964. As for Mk 4, but with the breech ring made of higher-quality steel.

Carriage:

Mk I: The standard humped box trail with platform See Data Table (p 32).

Mk II: Indian design with narrower wheel track and provided with a narrow No. 22 Firing Platform.

Mk III: Canadian origin. Had a narrow track and shield, and the trail was hinged in the middle to give an extra 30° elevation for high-angle fire. This also used the No. 22 Platform, and a special cranked sight bracket to correct the sight for the greater elevation. It was introduced late in 1944. The object of the narrow track on Mks II and III was (a) to be able to follow a jeep through jungle and (b) to enable the gun to be loaded into the C47 Dakota aircraft without dismantling, which was not possible with the Mk I carriage.

Mk IV: British design based on the Australian 'Short' Model (below), but with modifications to the recoil system to permit Super charge to be fired. Officially introduced 1 May 1945, declared

obsolete 1 September 1946, it is believed that only one or two were made.

Ordnance, QF, 25pdr Short Mark 1 (Aust), on Carriage, 25pdr Light Mk 1 (Aust). More familiarly known as the 'Baby 25pdr', this was developed in Australia early in 1943, after experience in the jungles of New Guinea indicated the desirability of portable artillery. The aim was to produce a weapon capable of being pack-transported, and by the time the design was finished, the only resemblance to the 25pdr was the breech mechanism, recoil system, cradle and sights; everything else was changed. The trail was greatly simplified, the wheels were smaller, and a castor wheel was fitted to the trail end for easier manhandling. The shield and platform were discarded, a heavy spade serving to anchor the gun in the firing position. The greatest change lay in the gun itself, which was drastically shortened to a bore length of 49.69in. To mitigate the effects of muzzle flash on the recoil system rods and on surrounding camouflage, a muzzle cap then had to be fitted, which gave the piece a total length of 63.79in. The equipment was capable of being broken into 14 pack loads, and the total weight in action was 3,015lb. The principal objection to this equipment was that it could not be used with Super charge; the lightened gun (810lb instead of 1,000lb) recoiled faster and built up too high a pressure in the recoil buffer cylinder. So the maximum range was restricted to 10,800 yards, though this was probably quite sufficient for the purposes envisaged. It was declared

obsolete for British service on 26 February 1946, though it lingered longer in the Australian Army.

Self-Propelled Equipments

Ordnance, QF, 25pdr Mks 2 or 3, on Carrier, Valentine, 25pdr Gun Mk 1. This was designed in 1941, using the chassis and hull of the Valentine tank. The turret was removed and replaced by a tall armoured barbette into which a modified 25pdr top carriage was fitted, complete with gun. An order was placed in October 1941 for 100 equipments, and these were sent to North Africa early in 1942. The principal defects resulted from the armoured barbette restricting the gun's elevation to 15°, which meant a maximum range of 6,400 yards, and the close and cramped conditions in which the gun detachment had to work. Nevertheless, they were a useful stopgap and they served to train regiments in the basics of SP gun handling and tactics. An Ordnance Board Mission to North Africa in June 1943 observed that 'Nothing good can be said of the Valentine SP, though the detachments are efficient.' Christened 'Bishop' (for no accountable reason) it continued in service throughout the Sicilian campaign and part of the early Italian campaign until replaced by the American M7 'Priest' equipment. It was declared obsolete on 24 November 1944.[18]

Ordnance, QF, 25pdr, Mk 2 or 3, on Carrier, Ram, SP 25pdr Gun Mk 1. Officially introduced on 6 September 1943, this was a modification of the Canadian Ram tank, the hull being built up into an armoured open-topped superstructure with the gun mounted on the front plate. This design allowed the full elevation to be reached and thus, the full range of the gun, and permitted 25° of traverse each side of zero. The recoil system was modified to give a constant recoil length of twenty inches at all elevations. Known as 'Sexton', production was carried out at the Montreal Locomotive Works, beginning early in 1943; the first equipment was tested by 19th Canadian Field Regiment at Petawawa range in April. By the time production ended in 1945, 2,150 had been built. It replaced 'Priest' in British service in 1944, and remained in use until the late 1950s, when the spare parts problem was becoming acute, and the 105mm 'Abbot' was within sight.

Design Projects and unadopted ideas

Once the 25pdr was in service and available, a number of projects were put forward, none of which reached service. Some of them, however, are worth recording.

1. A self-propelled mounting using the Loyd carrier as its basis. The gun was mounted in the front, in the area usually associated with a Bren gun. The whole idea was grossly impractical, since little ammunition could be carried and the two-man detachment were hopelessly cramped. Only one prototype was built.

2. The Alecto SP Mk 3. The Alecto was a self-propelled 95mm howitzer on the Harry Hopkins tank chassis (see under 95mm howitzer for further details)

and a version using the 25pdr Mk 2 gun was designed. It is possible that a prototype was built, but the entire Alecto project was abandoned before the 25pdr idea had been properly evaluated. It might have made a useful airborne assault gun.

3. The 25pdr Mobile Armoured Revolving Carriage (MARC). This was a towed equipment devised in Canada in 1942 by a Free French officer named Riboud. It consisted of a 25pdr Mk 2 gun, in an armoured turret on top of a highly modified and much strengthened trail. The forward end was supported on dual wheels in the normal axle position, and, in action, the rear end rested on two adjustable jacks so as to allow the turret to be levelled. For transport, a two-wheeled limber was attached to the trail end. It could be fired from its wheels in an emergency. A prototype was built and tested, but the idea was abandoned as impracticable and of limited usefulness in July 1944.

4. The Vauxhall Wheel Carriage. The Vauxhall Wheel was a solid-tyred, internally-sprung wheel developed by the Vauxhall Motor Company. The tyre was of leather and the whole thing was intended as a substitute for the normal pneumatic-tyred wheel in the event of a shortage of rubber. It was tested in 1943, but was found to give rise to excessive vibration, every nut and bolt on the carriage being loose after 27 miles of travel. After further testing, vibration caused one wheel bearing to collapse and the wheel fell off. The project was then terminated.[19]

5. The Australian Cruiser Tank Mk 3. The Australian Cruiser tank was, broadly speaking, an Antipodean version of the American M3, Grant, tank. Its history is of no importance here except to note that a Mark 3 version was proposed, using a 25pdr Mk 2 gun as the principal turret armament. One prototype was built in 1943, after which, the idea was dropped in favour of using a 17pdr gun, which became the Australian Cruiser Mk 4.

6. The American Gun Motor Carriage T51. After the first American M7 'Priest' 105mm SPs had been received by the British Army in the late summer of 1942, the General Staff, through the British Military Mission in Washington, asked if a similar design, mounting the 25pdr, could be produced. In July 1942, the US Ordnance Department built the T51, which was simply an M7 modified so as to take a 25pdr. Having done this, they then pointed out that there could be no hope of devoting any American production facilities to a weapon which the US Army would not use, which knocked the whole idea on the head immediately. It was a result of this decision that led to the Canadian Defence Department producing the Sexton.

7. Naval use. The first time the Royal Navy showed an interest in the 25pdr was in July 1943,[20] when they were offered it as a potential submarine gun. Their interest was aroused, but they objected to the separate-loading ammunition, and it was proposed to begin work to redesign gun and ammunition to accept a fixed round. But the idea was abandoned in favour of a new design of 3.5in gun.[21] In 1944,

Left: The Australian 'short' 25pdr gun.
Below, left: The Mk 3 carriage allowed the trail to be hinged to obtain an extra 30° of elevation, but a shallow pit was necessary to provide space for the breech to recoil. The trail joint was wrapped with rags to keep the hinges free from dirt.

Top right: The 'Bishop' self-propelled 25pdr, using the chassis of the Valentine tank. Note the armoured barbette, which restricted elevation thereby limiting the gun's range. Compare this with the 'Sexton', which used the Canadian Ram tank chassis, shown

in the lower right photograph. This design allowed full performance of the gun and, consequently, was a highly successful equipment. **Bottom:** The Canadian 25pdr MARC on tow.

the Mk 2 gun, fitted with a muzzle collar in place of the muzzle brake, was taken into naval service for the armament of special Landing Craft Guns, which were normal landing craft carrying turretted guns for use as close-support craft in the final minutes of a beach landing. Only one craft, the LCG(M) 103, was equipped, using two guns; the remainder of the projected fleet were equipped with 17pdrs. It was not used in action and was subsequently scrapped.

8. *The Ford Portee.* During 1942, the Ford Motor Company developed a 3 ton 4 × 4 chassis for carrying a 25pdr. By the time the development had been completed, the Army had no requirement for such an equipment, but since the project showed promise, it was decided to complete and test it. A trial was carried out in July 1943, which included firing the gun from the back of the vehicle, the vehicle recoiling five inches in the process. Unfortunately, there was no room on the chassis for the gun detachment to ride, nor for the carriage of a reasonable supply of ammunition, so on completion of the trial, the project was terminated.[22]

9. *A Monobloc gun with a five-port muzzle brake* was designed in December 1942 for a Vickers project for mounting the 25pdr into the hull of a Valentine tank. By the time the gun design was ready, the tank project had been abandoned, so that the gun never got past the paper stage.

Data Ordnance, QF, 25pdr Mk 2 or 3, on Carriage, 25pdr Mk 1

Weight of gun and breech mechanism: 1,000lb.
Total length, with muzzle brake: 106.72in.
Length of bore: 92.375in.
Rifling: 26 grooves, uniform RH 1/20.
Breech mechanism: Vertical sliding block, hand-operated, percussion fired.
Elevation: $-5°$ $+40°$.
Traverse: 4° right and left.
Recoil system: Hydropneumatic, variable, 20in to 36in.
Total weight in action: 3,968lb.

Performance *Firing standard high-explosive shell weighing 25lb:*
Maximum muzzle velocity: 1,700ft/sec (Charge Super).
Maximum range: 13,400 yards.
Firing armour-piercing shot, weighing 20lb:
Velocity: 2,000ft/sec (With Charge Super plus Increment).
Penetration: 70mm at 400 yards at 0° impact (proof figures).

Ammunition
Propelling Charge. The 25pdr propelling charge consisted of two basic units, the Normal Charge and the Super Charge. The Normal Charge consisted of three cloth bags of propellant in a cartridge case, fitted at the base with a percussion primer and closed at the mouth by a removable leather-board

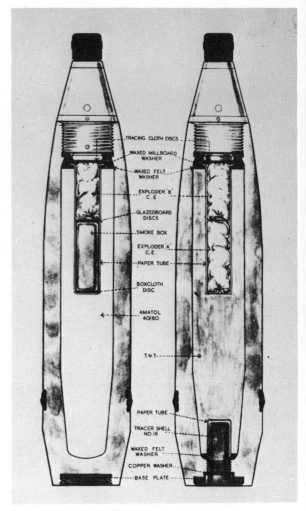

Above: HE shells for the 25pdr gun.

cup. The three bags were colour-coded; Charge 3 consisted of the full three bags, red, white and blue. For Charge 2, the blue bag was removed, and for Charge 1, both blue and white bags were removed, leaving the red bag in place, secured at the base of the case by a shellac cement.

The contents and shapes of the bags varied, since almost every service propellant, plus imported American propellant, was tested and approved as an alternative at some time or other. It would serve no useful purpose to tabulate the scores of variations; a representative example was the 'Cartridge, 25pdr Cordite W057 or WM061 and W016 or WM017 Mk 6 Foil' approved in 1943, which had 6oz 5drams of Cordite W016 or WM017 in Charge 1, 7oz 12drs W057 or W061 in Charge 2, and 13oz 3drs W057 or WM061 in Charge 3, giving a total charge weight of 1lb 11oz 4drs. The word 'Foil' in the nomenclature referred to the inclusion in the Charge 3 bag of a 7in × $2\frac{1}{2}$in sheet of lead or tin foil, .002in thick, which was consumed in the explosion and which assisted in keeping the bore clear of copper, deposited there by the passage of the shell driving band.

The Super Charge was a bundle of propellant placed in the cartridge case and there secured by a non-removable leather-board cup cemented in place. Again, there were innumerable variations; a representative one was the 'Cartridge, 25pdr Super Charge NQ/S Mk 1 Foil' which contained 2lb 13½oz of Cordite NQ/S in a bundle of 9.3in sticks, a 14in × 2½in piece of lead foil loosely crumpled on top, a percussion primer No. 11 and a sealing cup.

The standard cartridge case was of drawn brass, but much development work went into the perfection of a steel case against the probability of a brass shortage. Work on this had begun in 1937, but was dropped in favour of more important things. It was revived in 1939, and the Royal Ordnance Factory, Birtley and various private companies spent much of the war working on designs of drawn and fabricated cases. In November 1942, a design of built-up case, with a welded tubular steel body welded to a machined steel base, was approved for issue,[23] and a contract was placed for 200,000 to be made by New Crown Forgings of Landore. Additional contracts were later made, and a total of 380,000 were manufactured, of which, 39,000 were filled, but not issued. In December 1944, an acute shortage of 25pdr ammunition developed, and it was proposed to use the filled steel cases which were in store at an ammunition depot in Easingwold. 2,000 were issued for trial, half to the School of Artillery and half to the Ordnance Board, and they proved to be unsatisfactory, giving rise to jams and difficult extraction. Approval for service was withheld. In September 1945, there was a proposal to use them up for training, but in view of the failures in tests, the proposal was refused by the Ordnance Board and they were all scrapped. In post-war years, cases in wrapped steel and fibre-reinforced plastic were developed, but none were ever taken into service.

The four basic charges (1, 2, 3, and Super) were later augmented by 'Incremental Charges'. The first of these was the 'Super Plus', an addition charge to fit into the hollow of the closing cup of the Super Charge and thus impart more velocity to the 20lb armour-piercing shot. This was proposed early in 1942 after it had been decided to adopt a muzzle brake, and the first trials took place in September 1942. The original design was in a cambric bag, but, in the interest of water-proofing, it was changed to a celluloid capsule in February 1943. This, containing 5½oz Cordite NQ/S was approved on 16 June 1943 and issued thereafter; the design was later changed to 4½oz Cordite WM, after it had been found that the celluloid of the capsule was generating 15ft/sec velocity and several hundreds of pounds of extra pressure in the breech.

When the Italian campaign got under way, it was found that the normal and super charges did not give sufficient choice of trajectories to satisfy the requirements of gunnery in mountainous country. The trajectory for a given range at Charge 3 would

be so low as to strike the hill-top, while changing to Charge 2 to get the shell over the crest gave slightly too little range. To cure this, 'Intermediate Increments', 4oz bags of propellant, were provided. One increment could be used with Charge 1 to give, in effect, Charge 1½, while on or two could be used with Charge 2, to give Charges 2⅓ and 2⅔. The bags were striped red and white as a reminder that they were only to be used with the red and white bags of the normal charge. Provision of these increments was authorized in January 1944.[24]

There were only two designs of HE shell, and only one of those was ever issued. However, there were more than twenty different 'Method of Filling Designs' which covered different types of explosive and methods of arranging the exploders within the shell. The most important development in this line was the adoption of the 'Universal Filling', in which the explosive was formed with a large central cavity suitable for a proximity fuze; this was normally filled with a removable pellet of explosive, on top of which the conventional percussion or time fuze could be screwed into the nose of the shell. For use was a proximity fuze, the pellet was taken out and the shank of the fuze went into the deep cavity.

Shell, 25pdr HE Streamlined, Mk 1D. This was the standard projectile, weighing exactly 25lb when filled and fuzed. The original approved filling was 1lb 2oz of Amatol 60/40, but various percentage mixes of Amatol were later approved, and fillings of TNT, PE3, RDX/Beeswax and RDX/TNT were bought into use as the war went on.

Shell, 25pdr HE Streamlined, Mk 2DT. This was the Mark 1D with the addition of a tracer in the base. It was introduced in the spring of 1943. The original intention had been to use the shell for anti-tank shooting, the tracer being necessary in order to correct the aim, but this idea lapsed, and its official use was stated to be as a marker for indicating barrage limits at night. There is no record of it ever having been used in service.

Note: The letter 'D' behind the Mark number indicated the head shape of the projectile. This was a hang-over from the years when old designs with blunt heads were still in service, and it was necessary to distinguish between the two types. The system was abandoned at the end of the war when the older shells had all passed from service. The suffix letter 'T' indicates the presence of a tracer.

Smoke Shells. The issued smoke shells for the 25pdr were all of the base-ejection type, although a bursting type, filled with white phosphorus, was designed and approved for issue should there be a shortage of the ingredients for the base ejection smoke canisters.

Shell, Smoke, 25pdr, Base Ejection, Mk 1A. This was the original pattern, developed by the Chemical Warfare Research Establishment, Porton, in 1937. It was blunt-nosed (hence the letter 'A') and contained four canisters and an expelling charge. Time and Percussion Fuze 220 was fitted, which, at the

Above: The range of 25pdr projectiles; not all of these were available during the war.

end of the set time, ignited the expelling charge; this, in turn, ignited the canisters and forced them down the shell body, shearing off the shell base and ejecting the burning canisters.

Shell, Smoke, 25pdr, BE, Streamlined, Mks 1D to 6D. These had a tapering nose and streamlined base and contained three canisters; the shells were all fuzed T&P No. 221. They replaced the Mk 1A early in 1941, and because of their shape and weight (21lb 14oz) ranged closer to the HE shell than had the Mk 1. The difference between the various Marks was small, consisting solely of manufacturing and assembly details.

Shell, Smoke, 25pdr, BE, Mk 7D. This shell had a tapered nose and a cylindrical, non-streamlined base. It originated as a design for a chemical shell, and was adopted for smoke for the sake of production convenience. It ranged much differently from the streamlined shell, and for this reason alone, was heartily disliked by the gunners. It appears to have been restricted to training, and large stocks were still being used up for several years after the war.

Shell, Smoke, Coloured, BE, Mks 1D and 2D. These were streamlined smoke shells of the standard type, but having the canisters filled with compounds which emitted red, yellow, green or blue smoke. The purpose was to indicate targets for air strikes, or to mark barrage lines. Issued first in 1944. The only difference between the two Marks lay in the contour of the driving band.

Shells, Chemical. Development of chemical (gas) shells began in 1937, and ten different marks of base ejection and two of bursting shell were eventually designed and approved, the fillings ranging from tear-gas to thickened mustard gas. The quantity filled and stored was never very great. According to one source, the amount available at any one time during the war would have sufficed for about ten days of combat, after which, there would have been a pause of several weeks while the stocks of empty shell were filled. All the filled stock were sea-dumped as soon as the war ended.

Shell, Flare, Target Recognition, BE, Mk 1D. This was essentially similar to the coloured smoke shell, except that the canisters were filled with a magnesium compound which emitted a brightly coloured flame. Red, yellow and green were first issued, there being difficulty in developing a blue flare which burned sufficiently brightly and yet was recognizably blue, though this difficulty was eventually overcome.

Shell, Incendiary, BE, Mk 1D. Another variation on the smoke shell, the canisters being made of magnesium and filled with Thermite. The first design, based on the Smoke Shell Mk 1A, was developed in 1939 and approved for issue in September 1940. It is believed that few were made, since there appeared to be no requirement. A fresh design, of streamlined shape, was developed in 1944 against a demand for shell capable of igniting standing crops in Normandy to remove the cover from enemy machine-gunners. This appeared late in 1944 as the Mark 1D, but it seems to have been used very rarely in action.

Shell, Star, BE, Mk 1D. Developed in 1943, this used the non-streamlined Smoke Mk 7 body, and contained a parachute and canister. The star composition gave a light of 430,000 candle-power and burned for about 25–30 seconds during its fall, lighting up the ground beneath.

Shell, Propaganda, BE. This was never an issue shell as such. It originated in a local conversion of smoke shell in North Africa, developed by the Weapons Technical Staff Field Force, by simply unscrewing the base of a smoke shell, removing the canisters, and replacing them with rolled-up leaflets. Since topicality was the essence of good propaganda, it was unpractical to fill these shells in Britain and ship them to the scene of action, so it remained a local expedient, provision of the necessary shells and leaflets being left to local resources.

Shot, Armour-Piercing, Mks 1T to 6T and 8T. These were solid steel shot, the 'T' indicating the provision of a tracer. The differences between Marks were minor, and concerned the method of fitting the tracer or the contour of the driving band. All weighed 20lb.

Shot, Armour-Piercing, Capped, Mk 7T. This was first approved in January 1943, being a standard shot with the addition of a malleable steel cap over the point. It was developed in an attempt to improve the performance of 25pdr shot against face-hardened armour. After approval, it was pointed out that the effect of a cap was negligible except at velocities much greater than those which could be attained by the 25pdr. Moreover, while it improved the performance against face-hardened plate, it actually degraded the performance against homogeneous plate. In view of these objections the shot was never manufactured or issued, though it actually remained in the Vocabulary for several years before being struck off.

Experimental Ammunition

A considerable range of different types of ammunition was developed at various times, but for various reasons they never entered service. The following deserve mention if only to prove that the designers did not overlook much.

Shot and Shell, APCBC. Development of capped, ballistic capped shot and shell took place in 1942–43, a 25lb version being designed first and then a 20lb model, but the project was dropped when it was finally appreciated that the 25pdr could not fire them at sufficiently high velocities to make their adoption worthwhile.

High-Explosive, Anti-Tank (HEAT). In the early flush of enthusiasm for hollow-charge munitions, it was logical to develop a hollow-charge shell for the 25pdr. Work began in 1940 and continued throughout the war, the principal difficulty being the design of a suitably sensitive base fuze. Work was further hampered by insufficient knowledge of the fundamental principles of the hollow-charge phenomenon. Much basic research had to be done (a lot of which proved to be of value to other hollow-charge projects) but just as things seemed, at last, to be going well, it was discovered that spun shell were not the best vehicle for the hollow charge, and also that the Wallbuster Shell (see under the recoilless gun section for more information on this) showed greater promise as an anti-tank weapon. The HEAT project was therefore finally abandoned late in 1944.

Combined HE/Chemical Shell. Work on this began in December 1940, the aim being a shell with a cavity in the nose filled with high-explosive, and a base cavity filled with some chemical agent. Work proceeded at low priority, some trials were carried out, but the requirement was cancelled in November 1944.

Cast Iron HE Shell. In the hope of producing a cheap and easily made HE shell, a great deal of work went into developing a cast iron shell from 1939 onwards, but although several designs were tried, they all exhibited the same tendency to break up as soon as they left the muzzle. The project was finally abandoned in August 1944.

Long-Range Shell. Development of a 21lb shell in 24-ton steel, containing 3lb of high explosive and giving 20% better lethality and a range of 14,500 yards, began in September 1943. Work continued on a low priority and had not been completed by the end of the war.

Fuzes

The following fuzes were approved for use with shells as shown.

High-explosive shell. Percussion: 115E, 117, 117B, 119, 119B, 231, 232. Time and Percussion: 222, 213. Proximity: T97E6, T97E9.

Smoke, BE. Time: 221T. Time and Percussion: 220, 221.

Flare, Star, Incendiary and Propaganda. Time and Percussion: 221

Chemical, Bursting. Percussion: 119

Base Ejection. Time and Percussion: 221.

References in text:
1. Royal Artillery Committee Memorandum B141 of 25 Jan 1922.
2. RAC Memo B315 of 20 Aug 1924.
3. Ordnance Committee Memoranda B7327, B7401, B7558 and RAC Memo B319 of 3 Sept 1924.
4. RAC Memo B431 of 10 June 1925.
5. RAC Memo B561 of 3 March 1926 and B550 of 3 Feb 1926.
6. RAC Memo B716 of 27 Dec 1926.
7. RAC Memo B722 of 5 Jan 1927.
8. RAC Memo B1151 of 30 May 1928.
9. RAC Memo B1611 of 26 June 1929.
10. RAC Minute G702 of 13 Oct 1933.
11. RAC Minute G728 of 12 Dec 1933.
12. RAC Minute G862 of 12 Sept 1934.
13. List of Changes in Equipment, Para B584 of 26 Aug 1936.
14. List of Changes, Para B1638 of 11 Feb 1938.
15. List of Changes, Para B3218 of 7 Dec 1937.
16. List of Changes, Para B3217.
17. List of Changes, Para B7830 of 21 July 1942.
18. List of Changes, Para C459 of 24 Nov 1944.
19. Ordnance Board Proceeding AG1240 of 27 Oct 1943.
20. Ordnance Board Proceeding 23882 of 12 July 1943.
21. Ordnance Board Proceeding 25191 of 22 Oct 1943.
22. Ordnance Board Proceeding AG1204 of 8 Sept 1943.
23. Ordnance Board Proceeding 20487 of 18 Nov 1942.
24. Ordnance Board Proceeding 26932 of 13 March 1944.

3.7in Mountain Howitzer

Artillery for pack transport was always faced with the dilemma that a powerful gun was too big to form a single mule load, while a gun small enough to go on a mule's back was too weak to be of much use in mountainous country. The solution appears to have originated in Russia. In 1876, a Captain Kolokolzor, director of the Tsar's arsenal at Obuchov, suggested making the gun in two sections and screwing them together. This was kept secret in Russia until 1883. In Britain, a Colonel Le Mesurier, RA, had come up with the same idea. In 1879 he designed a rifled muzzle-loader, and 12 guns were made by the Elswick Ordnance Company for the Afghanistan Expedition in 1879. The efficiency of this 'RML 2.5in Jointed Gun' was sufficient to perpetuate the principle in Indian service for many years, and the last of the breed was the 3.7in, more usually known as the Pack Howitzer.

At the beginning of the century, the Indian Army was using a BL 10pdr jointed gun, but with the

Above and below: Two views of the 3.7in howitzer on Carriage Mk 4P. The gun shown below is the Mk 1/1 variant.

adoption of such modern weapons as the 18pdr, the Indian Government asked Woolwich Arsenal to develop a new pattern of jointed gun, a modern weapon using cased charges and with an on-carriage recoil system. Woolwich, having their hands full, passed the request on to Vickers Sons & Maxim, who produced the 3.7in in about 1910. Trials were conducted and the design was approved, but because of a shortage of funds, the Indian Government were unable to proceed further and the design was shelved. In 1915, with the Indian units in France demanding replacement weapons, finance was found, production began, and official approval was given in February 1917, though by then, the weapon had been in use for some months.

The barrel of the 3.7in separated into two portions, breech and chase, and these were joined together by a 'junction nut' inside an enveloping sleeve. The nut was operated by a worm screw at the top of the sleeve; the two sections were thrust together, the front end of the breech section entering the junction nut. The nut was then revolved by the worm screw so as to clamp the two halves together with the rifling in perfect register. There was, unfortunately, no practical way to interlock the firing mechanism with the junction nut, and so it was not unknown for the gun to be fired with the junction nut undone. The result was spectacular, though relatively harmless; the chase departed up the range after the shell.

The carriage was the first split-trail pattern to be adopted in British service. A hydropneumatic recoil system was fitted, and equipments used on the North-West Frontier of India usually had a large shield to protect the gunners from sniper fire. The whole equipment dismantled very rapidly into eight units for mule carriage.

After the First World War, its use was extended beyond the original mountain artillery role, and it became the equipment of 'Light Batteries, RA', intended to act as close support for infantry. This idea was abandoned in the late 1920s when the infantry were given the 3in mortar which enabled them to do their own close support. During the Second World War, the 3.7in was used principally in the Far East, though some pack batteries were usefully employed in Italy. By mid 1944, it was past its best, and a specification was issued for a replacement pack weapon of 3.3in calibre firing an 18lb shell. The development of this was passed to the Canadian Army and continued into the 1950s before it was finally abandoned. As a stopgap, more powerful propelling charges were suggested for the 3.7in, and I was involved in trials of these shortly after the war. The idea was not a success, the recoil being excessive and parts falling off the gun every time it fired, and the idea was dropped.

The ability of the 3.7in to come to pieces was of value when airborne artillery units were being formed, and it became one of the standard artillery weapons of airborne troops. It was also carried on warships for many years, having been adopted by the Royal Navy as their 'Landing Gun' to accompany shore parties, though it is doubtful if it was ever put to serious use in this role. The 3.7in howitzer was finally declared obsolete in February 1960.

Variants
Ordnance:

Mk 1: Two varieties of this existed; the first half-dozen or so guns had increasing twist rifling, but this was changed to uniform twist and the chamber was slightly enlarged without change of Mark number.

Mk 1/1: Introduced in 1944, had a simplified breech mechanism.

Mk 1/2: Introduced 1945, had new firing-pin unit.

Mk 1/3: This was declared obsolete in 1960, but no record of its introduction has been found and we are unable to say what the differences were.

Carriage:

Mk 1: Split trail, wooden wheels, shield. Pack carriage.

Mk 2: As for Mk 1, but with additional fittings for animal draught.

Mk 3: Fixed instead of movable spades, otherwise as for Mk 2.

Mk 4P: Pneumatic tyres, no shield, not capable of being dismantled into pack loads.

Mk 5: Lightened model for airborne troops.

Data
Weight of gun and breech mechanism: 451½lb.
Weight of breech section: 247lb.
Weight of chase section: 204½lb.
Total length: 46.8in.
Length of bore: 43.5in.
Rifling: 28 grooves, uniform RH 1/25.
Breech mechanism: Interrupted screw, percussion fired.
Elevation: $-5° +40°$.
Traverse: 20° right and left.
Recoil system: Hydropneumatic variable, 17½in to 35in.
Weight in action: 1,856lb.

Performance
Firing standard 20lb Shrapnel shell:
Muzzle velocity: 973ft/sec.
Maximum range: 6,000 yards.
Firing 20lb HE shell (restricted to Charge 4 or less):
Muzzle velocity: 798ft/sec.
Maximum range: 4,500 yards.

Ammunition separate loading, cased charges.
Propelling Charge. This was a five-part charge contained in a brass case 3.6 inches long and closed by a removable leather-board cup. Nominal weight of the full charge was 9oz of Cordite, though varying weights of different types of propellant were approved at different times. The bags were colour-coded. There was a small supplementary bag attached to Charge 5 which was removed to give a special

'Star Shell Charge' in which the velocity was slightly reduced so as to obviate the danger of the star parting company from the parachute when ejected, which would occur if the terminal velocity were too high.

Shell, HE, 3.7in Mk 3. A non-streamlined shell filled with Amatol and with the Percussion Fuze 101E, 106E, 44 or 45. This shell was restricted to firing with Charge 4 or less. Towards the end of the war, a streamlined shell was designed which, with a special 12oz 'Super Charge' could range to 7,000 yards, but it was not adopted for service.

Shell, Shrapnel, 3.7in Mk 6. The usual type of nose-ejecting shrapnel shell, filled with lead/antimony bullets, a gunpowder expelling charge, and with the Fuze Time and Percussion No. 80.

Shell, Smoke, Bursting, 3.7in Mk 3. A non-streamlined shell with a filling of white phosphorus and

fuzed Percussion No. 117 or 119. Weight 19lb 11½oz.

Shell, Smoke, BE, 3.7in Mk 1. A base-ejection shell with two smoke canisters, fitted with the Fuze Time and Percussion No. 83. Manufactured in small numbers and rarely seen.

Shell, Star, 3.7in Mk 3. This contained a single star unit suspended from a parachute, and used the Fuze, Time, No. 221T. Weight 21lb 13¼oz.

Shell, HEAT, 3.7in Mk 1. A hollow-charge shell of the usual type, with a hemispherical head and with the Fuze Percussion No. 233. It was developed in 1942 on a demand from the Indian Army. In order to keep it short so as to fit into the mule transport carriers, it was less effective than it might have been, but appears to have performed well against light Japanese armour. It weighed 15lb, and could pierce plate of approximately 2½ inches.

95mm Infantry Howitzer

The 95mm howitzer project was born in January 1942 with a proposal to develop a 3.7in self-propelled howitzer as a form of assault gun, and a similar weapon for use in tanks. It was to consist of a barrel machined from a 3.7in Mark 2 AA gun barrel liner, fitted with a modified 25pdr breech ring and mechanism with a lug on top of the breech ring to attach it to a recoil system. It would fire 3.7in Pack Howitzer ammunition, though for tank use a new, fixed round was to be developed. The entire gun was to be so designed that it would balance and fit into the standard 6pdr tank mounting, and use the 6pdr cradle and recoil system.

Bearing in mind the fact that in 1942, the average British tank was sadly under-gunned, there was an element of sense in this idea, but the weapon, as proposed and as finally produced, was so low-powered as to be useless as a main tank armament. It eventually appeared as a 'Close Support Howitzer' on Churchill, Cromwell and Centaur tanks, performed some useful work during and after the invasion of Europe in 1944 and remained nominally in service until 1954.

What concerns us here, however, is the towed version, which had a most chequered career. This appears to have been proposed some time in the summer of 1942, though we have been unable to find any sort of firm policy statement to indicate who suggested it or why. At that time, the idea of an 'Infantry Gun' was much in the air; the German and Russian armies both gave light artillery to their infantry for close support, and the American Army had formed 'Infantry Cannon Companies' and were equipping them with a truncated 105mm howitzer (see p. 63). And so a 95mm Infantry Howitzer was projected. The first record seems to be in an Ordnance Board Proceeding of 18 November 1942, in which it was noted that two versions

were under development; a 20-calibre howitzer on a Stevens carriage using the 6pdr recoil system, and a 15-calibre version on a field carriage 'now under design by CEAD' (Chief Engineer & Superintendent of Armaments Design).

By April 1942, two pilots, one of each of the above types, had been built and were sent to Shoeburyness for testing, and on 10 September 1943, the 20-calibre howitzer on the Stevens carriage was accepted for service by the Director of Infantry. Already, though, there were some doubts about the whole idea; an Ordnance Board Mission to North Africa in June 1943 had discussed the 95mm project with staff officers, divisional commanders and other interested parties, and reported that '. . . in no case was it welcome. All said that the battalion was already overloaded with a variety of weapons and that the only place for the infantry gun was in the support company. The opinion was expressed that if our infantry would learn to use their mortars and their radio sets for directing artillery fire, then there would be no need for an infantry gun.' Unfortunately, the days of the Consumer Research Council were far in the future, and no heed was paid to the voice of the front-line soldier; the 95mm Infantry Howitzer Mark 2 on Carriage Mark 1 went into production.

As noted above, the ordnance was based on the 3.7in AA gun loose barrel, suitably cut down and re-chambered. The 25pdr breech mechanism was used, the 6pdr hydro-spring recoil system, and a modified 25pdr sight bracket. The Stevens (named for the designer) carriage was a clumsy box trail of welded square section, ugly and cumbersome in action, and with a large shield to protect the detachment. The whole equipment could be dismantled into ten pack loads for mule transport. The exact number produced is not known, but it was quite considerable; propaganda photographs of 1944 showed rows and rows of them in ordnance depots. But production had begun prematurely, before all the trials had been completed, and as these trials followed their course, some serious defects became apparent. In May 1944, the report of the travelling trial showed that the wheel track was too narrow and the gun was unstable when being towed across rough country, frequently overturning. But the worst report came in November 1944 at the close of the endurance trials, during which, thousands of rounds had been fired from a series of guns. This revealed grave defects in the recoil system. 'The spring recuperator has failed throughout, in spite of every effort to find springs that will stand up to the work.' The Ordnance Board considered the system to be unsuitable and recommended that it be abandoned and a fresh design begun. These reports went to the Deputy Chief of the Imperial General Staff who, on 13 November, minuted to the Director-General of Artillery 'In view of the amount of re-design that would be necessary and also that, in its redesigned form, it will still not meet our requirements due its limited elevation, I consider the project should be abandoned and the carriage declared obsolete.' Acting on this, on 8 December 1944 the Ordnance Board ruled that all design and development work was to stop, with the exception

Right: A 95mm howitzer with detachment at the School of Infantry, 1944; and (bottom) in firing position. **Middle:** The 'Alecto' self-propelled 95mm howitzer.

of the redesign of the recoil system, which could be utilized in connection with other equipments. Finally, on 18 April 1945, the Deputy Director of Artillery announced that 'In accordance with a General Staff decision' the 95mm Infantry Howitzer was to be declared obsolete.

It might be noted that, in 1944, two further projects using this equipment were mooted. First, a lightweight version, without shield, for airborne use, and second, a version with greater elevation. Neither design was ever approved nor built.

Variants

Apart from the experimental projects mentioned above, there was never any variant model of the Infantry Howitzer, but for the sake of completeness, the full tally of 95mm models is given here.

Mk 1: Tank howitzer, nominally 20 calibres, actually 21.75. It was fitted with a muzzle counterweight. Used on Churchill Mks 5 and 8, Cromwell Mks 6 and 7, and Centaur Mk 4 tanks. 80 built. Had an elevation of 37°, hence a maximum range of 6,800 yards. Used fixed ammunition.

Mk 2: Infantry howitzer on towed carriage.

Mk 3: Self-propelled howitzer on Alecto Carrier (a modified Harry Hopkins tank chassis). Same gun as the Mk 1, but without muzzle counterweight, and using separate-loading ammunition.

Mk 4: Tank Howitzer. Conversion of Mk 1 to horizontal breech block with semi-automatic operation.

Mk 4/1: Conversion of some Mk 1 and all Mk 4, by enlarging the clearance in the breech ring mortise and fitting a new, oversized breech block. This took place in 1949.

Mk 5: New manufacture to Mk 4 standard.

Data Howitzer Mk 2, on Carriage Mk 1
Weight of gun and breech mechanism: 517lb.
Total length: 74.05in.
Length of bore: 69.0in (18.65cal).
Rifling: 28 grooves, uniform RH, 1/25.
Breech mechanism: Vertical sliding block, hand-operated, percussion fired.
Elevation: $-5°$ $+30°$.
Traverse: 4° right and left.
Recoil system: Hydro-spring, variable, to 30in.
Weight in action: 2,105lb.

Performance firing the standard 25lb HE shell
Muzzle velocity: 1,083ft/sec.
Maximum range: 6,000 yards.

Ammunition separate loading, cased charge.
Although originally it was hoped to utilize the existing designs of ammunition used with the 3.7in howitzer, this was soon found to be impracticable and a complete new range was designed. The tank gun ammunition was fixed; that for the SP and Infantry equipments was separate loading. Only the latter is listed here.

Propelling Charge. This consisted of three bags, coloured red, white and blue, carrying a total of 13oz 7dr of Cordite, in a brass case, 8.1in long, closed with a leather-board cup. Because of the different lengths of the towed and SP howitzers, their performance was slightly different.

	Mk 2 howitzer:	Mk 3 Howitzer:
Charge One	503ft/sec	523ft/sec
Charge Two	813ft/sec	839ft/sec
Charge Three	1,083ft/sec	1,111ft/sec

Shell, HE, 95mm Mk 1D. This was a non-streamlined (square-based) shell of normal pattern. It carried a filling of Amatol or TNT, and was fuzed Percussion No. 117 or 119. It weighed 25lb. This shell was also used with the tank rounds and, therefore, had a groove cut below the driving band, into which the mouth of the tank cartridge case was cannelured to form the fixed round.

Shell, Smoke, BE, 95mm Mk 1D. A base-ejection smoke shell similar to that for the 25pdr gun. It was non-streamlined, filled with three smoke canisters, and fuzed Time and Percussion No. 221. Shells used with tank rounds were fuzed Time No. 390, graduated in yards instead of seconds.

Shell, Flare, TRBE, 95mm Mk 1D. Similar to the smoke shell, but containing three flare canisters filled with a magnesium composition. ('TRBE' stands for Target Recognition, Base Ejection.) Although formally approved, it is doubtful if any were made.

Shell, HE/CF, 95mm Mk 1. This was a combined hollow-charge anti-tank and high-explosive anti-personnel shell, resembling the 3.7in pack howitzer.

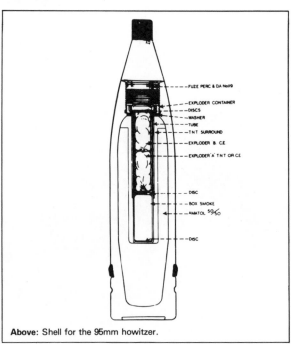

Above: Shell for the 95mm howitzer.

HEAT shell, but elongated to give greater explosive capacity. It carried a 233 Percussion fuze. The letters 'CF' indicated 'Combined Filling' to designate the dual function. It was not particularly successful and it is doubtful if any were ever issued.

4.5in Howitzer

In the aftermath of the South African War, the Field Howitzer Sub-Committee of the Royal Artillery Committee deliberated on a design to replace the elderly 5in BL howitzer. Their approach was a simple one; they specified the performance required, sent a letter to all the gunmakers, and then sat back to await results. Various designs duly appeared, the Committee conducted trials, and eventually settled on the 4.5in Howitzer produced by the Coventry Ordnance Works. It was approved for service on 19 March 1909, though issues actually began in 1908, and by the end of 1918, some 3,359 had been built. Production then stopped and the equipment remained in service until declared obsolete on 13 September 1944.

The 4.5in howitzer was a built-up gun using an 'A' tube, jacket, and 'B' hoop, all of nickel steel. The horizontal sliding block breech was the first of its type in British field service. The carriage was a box trail type with shield, using a hydro-spring recoil system. During the First World War, there were a number of accidents caused by the breech block 'setting back' on firing, and fracturing the breech ring, and this was cured in the Mark 2 gun by enlarging the radius of the corners of the breech ring mortise, in which the block slid. The breech block was also strengthened, and the rifling, which was originally of increasing twist, was changed to uniform twist in the interests of easier manufacture. In post-war years, the carriage was modernized by adding pneumatic tyres, and the sights were also improved, but, basically, the howitzer which went out in 1944 was little changed from the one which came in in 1908.

The 4.5in howitzer was to have been replaced by the 25pdr gun, but since deliveries of the latter were slow, several batteries of 4.5s were still in service in 1939, and the howitzer saw use in France in 1939–40. It was also used in the Eritrean campaign, and in the Western Desert in 1941–42, but the few survivors were withdrawn at the end of the North African campaign. Thereafter, it was used for training while ammunition stocks remained.

Variants

Ordnance:

Mk 1: Original Coventry Ordnance Works design, with increasing twist rifling.

Mk 2: Royal Gun Factory design, uniform twist rifling and strengthened breech.

Carriage:

Mk 1: Original; wooden wheels with steel tyres.

Right: 4.5in howitzer on Carriage Mk 1P. The version shown here was standard at the outbreak of war.

Mk 1R: Wooden wheels with solid rubber tyres.

Mk 1P: Steel disc wheels and pneumatic tyres.

Mk 1PA: As Mk 1P, but improved sights and recoil system.

Data

Weight of gun and breech mechanism: 972lb (Mk 1); 1,021lb (Mk 2).

Total length: 70.0in.

Length of bore: 60.11in (13.35 cal).

Rifling: 32 grooves. Mk 1: Increasing RH, from 1/41.31 at breech to 1/14.78 at 5.87in from the muzzle, thereafter uniform. Mk 2: uniform RH 1/20.

Breech mechanism: Horizontal sliding block, percussion fired.

Elevation: $-5°$ $+45°$.

Traverse: 3° right and left.

Recoil system: Hydro-spring, variable, 15in to 43in.

Weight in action: 3,010lb (Mk 1); 4,030lb (Mk 1P); 3,291lb (Mk 1PA).

Performance firing standard 35lb HE shell

Muzzle velocity: 1,010ft/sec.

Maximum range: 7,000 yards.

Ammunition separate loading, cased charge.

Propelling Charge. This was a five-part charge contained in a brass case, 3.4in long, the total weight of propellant being 15.875oz of Cordite. Muzzle velocities and maximum ranges through the zones were as follows.

Charge 1	480ft/sec	2,000 yards
Charge 2	630ft/sec	3,200 yards
Charge 3	700ft/sec	3,800 yards
Charge 4	820ft/sec	4,900 yards
Charge 5	1,010ft/sec	7,000 yards

The Percussion Primer No. 1 was standard.

Shell, HE, Mks 12 to 16. These were all 35lb non-streamlined shells filled with Amatol or TNT, and

Above: Rear of the 4.5in howitzer on the Mk 1PA carriage.

adapted to the Percussion Fuzes Nos. 44, 45, 101E, 106, 117 or 119. The differences between the Marks were minor and did not affect performance.

Shell, Smoke, Bursting, Mks 3 to 11. A 35.75lb shell, non-streamlined, and with a filling of white phosphorus. Normally fuzed 106E or 117, though the 45 could also be used by means of an adapter.

Shell, Smoke, Base Ejection, Mk 1. A 35.75lb non-streamlined shell with the usual three smoke canisters filled with Hexachloroethane/Zinc mixture and fitted with the Time and Percussion Fuze No. 83.

Shell, Star, Mk 3. A 35.75lb non-streamlined shell carrying a star unit and parachute, ejected over the target by a Fuze Time and Percussion No. 221.

 # 4.5in Medium Gun

The 4.5in was an odd weapon in some respects, falling into the medium category by virtue of its size and employment, but not really offering much improvement over its partner, the 5.5in gun. It was first suggested in about 1933 as a modification of the 60pdr in order to fire a modern design of shell and obtain a better range. The usual financial question intervened, and the redesign came down to no more than relining the barrel. In 1937, the first equipment was tested, giving a maximum range of 20,000 yards, a sizeable improvement on the 60pdr. The conversion was approved, work began, but it was then found that there were only 76 60pdrs available for conversion, a number insufficient to equip the expanding army. So in 1938, the Director Royal Artillery, on his own initiative and responsibility, authorized development of a fresh design of gun which would fit the new carriage then being designed for the 5.5in gun. This, the Mark 2 gun, was approved on 31 August 1939, but no production took place until late 1940, and guns were not issued until 1941.

In every respect except calibre and barrel length, the 4.5in was the same as the 5.5in, the same breech mechanism and the same carriage being used. The guns were issued to Medium Regiments RA, one battery generally using 4.5s and the other 5.5s and because of the 4.5's longer range, they were fondly referred to as the 'long-range snipers' of the regiment. But the extra range did not really compensate for the lighter shell, and the 4.5in was never as popular as the 5.5in. The Mark 1 and

Mark 1* guns were made obsolete in April 1944; the Mark 2 lingered until August 1959, but it was principally a training weapon during the post-war years.

Variants

Ordnance:

Mk 1: Conversion of 60pdr Mk 2 or Mk 2* by relining.

Mk 1:* Conversion of 60pdr Mk 2 or Mk 2* by insertion of an auto-frettaged loose barrel into the jacket, which was bored oversize to accommodate it.

Mk 2: New design to fit 5.5in carriage.

Data Gun Mk 2 on Carriage Mk 1 or Mk 2
Weight of gun and breech mechanism: 4,263lb.
Total length: 192.75in.
Length of bore: 185.0in (41 cal).
Rifling: 32 grooves, uniform RH 1/25.
Breech mechanism: Asbury, interrupted screw, percussion fired.
Elevation: $-5°$ $+45°$.
Traverse: 30° right and left.
Recoil system: Hydropneumatic, variable, 30in to 54in.
Weight in action: 12,880lb.

Performance firing standard 55lb HE shell
Muzzle velocity: 2,250ft/sec.
Maximum range: 20,500 yards.

Below: The 4.5in gun; only the barrel length distinguishes it from the 5.5in when on the same carriage. **Right:** Ammunition for the 4.5in.

Ammunition separate loading, bag charge.

Propelling Charge. This was produced in two different forms, each of which made up into a three-charge combination. The first pattern consisted of a Charge One unit of 'potato-masher' shape, containing 2lb 15oz of Cordite. Charge Two was a completely separate unit, cylindrical in shape, containing 6lb 7oz, while the Charge Three increment, a short cylinder tied to the end of Charge Two, contained 2lb 9oz.

The second pattern was entirely cylindrical and was filled with American NH powder. Charge One was 3lb 5½oz and was fired by itself. Charge Two, used independently of One, contained 7lb 12oz, and the Charge Three increment contained 3lb.

Shell, HE, S/L, 4.5in BL Gun Mk 1D. This was the only projectile issued for this equipment. It was a conventional streamlined shell weighing 55lb with the Fuze Percussion No. 117 or 119. The filling was either TNT or Amatol. The shell was prominently marked with a wide black band just above the driving band to distinguish it from the 4.5in Howitzer shell.

60pdr Gun

The 60pdr was another old soldier, dating from 1904 in its original form. It had been developed as an improvement on the Naval 4.7in guns used on extemporized field-carriages in South Africa, and was designed by the Elswick Ordnance Company. The Mark 1 version was so built that when hooked to its transport limber for horse draught, the gun and recoil system could be disconnected from their anchorage in the cradle and pulled back to rest on the trail, and so better distribute the weight between the gun wheels and the limber wheels. During the First World War, a simpler carriage, without retraction, was produced, but this weighed a ton more than the original and was a retrograde step. A fresh design restored the retraction feature, but simplified it by merely disconnecting the gun from the recoil-system piston rods.

In 1918, the entire carriage design was reworked by Vickers-Armstrong, and a completely new equipment appeared. The gun was five calibres longer and used an improved breech mechanism, while the carriage was lightened and simplified, the ring cradle and cumbersome recoil cylinders of the first design being replaced by a more compact recoil unit in a trough cradle under the gun. The retracting system returned to the original form, in which the recoil cylinders were disconnected from their housings in the cradle, and pulled back with the gun. The earlier models were scrapped as they wore out, and the new design, the Mark 2 gun on Mark 4 carriage, remained in service as the standard medium gun. By 1939, the 60pdr was obsolescent and was to be replaced by the 4.5in and 5.5in equipments, but in their absence, it had to continue in service. It saw its last actions in the Desert Campaign, notably in the hands of the Australians at Tobruk, but it was retained in Britain as a training equipment until late 1944.

Variants

Ordnance:

Mk 1: EOC design; wire-wound gun, 33.6 calibres long.

Mk 1*: Differed in construction, there being no breech bush and the breech screw engaged directly into threads cut in the rear end of the 'A' tube.

Mk 1**: Differed from Mk 1* by having a breech bushing let into the rear of the 'A' tube, and the breech threads cut into this bushing.

Mk 2: Vickers-Armstrong design, 37 calibres long, with Asbury breech mechanism.

Mk 2*: Slight changes in construction to prevent rotation of the inner 'A' tube from torque generated by the action of the shell on the rifling.

Carriage:

Mk 1: Original design. Maximum elevation 22°. Ring cradle and hydro-spring recoil system. Retraction.

Mk 2: Similar to Mk 1, but no retraction.

Mk 2*: Mk 2 locally modified to have retraction facility.

Mk 3: Mk 2 redesigned and incorporating retraction; new manufacture.

Mk 4: Completely new design with hydropneumatic recoil system, trough cradle, and retracting facility.

Data Gun Mk 2, on Carriage Mk 4
Weight of gun and breech mechanism: 4,900lb.
Total length: 192.25in.
Length of bore: 185.0in (37 cal).
Rifling: 32 grooves, uniform RH 1/30.
Breech mechanism: Asbury interrupted screw, percussion fired.
Elevation: $-4\frac{1}{2}°$ $+35°$.
Traverse: 4° right and left.
Recoil System: Hydropneumatic, variable, 21.6in to 54in.
Weight in action: 12,048lb.

Performance firing standard 60lb HE shell.
Muzzle velocity: 2,125ft/sec.
Maximum range: 16,400 yards.

Ammunition separate loading, bag charge.
Propelling Charge. This was a single bag containing 8lb 12oz of Cordite, or varying weights of other types of propellant to give the same ballistics. A gunpowder igniter was stitched to the rear end.

Shell, HE, Mark 9C. A nose-fuzed non-streamlined shell containing 6lb of Amatol and adapted to the Percussion Fuzes Nos. 101, 106, 119, or 231. Weight 60lb.

Shell, Shrapnel, Mk 5C. A nose-ejection shell of the usual shrapnel type, containing 397 lead/antimony bullets of 1oz each and with the Time and Percussion Fuze No. 88 or 220. Weight 60lb.

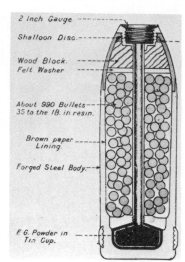

2 Inch Gauge
Shalloon Disc
Wood Block
Felt Washer
About 990 Bullets, 35 to the lB. in resin.
Brown paper Lining
Forged Steel Body
F.G. Powder in Tin Cup.

Left: Shrapnel shell for the 60pdr gun.

Opposite page, top: The 60pdr gun on Mk 4 carriage in firing position; (middle) retracted for travelling; and (bottom) positioned for direct-firing.

5.5in Medium Gun

In the early 1930s, it was decided to develop a new medium gun to replace the ageing 6in gun and 6in 26cwt howitzer, and after discussion, an Operational Requirement was issued in January 1939 calling for a 5in gun to fire a 90lb shell to 16,000 yards and to weight less than 5½ tons. But the best ballistic design of shell to match the range requirement turned out to be of 5½in calibre, and so the 5.5in gun was born.

No effort was spared to produce an up-to-date design as technically advanced as possible, but, looking back, one is inclined to think that the designers over-reached themselves by introducing complications which, when they failed, had to be designed out again. The gun was an auto-frettaged loose barrel in a short jacket, with an Asbury breech mechanism. So far, so good, but it was then given a 'Lock, Percussion 'L' in Slide Box 'AC'', a most involved semi-automatic firing lock which was difficult to strip and assemble, and which revealed innumerable ways of going wrong, undreamed of by the designers. Originally, it had been designed for naval turret guns, in which role it had performed well, but the dirt and grit of field service defeated it, and in mid 1941 it was removed and

replaced by the much simpier 'Lock Percussion 'K' and Slide Box 'Y'', which had served in various guns since 1917.

The carriage was a two-wheeled split-trail pattern which carried the gun in a trough cradle with the trunnions towards the rear so as to allow recoil, at full elevation. In order to balance the barrel mass, two hydropneumatic balancing cylinders were mounted vertically, bearing on the cradle. These gave an immense amount of trouble; they were prone to leak, and if one leaked it threw too much strain on the other, failed to balance, and twisted the cradle. They were difficult to adjust and maintain, and they were difficult and expensive to manufacture, and eventually they had to be discarded and replaced by a much simpler – and more efficient – spring design. These fitted in the same way and gave the equipment the characteristic 'horns' alongside the barrel.

A quick-loading gear was also fitted; this was a proven design and gave no trouble. The cradle was locked to the elevating arc by a spring bolt controlled by a lever alongside the cradle. When, at high elevation, the gun had fired, instead of the gun-layer having to wind furiously on a handwheel to

bring the gun down to a convenient loading angle, the lever was pressed and the cradle thus disengaged from the elevating arc. Pulling up on the rear end of the cradle allowed the gun to swing down to be loaded. While loading was in progress, the gunlayer could set a fresh elevation on the sights, and adjust the elevating arc without affecting the gun. When loading had been completed, a push on the cradle would swing the gun back until the spring bolt dropped into the hole in the elevating arc and locked the cradle and arc together once more; the gunlayer now made a final adjustment and the gun was ready to fire.

Because of difficulties with the design and with organizing production, it was not until May 1942 that the first 5.5in guns went into action in the Western Desert. They were highly successful and well liked, but during the Italian campaign, a rash of premature explosions gave the gun a bad reputation which took some time to live down. The cause was eventually traced to a variety of defects such as sideslap of the shell in worn barrels, erosive wear, and dirty ammunition, all of which had managed to come together with fatal effect. As soon as the faults had been isolated and rectified, the problem vanished and the 5.5 lived out its remaining years without complaint.

One objection to the 5.5 was lack of range, but this was cured in 1943 with the introduction of an 80lb shell. The utility and popularity of the 5.5 can be gauged by the fact that the guns with 21 Army Group in north-west Europe fired 2,610,747 rounds between 'D' Day and 'VE' Day.

Speaking personally, I never liked the thing. Although it weighed over six tons, we were still expected to fling it in and out of action as if it were a field gun. There was a brass plate on the trail end which bore the legend 'With spades off this equipment balances at 26 inches above the ground'. It may have done, but it was damned hard work getting it up those 26 inches.

Variants

The Land Service equipment was the Mk 3 gun; Mks 1 and 2 were Naval weapons introduced during the First World War, and they bore no relationship other than calibre. The Mk 4 was not introduced until 1948; the difference between this and the Mk 3 was solely in the angle of the 'shot seating', the taper at the front end of the chamber into which the driving band was forced when the shell was rammed.

Data
Weight of gun and breech mechanism: 4,120lb.
Total length: 171.6in.
Length of bore: 164.0in (30 cal).
Rifling: 36 grooves, uniform RH 1/25.

Opposite page: 5.5in gun at the Rotunda Museum of Artillery.

This page, below: 5.5in gun in firing position, with shell and cartridge at the ready on the loading tray. **Right:** This arrangement of shields for the 5.5in was an experiment that was not adopted.

Breech mechanism: Asbury interrupted screw, percussion fired.

Elevation: $-5°$ $+45°$.

Traverse: 30° right and left.

Recoil system: Hydropneumatic variable, 30in to 54in.

Weight in action: 13,646lb.

Performance
Firing standard 100lb HE shell:
Muzzle velocity: 1,675ft/sec.
Maximum range: 16,200 yards.
Firing 80lb HE shell:
Muzzle velocity: 1,950ft/sec.
Maximum range: 18,100 yards.

Ammunition separate loading, bag charge.
  Propelling Charge. As originally designed, the 5.5in had a four-charge system divided into Short Range and Long Range portions. The Short Range portion comprised Charge One, a 'potato-masher' shaped bag, with a Charge Two increment tied around the stem. The Long Range portion was Charge Three, a cylindrical bag, with Charge Four, a shorter cylinder, tied to the end. The Short Range portion was later re-designed into two cylindrical bags end-to-end. Only the One and Three bags carried igniters; the Two and Four increments could not be fired separately. Total weight of the Short Range portion was 4lb 4oz of Cordite, and of the Long Range portion, 9lb 2oz. These weights varied, of course, when different propellants were introduced during the war.
  With the adoption of the 80lb shell it was possible to introduce a 'Super' charge, a cylindrical bag containing 12lb 9oz of Cordite. This charge was fired by itself, never in conjunction with any part of the lower charges which it completely replaced, and it was prominently marked with a black band

Top: Direct shooting with the 5.5in gun. **Middle:** The breech of the 5.5in gun closed, showing the firing lock; and (bottom) open, displaying the Welin breech screw.

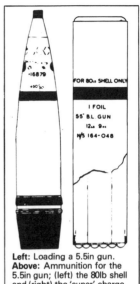

Left: Loading a 5.5in gun.
Above: Ammunition for the 5.5in gun; (left) the 80lb shell and (right) the 'super' charge.

around the bag (corresponding to the black band around the shell) and the inscription 'FOR 80LB SHELL ONLY'.

Performance with the various shells and charges was as follows.

Charge:	100lb Shell:		80lb Shell:	
	MV	Range	MV	Range
1	875ft/sec	6,800yds	950ft/sec	7,600yds
2	1,150ft/sec	10,600yds	1,250ft/sec	11,100yds
3	1,375ft/sec	12,900yds	1,525ft/sec	13,800yds
4	1,675ft/sec	16,200yds	1,825ft/sec	16,800yds
Super	—	—	1,950ft/sec	18,100yds

Shell, HE, S/L, 100lb Mk 1D. A streamlined shell with a single, wide, driving band, and filled with Amatol. It was supplied with the nose plugged, and could be fitted with the Fuzes, Percussion, 119 or 231. Weight when fuzed was exactly 100lb.

Shell, HE, S/L, 100lb Mk 2D. This was the same as the Mk 1D, but had double driving bands in order to provide better sealing in the gun bore, to reduce erosion and to distribute the torque more evenly through the shell walls.

Shell, HE, S/L, 80lb Mk 1D. This was almost the same size as the 100lb shell and it achieved its weight reduction by having a finer taper to the head, and by being made of higher-grade steel which allowed a thinner wall section. Double driving bands were fitted, and the filling was either Amatol or TNT. The weight when fired was 82lb. The rear portion of the shell, from the driving band to the base, was painted black to indicate that it was the 80lb shell and not the standard projectile for which the gun had been designed.

Shell, Smoke, BE, Mk 1D. Hundreds of ex-medium gunners will dispute this, but there actually was a base-ejection smoke shell designed and manufactured for the 5.5in gun, though it was rarely issued. It was of the usual type, containing four canisters of smoke composition, the topmost canister being shaped to fit into the shell's tapering nose. It was non-streamlined, weighed 82lb, and used the Time and Percussion fuze No 221. The muzzle velocity was 1,625ft/sec and the maximum range with Charge Four was 14,700 yards.

Shell, Coloured Smoke, BE, Mk 1D. Although developed during the war, production of this shell did not commence until September 1945, and the quantity made was small. It is unlikely ever to have been issued to service regiments. The design was exactly as for the screening smoke shell above, except for the chemical composition in the canisters. Red, green and blue smoke shells were approved, but there is no confirmation that any other than red were produced.

In addition to the above types, Chemical shell, Incendiary shell and a solid shot were approved. Four marks of chemical were designed, all filled with liquid gases and fuzed T&P No. 221; weight varied from 90lb to 98lb. The incendiary shell was based on the design of the BE smoke shell, and used four magnesium canisters filled with Thermite. It was first tested in January 1944 and was later approved for service, but it is doubtful if any were made.

The solid shot is something of a mystery. The only one I have seen was marked with a yellow band, indicating that it was for practice, and a brown band, indicating that it was of cast iron. The inference is, that if a practice shot were made, there must have been a service steel shot, but there is no evidence of any steel shot ever having been designed or approved. The 'approved' anti-tank projectile for the 5.5in was the 100lb shell fired without a fuze, the nose closed by the steel transit plug. Firing at moving targets with the 5.5in was far from easy, but the plugged shell had a devastating effect on tanks; it would lift the turret from any wartime tank with the greatest of ease.

6in 26cwt Howitzer

Like the rest of the British medium artillery in 1939, this dated from the First World War, having been developed in 1915 to replace an earlier design, the 6in 30cwt. This latter weapon had co-existed with another, the 6in 25cwt, which explains the insistence in putting the gun weight into the nomenclature.

Almost 4,000 of these howitzers were built before the Armistice, and they became the backbone of the medium artillery during the inter-war years. For their time, they were an advanced design, and the carriage incorporated the first hydropneumatic recoil system to be used in a mobile equipment in British service, a design so basically sound and reliable that with little modification it was used with the 4.5in and 5.5in guns of the 1940s.

The howitzer was of wire-wound construction, 13 calibres long and with an Asbury breech mechanism. The carriage was a simple box trail on wooden wheels; rubber tyres (Mk 1R) and pneumatic tyres (Mk 1P) were adopted in later years. It was used throughout the desert campaign and in Eritrea, but after 1942, its service was largely confined to the Far East, where it remained in constant use until the end of the war. It was finally declared obsolete in October 1945. Perhaps the most eloquent testimony to the essential rightness of the basic design was the fact that there were never any variant models; only the Mark 1, from start to finish.

Data

Weight of gun and breech mechanism: 2,856lb.
Total length: 87.55in.
Length of bore: 79.8in (13.3 cal).
Rifling: 36 grooves, uniform RH 1/15.
Breech mechanism: Asbury interrupted screw, percussion fired.
Elevation: 0° +45°.
Traverse: 4° right and left.
Recoil system: Hydropneumatic, variable, 24in to 54in.

Right: The 6in 26cwt howitzer; (below) on Carriage Mk 1P.

Weight in action: 9,262lb.

Performance firing standard 86lb HE shell
Muzzle velocity: 1,409ft/sec.
Maximum range: 11,400 yards.

Ammunition separate loading, bag charge.
Propelling charge. Two charges were provided. The 'Super' charge, for use with the 86lb shell, weighed 5lb 3oz and was divided into five charges.

'Normal' charge, for use with the 100lb shell, weighed 4lb 11½oz and was divided into three charges. Maximum performance with this charge and shell was 1,234ft/sec and 9,500 yards range.

Shell, HE, S/L, 86lb Mk 1D. A streamlined shell filled with Amatol or Lyddite and fuzed with any of the Percussion Fuzes Nos. 101, 106, 117, 119 or 231.

Shell, HE, S/L, 100lb Mk 1D. Similar to the previous shell, but about 3in longer and slightly thicker in the walls.

75mm Howitzer

The 75mm howitzer was designed as the answer to the Westervelt Board's request for a 3in Mountain and Pack weapon with a minimum of 5,000 yards range and capable of being split into four mule loads of about 225lb each. The first model was the M1920E, but this was unsatisfactory and redesign began in 1922. It was standardized and introduced as the Howitzer 75mm Pack M1 on Carriage M1 in 1927.

The whole equipment was an extremely ingenious design. The gun tube and breech ring were connected by an interrupted thread, and were separated for transport. On assembly, the gun and breech were dropped into a 'bottom sleigh', a trough-like unit on top of the cradle, and connected to the recoil system. The gun was then secured in place by the 'top sleigh', a hollow steel casing filled with lead, which dropped on top of the gun tube and was locked to the bottom sleigh by a quick-release catch. The cradle was trunnioned at the rear end, and a coil spring inside the trail pushed against the bottom of the elevating arc to balance the muzzle preponderance, assisted by the greater weight of lead at the rear end of the top sleigh.

The box trail had a hinged joint in its centre which allowed the trail to be folded for animal draught, or divided at the joint for pack loading. The breakdown for pack use was: tube; breech ring, mechanism and wheels; cradle and top sleigh; recoil system and bottom sleigh; front trail; rear trail and axle. Traversing was across the axle, controlled by a hand-wheel positioned around the axle. Wooden wheels with steel tyres were fitted.

Below: The 75mm howitzer on Carriage M8, being used in the anti-tank role by British troops.

Variants
Howitzer M1A1 Redesigned breech ring and block, not interchangeable with the M1.
Carriage M8 This was the designation of the M1 carriage when fitted with steel disc wheels and pneumatic tyres, and issued to airborne troops. It was adopted in British service in 1944 and used by airborne troops until the 1960s.

Data
Weight of gun and breech mechanism: 341lb.
Total length: 52.0in.
Length of bore: 47.0in (16 cal).
Rifling: 28 grooves, uniform RH 1/20.
Breech mechanism: Horizontal sliding block, percussion fired.
Elevation: $-5°$ $+45°$.
Traverse: 3° right and left.
Recoil system: Hydropneumatic, constant, 29in.
Weight in action: 1,269lb (M1) 1,339lb (M8).

Performance firing standard 14lb HE shell
Muzzle velocity: 1,250ft/sec.
Maximum range: 9,610 yards.

During the 1920s, it was decided to produce a 75mm howitzer for the use of horse artillery accompanying cavalry divisions, incapable of being dismantled, and this became the M3 carriage. The design was based on the M1 carriage, but had a split trail with tubular legs, a firing pedestal in front of the axle, and pneumatic-tyred wheels mounted on rotatable stub axles so that the wheels could be lifted from the ground to allow the gun to rest on the firing pedestal. Top carriage traverse was fitted, and the

barrel was balanced by means of two spring equilibrators alongside the cradle. All in all, it was a very luxurious design. However, it seems that relatively few of them were built, and few saw service, because the horse cavalry and their accompanying horse gunners were being replaced by tanks and mechanized artillery.

Variants
Carriage:

M3A1: Standard, described above.

M3A2: M3A1 with the addition of a shield.

M3A3: A1 or A2 fitted with divided-rim wheels and combat tyres.

Data
Ordnance as Howitzer M1.
Elevation: $-9°$ $+50°$.
Traverse: $22\frac{1}{2}°$ right and left.
Recoil system: Hydropneumatic, constant 32in.
Weight in action: 2,160lb.

Performance as M1.

Self-Propelled Mountings

Early in 1942, the Armored Force requested a howitzer-armed close-support tank. A quick and easy solution was an M3 half-track adapted to mount the M1 howitzer in similar fashion to the model using the 75mm gun (the T19 carriage). This became the Howitzer Motor Carriage T30, but it was not standardized, though a small number were issued. A better solution was reached by using the M5 light tank as the basic vehicle. The first conversion was to open out the hull top and construct a barbette shield, the result somewhat resembling a miniaturized M7. This was known as the HMC T41, but it too, was unsatisfactory; crew protection was minimal and the modifications to the tank structure so great that there would have been a considerable problem in production. The eventual solution was to take the hull of the M5 tank as it stood and drop on a new turret which mounted a 75mm howitzer in a tank-type mantlet mounting. The only modification to the vehicle was to move

the driver's hatches so that they did not foul the new turret. Originally designated T47, it was standardized as the HMC M8 on 23 April 1942. 1,778 were built by Cadillac before production stopped in January 1944.

In order to fit the M1 howitzer into a mantlet mounting with a ring cradle, it was necessary to fit a 'Tube Mounting Support' around the howitzer barrel. With this in place, the M1 howitzer became the M2. There were not enough existing spare howitzer barrels for the number of vehicles, so new barrels had to be made; these were made with the mounting support as an integral part of the design, and became the Howitzer M3. Their ballistic capabilities and dimensions were no different from the M1 pattern.

Ammunition semi-fixed, cased charges.

Propelling Charge. Ammunition for the 75mm howitzer was in the form of semi-fixed rounds. The cartridge and shell were separate units on delivery, but were assembled by placing the shell base into the mouth of the cartridge case, before loading as one unit. An exception was the HEAT round, which was fixed, since its propelling charge was not adjustable. The adjustable charge used with other rounds was contained in four bags; the base charge was held in the case by a clip retainer around the primer, and the other three bags were attached to the base charge by a length of twine. Data for the four charges was as follows.

Charge:	Weight:	Velocity (ft/sec):	Range (yards):
1	5.9oz	700	4,190
2	7.7oz	810	5,360
3	9.9oz	950	6,930
4	14.7oz	1,250	9,610

The HEAT round used a fixed charge of 6.6oz, which developed a muzzle velocity of 1,000ft/sec and a maximum range of 7,900 yards.

Shell, HE, M48. This was the same shell as was used in the 75mm gun, streamlined, nose-fuzed, and with a filling of 1.47lb of TNT. It was normally supplied with the Fuze PD M48 or M51, but the Fuze Time and Superquick M54 could be fitted if required. The shell weighed 14.7lb filled and fuzed, and the complete round, as fired, 18.22lb.

Shell, Chemical, M64. This used a similar shell body to the M48, and carried a central burster tube loaded with 1.75oz of Tetryl. The space in the shell around the burster carried the chemical filling: 1.35lb of white phosphorus (WP); or 1.51lb Titanium Tetrachloride (FS); or 1.04lb Mustard Gas (H). The shell weight varied with the filling: 15.25lb WP; 15.41lb FS; or 14.94lb H. Ballistics were also changed, the WP and FS shells having a maximum range of 9,630 yards and the H shell, 9,620 yards.

Shell, HEAT, M66. A hollow-charge shell with long tapering nose and with the Base Fuze M62. The filling was 1lb of Pentolite behind the conventional cone, and it was capable of piercing 3½in plate at any range.

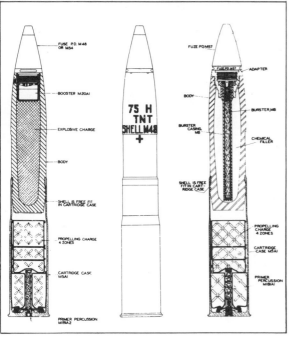

75mm Field Gun

In 1917, the US Army was provided with a 3in gun as the standard field piece, and for various reasons, principally standardization of supply, it was decided to change the standard calibre to 75mm and adopt the French 75mm M1897 gun as the field gun. The 3in M1916, then about to be introduced into service, was also converted to chamber the French 75mm ammunition, and quantities of British 18pdr guns, built in the USA, were also converted to become the 75mm M1917.

The Westervelt Board recommended the development of a new 75mm gun with a range of 15,000 yards, all-round traverse, and an elevation capability of 80°, in the hope that it could fulfil the dual role of field gun and AA gun, a popular theory of the time. As an interim measure, the Board recommended retention of the M1897 and M1916 guns.

In fact, all the wartime guns continued in service, the M1897 on issue and the others in reserve stocks, and they all appeared during the Second World War.

The design recommended by the Westervelt Board finally appeared in the early 1930s as the 'Divisional Gun' – the precise model number is not known – but it was an unpractical design and was abandoned in about 1937. As the illustrations show, it had three trail legs which formed a ground platform for all-round fire, or it could be used with two trail legs and a firing pedestal in the field-gun role.

75mm Gun M1916

Development of this weapon began just before the First World War, the object being to produce a field gun on a split-trail carriage, which would be well in advance of anything else in the world.

Left: The 75mm M1897 in its original French form.

Above: The 75mm 'Divisional Gun' of the 1930s in the all-round traverse and anti-aircraft mode, and (left) in the field-gun application.

Unfortunately, the result fell a long way short of his worthy aim; modification followed modification, and by the end of the war it was being called the 'Crime of 1916' instead of the 'Model of 1916', so much time and effort having been wasted on it. What concerns us here, though, is that in the end, some 810 were built and remained in service during the inter-war period, and in 1940, a number were bought by Britain and taken into use as the 'Ordnance QF 75mm 'S' Mk2 or Mk2*', indicating the split trail as opposed to the pole trail of all the other 75mm designs bought at that time.

There were six different models of the M1916, as a result of the frequent design changes incorporated in the production run, to remedy some defect or other; these were all of a constructional or manufacturing nature – e.g., the use of forgings instead of castings or vice versa – and need not be detailed here. The resultant guns were known as the M1916, M1916MI, M1916MII, M1916MII½, M1916MIII and M1916III½, all of which, in British service, became the Mark 2. All were fitted with the original American-designed hydro-spring recoil system. In 1917, because of problems with this system, the American Government contracted with a French designer for a hydropneumatic recoil system, at a fee reported to have been $60,000. This was adopted as the 'St Chamond' system, and guns fitted with it, took the suffix 'A1' after the model number, and became the M1916MIA1, MIIIA1 and MIII½A1. These, in turn, became the Mk 2* in British service.

Originally, the split-trail carriage M1916 had wooden wheels and was adapted to horse draught; when fitted with pneumatic tyres it became the M1916A1.

Data Gun M1916MIA1
Weight of gun and breech mechanism: 749lb.
Total length: 90.9in.
Length of bore: 84.0in (28.5 cal).
Rifling: 24 grooves, increasing RH 1/119 to 1/25.4.
Breech mechanism: Vertical sliding block, semi-automatic, percussion fired.
Elevation: $-7°$ $+53°$.
Traverse: 22½° right and left.
Recoil system: Hydropneumatic, constant, 46in.
Weight in action: 3,210lb.

Performance firing standard 14.7lb shell
Muzzle velocity: 1,900 ft/sec. Maximum range: 12,490 yards.

Below: The 75mm M1916 gun on its original wooden-wheeled split-trail carriage; and (right) showing the oval recoil-system casing and the unusual fixed shield protecting the elevating arc.

Right: The 75mm M1917, which was a worked-over British 18pdr. **Below:** The Gun M1897 on Carriage M1897A4, with its caisson.

75mm Gun M1917

This was the British 18pdr gun Mks 1 to 2*, relined to 75mm calibre and chambered for the French ammunition, apart from which it was identical with the standard British gun. The M1917 carriage was the British wooden-wheeled pole trail pattern; this was largely replaced in the 1920s by the M1917A1, which was adapted to high-speed towing by fitting steel wheels with pneumatic tyres. In British service, in 1940, the guns on M1917 carriages became the 'Ord QF 75mm Converted M–1' while those on the M1917A1 carriages were the 'Mark 1*'.

Data Gun M1917 on Carriage M1917A1
Weight of gun and breech mechanism: 995lb.
Total length: 88.2in.
Length of bore: 84.0in (28.5 cal).
Rifling: Increasing RH from zero at breech to 1/25.4 at 9.72in from muzzle, thereafter uniform.
Breech mechanism: Interrupted screw, percussion fired.
Elevation: $-5°$ $+16°$.
Traverse: $4°$ right and left.
Recoil system: Hydro-spring, constant, 49in.
Weight in action: 2,990lb.

Performance firing standard 14.7lb shell
Muzzle velocity: 1,900 ft/sec. Maximum range: 12,490 yards.

75mm Gun M1897

This was the original French 75mm gun adopted by the US Army in 1917, and subsequently considerably modified. It remained in service as the standard weapon during the inter-war years, and throughout the Second World War as a training weapon in the towed mode, though the ordnance was adopted for a number of self-propelled and tank mountings. Numbers were supplied to Britain in 1940, and were taken into service as the 'Ordnance QF 75mm Mark 1'.

The basic M1897 gun was of built-up pattern, using a Nordenfelt eccentric screw breech, and percussion fired by means of a hammer and lanyard. Because of the long recoil movement (which this gun pioneered), the muzzle carried a reinforcing band with two rollers beneath it; these engaged in the cradle slides during the latter part of the recoil stroke, and supported the gun in alignment with the cradle. Without these, the breech would have sagged down at the end of the recoil stroke, and the cradle guides would thus have been strained and deformed. The Carriage M1897 was of French design and manufacture, with a pole trail, wooden wheels, and a seven-piece shield. It was fitted with a rather unusual rod-operated brake system which could be swung beneath the wheels, and the gun could be heaved onto the brake shoes – 'en abatage' was the term used – so as to form a species of firing support.

During the years after the First World War, modifications were made as follows.

Ordnance:

M1897: Original French purchase; breech block rotated 120°.

M1897A1: As M1897, but of American manufacture.

M1897A2: No muzzle hoops or jacket. Breech rotated 156°.

M1897A3: As M1897A2, but slight modification to suit the Carriage M1897M1A2.

M1897A4: Rollers at muzzle removed and replaced by steel rails and bronze strips. 156° breech block.

Carriage:

M1897: Original French purchase. 2,800 bought.

M1897M1: American manufacture. Recuperator cylinder fitted with a 'respirator' instead of a plug. Four-piece shield, small changes to wheel-guards, towing hook, etc. Parts not interchangeable with M1897.

M1897A2: M1897 fitted with a handspike for traversing.

M1897M1A2: M1897M1 fitted with a handspike for traversing.

M1897A3: Design not adopted.

M1897A4: Any previous model fitted with high-speed adapter – i.e. pneumatic tyres, steel wheels and internal expanding brakes.

M2: New split-trail design. Pneumatic tyres, firing jack, equilibrator, variable recoil length, no shield.

M2A1: M2 with shield added and brakes modified.

M2A2: M2A1 with changed axle assembly and brakes.

M2A3: M2A2 with pivoted axle, firing segments instead of jack. Trails 19 inches shorter. Constant-length recoil.

Above: 75mm Gun M1897A2 on Carriage M2A3, in firing position.

Data 75mm Gun M1897A4

Weight of gun and breech mechanism: 1,035lb.
Total length: 107.13in.
Length of bore: 101.87in (34.5 cal).
Rifling: 24 grooves, uniform RH 1/25.6.
Breech mechanism: Nordenfelt eccentric screw, percussion fired.
Muzzle velocity: 1,955ft/sec.

Carriage Data and Performance firing standard 14.7lb HE Shell

	M1897–1897A3	M1897A4	M2A1,M2	M2A3
Weight in action (lb):	2,657	3,007	3,447	3,225
Recoil length (inches):	44.9	44.9	41.5–46	44.9
Maximum elevation:	19°	19°	46°	45½°
Maximum depression:	−10°	−10°	−10°	−10½°
Traverse right:	3°	3°	45°	30°09′
Traverse left:	3°	3°	40°	30°15′
Maximum range (yards):	9,200	9,200	12,780	13,950

Other Models of 75mm Gun

M2: Tank gun for mounting on M3 tanks. Barrel length 91.75in.
M3: Tank gun for mounting on M4 tank. Barrel length 118.38in.
M4: Aircraft-mounted gun.
M5: Aircraft-mounted gun.
M5A1: M5 with rifling changed to 1/22 in order to improve the shell's stability in aerial firing.
M6: Tank gun for mounting on M24 tank. Barrel length 129.2in.
T22: Anti-aircraft gun (See p 121).

Self-Propelled Mountings

T12: M1897A4 gun mounted in M3 half-track, facing forward. Standardized as the Gun Motor Carriage M3 or M3A1. The gun was fitted to the Mounting M3, a converted top carriage from the M2A3 field carriage, becoming the M3. Guns on Mounting M5, derived from the M2A2 field carriage, became M3A1. Sentenced Limited Standard in March 1944, and obsolete in September 1944.

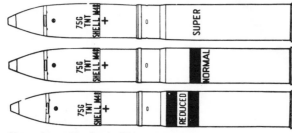

Above: Ammunition for the 75mm gun.

T27: M1897A4 gun on modified Mounting M5 on a Studebaker 4 × 4 'Swamp Buggy'. Gun centrally mounted, firing to the rear. Tried in 1941, abandoned.
T67: M1897A4 gun on high-speed tracked chassis derived from a Christie design. Abandoned in 1941.
T73: M3 (T27) using an M3 tank gun in place of the M1897A4; not adopted.

Ammunition fixed, cased charges.

As might be expected with a gun in service since 1917, there was a wide variety of ammunition standardized over the years. Most of these museum pieces were unloaded onto the British in 1940 – quite legitimately, since this was the ammunition around which the older guns had been designed. The difference between this and the later ammunition lay in the projectiles; the old shells were copies of the original French designs, with blunt heads, square bases and protuberant fuzes of the PD M46 and M47 types – which were, in fact, American improvements on original French designs. The later shells, developed in the 1930s, had streamlined noses and tails, and were adapted for modern pointed fuzes of the M48 type. In order to save space, the details below refer to representative rounds which were in service in 1944. Note that 75mm gun rounds were interchangeable between the field guns M1897 (all modifications), M1916, M1917; the tank guns, M2, M3 and M6; the aircraft guns M4 and M5, but not the AA gun T22.

Complete Round, Shell, HE, 75mm M48. This consisted of the HE Shell M48, the M18 cartridge case, M22A3 or M31A2 percussion primer, and a propelling charge. The steel cartridge case M18B1 was an approved alternative, except for aircraft gun use. The shell weighed 14.7lb filled and fuzed, and contained 1.5lb of TNT or 1.36lb of Amatol. The Fuze PD M48 or TSQ M54 was standard. Two types of round were supplied, Normal and Supercharge; Normal rounds carried a propelling charge of 1.05lb, the Supercharge, one of 1.93lb. A reduced charge round, loaded with 0.38lb of powder, was available for training.

Complete Round, Shell, Chemical, 75mm M64. This resembled the previous round, but the M64 shell weighed 15.25lb, had a filling of 1.34lb of white phosphorus, and was fuzed PD M57. Only one charge was available, loaded with 1.93lb of FNH powder. As a result of the slight change in balance and weight, the shell ranged less than the HE shell at all elevations. Maximum range with the M1897A4 gun was 13,730 yards with a velocity of 1,950ft/sec.

Complete Round, Projectile, APC, 75mm M61. This round consisted of an armour-piercing shell weighing 14.96lb and a 2.16lb propelling charge to give a velocity of 2,000ft/sec. The shell was capped and contained a 2.3oz charge of Explosive D, and a Base Fuze M66A1. It was claimed to be capable of piercing 70mm of homogeneous plate at 500 yards.

105mm Howitzer M1

The American 105mm field howitzer can trace its roots back even farther than the British 25pdr. In 1916, Colonel Charles P. Summerall was sent to France by Secretary of War Newton Baker to act as an observer and to report on the development of military equipment in Europe, with a view to obtaining information to guide future US weapon design and procurement policy. One of Summerall's recommendations was that the contemporary field guns of the 75mm/3in class were no longer sufficiently powerful, especially since the arrival of the tank, and that the future US standard weapon should be of 105mm calibre. At that time, the US Ordnance Department was striving to perfect the 3in M1916 gun, and Summerall's views were given short shrift.

At the end of the war, the Westervelt Board was convened 'To make a study of the armament, calibers, types of material to be assigned to a field army' and in their report, published 23 May 1919, they recommended 'A weapon of about 105mm caliber on a carriage permitting a vertical arc of fire from $-5°$ to $+65°$ and a horizontal arc of 360° . . . The projectile should weigh about 30 to 35lb and should include both shrapnel and shell. A maximum range of 12,000 yards would be satisfactory. Semi-fixed ammunition and zone charges should be used.' At the same time, the Board also recommended 'A gun of about 3in caliber . . .' so that all the divisional eggs were not to be in one basket.[1]

Development of a 105mm weapon began forthwith, and in the following year, the Howitzer M1920 on Carriage M1920E appeared. Four pilot models were built, varying slightly in details, but all of 22 calibres length, with horizontal sliding breech blocks, mounted on split-trail carriages giving $-4\frac{1}{2}°$ to $+80°$ elevation, and 30° of traverse. A carriage M1921E was also produced; this used a box trail, giving elevation 0° to $+51°$, and 4° of traverse on each side. The Field Artillery Board examined all the pilots, condemned the M1920E carriage as too cumbersome and complicated, and called for a fresh design using the M1921E carriage as a basis. This resulted in the Howitzer M1925E on Carriage M1925E1, a simplified box-trail design, in which the most significant feature was that the trunnions were well behind the centre of balance, and the muzzle weight was counterbalanced by an equilibrator spring. This prevented the breech coming too low when the gun was elevated, and thus allowed the gun to fire at high angles without the breech striking the ground.

At the same time, a design of simplified split-trail carriage was being worked on, as the Howitzer T2 on Carriage T2, and this was eventually standardized in 1928[2] as the Howitzer M1 on Carriage M1. It used a 6-part propelling charge, had a muzzle velocity of 1,550ft/sec, and a maximum range of 12,000 yards, traverse of $22\frac{1}{2}°$ right and left, and elevation $-5°$ $+65°$. Although standardized, none were ever manufactured beyond the prototypes, since no money was available, but the design was prepared for production when circumstances allowed.

During the early 1930s, the mechanization of the US Army got under way, and one task was the conversion of all horse-drawn equipment. In 1933, the carriage M1 was called in for re-designing, but because of pressure of other work, the project lapsed and was not revived until 1936.[3] On examination of the problem, it seemed simpler to make a fresh start than to try to modify the M1 carriage, and a fresh project was begun, resulting in the T3 and T4 carriages. Both were split-trail types with pneumatic tyres, the differences lying in the application of firing pedestal, spades, and types of elevating gear. Neither was entirely satisfactory, but the T4 was taken as a starting point and improved through the T4E1 and T5 models until it was standardized as the M2 carriage early in 1940.[4]

In 1934, the M1 howitzer was modified to permit the loading of the shrapnel round as a fixed unit, and was then standardized as the Howitzer M2,[5] but this approval was rescinded in January 1935, since the shrapnel shell was no longer considered to be the primary projectile. Nevertheless, the M2 remained the standard, but in the course of adapting it to suit the M2 carriage, some more changes were made, principally in minor dimensions, and the result became the M2A1 howitzer, standardized in March 1940.

Production of the standardized design got under way immediately, and some 8,536 equipments were built during the war years. There were few major

Above: The M1920 howitzer on Caterpillar Mount Mk 4, in 1921. It was one of several post-war self-propelled prototypes.

References:
1. *Journal US Artillery*, Vol. 51, No. 1, July 1919, pp. 72–109 'The Westervelt Board Report'.
2. Ordnance Committee Minute (OCM) 6684 of 5 January 1928.
3. OCM 13109 of 4 September 1938.
4. OCM 15639 of 23 February 1940.
5. OCM 11395 of 5 April 1934.

design changes, though some small modifications led to variant model numbers (see below). It became the standard divisional artillery piece, and during the post-war years was supplied to countries throughout the world. In revised form it is still the standard US field artillery piece.

Variants

Howitzer:

M1: Original, Standardized 1928, obsolete 1935.

M2: M1 with chamber dimensions changed to permit loading fixed rounds. Standardized 1934.

M2A1: Redimensioned; new trigger shaft; new breech ring with bronze bearing strips underneath. Standardized 1940.

M2A1E3: Rifled uniform RH 1/27. Two made in 1943 to investigate the effect of rifling twist upon accuracy.

M3: See separate entry p. 63.

M4: Modified M2A1 used on the self-propelled carriage M37 to allow it to be used in a ring cradle. Breech ring modified to use shorter block, electric firing solenoid fitted, breech operating lever repositioned.

T12: Lightweight 30-calibre model for mounting in aircraft. Pilot model made February 1944; project cancelled September 1945.

T51: Modified tank pattern for use in HMC T87. Differed from T12 in length of recoil slide surface. Begun in March 1945, it was installed into the GMC T88E1 in the following month. Project cancelled September 1946.

Carriage:

M1: Original horse-draught model. Fourteen were made.

M1A1: Modified M1, thirteen of the originals were altered. Eliminated the horse-draught items, added pneumatic tyres, and towing attachment for truck trailing.

M2: Fresh design for high-speed towing. Additional elevating handwheel, trunnions seated by the elevating arcs, firing segments discarded, electric brakes.

M2A1: Following an Army Ground Forces Board decision not to have brakes on equipments weighing less than 5,000lb, the electric brakes were removed in 1942.

M2A2: Larger shield, larger recoil buffer, enclosed screw traverse. Standardized 1943.

M2E4: Modified M2A2 with jointed trail legs to reduce length to 72 inches for air-loading. Passed trials in November 1943, but there was no requirement since the standard carriage could easily be loaded into the C47.

M3: Non-alloy steel tubular trail legs, saving 11½ in weight. In January 1944 found to be insufficiently rigid and had to be redesigned. Cancelled in 1945.

M3A1E2: M3 with magnesium alloy trail legs. Cancelled 1946.

T15: Standard design in light alloy to save weight. Tried in 1943, but not adopted.

Set, Harness, T1: An attachment set for mounting the howitzer on the cargo deck of a DUKW

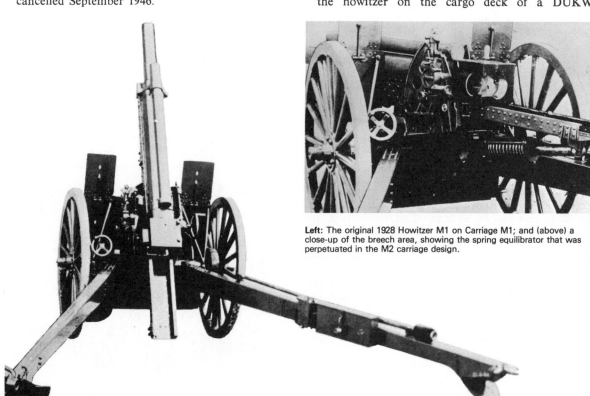

Left: The original 1928 Howitzer M1 on Carriage M1; and (above) a close-up of the breech area, showing the spring equilibrator that was perpetuated in the M2 carriage design.

amphibious truck. In March 1943, 200 sets were procured, but there is no record of their employment.

Self-propelled equipments: *

T9: Project to mount an M2A1 howitzer on a Cletrac MG–2 tracked tractor.

T19: M2A1 on pedestal mount in the half-track M3, firing over the cab. Developed in 1942, it was not standardized, but 324 were built and a number were used in the North African campaign. It was not particularly successful, being too much cannon for too little carriage.

T32: Standardized as M7. (See below).

T34: Project for an M2A1 on pedestal mount on the Mack T3 half-track carrier.

T45: Project for M2A1 on Mack full-track chassis.

T76: Standardized as M37. (See below).

T87: Amphibious; M21 in open-topped turret on amphibious chassis based on the M18 Tank Destroyer chassis.

T88: Similar to the T87, but on the M18 chassis without amphibian capabilities.

M7: M2A1 Howitzer on Mount M4 in modified Medium Tank M3 chassis. Standardized in November 1943. It began as the T32 in June 1941, the M3 chassis being fitted with an open-topped hull. The Mount M4 resembled the trail legs of the field carriage cut down and spread across the fighting compartment in order to distribute the recoil forces. The first vehicles were sent straight to Egypt and were used by the British Army at the Battle of Alamein in October 1942. They remained in British service until replaced by the 25pdr Sextons. Those in US service continued until replaced by the M37. More than 3,500 were built.

M7B1: M7 based on the chassis of the M4A3 tank.

M7B2: M7B1 using horizontal volute spring suspension and a 23in wide track.

M37: Based on the chassis of the M24 light tank, the M37 was lighter, more mobile and less expensive than the M7. Shorter and wider, it gave more working space for the detachment and more ammunition stowage space, and was also better armoured. The general layout was similar to that of the M7, but the howitzer was carried in the Mount M5, a ring cradle with hydro-spring recoil system. The howitzer itself was slightly modified to suit the mount; the breech ring was repositioned and the block shortened and modified to accept an electrical solenoid-operated firing mechanism. The position of the breech operating lever was also changed. All these modifications changed the howitzer to the M4 model. The M37 was standardized in January 1945 and remained in service until the 1950s.

*All self-propelled equipments were known as Howitzer Motor Carriage (HMC).

Data Howitzer M2A1, on Carriage M2A2
Weight of gun and breech mechanism: 1,064lb.
Total length: 101.4375in.
Length of bore: 93.0in (22.5 cal).
Rifling: 34 grooves, uniform RH 1/20.

Above: Top view of the M7, showing the method of mounting the 105mm howitzer. **Top right:** The 105mm howitzer Motor Carriage T19, as used during the Tunisian campaign. **Bottom right:** British troops with their 105mm HMC M7 in Italy. Note the anti-aircraft machine-gun 'pulpit', which caused the British to christen the equipment 'Priest'.

Breech mechanism: Horizontal sliding block, percussion fired.
Elevation: $-4°45' +66°13'$.
Traverse: 23° right and left.
Recoil system: Hydropneumatic, constant, 42in.
Weight in action: 4,980lb.

Performance
Firing standard 33lb HE shell:
Muzzle velocity: 1,550ft/sec.
Maximum range: 12,205 yards.
Firing 29.29lb HEAT shell:
Muzzle velocity: 1,250ft/sec.
Maximum range: 8,590 yards.
Penetration: 115mm at all ranges.

Ammunition semi-fixed, cased charge.
Ammunition for the 105mm howitzer was of the type in which shell and cartridge were supplied as separate units, but were fitted together after adjustment of the charge, and then loaded as a fixed unit. An exception to this was the HEAT anti-tank round (see below).

The cartridge case was of brass (M14) or copper-plated drawn steel (M14B1) and both were 14.64in long. Primer Percussion M1B1A2 was standard, and was press-fitted into the base of the case. The standard charge was sub-divided into seven zone charges, each in its own bag of cloth, the nominal weight of the full charge being 3.04lb. The bags were not colour-coded, but were stamped with the number of the charge zone and were connected by a length of twine. The base increment (Zone 1) was secured in the cartridge case, either by brass hooks fixed inside the base of the case or by various types of charge retainer, metal clips or spring discs which snapped around the stem of the primer and held the bag in place. Early models of charge retainer had a habit of coming loose on firing and lodging in the bore, to the detriment of the next shell fired, and they were withdrawn in favour of the M3A1, a clip of phosphor-bronze spring wire.

The HEAT round was fixed, and had a fixed charge weight of 1.5lb of FNH powder, enclosed in a cloth bag and tied to the M3A1 retainer.

Shell, Semi-Fixed, HE, M1. The standard projectile, a streamlined shell weighing 33lb. It was filled with 4.8lb of TNT and was normally issued fuzed with the Point Detonating Fuze M48 or M51. The Time and Superquick Fuze M54 was available for airburst fire, and, towards the end of the war, a deep cavity filling was adopted, with removable supplementary charge, to allow insertion of the Proximity Fuze T80E6. Fillings of Trimonite and Amatol were authorized as alternatives, but these were generally used up in training and were rarely met in the field.

Shell, S/Fxd, Chemical, M60. This was a bursting shell, having a central burster tube filled with Tetryl, and the chemical filling in the surrounding space. The Percussion fuze M57 was standard. The filling most generally encountered was 4.1lb of White

Phosphorus, this shell being used for producing smoke screens. Other fillings were 4.61lb of Titanium Tetrachloride smoke composition or 3.17lb of HS (Mustard) gas. Of these, the Titanium (known as FS) was substitute standard for smoke screen purposes, while the HS, like other gas shells, was never used. The M60 shell weighed 34.86lb when filled FS; 34.34lb filled WP; and 33.42lb filled HS. Because of the weight variation, they all ranged differently; the FS to 12,319 yards; the WP to 12,281 yards and the HS to 12,243 yards. The propelling charge used with these shells was of the same design as that used with the HE shell, but weighed 2.94lb.

Shell, S/Fxd, Chemical, BE, M84 and M84B1. This was developed during the war, the design being taken from that of the British 25pdr base-ejection smoke shell. It contained three canisters of HC smoke composition and a gunpowder expelling charge. The shell weighed 32.87lb and was fuzed with the Time and Superquick Fuze M54. The M84 shell had the body made from steel tubing and had a nose adapter; the M84B1 was a one-piece forging. The 7-zone propelling charge weighed 3.04lb and the maximum range was 12,243 yards.

In addition to the standard white smoke canisters for screening purposes, coloured smoke, for signalling and indicating targets, was also provided.

Shell, HEAT, M67. This was a hollow-charge shell with a long tapering nose and a base fuze M62A1. The body of the shell carried the customary copper cone, behind which was a filling of 2.93lb of Pentolite.

Shot, Canister, Separate Loading, T18. This projectile consisted of a segmented steel container with a steel closing disc at the base, and a steel disc and terne-plate disc at the nose. This was enclosed in an outer terne-plate cylinder with turned-over ends. Into this container went approximately 400 steel balls set in a resin matrix; the number of balls was not fixed, the shot being filled to a constant weight of 33lb. A special propelling charge of 1.67lb of FNH powder in a standard cartridge case was provided for use with the canister shot. It was developed for use in the Pacific theatre, for clearing fields of fire in thick grass, and for clearing snipers from areas of bush and trees. It was never issued to the European Theatre of Operations.

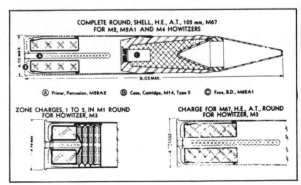

105mm Howitzer M3

In 1941, the US Army requested a 105mm howitzer suitable for carriage by air, and, as a rough guideline, a weight of 2,500lb and a range of not less than 7,000 yards were stipulated. In response, the M2A1 howitzer was cut down in length by 27 inches, to become the Howitzer T7. The carriage of the 75mm Howitzer M3A1 was adopted as the Carriage T6, and the recoil mechanism of the 75mm Pack Howitzer, much modified, became the Recoil Mechanism 105mm Howitzer T13. Surprisingly, when it was all put together it worked quite well and required very little further modification, and the design was standardized as the Howitzer M3 on Carriage M3 in February 1943. Trials of production models revealed a lack of strength of the carriage, so those converted from 75mm matériel remained the M3, while a newly-manufactured design, with thicker metal in the trail, became the M3A1.

While the original intention was for airborne use, in 1941–42 the idea of forming 'Infantry Cannon Companies' for forward artillery support took root, and the M3 was selected for this role. An M3A2 carriage, which had shields, was produced for this application, and the cannon companies were deployed during the North African campaign. They were not a success and the idea was discontinued in 1943. Thereafter, the M3 reverted to use solely by airborne units, and the M3A2 carriages had their shields removed.

The M3 was an effective weapon within its limitations, but as a result of the short tube, light recoil system and limited elevation, its greatest limitation was its short range. Nevertheless, 2,580 were built, and it remained in service throughout the war, being rapidly declared obsolete thereafter.

Variants

T10: A modified M3 on a redesigned carriage, reducing the total weight so that it could be carried as pack loads by four men. The project was begun in November 1943 and pilots were made in 1945 for tests in January 1946. It was subsequently cancelled.

T10E1: As T10, but with a different breech mechanism.
Self-propelled equipments:
The short barrel of the M3 made it an attractive proposition for mounting in armoured vehicles, and a number of projects were put forward:

HMC T38: Mounted on the Half-Track M3 in similar manner to the M2A1 Howitzer in the HMC T19.

T39: Mounted in the T13 armoured car.

T47: Mounted in the M5A1 tank chassis with open-topped hull, the general appearance being that of a shrunken M7.

T82: Revised version of the T47 intended for use in jungle.

None of these ever got past the project stage.

Data

Weight of gun and breech mechanism: 955lb.
Total length: 74.35in.
Length of bore: 68.2in (16.5 cal).
Rifling: 34 grooves, uniform RH 1/20.
Breech mechanism: Horizontal sliding block, percussion fired.
Elevation: $-9°$ $+69°$.
Traverse: $22\frac{1}{2}°$ right and left.
Recoil system: Hydropneumatic, constant, 29in.
Weight in action: 2,495lb.

Performance firing standard 33lb HE shell
Muzzle velocity: 1,020ft/sec.
Maximum range: 8,295 yards.

Ammunition

The ammunition was the same as that provided for the M2 howitzer, except that the propelling charge consisted of 5 zones instead of 7, and the powder granulation was smaller so as to achieve more rapid combustion in the short barrel. Nominal weight of the full charge was 21.3oz. In emergency, the standard M2 ammunition could be used, but only charge zones 1, 2 or 3.

The HEAT round was fixed and had a fixed charge weight of 1.20lb to give a velocity of 1,020ft/sec. and a maximum range of 8,490 yards.

Above: The 105mm M3 howitzer; the Indian soldier is looking into the Panoramic Telescope.

4.5in Field Gun

In 1919, the Westervelt Board recommended development of a 4.7in medium field gun to supplement the 155mm howitzer as divisional heavy artillery, and in 1920, the 4.7in gun M1920 on Carriage 4.7in Gun and 155mm How M1920 appeared. This was a 47.5 calibre gun firing a 50lb shell at 2,450ft/sec, mounted on a split-trail carriage. It was considered unsatisfactory and was re-designed as the Gun M1922E on Carriage M1921E; this was a 42 calibre gun firing the same shell at the same velocity to give a range of 20,500 yards. The Field Artillery Board recommended standardization, but decision was postponed while some modifications were made, and in August 1928, the project was placed in abeyance.

With war looming up in 1939, the design was revived with a proposal to develop a gun capable of reaching 20,000 yards, and on a carriage using as many components as possible of the 155mm How M1 carriage. The 4.7in Gun T3 was produced, which was exactly the same as the M1922E, and it was recommended for standardization by OCM 15556 of 4 January 1940. By this time, though, it was becoming obvious that sooner or later, the British and American armies were going to be operating together and it was suggested that if the calibre were changed to 4.5in, this would allow interchangeability of ammunition between the existing British 4.5 and the American gun. The idea met with approval and in April 1941, the T3, rebored to 4.5in calibre, was standardized as the 4.5in Gun M1.

The carriage was that of the 155mm How M1, with minor modifications. A small number of guns were also mounted on the carriage MkII M1918, which was that of the old 6in Gun (long obsolete), a box-trail carriage arranged for horse draught. Why this was done is obscure; possibly as a training equipment; it was mentioned in an Ordnance School Text of 1943, but no picture has ever been seen of it. When the 155mm How carriage was modified by replacing the electric brakes with air brakes, the same modification was done to the 4.5in carriage, advancing the nomenclature to M1A1.

The 4.5in gun served throughout the war, largely as a training weapon, though a small number were used in Europe. It was not well liked because of the relatively inefficient shell, a 55pdr designed in Britain to utilize low-grade steel and thus having inside it too little explosive for the Americans' liking. It was declared obsolete in September 1945, largely on the grounds of the insufficient lethality of the shell.

Variants

No variant model entered service, but there were a number of interesting proposals. In late 1943, the Gun Motor Carriage T16 was proposed, mounting the 4.5in gun on a chasis constructed largely from components of the M3 (Stuart) light tank. This was dropped in favour of the T16E1 which was to use the torsion-bar suspension of the T24 light tank. One pilot model was planned, but the question was raised as to whether such a weapon was actually wanted by the army. The answer, apparently, was 'no', and the idea was cancelled in July 1944.

In February 1945, there was a proposal to produce a new self-propelled gun to use a fixed round of ammunition. Work began on the round, and on a new breech mechanism, but it was decided to cancel the project because (a) it would remove the advantage of interchangeable ammunition between US and UK forces, and (b) 'Under existing priorities while feasible it could not be accomplished in time to be used during the war' (OCM 26248 of 15 February 1945).

Data

Weight of gun and breech mechanism: 4,070lb.
Total length: 197.6in
Length of bore: 189.6in (42 cal).
Rifling: 32 grooves, uniform RH, 1/25.
Breech mechanism: Interrupted screw, slow cone, percussion fired.
Elevation: 0° +65°
Traverse: 26½° right and left.
Recoil system: Hydropneumatic variable, 29in to 42in.
Weight in action: 12,444lb.

Performance firing standard 54.9lb HE shell:

	Muzzle velocity:	Maximum range:
Normal Charge M7	1,820ft/sec.	16,650 yards
Super Charge M8	2,275ft/sec.	21,125 yards

Ammunition

Propelling Charge. This was bagged, and two types were used. The Normal Charge M7 consisted of 7.44lb of powder in a bag 22.8in long, with a black powder igniter stitched to the base.

Alternatively, the Charge M8 could be used. This was a two-part base and increment unit of two bags. The Base Charge M8 consisted of one bag, 16.1in long, containing 8.328lb of powder. This was of a different formulation and granulation from the powder in the M7 charge, and thus, although the size and weight were different, it gave exactly the same ballistics as the M7. For greater range, the M8 Increment Section was added to the M8 Base Section and secured with tapes. This brought the total charge weight up to 11.06lb. The increment did not have an igniter and could not be fired by itself.

Of the two charges, the M7 was more regular in its performance and delivered better accuracy than the M8 Base Section; but it was impossible to make

Top left: The 4.5in gun at maximum elevation, showing the firing pedestal in front of the axletree; and (top right) in marching order. Note the travelling lock, which holds the barrel securely against vibration. A peculiarity of this gun was the way that the breech 'stuck out' clear of the cradle, giving the appearance of having failed to return to battery properly. This feature was so designed in order to balance the gun in the carriage. **Middle right:** The Normal Charge M7 for the 4.5in gun. **Right:** The 4.5in gun in firing position.

a Super Charge out of the powder type used in the M7, since this would have exceeded the safe chamber pressure (40,000lb/in²) and this led to the adoption of the M8 charge.

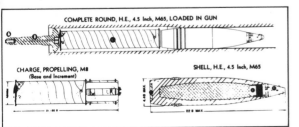

Shell, HE, 4.5in M65, M65B1 and M65B2. This was the British design of streamlined shell, differing only in the pitch of the screw-threads in the nose for American fuzes. It weighed 54.9lb and was filled with 4.49lb of TNT and fuzed PD M51 or TM M67. The shell M65 was made from a steel casting and had an inlet steel baseplate; the M65B1 was a steel forging and had the same type of baseplate. Both of these were of British design and were made in Canada. The M65B2 was a steel forging with an American pattern of welded base cover and was made in the USA.

No other ammunition was ever provided for the 4.5in gun.

155mm Howitzer M1917 and M1918

As the model number indicates, this equipment originated during the First World War. It was originally designed by Schneider et Cie for the French Army and was then adopted by the American Army on their entry into the war. The story of the gun's adoption and subsequent manufacture in the USA is long and involved, but unfortunately has no place here; interested readers are directed to *America's Munitions 1917–1918* by Benedict Crowell for the official story, and to *Signposts of Experience* by General Snow for the unofficial, but vastly more revealing tale.

The role of the M1917/18 howitzer during the Second World War was largely that of a training weapon, though numbers were in use in the Far Eastern theatres, and a quantity were sent to North Africa to supply the British Army there in June 1941. These served as a stopgap until they could be replaced by the 5.5in Gun in May 1942. Although by then virtually obsolete, it served well, though it was not particularly well-liked by the gunners of the Eighth Army.

Variants

Howitzer:

M1917: Original Schneider manufacture, issued to the AEF in France as complete equipments.

M1917A1: Schneider manufacture, shipped as guns only to the USA for assembly.

M1917A2: A1 adapted to take the M1918 breech mechanism.

M1918: US manufacture with a modified breech

Left and bottom: The M1918 howitzer on Carriage M1917A3; and (middle right) the 155mm howitzer M1918 on Carriage M1918.

mechanism which had a screw-in firing lock in place of the French continuous-pull mechanism.

Carriage:

M1917: Schneider manufacture. Box trail, wooden, steel-tyred wheels, curved shield.

M1917A1: 1917 modified by straight shield, rubber tyred wheels and US sights.

M1917A2: A1 with cradle lock and drawbar for mechanical draught.

M1917A3: M1917 with high-speed axle, pneumatic tyres, drawbar and cradle lock.

M1917A4: A2 with torque rods to protect the traversing mechanism while travelling.

M1918: US manufacture. Similar to 1917, but with a two-piece straight shield.

M1918A1: Converted for high-speed towing by pneumatic tyres and air brakes. Standardized in 1936.

M1918A2: No record; believed number not allotted.

M1918A3: As for A1, but with the addition of torque rods to protect the traversing mechanism.

Data

Weight of gun and breech mechanism: 2,740lb.
Total length: 91.81in.
Length of bore: 83.24in (13.64 cal).
Rifling: 48 grooves, uniform RH 1/25½.
Breech mechanism: Interrupted screw, Schneider, percussion fired.
Elevation: 0° to +42°20′.
Traverse: 3° right and left.
Recoil mechanism: Hydropneumatic, constant, 51.4in.
Weight in action (M1918A3 carriage): 8,184lb.

Performance Firing the standard 95lb high-explosive shell
Maximum muzzle velocity: 1,475ft/sec.
Maximum range: 12,400 yards.

Ammunition

Propelling Charge. This was in two distinct portions, the 'Green Bag' or short-range portion, and the 'White Bag' long-range portion. The Green Bag charge M1A1 was made up of a Base Section and four increments to give five possible charges or 'zones'; nominal weight of the complete five-charge unit was 4.00lb and the maximum range attained was 9,415 yards, the muzzle velocity with Charge 5 being 1,082ft/sec.

The White Bag charge M2A1 was similarly made up of a Base Section and four increments to give five charges; nominal weight was 8.09lb. The Base Section of the White Bag charge was ballistically the same as Green Bag Zone 3, and for the next two zones there was an overlap; i.e. Green Bag Zone 4 and White Bag Zone 2 were the same, as were Green 5 and White 3. But white and green bags could not be mixed to concoct a non-standard charge. The charges or zones were actually numbered from 1 to 7, with 3, 4 and 5 duplicated.

Shell, HE, 155mm M102. This was the standard projectile and weighed 95.3lb. It contained 15.13lb

of TNT and was fuzed PD M48, PD M57 or TSQ M55. It was of conventional streamlined form, but had a narrow driving band and was not normally used in any other 155mm equipment, though in a dire emergency it was possible to fire it from the M1 howitzer. No other 155mm shell from other weapons could be used with these howitzers.

Shell, Chemical, 155mm M105. This projectile was available filled with 15.6lb of white phosphorus (WP) smoke composition, 16.9lb of sulphur trioxide (FS) smoke composition, or 11.70lb of mustard gas (HS). The design was of the usual bursting pattern, having a central tube containing 0.36lb of Tetryl and the payload packed around it. The WP shell had a total weight of 97.68lb, velocity 1,476ft/sec and maximum range of 12,783 yards; FS weighed 99.23lb, velocity 1,476ft/sec and maximum range 12,791 yards; HS weighed 93.78lb, velocity 1,476ft/sec and maximum range 12,773 yards. All shells were fitted with Fuze PD M57 or M51.

Shell, Smoke, Base Ejection, 155mm M115 and M115B1. After adoption of the base-ejection smoke shell for the 105mm howitzer, the design was then extended to the 155mm calibre. The M115 had a body of drawn steel tube with a shaped ogive (nose) section screwed in; the M115B1 had a one-piece forged body. Four smoke canisters were carried, three parallel-sided M1 and one conical M2 which fitted inside the shell's ogive. The shell baseplate was secured by a screwed-in lock ring. The time fuze TSQ M54 was fitted. The M115 weighed 94.88lb, the M115B1 94.14lb. Both had a maximum muzzle velocity of 1,476ft/sec and a maximum range of 12,405 yards. Only white smoke was available.

Limited Standard Designs. Numbers of earlier projectiles, the HE Shell MkIA1 and the Chemical Shell MkIIA1 were in stock at the outbreak of war and were sentenced Limited Standard, to be used for training, when the M102 and 105 designs appeared. Large quantities were supplied, with the howitzers, to the British Army in 1941. The principal difference lay in the fuzing; these earlier shells were fitted with the Fuze PD M46 (Superquick) or PD M47 (Delay) which had been developed from the original French RYG24/31 fuzes of the First World War. These had a narrower screwed shank and the shell nose was fitted with an adapter to take them. By and large, the later shells were simply the same design, but with the adapter removed and a two-inch threaded hole for the later patterns of fuze.

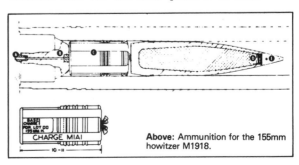

Above: Ammunition for the 155mm howitzer M1918.

155mm Howitzer M1

One of the principal defects of the M1917 carriage was the limited traverse, which meant that the whole equipment had to be manhandled for switches of greater than 3°, and the mechanical arrangement of the traverse which, by means of a screw mechanism, slewed the entire carriage across the axle. This system is just acceptable in a light field gun, but in an equipment as big as the 155mm howitzer it was grossly out of place. In the early 1930s, a number of ground platforms were devised and tested in the hope of improving the horizontal arc of fire, but none were acceptable to the army, and in 1934, development of a new split-trail carriage, the T2, was begun. The specification called for 30° of traverse each way, a range of 16,000 yards, 65° of elevation, and a carriage weight of not more than 11,000lb. This development was proceeding quite well until in 1939, somebody pointed out that there was little profit in designing a beautiful new carriage and then putting it underneath an ancient howitzer, so the whole project stopped and work began afresh on designing a complete new equipment.

The new models were the Howitzer T3 and Carriage T2, the carriage to be suitable for use with either the 155mm howitzer or the new 4.7in gun then being designed. Work went ahead quickly, and the standardization of the Howitzer M1 on Carriage M1 was authorized by OCM 16724 of 15 May 1941.

The principal changes on the howitzer were the lengthening of the barrel to 20 calibres and the fitting of a new breech mechanism; this was notable for being the only 'slow-coned' mechanism in use anywhere in an equipment designed after 1920. The obturating pad in the breech screw was so contoured that the first movement of the breech operating lever had to withdraw the block and pad axially before it could be unlocked and swung open. This is in distinction to the 'steep cone' mechanism where rotation and withdrawal are simultaneous. No explanation for the selection of this type of mechanism has ever been found, and it was perpetuated (perhaps, in this instance, perpetrated might be a better word) in the SP M44 equipment introduced in the 1950s.

Rather more than 6,000 M1 howitzers were produced, and it has been widely adopted in other countries since the war.

Variants

Howitzer: None.
Carriage:
M1A1: As M1, but with the Warner Electric Brakes removed and replaced by Westinghouse Air Brakes. Both M1 and M1A1 carriages were fitted with a mid-axle firing pedestal which was extended into place by a ratchet.
M1A2: M1A1, but with the firing pedestal operated by a screw jack system and with a modified travelling lock.
M1A1E1: Modified M1A1 carriage with the wheels removed and a free-rolling tracked suspension unit fitted, intended for use in mud and jungle conditions. Project was begun late in 1944, but was ended in August 1945 without having reached a successful conclusion.
T9: Modified M1 carriage with screw-type elevating and traversing gears, redesigned trunnions and reinforced trail legs made from low-alloy steel. Begun in 1943, but ran into manufacturing difficulties; pilot-tested in April 1944, project terminated April 1945. The design had been put together to try and overcome certain features of the M1A1 carriage which were considered objectionable by theorists; but as the actual carriages performed well in action, and the theorists never got their design to function properly, there seemed no point in continuing.
T10: Similar to T9, but of low-carbon steel, the project being started when there appeared to be the possibility of an alloy steel famine. By the end of 1943, the steel situation had improved and the project was closed down.
T16: Development of a lightweight carriage of high-yield steel, estimated to save 1,200lb weight. Work began in July 1945 and continued after the war, though nothing appears to have come of it.

Self-Propelled Equipments

Remarkably, only one self-propelled equipment was built around the 155mm howitzer. This began as the T64, using the M5 light tank chassis, in mid 1943. In January 1944, this was dropped in favour of the T64E1, using the chassis of the T24 light tank, a project which had also begun in mid 1943, but which had gone into abeyance waiting for a firm statement of requirement for such an equipment. A pilot model was built in February 1944, and it was standardized as the HMC M41 by OCM 27661 of 17 May 1945. Procurement of 500 equipments was authorized in July 1944, though this was later reduced to 250 and the final production figure is believed to be less than 100.

Data Howitzer M1, on Carriage M1A1
Weight of gun and breech mechanism: 3,825lb.
Total length: 150.0in.
Length of bore: 122.04in (20 cal).
Rifling: 48 grooves, uniform RH 1/25.
Breech mechanism: Interrupted screw, percussion fired.
Elevation: −2° +63°.
Traverse: 25° right, 24° left.
Recoil system: Hydropneumatic, variable, 41in to 58in.
Weight in action: 11,966lb.

Performance firing standard 95lb HE shell
Muzzle velocity: 1,850ft/sec.
Maximum range: 16,355 yards.

Ammunition separate loading, bag charge.

Propelling Charge. This came in two sections, the 'Green Bag Portion M3' and the 'White Bag Portion M4', each unit being coloured accordingly. The Green Bag was divided into a Base and four increments, with a nominal weight of 5.13lb, while the White Bag was divided into Base and four increments of nominal weight 13.26lb. Green Bag gave Zones (Charges) One to Five, with maximum velocity 1,220ft/sec and maximum range 10,780 yards, while White Bag overlapped to give Zones Three to Seven.

Shell, HE, 155mm M107. This was virtually the same as the M102 shell, except for the driving band, which was broader and slightly greater in diameter. The filling was 15.13lb TNT, and the total weight was 95.01lb. Standard fuze was the PD M48 or M51 or the TM M67.

Shell, Chemical, 155mm M110. This, too, was similar to the M105 shell for the earlier howitzer, except for the heavier driving band. It was available with white phosphorus (WP) filling (total weight 98.4lb), titanium tetrachloride (FS) filling (99.4lb) or distilled mustard gas (HS) filling (94.21lb), and used the PD Fuze M51 as standard. As a result of the different weights, ballistic performance changed, the maximum range being 16,355 yards for WP and FS, 16,375 for HS.

Shell, Smoke, BE, 155mm M116 or M116B1. This resembled the M115 and M115B1, except for the driving band. The M116 contained four smoke canisters, and was made in two portions, the parallel-walled body and the tapering nose, screwed together. The M116B1 version was a one-piece forging which weighed very slightly less than the two-piece shell. M116: 95.1lb; M116B1: 94.36lb. Only white smoke, for screening, was available during the war, though coloured signalling smokes were produced during the post-war years.

Left: Ammunition for the 155mm howitzer M1. **Below:** The 155mm howitzer M1 on Carriage M1 in firing position.

SHELL, H.E., 155 mm, M107

CHARGE, PROPELLING, M3

27.54 MAX.

14 – 15

Ⓐ Primer, Percussion, Mk. IIA4
Ⓑ Obturator Spindle
Ⓒ Charge, Propelling, M4A1
Ⓓ Booster, M21A2
Ⓔ Fuze, P.D., M51A3 (.15 sec.), or Fuze, M.T., M67A1

Anti-Tank Artillery

In 1916, the machine-gun was the thing to beat, and so the tank appeared on the battlefield. In 1939, the tank was the thing to beat, and a great deal of worry and sweat went into the question of providing anti-tank guns.

The tank and the anti-tank gun represent the opposite ends of a see-saw for superiority which went up and down at varying speeds and at varying times during the war years, but, by and large, the first half of the war saw the Western Allies with their guns at the bottom of the see-saw. One reason for this was that in pre-war years, the design of anti-tank guns was closely tied to the design of tank guns, since it was argued that

Below: Business is slack today; two GIs with a 37mm gun waiting for customers in North Africa, 1943. (See data page 83.)

they both had to do the same job and that it was economical to provide one gun for both applications. Unfortunately, this tied the gun designer to the dimensions of the tank turret or fighting compartment, which left him little scope. Another common failing was to take the 'home' tank instead of the 'away' tank as the optimum target, and so long as the tanks of one's own army were relatively thin-skinned, a small gun was all you could expect. Then, too, there was the argument, paralleling that heard in anti-aircraft circles, that the tank's enemy was another tank, and that anti-tank guns were unnecessary; when the infantry pointed out that it was not unknown for tanks to sneak past the opposition and start raising hell in the rear areas, they were given a powerful rifle and told to shut up.

All these arguments were heard in other countries as well, but Britain and America had the additional burden of tight finance, and smaller guns were cheaper than big ones. So both countries began the war with light-weight weapons, easily manoeuvred and concealed, capable of piercing the armour of the German tanks of 1939, but which were soon to be at a disadvantage when tank armour became thicker and tanks began to mount more powerful weapons. The Desert Campaign of 1941–42 was largely fought

with the 2pdr, an excellent weapon when designed but, by 1942, no match for the opposition which could stand off out of danger and shell the 2pdr into silence with their 50mm and 75mm guns, firing high-explosive.

The lesson was eventually learned, and gun designers began producing bigger and better guns, to the extent that by the end of the war, they were offering weapons which weighed about as much as a medium field-gun and were about as mobile and handy in action as a brick outhouse. Like the dinosaur, the anti-tank gun finally succumbed to its own weight.

What saved the day was not gun design, but ammunition design. The development of tungsten-cored projectiles and squeeze-bore guns is covered in the general introduction, and need not be repeated here, but it was this development which enabled guns to improve their performance so that they could still beat the opposition without having, at that time, to go to extremes of weight and size. By the time the see-saw had swung again, and the size of guns was having to go beyond the bounds of practicality, the recoilless gun came along and proved to be the post-war solution to the dilemma of performance versus size.

Again, it was ammunition which saved the situation; no recoilless gun could have fired discarding sabot projectiles at a worthwhile velocity, but the development of the hollow-charge and squash-head shells provided chemical instead of kinetic energy, and allowed low-velocity guns to deliver killing blows against the hardest armour.

The hollow-charge shell was also the means of providing field artillery with an anti-tank capability, for use in the not uncommon circumstance of a tank evading the anti-tank specialists. The American artillery adopted several hollow-charge shells, but the British, though being the first ever to put a hollow-charge munition into service (the Rifle Grenade No. 68), never adopted it for serious anti-tank work. Their development programme brought out the fact that spinning a hollow-charge shell degraded its performance; the 25pdr used a first-rate piercing shot which was quite capable of seeing off most tanks if the gunner held his fire (and his breath) until the target was close enough. Only the 3.7in howitzer and some of the more weird Home Guard weapons were given hollow charge, since this was their only hope of dealing with tanks, and the likelihood of their being called upon to prove it was remote.

The tactics of anti-tank work also went through various phases. At first, it was purely an infantry self-protection affair; then the 'Tank Destroyer' idea took hold, and the thing was to go looking for tanks, preferably on some sort of self-propelled mounting. Finally, the tactics stabilized at something between the two: moderate tank hunting, with a solid backing of skilfully deployed guns covering the avenues of approach, that experience and commonsense determined an enemy tank would use. It was a demanding job, whichever way you went about it, one of the most dangerous and highly skilled that gunners were called upon to do throughout the war. They had few illusions about it. Some years ago, I knew a man who had been a gunner on a 2pdr with an anti-tank regiment in the Western Desert. 'What were you in the Desert, Tex,' I asked, 'A 2-pounder gunner?' 'Yes,' he said, 'And I was the fastest bloody runner in the Eighth Army.'

Right: 2pdr gun on the Mk 1 carriage, using screw-jacks at the end of the trail legs.

2pdr Anti-Tank Gun

On the day it was formally approved, 1 January 1936, the 2pdr was undoubtedly the best anti-tank gun in the world. Unfortunately, by the time it had to earn its keep, it was no longer capable of dealing with the opposition quite so effectively, and as a result it has come in for more than its fair share of criticism and opprobrium over the years.

The 2pdr was developed in accordance with pre-war tactical thought which called for a light-weight gun capable of being manhandled by front-line infantry. Sufficient trials had been carried out in the 1920s to indicate what was desirable in a gun intended solely for the defeat of tanks, and one of the highest priorities was the ability to swing rapidly through a wide arc so as to be able to deal with targets in any quarter. This led to the three-legged mounting above which the gun could traverse through a complete circle. In similar fashion, a demand for a high rate of fire led to a semi-automatic breech mechanism, and a call for accuracy in poor light led to an excellent telescope sight. Unfortunately, the outcome was a weapon which weighed twice as much as any of its contemporaries. This difficulty was overcome, to some extent, in 1938, when the responsibility for anti-tank defence was taken from the infantry and given to Anti-Tank Regiments, Royal Artillery; these could afford men better than the hard-pressed foot, and their tactical doctrines resulted in rather less manhandling.

By 1939, the 2pdr was in service in some numbers, and it was fast approaching the end of its useful life, since tank design had moved on during the five years since the original specification had been drawn. In 1940, more than 500 guns were left behind in France, and in order to equip the army in Britain as rapidly as possible, the 2pdr continued in production for another year. During the Desert campaign of 1941–42, its weaknesses were revealed, notably its high silhouette which made it difficult to conceal. This allowed German tanks to stand well away and shell the gun into silence. It took aggressive handling and ingenious tactics to get a 2pdr close enough to a German or Italian tank to be sure of stopping it.

After the summer of 1942, the 2pdr was replaced in anti-tank regiments by the 6pdr, and the 2pdr returned to the infantry; a number were also issued to the Home Guard in Britain. It was retained by RA units in the Far East where its performance was still quite sufficient to cope with Japanese tanks. It was finally made obsolete in December 1945.

The gun was a conventional monobloc with vertical sliding breech. The carriage consisted of a basic structure of three trail legs, two of which folded upwards alongside the gun barrel, and an axle suspended by a transverse leaf spring. The wheels were fitted with quick-release gear and could be removed when putting the gun into action with all three trail legs on the ground. In an emergency, the gun could be fired from its wheels, but the presence of the folded trail legs limited the traverse.

Above this basic structure was a turntable which carried the gun, shield, ammunition locker and gunlayer's seat. A two-speed traversing gear was fitted, allowing fast movement to pick up a target, and fine movement for accurate laying. The gunlayer could fire the gun by foot-pedal or hand firing lever, and a second firing lever alongside the breech could be operated by the detachment commander in the event of a defect in the layer's gear. A frontal shield was standard, and side shields to give full protection to the gunners were available, though they appear to have been rarely seen outside of training establishments.

Left: Another variant of the Mk 1 carriage, with screw-jack pickets on the trails for digging into soft ground.

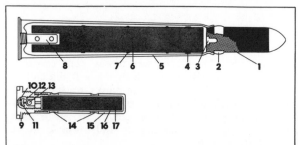

Above: Ammunition for the 2pdr gun.
1. Shot; 2. Driving band; 3. Tracer plug; 4. Tinfoil; 5. Case; 6. Cordite;
7. Silk thread; 8. Primer; 9. Head; 10. Cap; 11. Detonator;
12. Anvil; 13. Copper ball; 14. Flash holes; 15. Magazine;
16. Paper; 17. Gunpowder pellets.

Right: The 2pdr mounted on a Loyd carrier; few were made.

In order to save wear and tear, it was normal to carry the equipment 'en portée' in the back of a truck and remove it on reaching the scene of action. In the desert it became common practice to leave the gun on the truck at all times, the truck bed being suitably reinforced to take the firing shock, and the trail being folded down to give full traverse.

A variety of self-propelled mountings were developed, usually using the Universal or Loyd carriers as the basic chassis, but few of them appear to have had official backing and none were ever adopted for service; probably because by the time they had been perfected, the 2pdr was obsolescent.

An interesting derivative of the 2pdr was the Canadian 'David' high-velocity gun. This was designed in 1942 and was essentially a 2pdr with an enlarged chamber and a 6pdr breech, firing a round which comprised the 2pdr shot and a 6pdr cartridge case. Development was slow, because of problems in ammunition design. A gun and ammunition were sent to Britain for trials, but these were still in progress when the war ended. The project was finally abandoned, but it had yielded much useful information on high-velocity guns which proved useful in other applications.

Variants
Mk 9: Original design with auto-frettaged barrel.
Mk 9A: Approved in 1940 in order to speed up

Left: 2pdr gun on Mk 2 carriage, the model most commonly issued; this used pads at the end of the trail legs, disc wheels, and had some manufacturing simplifications. **Below:** The 2pdr prepared for action.

production, this was the same as the Mk 9, but non-auto-frettaged and with some dimensional tolerances relaxed.

Mk 10: Approved in 1936; as Mk 9, but of higher grade steel, and not auto-frettaged.

Mk 10A: As Mk 10, but with dimensional tolerances relaxed.

Mk 10B: As Mk 10A, but fitted for the Littlejohn muzzle adapter. This was a squeeze-bore attachment used with armoured cars and light tanks, in conjunction with a special skirted projectile.

Data

Weight of gun and breech mechanism: 287lb.
Total length: 81.95in.
Length of bore: 78.75in.
Rifling: 12 grooves, uniform RH 1/30.
Breech mechanism: Vertical sliding block, semi-automatic, percussion fired.
Elevation: $-13° +15°$ on platform; $-5° +23°$ on wheels.
Traverse: 360° on platform; 14° left, 10° right on wheels.
Recoil system: Hydro-spring, constant, 20in.
Weight in action: 1,757lb.

Performance firing standard 2lb AP shot.
Muzzle velocity: 2,650ft/sec.
Maximum range: 8,000 yards.
Penetration: 42mm/1,000yds/30°

Ammunition fixed, cased charge.

Propelling charge. The propelling charge was contained in a brass cartridge case; its weight varied with the type of projectile and type of propellant powder, but representative charges were 10oz 15drachms with the HE shell, and 9oz 12dr with the AP shot.

Shot, AP, Mk 10T. A solid steel shot weighing 2lb and with a tracer in the base.

Shot, APCBC, Mk 9BT. Solid shot, with penetrative and ballistic caps and tracer.

Shell, AP, Mk 1. This shell was part of the original specification for the gun, and was a piercing projectile with a tiny filling of Lyddite and the Base Fuze No. 281, which carried a tracer. Experience revealed that on impact, the fuze tended to part company with the shell and thus failed to initiate the filling. Moreover, even when it worked correctly it appeared to do no more damage than a plain steel shot, which was easier to manufacture. As a result, the AP shell was withdrawn.

Shell, HE, Mk 2T. Contrary to many published statements, there *was* a high-explosive shell for the 2pdr gun, though it appears not to have been issued to tanks. It was a pointed shell with a small filling of TNT and a Base Percussion Fuze No. 243. Its penetrative performance was zero, since it was intended for attacking soft vehicles and defended positions.

 # 6pdr Anti-Tank Gun

The need of an eventual replacement for the 2pdr anti-tank gun was appreciated almost as soon as the 2pdr had been issued, and a 6pdr of 57mm calibre seemed a logical step, since this calibre had been in service since the 1880s so that barrel-making machinery, ammunition production capacity and ballistic knowledge were all available. As a result, the design was completed in 1938, and in 1939, a Mark 1 gun was made and fired, after which the design was sealed and put to one side to await the day it was needed.

Unfortunately, when that day dawned, the situation was so grim that the design had to stay on the shelf a little longer. In 1940, the grave losses in 2pdr guns led to the suggestion that now was the obvious time to produce the 6pdr, but to place the 6pdr in production would have taken considerable time and it would have absorbed almost all the facilities then in use for producing the 2pdr. In the summer of 1940, a gun in the field was better than any number in the production schedules; moreover, the 2pdr was a weapon with which the troops were familiar, whereas the 6pdr would demand extensive retraining before it could become a viable service weapon. So the 2pdr stayed in production at the expense of the 6pdr. Although a contract for 400 6pdr guns was issued in June 1940, it had to wait until the demand

for 2pdrs was satisfied and production capacity could be allocated, and it was not until November 1941 that the first guns were made. By May 1942, more than 1,500 guns per month were being turned out from the factories.

Once issued, the 6pdr went to anti-tank regiments to replace the 2pdr, and later, when stocks allowed, numbers were issued to infantry battalions, the issue increasing in 1943, when Royal Artillery units began to receive the 17pdr gun. Numbers were also given to the Soviet Army and to the US Army, who copied it as their 57mm Gun (p. 85). Though it was little in evidence in post-war years, it was not declared obsolete until July 1960.

The 6pdr was a conventional monobloc gun with vertical sliding breech block. The carriage was a split-trail model with 90° of traverse; this was originally controlled by a handwheel, but during user trials in March 1941, it was suggested that a better method would be to allow free traverse, controlled by the gunlayer tucking a shoulder-pad under his arm and pushing the breech end from side to side, a system which had been used for many years in coast and naval light guns. The idea was approved and was incorporated into the production carriages.

The performance of the 6pdr was vastly improved by the adoption of new types of projectile (see

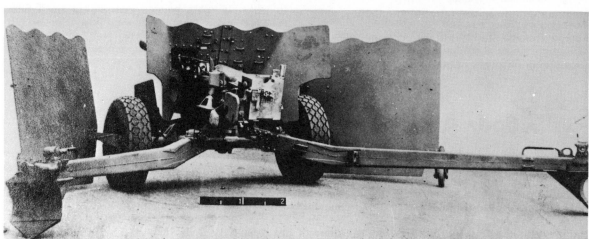

Top: The 6pdr with split-trail carriage, and shoulder-pad for the gunlayer. Middle: Rarely seen—the auxiliary shields for the 6pdr. Below: The Mk 4 6pdr with short spades and trail legs closed, ready for travelling.

below) but, in addition, a squeeze-bore Littlejohn adapter was developed in 1942. This used a special skirted projectile and had an emergent calibre of 1.68in (42.6mm), but after trials, it was decided that no service requirement existed and the project was abandoned. An improved gun, known as the '6pdr Canuck' was placed under development in Canada, but this project had not been completed before the end of the war and was eventually cancelled.

In addition to its artillery use, the 6pdr was, of course, the principal British tank gun for most of the war. It was also hoped to develop a fast and well-armoured 'tank destroyer' using the 6pdr gun, fitted with an automatic loading device to allow one-man operation (in order to keep the size of the vehicle to the minimum). The Molins Machinery Company, who had invented the fuze-setter-rammer for the 3.7in AA gun, produced a suitable autoloader in only five months. But by that time, the 17pdr gun was in service and the army had decided against the tank-destroyer idea. The Royal Navy now appeared and took the gun and autoloader over, with slight modifications, as armament for fast coastal craft, in which role, it was highly successful.

The Royal Air Force now showed an interest, since their 40mm 'S' gun mounted in aircraft was no longer sufficiently powerful and they were looking for an anti-submarine weapon. The 6pdr was fitted into a Mosquito aircraft and proved to be satisfactory; twelve guns were eventually fitted, and these aircraft operated over the Atlantic Ocean with some success, at least one submarine falling victim to the 6pdr gun. But the Air Ministry then decided to develop rocket weapons for the anti-submarine task and the 6pdr Mosquito was retired from service.

It should be mentioned that a possible replacement for the 6pdr, suggested in 1942, was an 8pdr of 2.33in calibre. This was suggested as a method of producing a better performance while keeping the gun dimensions the same as those of the 6pdr, and thus allow the 8pdr to be used in the same carriages and tank mountings. The original design was for a 59-calibre gun which gave the same penetrative performance as the 6pdr, but at a 28% better range; or, conversely, gave better penetration at the same ranges. However, this length of gun was impossible to balance in either the towed carriage or in tank mountings; it was, therefore, reduced in length to 48 calibres, whereupon, the performance declined to that of the 6pdr. There being no point in continuing, the project was cancelled in January 1943.

Variants
Ordnance:
Mk 1: Original development model. A few were made in 1939, but none were issued to service.
Mk 2: Production model for towed carriage.
Mk 3: For tanks. As for Mk 2, but with lugs on the breech ring to suit the tank mounting and recoil system.
Mk 4: As Mk 2, but with the barrel 16in longer in order to improve muzzle velocity, and with a muzzle brake. For towed carriages.
Mk 5: As Mk 3, but 16in longer and with a muzzle counterweight. For use in tanks.
'C' Mks 3, 4, 5: As Mks 3, 4 and 5, but of Canadian manufacture.
Carriage:
Mk 1: Original split-trail production model.
Mk 1A: As Mk 1, but different axle-tree and wheels.
C Mk 1: Mk 1 of Canadian manufacture.
Mk 2: Slightly simplified design intended as a production alternative to Mk 1, but which was not adopted.

Mk 3: Generally as Mk 1, but lightened for air-dropping or glider carriage by airborne batteries.

Data Gun Mk 2, on Carriage Mk 1
Weight of gun and breech mechanism: 768lb.
Total length: 100.95in.
Length of bore: 96.2in (43 cal).
Rifling: 24 grooves, uniform RH 1/30.
Breech mechanism: Vertical sliding block, semi-automatic, percussion fired.
Elevation: $-5° +15°$.
Traverse: 45° right and left.
Recoil system: Hydro-spring, constant, 30in.
Weight in action: 2,521lb.
Note: Mk 4 gun as above except
Length of gun: 116.95in.
Length of bore: 112.2in (50 cal).

Performance firing standard 6lb AP shot
Muzzle velocity: 2,693ft/sec.
Maximum range: 5,500 yards.
Penetration: 74mm/1,000yds/30°.

Ammunition fixed, cased charge.
Propelling Charges. These varied with the projectile and are detailed below. The charges were of Cordite, bundled and tied, or of nitro-cellulose powder loosely poured into the case. The Percussion Primer No. 15 was standard.

Shot, AP, Mks 1 to 7T. These were all plain steel solid shot, the differences being principally in the composition of the tracer and the attachment of the driving band. The tracer was pressed into a hole in the shot base and burned for about 2–3 seconds. The propelling charge was 1lb 13½oz Cordite or 2lb 5½oz of NC powder.

Shot, APC, Mk 8T. Similar to the AP shot, but with the addition of a penetrative cap in order to attack face-hardened plate. Propelling charges as for AP shot. Weight 6.25lb.

Shot, APCBC, Mk 9T. As for APC, but with a light ballistic cap. Penetration with this, because of the better ballistic shape, was improved to 88mm/1,000yd/30°. Muzzle velocity 2,775ft/sec. Weight 7.0lb.

Shot, APCR, Mk 1T. Provided in small quantities in October 1943, this consisted of a tungsten core built up to full calibre by a light allow body. It weighed 3.97lb and developed a muzzle velocity of 3,528ft/sec. At short range, its penetration was far better than that of steel shot, but because of its light weight and poor weight/diameter ratio, the performance fell off until at 1,000 yards range it was little better than that of the APCBC shot.

Shot, APDS, Mk 1T. Issued in June 1944, this used a tungsten core in a light steel sheath, built up to full calibre by a four-piece light alloy sabot unit which discarded at the muzzle. The complete shot weighed 3.25lb, developed 4,050ft/sec and could defeat 146mm of plate at 1,000 yards range. The propelling charge was 2lb 5¼oz of NC powder. In order to permit the firing of this shot, the muzzle brakes had to be bored out slightly so that the discarding portions did not foul as they passed through.

Shell, HE, Mk 10T. A nose-fuzed high-explosive shell filled with TNT and fitted with the Tracer No. 13 and the Percussion Fuze No. 243. Propelling charge 2lb 5oz NC powder. Muzzle velocity 2,700ft/sec.

Self-Propelled Equipments

Although a number of proposals were mooted, only two reached production, the 'Firefly' and the 'Deacon'. 'Firefly' was a four-wheeled Morris armoured car with the gun frontally-mounted alongside the driver, and fitted with the Molins autoloader so that the driver was the sole crew, and could aim the gun by pointing the car and fire it from the driving seat. Very few were made, since the Army had decided against the 'tank destroyer' tactical theory before the design was completed. These few were employed only in Home Defence.

'Deacon' was more ambitious, a turntable-mounted

gun, well shielded, on the back of an armour-protected AEC 'Matador' truck. 175 of these were built in 1942, and the majority were sent to the Middle East. Though well engineered they suffered from a high silhouette and poor cross-country performance, particularly in sand, and in spite of some gallant actions by their crews, they were not particularly successful. They were withdrawn at the end of the North African campaign.

An unusual experimental project by the Wheeled Vehicle Experimental Establishment (WVEE) was the 'WVEE Carrier', a peculiar, wheeled chassis onto which a towed gun could be quickly and easily manhandled, after which, the carrier could be driven off with the gun 'en portée'. In extreme emergency the gun could even be fired from the carrier, but it was basically only a transport system. But by the time the carrier had been perfected, the Desert campaign, home of the portée gun, was over and the 17pdr was replacing the 6pdr, so the carrier project was abandoned.

Top, left: The 6pdr on portée mounting. Top, right: 'Deacon', a 6pdr gun mounted on an armour-protected AEC 'Matador' truck. Middle, left: 'Firefly', a 6pdr tank destroyer. The muzzle carries a counterweight, several discs bolted together, since the gun is trunnioned well back. Middle, right: The WVEE carrier, having delivered the gun, using its own wheels; and (left) with the trails slung on to the carrier and the carrier rear wheels removed.

17pdr Anti-Tank Gun

The 17pdr gun was the result of a meeting at Adelphi House, London, on 21 November 1940 at which the question of a heavier replacement for the 6pdr was discussed. One school of thought argued for an 8pdr which would improve performance, but keep the physical size of the weapon the same, but the consensus was for something a good deal more powerful. Various ballistic solutions had been calculated, and a 3in calibre gun firing a 17lb shot was thought to show the greatest promise. Accordingly, instructions were given to the Armaments Design Department to prepare a design and a wooden mock-up.

This was done in fairly short time, but there were some misgivings at the result; the Director of Artillery was 'Perturbed at thè massiveness of the gun'. Nevertheless, since it was to be truck-drawn, this was not held to be a valid argument against it and four pilot models were ordered in July 1941; these were to incorporate three different designs of barrel each having different factors of safety.

By early 1942, the pilots had been tested and final decisions had been taken on the production pattern, and the 17pdr was formally approved for service on 1 May 1942. Originally, it was provided with a plain steel shot, but very shortly afterwards a capped shot and, later, an APCBC shot were provided, and by 22 June 1942 the question of a discarding sabot shot was being explored. This was developed during 1943 and the design was approved 'For immediate provision' on 21 April 1944, first supplies reaching the troops in August of that year.

The gun was a straightforward design of auto-frettaged barrel in a short jacket, with semi-automatic vertical sliding breech and percussion firing. The carriage was a two-wheeled split-trail type, somewhat massive in order to withstand the recoil of such a powerful weapon, and the design caused some delays in the provision of the first supplies. This was

in the autumn of 1942 and by then, Army Intelligence sources had got wind of the forthcoming appearance of the new German 'Tiger' tank in North Africa. Since the 17pdr looked like being the only gun which could deal with the Tiger except at suicidally short ranges, it became a matter of urgency to get the guns – which were coming off the production line in increasing numbers – on to some sort of carriage. As an interim measure, a gun was mounted on to the standard 25pdr Mark 2 carriage, and test fired in September 1942. To the surprise of many, the carriage stood the strain, and the jump and accuracy of the gun were within acceptable limits. A number of guns, therefore, were mounted on 25pdr carriages and sent to North Africa late in 1942, where they were successful in stemming the tide until the correct combination of gun and carriage could be provided.

Variants

Ordnance:

Mk 1: Service original issue, with muzzle brake.

Mk 2: As Mk 1, but with a muzzle counterweight instead of a brake. For use in tanks. The counterweight was removed and replaced by a muzzle brake from March 1944 onward.

Mk 3: Introduced in 1943, this was a Mk 1 modified by having the semi-automatic gear removed from the breech, converting it to hand-working only. This model was adopted by the Royal Navy for use in turrent mountings (Mounting 17pdr No. 2 Mk 1, Port or Starboard) on Landing Craft Gun (M).

Mk 4: For tanks. As Mk 1, but with new breech ring to suit the tank turret, the block moving horizontally.

Mk 5: For fitting to US M10 SP equipments. Generally as Mk 1, but with alterations in the breech ring.

Below: 17pdr Mk 1 on Carriage Mk 2, the 25pdr carriage version.

Mk 6: As for Mk 4, but with differences in breech ring and semi-automatic gear. Used a shorter breech block than any other Mark. For tanks.

Mk 7: Generally as Mk 4, but with different breech ring. For tanks.

Data
Weight of gun and breech mechanism: 1,822lb.
Total length: 180.35in.
Length of bore: 165.45in (55 cal).
Rifling: 20 grooves, uniform RH 1/30.
Breech mechanism: Vertical sliding block, semi-automatic, percussion fired.
Elevation: $-6°$ $+16\frac{1}{2}°$.
Traverse: 30° right and left.
Recoil system: Hydropneumatic, constant, 40in.
Weight in action: 4,624lb.

Performance
Firing standard 15.4lb HE shell:
Muzzle velocity: 2,875ft/sec.
Maximum range: 10,000 yards.
Firing 16lb 15oz AP shot:
Muzzle velocity: 2,900ft/sec.
Penetration: 109mm/1,000yds/30°.
Firing 17lb APC shot:
Muzzle velocity: 2,900ft/sec.
Penetration: 118mm/1,000yds/30°.
Firing 7lb 10oz APDS shot:
Muzzle velocity: 3,950ft/sec.
Penetration: 231mm/1,000yds/30°.

Ammunition fixed, cased charge.
Propelling charges. These varied with the projectile and are given below.
Shell, HE, Mk 1T. A conventional nose-fuzed shell loaded with TNT and fitted with the Nose Percussion Fuze No. 244. A Tracer No. 13 was fitted to the shell base. Propelling charge 7lb 2oz of NH powder.

Shot, AP, Mk 3T. A plain steel shot with a tracer filling pressed into a cavity in the base. Propelling charge 8lb 2oz NH powder.

Shot, APC, Mk 4T. Similar to the 3T, but with the addition of a penetrative cap soldered to cover the point. Propelling charge as for 3T.

Shot, APDS, Mk 1T. This consisted of a tungsten-carbide core enclosed in a light steel sheath which carried a tracer unit in the base. This was then enclosed in a light alloy sabot unit so made as to split into four sections on firing and discard at the gun muzzle. Propelling charge, 6lb 10oz; weight of shot as fired, 7lb 10oz.

Self-Propelled Equipments
The first 17pdr SP gun was 'Archer', which mounted the gun facing to the rear of a converted Valentine tank chassis. An open-topped superstructure over the fighting compartment protected the gunner, but space was so confined that the driver had to get out of his seat before the gun could be fired in order not to be decapitated by the recoiling breech. A total of 665 Archers were built, and they continued in service after the war. In spite of looking rather awkward, they were a nimble and easily concealed weapon which did great execution.

The second equipment was the American M10 and M10A1 3in SP equipment. This was used for some time in British service as it stood, but there was some dissatisfaction with the gun and late in 1944, they were withdrawn from service and refitted with 17pdr guns, being known thereafter as 'Achilles'. These were fast and potent weapons, though their silhouette made them conspicuous in comparison with 'Archer'. They, too, remained in service for some years after the war.

Opposite page: 17pdr gun in travelling order. **This page, left:** It looks like a 25pdr at first glance, but the breech closing spring casing on the left of the breech ring gives the clue; the rear view of the 17pdr conversion. **Below, left:** 'Archer' in action in Germany, 1945. **Below:** Top view of the Straussler conversion. This was the invention of Nicholas Straussler, an Hungarian engineer who later adopted British nationality. He had designed armoured cars for Alvis in pre-war days, and his principal contribution to the war effort was the invention of the 'DD' swimming tank which proved invaluable on D-Day. The 17pdr conversion was developed in 1943-44 and involved lengthening the gun axle and adding an engine, transmission and driving controls at the right side of the shield. The trail ends were supported by detachable wheels, and the whole equipment then could be driven about and manoeuvred when separated from its tractor. The principal military objection was the sheer size of the equipment, which led to problems in digging it in to a pit or trying to conceal it in the manner necessary for successful anti-tank deployment. For this reason it was turned down for military use and the development was abandoned.

32pdr Anti-Tank Gun

Once the 17pdr design had been approved, thoughts turned to the day when it would have to be replaced, and in October 1942, the General Staff demanded a weapon with a 25 per cent increase in performance over the 17pdr. The solution produced by the ballistic experts was a 4.45in gun of 50 calibres, firing a 55lb shot at 2,600ft/sec; or, in other words, a 4.5in AA gun made over into an anti-tank weapon. What the resulting weapon might have looked like is, mercifully, not known, since in March 1943, the Ordnance Board pointed out that using discarding sabot shot in the 17pdr gun would produce better results than would the proposed 55pdr gun. In April 1943, the 55pdr project was abandoned in favour of a new design, a 30pdr gun.

This, in fact, was little more than the 3.7in AA gun given the same treatment as that proposed for the 4.5in. The 30pdr was to be of 3.7in calibre, and to be rifled 1/30, and in September 1943, approval was given for a pilot equipment to be built. In

January 1944, the specification was changed to have the gun rifled 1/25, since this made the design of discarding sabot shot easier. At the same time, it was predicted that a 37lb shot would give the best performance, and so the gun was provisionally named the 'Ordnance QF 37pdr EX1'; designs for a self-propelled version, EX2, were also approved. But in June 1944, firing trials showed that the 37lb shot fell short of its promised performance; a 32lb shot was designed and the gun was rechristened 'Ordnance QF 32pdr'.

The carriage was to be a split-trail two-wheeled pattern and in August 1943, two designs were approved. One was designed by the Armaments Design Department and used a conventional recoil system in conjunction with a special muzzle brake of 75% efficiency on the gun; in other words, the brake would cut the recoil force by 75%. The other carriage was designed by a Mr. Stevens and employed a single cylinder recoil system of his own devising, which incorporated a pressure system allowing the gun to be run back in its cradle and locked to the trail legs for travelling. This system was so good (it was claimed) that a 40% efficiency muzzle brake would suffice.

Development work continued in 1945, but by the time the war ended, the pilot models showed that the towed conventional anti-tank gun had now got to a point where it was too cumbersome to be practical.

In September 1945, the General Staff stated 'No requirement exists' and in October, the Director of Artillery's department said 'It is not being perpetuated in service and only certain trials will be carried out . . .' These trials were completed in 1946, and the equipments were then disposed of; the Stevens carriage model was retained as a museum piece, the other was scrapped.

The self-propelled version, known as 'Tortoise', was a massively armoured 78-tonner with limited traverse and even more limited application in battle. The German 'Ferdinand' had demonstrated the hazards of armoured vehicles incapable of all-round protection, while the sheer size of the vehicle posed logistic problems. It, too, was abandoned after trials; six were made, and two now remain in the RAC Museum.

It is regretted that full data for the 32pdr is not available. The basic dimensions of the gun were much the same as those of the 3.7in Mk 1 AA gun. It fired a 32lb APCBC shot by a 13lb 1oz propelling charge. The ammunition was separate loading, with a cased charge in a parallel-sided brass case, 35.8in long. Muzzle velocity was 2,880ft/sec. It was forecast that 4,000ft/sec would be possible with an APDS shot, but it is unlikely that any such shot was ever made.

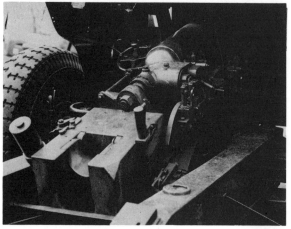

Above: Close-up of the breech of the 32pdr. The apparatus to the right front of the breech ring is a valve unit for pumping the gun back in its cradle for travelling.

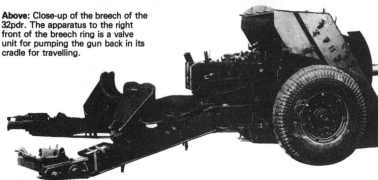

Left: Side view of the 32pdr gun. **Below:** This view of the 32pdr (at the Rotunda Artillery Museum) gives an idea of its bulk in comparison with the 5.5in gun alongside. The 'box' on the front of the shield is actually the front and side skirts folded up for travelling. The box beneath the mounting merely takes the weight off the tyres.

37mm Anti-Tank Gun

Development of this gun began in 1937, with the belated realization that the US Army owned nothing specifically designed as an anti-tank weapon. The matter appeared urgent and, to give the designers some guidance, two German 37mm PAK36 guns were bought for study. Two development models were authorized, the T7 which used a sliding breech block with semi-automatic gear, and the T8 which used a Nordenfelt Screw breech copied from that of the 75mm Gun M1897. The T7 was dropped and the T8 turned into the T10, using a vertical sliding breech block, hand operated. In fact, the designers, after some exploration of byways, had arrived back at the German PAK36 design, and in October 1938 the T10 was standardized as the M3 gun.

The M3 was a simple monobloc weapon, and the Carriage M4, on which it was mounted, was a two-wheeled split-trail design with shield. A prominent perforated shoulder guard protected the gunlayer from the recoiling breech. It was produced in some large quantity and was widely used, but in truth, it was obsolete before Pearl Harbor. However, it was still capable of dealing with light tanks and thus it was usefully employed in the Pacific theatre until the end of the war. Although used in Europe, it was of less value there and was generally superseded by heavier equipments.

Variants

Gun M3A1: M3 with the muzzle threaded and fitted with a 5-port Solothurn pattern muzzle brake. Although authorized in 1941, the brake was never used, but all production guns had the thread cut at the muzzle and were thus known as M3A1.

Carriage M4A1: M4 carriage with a quick-release clutch in the traversing mechanism which allowed the gunner to disengage the traversing handwheel and swing the gun by pulling and pushing on the shoulder guard. Standardized in January 1944, it is doubtful if many were made.

Self-Propelled Equipments

Apart from the use of the 37mm in tanks, which is a separate subject, the 37mm M3 was inserted into a wide variety of motor vehicles during the early war period when the 'tank destroyer' idea was at its height. In numerical order the various proposals were as follows.

T2: Pedestal-mounted gun in the rear of a ¼ton 4x4 American Bantam 40BRC 'Jeep'.

T2E1: The same, but firing to the rear.

T8: Gun firing forward on a Ford 'Swamp Buggy'. Engine and driver were at the rear.

T13: Gun firing forward on a Willys 6x6 modified Jeep chassis.

T14: Gun firing rearward on a lengthened Ford 6x6 Jeep.

T21: Gun firing rearward on Dodge ¾ton 4x4 weapons carrier; later standardized as the M6 (see p 84).

T22: Gun on Ford 6x6 chassis. Became the Armored Car T22.

T23: Gun on Fargo 6x6 chassis. Became the Armored Car T23.

Above: The 37mm gun in the action position.

T23E1: Gun on Fargo 4x4 chassis. Became the Armored Car T23E1.

T33: Gun on Ford ¼ton 4x4 chassis based on the Model GAJ cargo truck.

T42: Gun on T9 light tank chassis, open topped.

T43: Gun on Studebaker 6x4 chassis; became Armored Car T21.

T44: Gun firing rearward on Ford ¼ton 4x4 chassis based on a cargo truck. Later replaced by 57mm gun.

All these appeared in 1941 and early 1942 and disappeared very rapidly. The only design to be standardized was the T21 which became the M6 in February 1942. The gun was mounted on the chassis of the standard ¾ton 4x4 Dodge truck by means of the Pedestal Mount M25 or M26 bolted to the floor. The top-carriage assembly was identical to that of the M4 towed carriage. Elevation of −10° +15° was possible, with a traverse of 360°. A ¼in armour-plate shield, shaped to give flank and overhead protection, was fitted. The vehicles were built by the Fargo Division of General Motors. They saw little active service, were declared Limited Standard in September 1943 and obsolete in January 1945.

Data Gun M3 or M3A1, on Carriage M4 or M4A1
Weight of gun and breech mechanism: 191lb.
Total length: 82.5in.
Length of bore: 77.93in (53.5 cal).
Rifling: 12 grooves, uniform RH 1/25.
Breech mechanism: Vertical sliding block, percussion fired.
Elevation: −10° +15°.
Traverse: 30° right and left.
Recoil system: Hydro-spring, constant, 20in.
Weight in action: 912lb.

Performance firing standard 1.92lb AP shell
Muzzle velocity: 2,900ft/sec.
Maximum range: 12,850 yards.
Penetration with AP shot: 36mm/500yds/0°.
Penetration with APC shot: 61mm/500yds/0°.

Ammunition fixed, cased charge.
Propelling Charge. The charges differed with the projectile and are detailed with them below. All rounds used the Cartridge Case M16 (brass) or M16B1 (steel) which was 8.75in long. This case was only for use with the M3 towed and M5 and M6 tank guns, and could not be used with the AA or aircraft pattern 37mm guns.

Shell, HE, M63. This projectile weighed 1.61lb and was flat-based and had a long tapering nose. The filling was 1.36oz of flaked TNT, and the Base Fuze M58 was fitted. The propelling charge used was 7oz of NH powder, giving a velocity of 2,650ft/sec.

Shot, AP, M74. This was a solid steel shot weighing 1.92lb, with flat base and blunt nose. A tracer cavity in the base was filled with tracing composition but there was no explosive filling or fuze. The charge was 8.1oz of NH powder, giving a velocity of 2,600 ft/sec.

Shot, APC, M51B1 and M51B2. This was a capped, ballistic capped, solid shot weighing 1.92lb. The two models differed only in the ballistic cap, that of the B1 being pointed and that of the B2 being rounded. A tracer giving a three-second burning time was fitted in the shell base. The charge was 8.5oz of FNH powder giving 2,900ft/sec.

Shot, Canister, M2. This was primarily a tank gun anti-personnel round, but it was occasionally used by the towed guns, notably in the Pacific theatre where it was extremely useful for scything down fields of fire in thick grass, and also for flushing snipers from bushes and trees. The projectile was made of terne-plate in the form of a cylinder and contained 122 ⅛in steel balls embedded in resin. On firing, the cylinder split open and the remains, and the steel balls, were discharged shot-gun fashion. The effective range was about 250 yards. The canister weighed 1.94lb and was 6.5in long; the charge was 8.25oz, giving a muzzle velocity to the fragments of about 2,500ft/sec.

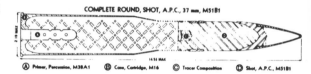

COMPLETE ROUND, SHOT, A.P.C., 37 mm, M51B1

Ⓐ Primer, Percussion, M38A1   Ⓑ Case, Cartridge, M16   Ⓒ Tracer Composition   Ⓓ Shot, A.P.C., M51B1

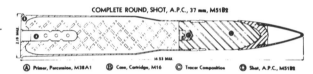

COMPLETE ROUND, SHOT, A.P.C., 37 mm, M51B2

Ⓐ Primer, Percussion, M38A1   Ⓑ Case, Cartridge, M16   Ⓒ Tracer Composition   Ⓓ Shot, A.P.C., M51B2

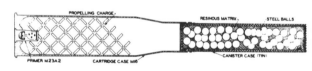

CANISTER, M2

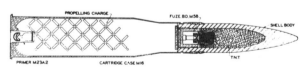

SHELL, HE M63

Above: Internal details of ammunition for the 37mm gun. **Below:** The 37mm Gun Motor Carriage M6.

57mm Anti-Tank Gun

By 1941, the US Army realized that the 37mm anti-tank gun was no longer capable of defeating the latest types of tank except in extremely favorable circumstances, and a search began for a suitable replacement. The quickest solution was to adopt an existing design and put it into production as fast as possible, and the British 6pdr was selected as the model. Drawings were obtained from Britain, and on 20 February 1941, the Ordnance Committee authorized the preparation of production drawings based on the British design, but converted to American standard tolerances, thread and gear sizes. On 15 May 1941, the design was approved and standardized as the 57mm Gun M1.

At the time, a completely American 57mm design was being worked on; this, the 57mm Gun T2, was little more than a scaled-up version of the 37mm M3. Two pilot models were built using the recoil mechanism of the 75mm howitzer, and two using a newly designed hydro-spring mechanism. It has been claimed that the performance of these was superior to that of the 57mm M1 (though no figures are ever produced to prove this contention), but by the time the pilots had been tested, production of the M1 was under way and the T2 design was dropped.

The only significant difference between the British gun and the American was that the American design was 16in longer in the barrel. This was because the British design had been tailored to available machinery, while the Americans had longer gun

lathes readily available. They therefore lengthened the gun to 50 calibres, gaining an additional 100 ft/sec muzzle velocity. It should be noted that this was, in fact, the length of the British Mk 1 gun, but the shorter option was selected in Britain for production convenience in 1941. As soon as longer lathes were available in Britain, the 50 calibre design was adopted there.

The carriage design also began as a straight copy of the original British carriage with handwheel traverse, and it was then modified in the light of experience.

The 57mm served throughout the war in all theatres. Towards the end, it was too small for the current German tanks and it also suffered, in Europe, from an excess of confidence in Allied tank strength, which led many American infantry units to leave their guns behind when advancing, an action they were to regret. But, in default of a replacement, it had to serve, and, in general, it served well.

Variants

Gun M4: M1 with muzzle brake added. Rarely seen.
Carriages:
M1: Original model; used handwheel traverse and commercial wheels and tyres.
M1A1: As M1, but with divided-rim wheels and combat tyres.
M1A2: M1A1 with free traverse controlled by gunner's shoulder-rest.
M1A3: M1A2 with modified trail lock and towing

eye to reduce the turning circle when being towed.

M2: Fresh design incorporating all modifications and designed to simplify manufacture. Approved January 1944, but few were made.

Self-Propelled Equipments

GMC T44: Gun on pedestal mounting, firing rearward, on a Ford ¾ton 4x4 chassis based on the Cargo Truck GAJ.

GMC T48: Gun on pedestal in the rear of a half-track M3. Built by the Diamond-T company, it was never standardized, but several hundred were built and all were given to the British Army in 1943. I cannot imagine what we did with them.

GMC T49: Gun mounted on a Christie-pattern high-speed tracked chassis.

None of these designs prospered; it is obvious that by the time the 57mm gun had got into production, the 'tank destroyer' fever had abated.

Data

Weight of gun and breech mechanism: 755lb.
Total length: 117.0in.
Length of bore: 112.2in (50 cal).
Rifling: 24 grooves, uniform RH 1/30.
Breech mechanism: Vertical sliding block, semi-automatic, percussion fired.
Elevation: −5° +15°.
Traverse: 45° right and left.
Recoil system: Hydro-spring, constant, 29.75in.
Weight in action: 2,810lb.

Performance firing standard 6.28lb AP shot
Muzzle velocity: 2,800ft/sec.
Maximum range: 10,260 yards.
Penetration: 73mm/1,000yds/20°.

Ammunition

Propelling Charge. This was contained in the Cartridge Case M23A2 (brass) or M23A2B1 (steel) and consisted of 2.6lb NH powder with the AP shot, or 2.58lb with the APC shell.

Above: The 57mm Gun Motor Carriage T48. Below: Internal details of ammunition for the 57mm gun.
A. Primer, Percussion, M1B1A2   B. Case, Cartridge, M23A2
C. Tracer Composition   D. Shot, A.P., M70

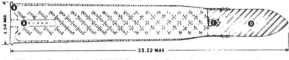

A. Primer, Percussion, M1B1A2   B. Case, Cartridge, M23A2
C. Fuze, B.D., M72   D. Projectile, A.P.C., M86

Shot, AP, M70. A plain steel shot with blunt point and a filling of tracer composition in the base. Weight 6.28lb.

Projectile, APC, M86. This was a piercing shell with penetrative and ballistic caps. A filling of 1.2oz of Explosive D was initiated by the Base Fuze M72 which also carried a 4.5sec tracer unit. Weight of this projectile was 7.27lb and it had a muzzle velocity of 2,700ft/sec. Penetration was the same as that of the AP shot against homogeneous plate; against face-hardened plate it could defeat 79mm/1,000yds/20°.

HE Shell. According to some reports, a high-explosive shell was developed for the 57mm gun, weighing 6.57lb, having a velocity of 2,720ft/sec and a maximum range of 12,670 yards. However, no official nomenclature list of the war years mentions it and no such shell appears to have been standardized.

 # 76mm Anti-Tank Gun

The development of the 76mm gun is rather involved, since much of it was concerned with tank armament, but we will try to simplify it a little. The original demand was for a gun with better muzzle velocity and penetrative performance than the 75mm tank gun. The 3in appeared likely to fill the bill, but it was too big and took up too much room inside the tank's turret, while the ammunition was bulky. The solution, designated 3in Gun T16, was the 3in barrel, a modified 75mm Gun M3 breech ring and mechanism, and a new cartridge case, thinner and slightly shorter than the 3in gun case. In July 1942, this was re-named the 76mm Gun T1, and it was standardized as the M1 in August 1942. This then became the primary armament of the later M4 tanks and of the M18 SP gun.

In June 1943, a proposal to mount the 76mm M1 in a wheeled carriage was put forward and approved. This became the T3 gun, with a semi-automatic breech and a muzzle brake. Two patterns of carriage were developed, the T4, which was a scaled-up version of the 57mm M1A3 carriage, and the T5, in which the shield formed the basic member and the trail legs were hinged to it. Both were unsatisfactory. The T4 had inadequate muzzle clearance when being towed, the wheels were too small, and the firing mechanism linkage was faulty. The T5 suffered from too small wheels and poor sights.

Work continued on E1 and E2 modifications to both designs until July 1944, when they were both scrapped and the T7 series was begun. In fact, the T7 was a T5E1 with better wheels and sights and increased muzzle clearance. A T3 carriage had also been briefly tried, which was basically a 3in M5 carriage with the addition of a castor wheel on the trail, but this had been cancelled in December 1943.

No 76mm towed gun, therefore, reached service before the war ended, though the Gun T3 on Carriage T7 was on test in August 1945 and was subsequently taken into service in limited numbers.

The self-propelled equipment, Gun Motor Carriage M18, was unique among wartime SPs because the chassis was actually designed from the start as a tank destroyer and was not a hacked-about tank like every other SP chassis. It stemmed from a lightweight Christie chassis intended for a 37mm gun in 1941. In 1942, this was upgunned to take the 57mm and became the GMC T49. It was then given the 75mm Gun M3 and became the GMC T67. Finally, late in 1942, it was redesigned around the 76mm gun and became the T70. It was ordered into production in January 1943 and standardized as the M18. The initial order was for 1,000, but 2,507 were eventually built before production ceased in October 1944.

Variants

Ordnance:

M1: Original design. 3in M3 gun tube. The first 1,000 made all failed proof and were scrapped because of faulty forgings.

M1A1: As M1, but shortened by 15 inches to improve balance.

M1A1C: M1A1 with a muzzle brake.

M1A2: Muzzle threaded for brake, rifling changed to 1/32.

M1A3: M1A1 withdrawn and threaded for muzzle brake. The designation was later changed to M1A1C.

M1E5: Experimental gun made from high-strength casting.

M1E6: M1 with rifling changed to 1/32 to give better stability to the projectile. Standardized as M1A2.

T3: M1A1 modified for use on wheeled carriage.

T3E1: T3 with rifling 1/32.

T3E2: T3 with alternative design of breech mechanism.

T3E3: T3 with new type of breech-operating mechanism.

Carriage:

T3: Similar to 3in M5 anti-tank.

T4: Scaled-up 57mm. Unsatisfactory.

T4E1: T4 strengthened, new travelling locks and trail ends.

T4E2: T4E1 improved on basis of test results.

T5: Unorthodox design; unsatisfactory.

T5E1: T5 with stronger elevating and traversing gears.

T5E2: Redesign of T5E1 on basis of test results.

T7: As T5E1, with increased muzzle clearance and other small modifications. Development continued post-war.

Data Gun T3, on carriage T4

Weight of gun and breech mechanism: 1,212lb.

Total length: 163.75in.

Length of bore: 155.0in (52 cal).

Rifling: 28 grooves, uniform RH 1/40.

Breech mechanism: Horizontal sliding block, semi-automatic, percussion fired.

Elevation: $-10°$ $+15°$.

Traverse: 29° right and left.

Recoil system: Hydropneumatic, constant, 28in.

Weight in action: 3,820lb.

Performance firing standard 13lb HE shell

Muzzle velocity: 2,700ft/sec.

Maximum range: 10,000 yards.

Ammunition

The projectiles used were those for the 3in gun (see p 90). The cartridge case M26 (brass) or M26B1 (steel) was used, which was 21.3in long. The propelling charges were slightly smaller than those used in the 3in gun; 3.75lb with both the HE shell M42A1 and the APC shell M62. Penetration figures were the same as those for the 3in gun.

Above: A post-war design, but based on the 76mm T3 gun on T4E2 carriage.

3in Anti-Tank Gun

The 3in gun was born of a demand, in September 1940, for a weapon capable of stopping any tank in the world. The Ordnance Department considered the matter and concluded that the only way to produce a quick answer was to adapt existing components, and they put together a design comprising the barrel of the 3in AA Gun T9, the breech mechanism of the 105mm howitzer M2, and the 105mm howitzer carriage. With some sawing and filing, all this fitted together quite well and the result was standardized in December 1941 as the 3in Gun M5.

The gun turned out better than might have been expected from such a hurried concoction, but its promise was betrayed by its ammunition. Techniques of fuze and projectile design which were adequate in 37mm calibre or at the longer ranges and larger calibres associated with attacks on ships by coastal defence guns, were insufficient when applied to the peculiar demands of hard armour, high velocities and short ranges. As a result, the 3in was plagued with faulty ammunition from its introduction in late 1942 until early in 1944; the principal problem area being in the fuzes. Penetration rarely reached the theoretically possible figure and, as a result, confidence in the gun evaporated. Another factor was Tank Destroyer Command's stated preference for self-propelled weapons, and after the M5 had been standardized, production was delayed while the TD Board developed and tested the Gun Motor Carriage M5 (see below). When this project failed to produce a practical result, the towed gun was reluctantly revived and put into production. Had this delay period been employed in overhauling the ammunition design, the 3in might have got away to a better start.

Eventually the ammunition problems were solved, and the 3in went to war. Some commentators have said that it was rarely used in action, but this is belied by the figures; the US 1st and 3rd Armies in Europe had 301 guns which, between them, managed to dispose of 399,834 rounds between 'D' Day and 'VE' Day. The only real drawback, apart from the unfortunate ammunition problem, was lack of enthusiasm during the early stages of its service.

Variants
Ordnance:
T14: A high-velocity development intended to give 3,000ft/sec, for tank or SP mounting. Suspended in 1944.
T15: Super-velocity gun for ballistic studies, using pre-engraved driving bands to achieve 3,850ft/sec. 90 calibres long. Development continued post-war.
T16: High-velocity development to give 3,000ft/sec, to be mounted on wheeled carriage similar to that of the 90mm T9. Development suspended in 1944.
T18: Super-velocity gun to achieve 3,850ft/sec, by

using over-sized chamber and reduced-weight, composite projectile. Preliminary studies were made in October 1944, but the design was not followed up.
Carriage:
M1: Original 105mm howitzer type with flat shield.
M1A1: Sloping shield; axle stops and firing segments added. Changes recommended by TD Command in 1943 and were applied to existing M1 carriages.
M6: New manufacture to M1A1 design.
T5: Modified 90mm Carriage T9 to mount 3in Gun T16.

Self-Propelled Equipments
Since the 3in was early on the scene, it was seized upon by the 'tank destroyer' designers with great avidity.
Gun Motor Carriage:
T1: Gun mounted on Cletrac MG-2 tractor. Standardized as M5.
T1: Gun mounted on 'Trackless Tank' wheeled chassis.
T15: Gun mounted on Ford 6x6 truck chassis.
T20: Gun on M3 light tank chassis; project only.
T24: Gun on M3 Medium Tank chassis in special open-topped octagonal barbette structure.
T35: Gun on M4 Medium Tank chassis.
T35E1: Standardized as M10 (See below).
T40: Standardized as M9 (See below).
T50: Project for gun on new high-speed chassis.
T55: Gun on Allied Machinery/Cook 8x8 armoured car chassis.
T56: Gun with shield on M3A3 Light Tank.
T57: As T56, but without the shield.
M5: The M5 was one of the TD Board projects which delayed introduction of the towed gun. It consisted of a turntable-mounted gun with a light enveloping shield mounted on the rear end of a Cleveland Tractor Co. Cletrac MG-2 tractor. Seats were provided for two gunlayers, but the rest of the detachment had to ride on an accompanying vehicle which also carried the ammunition. It worked, but it was not practical, and although standardized it was never put into production or service.
M9: The other TD Board project. This was an M3 Medium Tank chassis with the turret removed and the hull opened out until it resembled a 'Sexton' 25pdr, though the gun was the 3in. It was standardized in the belief that 50 barrels would be made available, but only 28 barrels were allocated and the vehicle never went into production.
M10: This had the gun mounted in an open-topped turret on a diesel-engined M4A2 Medium Tank chassis, the hull being very slightly modified. Later production used the petrol-engined M4A3 chassis, and these became the M10A1. When installed in this mounting the gun took the nomenclature M7.

Top: 'Dignity and impudence' the 3in M5 alongside a 37mm gun M3A1; a rare photograph showing the five-port muzzle brake on the 37mm gun. **Middle:** 3in Gun Motor Carriage T40, standardized as the M9, but never produced in quantity. **Right:** The 3in Gun M5 in firing position.

The M10 and M10A1 proved to be very good equipments, but by late 1944 the 3in was no longer capable of defeating the heavier German tanks and it was replaced by the 90mm Gun M36. The M10 in British service was originally known as 'Wolverine'; it was then re-fitted with 17pdr guns and was known as 'Achilles'.

Data Gun M5, on Carriage M1, M1A1 or M6
Weight of gun and breech mechanism: 4,875lb.
Total length: 158.4in.
Length of bore: 150.0in (50 cal).
Rifling: 28 grooves, uniform RH 1/25.

Breech mechanism: Horizontal sliding block, percussion fired.
Elevation: $-5°$ $+30°$.
Traverse: $22\frac{1}{2}°$ right and left.
Recoil system: Hydropneumatic, constant, 42in.
Weight in action: 4,875lb (M1); 5,870lb (M6).

Performance firing standard 15.4lb AP shell
Muzzle velocity: 2,600ft/sec.
Maximum range: 16,100 yards.
Penetration: 100mm/1,000yds/0°.

Ammunition fixed, cased charge.

Propelling Charge. The weight of propelling charge varied with the projectiles and is detailed with them below. The Case, Cartridge MkIIM2 (brass) or MkIIM2B1 (steel), 23in long, was standard.

Shell, HE, M42A1. This was the same round as was used with the AA gun. The shell was non-streamlined, 12.87lb in weight, and fitted with the PD fuze M48. The propelling charge was 4.56lb, developing 2,800ft/sec and a maximum range of 14,780 yards.

Shot, AP, M79. A solid shot of the usual form, with a three-second tracer in the base. Weight 15lb. The charge was 4.62lb, giving 2,600ft/sec velocity and a maximum range of 12,770 yards. Penetration at 1,000 yards was 100mm of homogeneous plate or 70mm of face-hardened plate.

Projectile, APC, M62A1. This was a piercing shell with penetrative and ballistic cap, filled with ·2.3oz of Explosive D and fitted with a Base Fuze M66A1. The projectile weighed 15.43lb and the propelling charge was 4.62lb.

Shell, Smoke, HC, BI, M88. This was a rather unusual round developed principally for use by the SP guns, but also available to the towed guns. It consisted of a cylindrical steel body filled with HC (hexachloroethane/zinc) smoke mixture. A hole bored through the base of this shell carried an ignition and delay unit. There was no fuze. The shell was fitted into the usual cartridge case with a charge of only 3½oz of powder. On firing, the flash of the propellant lit the ignition system in the shell base; this burned through the delay unit and ignited the smoke composition which then escaped through the

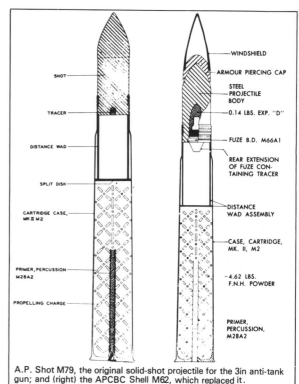

A.P. Shot M79, the original solid-shot projectile for the 3in anti-tank gun; and (right) the APCBC Shell M62, which replaced it.

base hole. The small charge and square nose of the shell ensured a short flight; its purpose was to produce a rapid smokescreen behind which the gun could make an escape.

90mm Anti-Tank Gun

After the successful German conversion of their 88mm AA gun to an anti-tank weapon, and the American conversion of their 3in AA gun, it seemed logical, once production had become ample, to try to convert the 90mm AA gun in a similar manner. This project began early in 1943 and by the end of the year, two carriages and guns had been built for trial. The T5 carriage was of orthodox split-trail pattern, two-wheeled and with a shield and folding spades. The all-up weight was 7,700lb, which was too heavy, and it was re-worked as the T5E1 to get the weight down to 6,980lb. This was tested in mid 1944 and again reworked into the T5E2 to rectify various faults which had appeared during the trials. The project was then closed down in favour of a totally fresh design, since there seemed to be no end to the re-working and little result from it.

The new project was the T13 gun on T9 carriage. The gun was similar to the M3 gun, but incorporated a semi-automatic breech and a muzzle brake. The carriage was most unusual; the shield was the basic structural member, and the trail legs were hinged to

its top corners. Two wheels were fitted, and these were lifted from the ground when firing, the gun resting on a central firing jack. For travelling, the trail legs folded forward and the barrel was depressed so as to lock to them and form a rigid towing unit.

Work on this design began in January 1944 and a pilot was built, but the project was halted in July since the design staff were needed for the 3in T5 project. Work began again in September 1944 and trials took place, but development had not been completed when the war ended.

In August 1944, the T5 carriage project was revived, and procurement of 600 was authorized. Production was slow in starting, and in August 1945 the order was reduced to 200 equipments. These were produced and issued after the war, but they were never standardized and remained the Gun T8 on Carriage T5E2 throughout their short service life.

Variants
Ordnance:
T7: Modified AA M1 gun for fitting into tanks and

Above: 90mm Gun T13 on Carriage T9, in firing position.

Right: The 90mm Gun Motor Carriage M36.

SP mountings. Standardized as the M3.

T8: Modified AA M1 gun for use on wheeled carriages.

T13: T7 with muzzle brake and new breech, for Carriage T9.

T14: Similar to M3, but modified to use a concentric recoil system in SP mountings, and fitted with Muzzle Brake T9.

T15: New design to give 3,200ft/sec and improve on the M3.

T15E1: T15 with reduced diameter chase.

T15E2: T15 using separate-loading ammunition, for the . T26 tank. Procurement of 1,000 guns was authorized in April 1945, but rescinded in June when it was found that no production had been planned for the tank.

T15E3: T15E2 made from an undersized forging.

T18: High-velocity anti-tank project to give 3,500 ft/sec.

T19: M3 with a 64in Crane Liner to reduce wear.

T20: New design to improve on the T8 gun and fit the T5E1 carriage. Horizontal sliding breech and muzzle brake. Six guns ordered September 1944; project later cancelled.

T21: T15 modified for use on a wheeled carriage. To have a larger chamber and fire tungsten-cored shot to achieve 3,150ft/sec.

T22: 90mm gun with 105mm gun chamber dimensions for high-velocity anti-tank use. Abandoned in favour of T54.

T54: T15E2 with short chamber, delivering 3,750 ft/sec with tungsten-cored shot, and giving penetration of 300mm at 1,000 yards. Development continued post-war.

T60: T54 to use fixed ammunition and a 25lb APC shot.

Carriage:

T5: Split trail, conventional design. For T8 gun.

T5E1: Lightened T5.

T5E2: T5E1 lightened and with improved suspension.

T9: Unorthodox pattern for T13 gun.

T9E2: T9 designed to split into eight loads for air transport.

T10: New and better-balanced version of T9.

T14: T5E2 redesigned to suit the T20 gun.

T15: Copy of the 3in M6 carriage, to mount the T20 gun.

Self-Propelled Equipments (Gun Motor Carriages)

T53: 90mm AA gun with shields, pedestal-mounted at the rear of an M4 tank chassis.

T53E1: As T53, but with the gun centrally mounted.

T71: M3 gun in an open-topped turret on M10 chassis.

T71E1: As T71, but using the M10A1 chassis; standardized as the M36 (See below).

T78: M3 gun on chassis of Light Tank M24. Project only.

M36: Because of the shortcomings of the 3in M10 self-propelled equipment, it was decided to replace the gun with the 90mm M3. The original plan was to produce 500, 300 of which would be built new, using M10A1 chassis, and 200 would be conversions of M10A1s withdrawn from service units. In March 1944, in order to increase this number, authorization was given for the conversion of M10 chassis as well. Eventually, 2,324 were built. When fitted with the 90mm gun, the M10 became a formidable weapon, capable of defeating any German tank, though whether it was better than the British 17pdr conversion of the M10 is debatable.

M36B1: Conversion of M4A3 tank to M36 specification, to provide for an urgent requirement in October 1944, and to supplement normal production. 187 were built.

Below: T9 carriage in travelling position.

M36B2: Conversion of 3in M10 by fitting the M36 turret and gun assembly.

Data Gun T8, on Carriage T5E2
Weight of gun and breech mechanism: 2,290lb.
Total length: 186.0in.
Length of bore: 181.0in.
Rifling: 32 grooves, uniform RH 1/32.
Breech mechanism: Vertical sliding block, semi-automatic, percussion fired.
Elevation: $-10°$ $+21°$.
Traverse: 30° right and left.
Recoil system: Hydropneumatic, constant, 42in.
Weight in action: 6,800lb.

Performance firing standard 24.5lb APC shell
Muzzle velocity: 2,800ft/sec.
Maximum range: 21,400 yards.
Penetration: 122m/1,000yds/0°.

Ammunition
The ammunition provided for this gun was the same as that used for the 90mm AA guns (see p 129).

105mm Anti-Tank Gun

Late in 1943, work began on the 105mm Gun T5, a 48-calibre weapon for use in tanks. In mid 1944, its barrel was lengthened to 65 calibres in order to reach 3,000ft/sec, and later in 1944, the idea arose of mounting it on to a wheeled carriage to produce an anti-tank gun with a secondary role of long-range field gun. Development continued throughout 1945 until after the war had ended, although the army had said that they could see no requirement for it. Two pilots were made and tested in February 1946, after which, the project was closed down. One example, shown here, is preserved at Aberdeen

Proving Ground. As the drawings show, there were various proposals for the carriage, but only the T19 was built.

Data Gun 105mm T8, on Carriage T19
Weight of gun and breech mechanism: 6,500lb.
Length of bore: 268.7in (65 cal).
Rifling: uniform RH 1/30.
Breech mechanism: Vertical sliding block, semi-automatic, percussion fired.
Elevation: $-7°$ $+46°$.
Traverse: 30° right and left.

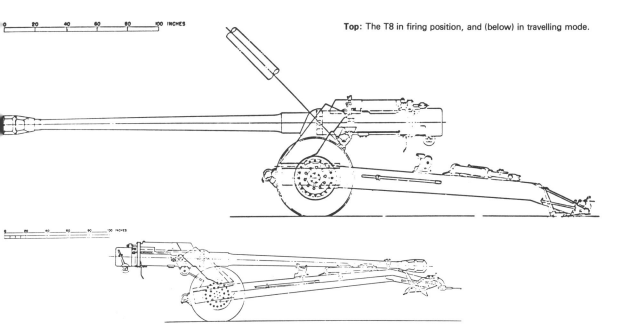

Recoil system: Hydropneumatic, constant, 20in.
Weight in action: approx 16,000lb.

Performance firing standard 35lb HE shell
Muzzle velocity: 3,100ft/sec.
Maximum range: 27,000 yards.

Ammunition

The ammunition was never standardized, and little information is available today. The round was separate-loading, the standard propelling charge being 14.75lb of FNH powder contained in a brass case. Projectiles developed included an HE shell of 35lb, an APC shell of 39lb and an APC shell of 41lb. Penetration was estimated as being 210mm of homogeneous plate at 100 yards range.

Above: Rear view of the T8. Note that the sights are arranged for two gunlayers, one on the left for line and the other on the right for elevation. While theoretically quicker, this division of responsibility is not a good thing in anti-tank gunnery. **Right:** Front view of the 105mm Gun T8, on display at Aberdeen Proving Ground, Maryland.

Anti-Aircraft Artillery

At the end of the First World War, the anti-aircraft defences of both Britain and the USA were dismantled almost overnight. The popular theory was that the natural enemy of the aeroplane was another aeroplane, and that anti-aircraft guns were a hasty solution thrown up by the war's pressures and not one to be perpetuated. The gunners knew better, however, and they worked away behind the scenes, trying to solve some of the complex problems of vertical gunnery, and trying to design guns which would turn their solutions into practical form. Eventually, in the early 1930s, when 'The Bomber Will Always Get Through' became the politician's cry, money became available and the guns began to appear.

While the guns were the outward and visible sign of air-defence, it must always be remembered that guns by themselves were useless unless they

Right: 3.7in gun on a Mk 2C mounting at practice, Manorbier School of AA Artillery, 1953. (See data page 107.)

could find their targets. Some of the most fundamental research was that concerned with detection of aircraft and with translating the knowledge of an aircraft's position in the sky into
information on range, bearing and altitude which
could be used on the gun in order to put a shell
into the air. In the early days, detection relied
entirely upon the sound emitted by the machine
as it flew through the air, and sound detectors of
varying complexity and size were produced,
culminating in the massive, fixed concrete
mirrors, emplaced in the south-east of England
(and still to be seen there) which could, on a good
day, pick·up an approaching aircraft at a range
of ten miles or so.

Fortunately, as every schoolboy knows today,
radar was discovered at the proverbial eleventh
hour, and came to the rescue of the air-defence
organizations to give early warning and, later, to
give precise data about the aircraft's position.
This raw material was then processed through the
'predictor' (or, in American terminology, 'director') which took the basic fact of the aircraft's
location, added to it some information about
temperature, wind direction, gun muzzle velocities and so forth, calculated the aircraft speed
and course, and then determined where the aircraft would be by the time the shell got up there;
from this it determined the necessary bearing,
elevation and fuze length to be applied to the
gun and fuze so that shell and target would
eventually coincide in space.

As the predictor was improved, so the design
of sighting systems on the guns changed. During
the First World War, the gun was an independent
unit, capable of doing the acquisition, prediction
and pointing, albeit badly. Following this line
during post-war years led to guns with five
gunlayers and only two men actually loading and
firing, a division which put a premium on highly-
trained men – and that at a time when armies
were shrinking in size. The arrival of the predictor allowed all the mathematics to be done in
one place, and cleared a lot of the work off the
gun, leaving room for the loaders to work, and
improving the rate of fire. All the layer had to
do was to set pointers against scales in accordance with instructions passed to him from the
predictor. At first, this was done by voice, but
data transmission systems soon appeared which
permitted electrical transmission to dials on the
gun mounting.

The next logical step, which made its first
tentative appearance in about 1929, was to provide the gun with power to elevate, traverse and
set fuzes, and then control the movements by
electrical signals from the predictor – a system
known as Remote Power Control (RPC). Like so
many ideas, the theory was impeccable, but
actually making the necessary apparatus took a
long time and demanded new techniques in industry, so it was not until the war had begun that

RPC came into service; if this seems a long delay, reflect upon the accuracy demanded. Using conventional optical sighting systems it was possible to point a gun to an accuracy of five minutes of arc, and not until a remote system was able to duplicate this consistently were the gunners willing to see it in service.

In the early 1920s, an anti-aircraft gun was an anti-aircraft gun and that was the end of it, but the rapid improvements in aircraft performance soon indicated that there would have to be sub-divisions. The gun capable of engaging a bomber at 20,000ft and 150mph was not well suited to shooting at a fighter-bomber doing 200mph at 2,000ft, since the speed of swing and pointing had to be very fast indeed to catch such a fleeting target. The only hope was to use a gun with a high rate of fire so as to get as many hits as possible while the target was within range. From this came the demand for light anti-aircraft guns, and it was brilliantly answered by AB Bofors of Sweden with their famous 40mm gun, which first appeared in 1929.

In similar fashion, as bombers flew higher, so guns of greater power were needed to reach them, and, during the war, it was belatedly realized that there was a gap in the sky which the light guns could not reach and the medium and heavy guns could not get down to, and this led to attempts to develop an 'Intermediate' gun; both Germany and Britain tried this and both failed, because the demand was too difficult for the current technology.

The last refinement for anti-aircraft shooting came with the arrival of the proximity fuze which is discussed in some detail elsewhere. Not only did this fuze promise greater accuracy in positioning the burst, it also promised faster rates of fire because there would be no need to set the fuze before loading. But the gun's last refinement carried within it the seed of the gun's replacement; the electronic technology which had produced the proximity fuze was to go on to produce the guided missile, and once that had been perfected, the days of the heavy gun were numbered. The light gun has managed to survive into the late 1970s, but there is every likelihood that the next generation of light-weight one-man missiles may well put an end to the last trace of anti-aircraft artillery.

Below: Indian gunners operating a 40mm Bofors gun. Note the 'Stiffkey Stick' in use.

40mm Bofors Anti-Aircraft Gun

The Swedish company, Aktiebolaget Bofors, developed their 40mm automatic light anti-aircraft gun in the late 1920s, and placed it on the international market in 1931. Within eight years, it was in use in 18 countries, 11 countries had purchased licenses to build it, and an updated version is in use by more than 20 different nations today. The Bofors Gun (although AB Bofors have made scores of different guns, the 40mm is always 'The Bofors Gun') is one of the most successful guns ever built.

British employment of the Bofors began with a War Office decision, on 23 April 1937, to buy 100 guns and 500,000 rounds of ammunition from Sweden in order to give the necessary low-level protection to the Army. This was followed by negotiation of a license to build them in Britain, and by the purchase of a further quantity of guns from Poland; the Poles had taken out a license in 1935, and after supplying their own needs, the Polish State Arsenal at Starachowice manufactured them for export. Thereafter, the British Army developed their own variations and manufacture took place in Britain and Canada. A special predictor, the Kerrison (or No. 3) was developed, the auto-loader was simplified, the sights underwent several changes and, towards the end of the war, remote power control was perfected. Although designed to be lowered to the ground for emplacement, it was quite possible to fire it from its wheels, and on the move, the gunlayers and loader often rode on the gun so as to be able to open fire with the least delay.

The gun was recoil operated and had a vertical sliding breech block. An 'auto-loader' unit behind the breech accepted rounds in chargers of four and fed them down into line with the breech, whence they were rammed by a spring rammer. The fired cases were ejected straight back and then deflected down a guide chute to be thrown clear at the front of the mounting. Balancing springs compensated the barrel weight, and the whole mounting revolved on a ball-race on the carriage, which had four outriggers and two axles.

A wide variety of sights were employed at different times. The first to be widely used was the 'Polish Course and Speed Sight' which used a reflector with illuminated graticules. A 'corrector box' could be set with speeds up to 350mph and ranges up to 4,400 yards and the box then rotated to align with the target's course, which automatically displaced the sight graticules to the correct aim-off. It was an excellent sight, but it was difficult to manufacture and demanded a high state of proficiency from the gunlayer. This sight was removed in 1940 and replaced by the much simpler 'Forward Area Sight', a wheel-type vertical foresight, a gate-type lateral foresight and crosswire hindsights. Simple range settings were used, and aim-off was estimated from the sights themselves. In 1943, the foresights were replaced by cartwheel sights with three rings for aim-off at target speeds of 100, 200 and 400mph.

In 1944, the 'Stiffkey Stick' or Sight, Correctional Mk 4 was introduced. An operator (not the gunlayer) aligned the 'stick' with the target's course and set in its estimated speed by a ratchet lever. A linkage then resolved the deflection equations and displaced the foresights by an appropriate amount. In this way, the gunlayers did nothing but aim the gun, the running adjustment being made by the stick operator. (Stiffkey, which should be pronounced 'Stookey', was a Light AA training camp and firing range on the north Norfolk coast, where this sight was evolved.)

Variants
The number of variant models is quite involved, since the make-up of a complete equipment involved a gun, an auto-loader, a mounting and a carriage or platform. For simplicity they are treated separately.
Ordnance:
Mk 1: Original Swedish manufacture. Used Type 'A' Auto-loader.
Mk 1*: Similar to Mk 1, but would accept any type of auto-loader.
C Mk 1: Mk 1 pattern, but of Canadian manufacture.
C Mk 1*: Mk 1* pattern, but of Canadian manufacture.
Mk 1/2: Conversion of Mk 1* by removal of the flame guard at the muzzle, and the fitting of a double-baffle muzzle brake. For use on airborne mountings Mks 7 to 10.
Mk 2: Number allotted to a naval design, but then withdrawn in order to avoid confusion with the American M2 model.
Mk 3: Wartime production model, designed to accept the simplified designs of auto-loader.
Mk 4: Naval; water-cooled, for twin mountings.
Mk 5: Naval; water-cooled, for single mountings.
Mk 6: Generally as Mk 1, but with changes to suit mounting in tanks. Used with Mounting Mk 6 in Crusader AA Tanks. The cartridge deflector ejected upwards.
Mks 7 to 11: Naval patterns.
Mk 12: Differed from Mk 1 in having cut-out switches on the elevating arc. For mountings with remote power control.
Mk 12/1: C Mk 1 modified as for Mk 12.
Auto-Loaders:
Type A: Swedish pattern using a central guide and ten mechanically-operated feed pawls. Took two 4-round chargers, the empty chargers being ejected to the left side of the breech casing.
Type A*: Type A with an adjustable peep-sight in the rear guide. Used only with the Mk 6 gun on tanks.
Type B: Simplified design without a central cartridge guide. Took three 4-round chargers and ejected them to the right.

Right: One of the earliest Bofors guns, the 40mm Mk 1 on Mk 1 carriage, at the Rotunda Artillery Museum. **Below:** Bofors gunners taking their posts in the battle against the 'flying bombs'. **Opposite page, left:** Breech end of the Bofors gun; note the 'Stiffkey Stick' and the cover over the auto-loader. **Right:** Mk 1/2 gun on the Platform C Mk 1 for airborne use.

Type C: A non-standard variation of Type B made by the Chambon Company.

Type M: Type B modified to be more reliable.

Type M*: Type C modified to be more reliable.

Mountings:

Mk 1: Original Bofors design, direct laying. Prepared for data-receiving dials, but not fitted with them.

Mk 1A: Polish design. As Mk 1, but not prepared for dials.

Mk 1B: British design. Similar to Mk 1, but with the elevating and traversing gears designed for hand or remote power operation. Only two were made.

Mk 2: Mk 1 modified for remote power control. None made.

Mk 3: British design, for remote power control.

C Mk 3: Canadian manufactured Mk 3.

Mk 3A: As for Mk 3, but small changes in the hand controls.

Mk 3B: As for Mk 3A, but with modified platform.

Mk 4: Similar to Mk 3B, but with 'cease firing' switches to prevent inadvertent firing at dangerous elevations.

Mk 4A: As Mk 4, but with elevating and traversing gears made by the Linotype Company.

Mk 5: As Mk 4, but modified for mounting on the Morris SP Carrier.

C Mk 5: Canadian manufactured Mk 5.

Mk 5/1: Mk 5 with the remote power control removed.

Mk 6: Similar to Mk 4, but modified for use in Crusader AA tanks.

Mk 7: Mk 3 converted to fit on airborne two-wheel carriage.

Mk 8: Mk 4 converted to fit on airborne two-wheel carriage.

Mk 9: C Mk 3 converted to fit on airborne two-wheel carriage.

Mk 10: Mk 4 of Canadian manufacture, modified to fit the airborne two-wheel carriage.

Platforms (Carriages):

Platform Mk 1: Original Bofors design. Riveted girder construction, Ackermann steering, independent suspension, 6in x 20in pneumatic tyres, hydraulic brakes on the rear wheels.

Platform Mk 1A: Polish design. Similar to Mk 1, but with the wheels attached by five studs instead of six.

Platform Mk 2: British design. Fabricated construction with tubular side girders. Trolley steering, 9in x 13in pneumatic tyres, no springing.

Platform C Mk 2: Canadian manufactured version of Mk 2.

Platform Mk 3: Similar to Mk 2, but with mechanical over-run brakes on the front wheels only.

Platform Mk 4: Mk 2 converted for close stowage in aircraft or gliders. Could be broken down into ten major units.

Platform 2-wheeled C Mk 1: Light 2-wheeled, sprung, travelling and firing platform, of Canadian design, for air transportation and Jeep towing. Two girders hinged together to form the towbar and the third girder telescoped into the centre section. Levelling jacks were fitted at the end of the girders. Electric brakes.

Carriage Transporting Mk 1/India: Two-wheeled carriage, capable of air transportation and Jeep towing, for use in Far East. For Indian Army use.

Carriage Transporting Mk 2/India: As Mk 1, but lighter, without brakes, and the axle 6in shorter.

Carriage Transporting Mk 2/1: As Mk 2, but with brakes. For British Army use in Far East.

Holdfast Mk 1: For concrete emplacement; four steel beams with eight holding-down bolts.

Platform Firing Mk 1: Temporary wooden structure for emergencies.

Platform Firing No. 16: Steel platform for use with the Mk 3 mounting in the Maunsell Forts in the Thames and Mersey estuaries.

Self-Propelled Mountings

Carrier, Morris, 40mm AA Mk 1. A 3-ton, four-wheeled Morris-Commercial truck chassis with the Mk 5 mounting secured to the cargo bed.

Crusader III, AA Tank, Mk 1. A Crusader III cruiser tank with the turret removed and replaced by an armoured barbette carrying a single gun. Operation was by hydraulic power, generated by a two-stroke petrol engine and pump, and the one gunlayer controlled the gun in both elevation and traverse by means of a joystick control. Hand controls existed, but the handles were normally removed because of the confined space within the barbette.

Data Mark 1 Gun, on Mounting Mark 1
Weight of gun and breech mechanism: 966lb.
Total length: 117.7in.
Length of bore: 88.58in (56.25 cal).
Rifling: 16 grooves, increasing RH twist, 1/54 to 1/30.
Breech mechanism: Vertical sliding block, automatic, percussion fired.
Elevation: $-5°$ $+90°$.
Traverse: 360°.
Recoil: Hydro-spring, constant 7.87in.
Weight in action: 4,368lb.
Rate of fire: 120rpm.

Performance firing standard 2lb HE shell
Muzzle velocity: 2,700ft/sec.
Maximum horizontal range: 10,800 yards.
Maximum ceiling: 23,600ft.
Effective ceiling: 5,000ft.

Note: The maximum range to self-destruction of the shell was approximately 16,500 feet, but fire control at this range was ineffective, and only harassing fire could be employed. 5,000 feet was considered to be the maximum range for effective aimed fire, this being governed by the predictor and sighting systems.

Ammunition fixed, cased round.

Propelling Charge. This consisted of 8.75oz Cordite in a brass case 12.25in long and fitted with percussion primers of various types. The case was unusual in that, for clipping it into the charger, it had a deep groove in the base, surrounding the primer, and a deep cannelure in front of the rim.

The AP Shot cartridge used a charge of 11.25oz.

Shell, HE, Mk 4T. A streamlined shell with a filling of 2oz 6drs TNT, a Percussion Fuze No. 251 or 255, and a tracer-igniter in the base. Different tracers gave self-destruction at ranges of 3,400 or 5,500 yards. Weight of projectile 2lb.

Shot, AP, Mk 6T. A plain steel shot, fitted with an internal tracer. Total weight 2lb 12oz.

Above: Ammunition for the 40mm Bofors gun. **Below:** The self-propelled Morris carrier.

2pdr Anti-Aircraft Gun

During the early 1930s, there was a great deal of hunting about for a suitable weapon to deal with low-flying attacks. Many European nations opted for 20mm automatic cannon of various types, but the British Army considered them to be of little value, since they fired an inadequate shell. (During the late war years, the British Army did adopt a number of 20mm cannon, but they were never very highly regarded.) Eventually, in 1936, it was decided to adopt the Naval 2pdr Pom-Pom for use in defended ports and for selected locations in the Air Defence of Great Britain. On 24 April 1937, the decision was taken to use the 2pdr Mk 8 gun on a modified Naval twin mounting, and then to proceed with the design of a fresh twin mounting which would be more portable than the Naval type.

At that same meeting, the 40mm Bofors gun was also adopted; experience soon showed that the Bofors was far more effective, and, as a result, the decision to adopt the 2pdr was rescinded and fewer than 60 equipments were ever made. They were installed at various ports and base areas in 1938–39, but once production of the 40mm Bofors was sufficient, the 2pdrs were replaced. In May 1943, they were declared 'Obsolete for Land Service' and transferred to the Royal Navy to be converted to shipboard mountings.

The 2pdr was automatic, operated by recoil, the barrel being water-cooled. In many respects it looked like an oversized Maxim machine-gun, though the mechanism was much different, using a vertical sliding breech block. The mounting carried two guns, one above the other, the top gun feeding from the left and the bottom gun feeding from the right, the feed being from flexible belts of 14 rounds. It was a static mounting, revolving on a base plate anchored in concrete. For moving, there was a special 'Carriage Transporting 2pdr AA Equipment Mk 1', but it was not possible to fire the weapon from this. Two mounting types existed, the Mk 1 and Mk 2; Mk 1 was the first design, based on the original Naval mounting, while Mk 2 rapidly succeeded it and incorporated several small improvements which experience with the Mk 1 had shown were desirable.

Data 2pdr QF Gun Mk 8, on Mounting Mk 1
Weight of gun and breech mechanism: 125lb.
Total length: 96.0in.
Length of bore: 62.0in.
Rifling: 12 grooves, uniform RH 1/30.
Breech mechanism: Vertical sliding block, automatic, percussion fired.
Elevation: $-10°$ $+80°$.
Traverse: 360°
Recoil: Hydro-spring, constant 7.4in.
Weight in action: 16,688lb (7.75 tons).
Rate of fire: 60rpm per gun.

Above: Twin Mk 8 guns on Mounting Mk 1. Note the belt boxes and ejection chutes.

Performance firing standard 2lb HE shell
Muzzle velocity: 2,275ft/sec.
Maximum horizontal range: 7,500 yards.
Maximum ceiling: 16,000ft.
Effective ceiling: 6,000ft.

Ammunition fixed, cased charge.
Propelling Charge. This consisted of 4oz 11drs Cordite HSC/T in a brass or steel cartridge case carrying a percussion primer No. 16.
Shell, 2pdr, HE, HV, Mk 1T. This was the same shell as was used with the anti-tank gun, but filled with TNT and fitted with a Percussion Fuze No. 243. A tracer No. 7 or No. 10 was screwed into the base, and gave self-destruction to the shell.

6pdr 6cwt Anti-Aircraft Gun

In 1940, the War Office came to the conclusion that a fresh type of anti-aircraft gun was needed. The 40mm could deal quite well with aircraft up to about 6,000ft; the 3.7in and larger guns could deal with those above 10,000ft. But the middle layer of sky was poorly defended, since the small weapons could not reach it and the heavy weapons could not swing and elevate fast enough to keep up with the rapid angular movement of an aircraft at about 8,000ft altitude. The 3in 20cwt *could* cover this area of sky, but its rate of fire was not good enough and, of course, it was an obsolescent weapon. Much of the trouble arose from the designs of predictor then in use, and development of new predictors and improvements in radar technology were urged as being the only long-term solution, but the more immediate problem could be solved by adopting an 'Intermediate AA Gun'. Two solutions put forward were a 3pdr, then under development for the Navy, and a 57mm 6pdr which had been designed before the

war by Bofors, and which was more or less an enlargement of the 40mm gun. The 3pdr was turned down because the shell was not thought to be large enough, while the Bofors design was only available on a Naval pattern of twin-gun mounting.

In January 1941, it was decided to develop a 6pdr gun, and a General Specification was issued, calling for a weapon giving a ceiling of 10,000 feet, a time of flight to that height of 5 seconds, and automatic fire at 100rpm. By the end of that year, a two-barrelled equipment on a three-wheeled carriage had been designed, and a pilot model was built during 1942. In December 1942, the Director-General of Artillery asked for a single-gun model to be developed, using an automatic loader which the Molins Company had developed for use with the 6pdr anti-tank gun. The first designs for this were submitted in April 1943, but they were considered unsuitable for various reasons, and the work began again. Fresh designs were submitted in December 1943 and it was then

Below: The 6pdr twin gun in firing position; and (right) on three-wheeled carriage, ready for travelling.

decided to build six pilot models, three fitted with electric remote power control, and three with hydraulic RPC, both achieving a traverse speed of 25° per second.

In February 1944, a new complication was added by a General Staff decision that the weapons had to be suitable for the dual role of AA guns and anti-motor-torpedo-boat (AMTB) guns, and this was further confused by a decision in June 1944 to modify the existing twin 6pdr coast AMTB guns to allow them to fire in the AA role.

The next problem arose in October 1944 when the Director Royal Artillery, pointing to the increased speed of jet aircraft, demanded that the equipment be capable of accurate fire against 600mph targets at 400 yards range; this meant a gun capable of traversing at 45° a second and it put the existing designs clean out of the running. In December 1944, it was decided to build twelve prototype single-gun equipments utilizing various RPC systems and different designs of carriage – sprung, partially-sprung and unsprung suspension – in the hope of hitting on a combination which would fill the bill.

To recapitulate this tangled story: by December 1944, two twin-gun equipments had been built, one with automatic loading and one without; a dozen single-gun prototypes had been authorized; the twin equipments were being re-designed in order to give them an AMTB capability; and, in the reverse direction, the existing 6pdr AMTB equipment was being re-designed to give it an AA capability. None of the weapons so far built had been satisfactory from the ballistic point of view or from the standpoint of mechanical reliability; they were extremely cumbersome and could not deliver the volume of fire desirable in this role, probably because the whole project relied on developing a high-speed loading system for a gun which, originally, had been designed for hand loading. The mechanical loading gear on the twin mounting was a staggering piece of complexity which rarely managed to perform for any length of time without breaking down.

Finally, on 30 March 1945, the War Office decided that 'Owing to the difficulties in obtaining satisfactory reliability with the 6pdr AA Twin equipment, and since the designed performance is out of date with modern high speed aircraft targets, together with the planned development of a fully automatic single 6 pounder equipment, the twin equipment will not be introduced into Land Service.'

Development of the single gun continued for some time after the war, but with the rapid development of jet aircraft the 1941 Specification became even more out of date, and the project was finally abandoned as a potential gun, although work on the automatic loading gear did continue, since this yielded considerable amounts of fundamental research information for a post-war project on high-speed loading systems known as 'Project Ratefixer'. But, as the German Army had also found out, the Intermediate AA Gun was an extremely difficult proposition, which had been solved by neither country during the war years, and which, perhaps fortunately, was eventually to be resolved by the guided missile.

The 6pdr AA gun was properly known as the 6pdr 6cwt in order to distinguish it from the anti-tank 6pdr 7cwt, and the coast defence 6pdr 10cwt. It was broadly based on the 6pdr 7cwt, but was larger and had a larger chamber taking a bigger cartridge case. The carriages were three-wheeled, with removable axles, the two front wheels having Ackermann steering. Four outriggers could be lowered, and hydraulic jacks could be used to level the mounting after the wheels had been removed. Remote Power Control gear was fitted in addition to hand-operated elevating and traverse gears, and a hand-fed hopper behind the guns held 8 rounds. The automatic loading gear was behind the gun and was driven by the recoil force.

Variants
Ordnance:

Mk 1: Hotchkiss gun of 1917 vintage, originally designed for use in tanks, and used in this connection simply because it was readily available as a starting-point for the project. Monobloc gun.

Mk 2: Hotchkiss Mk 2 of the same vintage, but a built-up gun. Both Mks 1 and 2 were shorter than Mk 3.

Mk 3: New manufacture. Monobloc gun without muzzle swell. The first four made were rifled 1/30, but this was subsequently changed to 1/28.

Mk 3/1: As for Mk 3, but with various fittings to suit auto-loading.

Mountings:

Mk 1: Twin mounting with rear trunnions and spring balancing gear. Generally as described in text.

Mk 1/1: As Mk 1, but with semi-automatic ramming gear.

No other mountings were ever officially recognized, though several experimental variants were made. Although never officially introduced for service, all 6pdr AA equipments were formally declared obsolete in February 1948.

Data (Twin Equipment)
Weight of gun and breech mechanism: 700lb.
Total length: 130.3in.
Length of bore: 125.55in (56 cal).
Rifling: 24 grooves, uniform RH 1/28 or 1/30.
Breech mechanism: Vertical sliding block, semi-automatic, percussion fired.
Elevation: $-5°$ $+85°$.
Traverse: 360°.
Recoil system: Hydro-spring, constant length.
Weight in action: 24,650lb.
Rate of fire: 35rpm per gun.

Performance firing standard 6lb HE shell
Muzzle velocity: 3,100ft/sec.
Maximum horizontal range: 15,000 yards
Maximum ceiling: 34,000ft.
Effective ceiling: 21,000ft.

Ammunition fixed, cased charge.

Propelling charges. There were two standard charges. The first was 2lb 14oz Cordite for use with the HE shell, the second, 2lb 12.75oz nitro-cellulose powder for use with the APC shot. The cartridge case was of brass, 20.25in long, and was fitted with the Percussion Primer No. 34.

Shell, HE, Mk 1CT. A flat-based shell with two driving bands, the front band having an abnormally high flange. The shell was filled with 8oz TNT and carried the Percussion Fuze No. 370. A Tracer and Igniter No. 14 in the base traced the trajectory and self-destroyed the shell after 12 seconds flight. Total weight 6lb.

Shot, APC, Mk 3T. A capped steel shot with an internal tracer, for use against tanks and ships. Total weight 17lb 1.6oz. Muzzle velocity 2,925ft/sec. Penetration 75mm/1,000yds/30°.

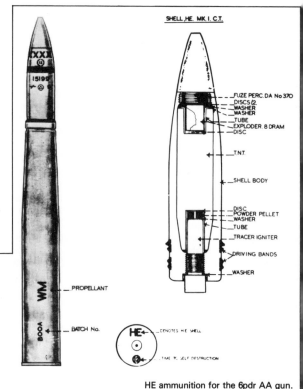

HE ammunition for the 6pdr AA gun.

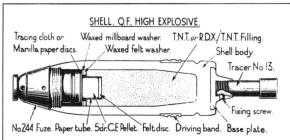

3in 20cwt Anti-Aircraft Gun

The 3in 20cwt gun was developed under Royal Navy sponsorship before the First World War, and was accepted for service in March 1914 as the common anti-aircraft gun for both navy and army. By the end of the war, it had supplanted most of the extemporized anti-aircraft guns and was the inter-service standard. It survived into the Second World War because there were plenty of them; because the 3.7in gun was not available in sufficient quantity, and because its light weight, easy mobility, good rate of fire and rapid traverse and elevation were particularly appreciated in forward areas. Eventually, as aircraft performance improved, it could no longer meet requirements, but it was not actually declared obsolete until 1946.

Originally, the gun was of wire-wound construction, later Marks being monobloc and, still later, loose-barrel types. On the first guns, the breech block was a vertical sliding block with semi-automatic closing, but this was changed in 1916 to a simpler, interrupted screw, which was quicker to make; examples of both types were still in service in 1939–40. The mounting was a static pedestal intended for anchoring in concrete, but it was later adapted to a variety of mobile lorry-borne or towed platforms. Sighting was direct, by means of rocking-bar,

open sights, though some guns had data-receiving dials fitted in the late 1930s and could thus be used with predictors.

As the guns were phased out of first-line service the barrels were put to other uses. Fifty were installed in Churchill tanks in 1942 to become the 'Churchill Gun Carrier' and another fifty were fitted to 17pdr anti-tank gun carriages as Home Defence weapons. Little is known of this latter application; it was never given official nomenclature or formal approval and was never authorized or recognized by the Ordnance Board. No handbook or official publication has ever been seen. According to some reports, 25 guns were kept in Britain for Home Defence while the other 25 were sent to the Middle East, but there is no record of their employment there.

Variants

Ordnance:

Mk 1: Wire-wound gun, vertical sliding breech, rifled 1/30.

Mk 1*: As Mk 1, but rifled 1/40. Later re-lined and rifled 1/30.

Mk 1**: Mk 3 converted back to Mk 1 breech mechanism in 1923.

Above: A show of military strength on Westminster Bridge in August, 1938. This Mk 1 3in gun is mounted on a Peerless lorry. **Below:** 3in gun on a four-wheeled platform. Note detachment members personal firearms attached to the front of the platform.

Mk 1***: Mk 3* converted back to Mk 1 breech mechanism in 1923.

Mk 1A: Mks 1 to 1*** repaired by removal of the 'A' tube and wire and the insertion of an auto-frettaged loose liner in 1933.

Mk 1B: New manufacture with auto-frettaged loose liner, 1933.

Mk 1D: Naval. Auto-frettaged monobloc barrel. 1941.

Mk 1E: Naval. Non-auto-frettaged monobloc barrel of high-yield steel. 1941.

Mk 2: Naval. As Mk 1, but slight differences in breech ring to suit the naval pattern of mounting. 1915.

Mk 2*: As Mk 2, but rifled 1/40. 1918.

Mk 2C: Mk 2 repaired as for Mk 1A. 1933.

Mk 3: As Mk 1, but with screw breech mechanism. 1917.

Mk 3*: As Mk 3, but rifled 1/40. 1918.

Mk 3A: Mk 3 or Mk 3* repaired as for Mk 1A. 1933.

Mk 4: Monobloc gun with Welin screw breech. A wartime alternative to Mk 3 made in 1916, obsolete in 1926.

Mk 4*: As Mk 4, but rifled 1/40.

Mountings:

Mk 1: Pedestal, variable recoil, two-speed elevating gear. Trunnion axis canted $2\frac{1}{2}°$ to compensate for drift.

Mk 2: Generally as Mk 1, but single-speed elevating gear and constant length recoil.

Mk 3: Simplified version of Mk 2 for wartime production (1916).

Mk 4: Added 'run-out control' to improve the working of the semi-automatic breech.

Mk 4A: Without run-out control, to suit guns with screw breeches.

Platforms:

Lorry, Peerless, AA: Commercial truck carrying the Mk 4 mounting. Solid tyres, firing-support jacks.

Platform 2-wheeled Mk 1: Introduced 1916, a square platform with single axle and short outriggers. Originally with solid tyres, pneumatics fitted after 1938.

Platform 4-wheeled Mks 1 and 2: Introduced 1928, pneumatic tyres, cone jacks for levelling and support.

Platform 4-wheel Mk 3: As Mk 2, but with mechanical 4-wheel brakes.

Platform 4-wheel Mk 3A: As Mk 2, but with Warner Electric brakes.

Platform 4-wheel Mk 3B: Similar to Mk 3A, but different pattern of Warner brakes.

Platforms 4-wheel Mks 4, 4A, 4B: Similar to Mks 3, 3A and 3B, but with a different jacking system.

Data Gun Mk 1, on Mounting Mk 1

Weight of gun and breech mechanism: 2,250lb.

Total length: 140.0in.

Length of bore: 135.0in (45 cal).

Rifling: 20 grooves, uniform RH 1/30.

Breech mechanism: Vertical sliding block, semi-automatic, percussion fired.

Elevation: $-10°$ $+90°$.

Traverse: 360°.

Recoil system: Hydro-spring, variable, 11in to 20in.

Weight in action: 6,000lb.

Rate of fire: 20–25rpm.

Performance firing standard 16.5lb HE shell

Muzzle velocity: 2,000ft/sec.

Maximum horizontal range: 12,400 yards.

Maximum ceiling: 25,200ft.

Effective ceiling: 15,700ft.

Note: An earlier pattern of 12.5lb shell gave the following performance.

Muzzle velocity: 2,500ft/sec.

Maximum horizontal range: 10,900 yards.

Maximum ceiling: 37,200ft.

Effective ceiling: 23,500ft.

Ammunition fixed, cased charge.

It is doubtful if any gun in British service has ever had so many different varieties of ammunition issued as the 3in 20cwt gun. The List of Changes in Matériel and War Stores for 1914–18 alone shows 215 different combinations of charge and shell, a figure capable of infinite permutation when all the possible variations of fuze are taken into account, while a 1943 inventory gives a total of 66 different complete rounds still in service. It would be pointless to tabulate all these, and the following are brief details of representative rounds.

Propelling Charges. The standard Full Charge was 2lb 2oz 10drs of Cordite W, contained in a brass case 16.5in long, and with the Percussion Primer No. 1. A 'Burst Short Charge', giving a velocity of 800ft/sec, consisted of 5oz 11drs Cordite MDT. Guns on tanks and on the 17pdr carriage used a piercing shot cartridge in which the charge was 2lb 13oz, giving a velocity of 2,600ft/sec.

Shell, HE, Mk 2B. This was a flat-based shell with a filling of TNT and carrying the Time Fuze No. 199. Total weight was 16lb $9\frac{1}{2}$oz.

Shell, Shrapnel, Mk 2BT. Used against low-flying aircraft, this contained 239 bullets and was fitted with the Time Fuze No. 199. A Tracer was fitted in the base. Total weight 16lb 5oz.

Shot, AP, Mk 2T. A plain steel shot fitted with an integral tracer and weighing $12\frac{1}{2}$lb. Penetration was 84mm at 1,000 yards at 30° angle of impact.

Opposite page: 3.7in gun on Mobile Mounting Mk 3.

3.7in Anti-Aircraft Gun

During the 1920s, the British Army investigated a number of AA gun designs, of 3.3in, 3.6in and 4.7in calibre, without coming to any really satisfactory conclusion. In 1928, after studying reports of what had been done, the RA Committee suggested that 'A 3.7in gun firing a 25lb shell with a ceiling of, say, 28,000ft, would be effective and would fill the gap between the medium 4.7in and the 3in weapons . . .' (RAC Minute B1307 5 November 1928). After theoretical calculations had been made, a General Service Specification was issued in 1933, calling for a 3.7in gun weighing 8 tons, capable of being put into action in 15 minutes and of being towed at 25mph. In 1934, designs were put forward by Woolwich Arsenal and by Vickers-Armstrong Ltd. The Vickers design was accepted, and their first pilot model passed proof in April 1936. Production was authorized in April 1937, and the first production guns were delivered in January 1938. From then on, production continued until 1945, reaching its peak in March 1942, with a delivery rate of 228 guns per month.

The 3.7in was an extremely advanced weapon for its time and the carriage was particularly compli-

cated. It was well over the specified 8 tons and, as a result, it was, at first, not well liked by people accustomed to the lighter and handier 3in 20cwt gun, and this latter gun still accompanied the field army, leaving the 3.7in for the defence of Britain. But its vastly better performance soon made people forget its bulk and, by the middle of the war, it was acclaimed as one of the best guns of its type in existence. It was constantly being improved, and the most important advance came with the adoption of the Molins Fuze Setter No. 11. This device, designed by the Molins Machinery Company (who normally manufactured cigarette-making machinery, but who displayed an amazing aptitude for automatic-loading mechanisms) was a combined fuze-setter and loading mechanism; a cartridge was dropped into a tray and the operating switch flap (known affectionately as the 'Pig's Ear') was slapped. From then on, operation was entirely automatic. The fuze setter descended onto the shell, set the fuze and retracted; the tray swung over in line with the breech; the round was rammed; the breech closed; the tray retracted and the gun fired. Not only did this device lighten the work of the gunners and speed up the

rate of fire, but it also determined a fixed 'dead time' between setting the fuze and firing the gun, which could then be taken into account in the prediction process.

Considering that it was the outcome of a 1928 specification, the 3.7in gun coped well with the air attacks of 1940, but in January 1941, the War Office, looking ahead, demanded a fresh design of gun, asking for a ceiling of 50,000 feet, a time of flight to that height of 30 seconds, and the ability to fire 3 rounds and have a fourth loaded in 20 seconds. The ballistic experts considered this and proposed four possible solutions. The Naval 5.25in gun could be adopted as it stood. The 5.25in could have its bore lined down to 4.5in calibre. The 5.25in could be

lined down to 3.7in calibre. The existing 4.5in gun could be lined down to 3.7in calibre. The 5.25in gun was chosen as the long-term answer (See p 113) but, as a stop-gap, until sufficient 5.25s became available, the 4.5in lined down to 3.7in was chosen.

Since a high velocity was demanded, a new system of rifling was proposed. Known as 'RD' (Research

Below: 3.7in gun on Static Mounting Mk 2C.
Right: Close-up of the Mk 2C mounting and the Molins Machine Fuze Setter No. 11.

Department) Rifling, it was designed by Colonel G. O. C. Probert of that Department, and it worked in conjunction with a specially-designed shell. The rifling commenced at zero depth, and the lands gradually assumed their full height at just over four inches from the commencement of rifling. Towards the muzzle the groove depth gradually reduced until at 11 inches from the muzzle, the bottom of the grooves had come up to meet the top of the lands and the gun was a smoothbore. The shell was fitted with a high-efficiency driving band, and twin centring bands at the shoulder. These had the effect of dividing the torsional stress of spinning more evenly along the length of the shell, and centring the projectile more perfectly on the axis of the gun barrel. As the rifling grooves decreased, the copper of the driving and centring bands was squeezed into cannelures in the shell body, and on leaving the muzzle, these copper bands, which normally protruded into the airstream and degraded the shell's flight, were smoothed flush with the shell wall to permit an unbroken air flow over the shell, which helped to sustain the velocity.

This RD Rifling was highly successful, and the gun was introduced in 1943 as the Mk 6 gun, the construction being a 65-calibre 3.7in liner inserted into the jacket of a 4.5in Mark 2 gun, and assembled on a 4.5in static mounting. This mounting was chosen in order to expedite production, since it took only 5,150 man-hours to make, against 9,500 man-hours for a mobile mounting. Although only a stop-gap, the Mk 6 gun performed so well that it remained in service for the remainder of heavy anti-aircraft's gunnery days, being declared obsolete in 1959.

Other modifications to the 3.7in design included simplified mobile and static mountings, partly because of the complexity of the original mobile mountings, and partly because of the demand for static guns for home defence. Remote power control was developed in 1943 and entered service in 1944, and the combination of this with advanced radar, predictors and the proximity fuze, gave the guns an 82% success rate against flying bombs in 1944. The average number of rounds fired to bring down a V-1 missile was about 150, a far cry from the 18,500 rounds-per-bird of the 1940 night blitz, when radar was in its infancy and powder-filled fuzes were standard.

Variants*

Ordnance:

Mk 1 1937: Used a loose barrel liner in a full-length jacket and the Mk 1 breech mechanism.

Mk 1/1 1948: Mk 1 modified by radiussing the rear corners of the breech-block mortise.

Mk 2 1937: Loose barrel in short jacket; may have had a Mk 1 (auto-frettaged) or Mk 2 (non-auto-frettaged) barrel. May have had Mk 1 or Mk 2 breech mechanism. This was the gun most commonly used.

C Mk 2 1944: Mk 2 of Canadian manufacture.

*Some are post-war, but all are included for the sake of completeness.

Mk 2A 1945: Mk 2 adapted to suit Mountings 2B or 3A, the change being in the breech ring and block.

Mk 2/2 1948: Conversion of Mk 2 by radiussing breech-ring mortise.

Mk 2/3 1948: Conversion of Mk 2A as for Mk 2/2.

Mk 2/4 1951: Conversion of Mk 2/2 or Mk 2/3 to accept electric firing gear so as to suit Mk 4 mountings.

Mk 3 1938: Mk 1 gun with Mk 2 breech mechanism. Made in limited numbers.

Mk 3/1 1948: Conversion of Mk 3 by radiussing breech-ring mortise.

Mk 3/2 1947: Conversion of Mk 3 for use with Mk 3A or Mk C3A mounting.

Mk 3/3 1947: Conversion of Mk 3/1 as for Mk 3/2.

Mk 3/4 1951: Conversion of Mk 3/1 or Mk 3/2 as for Mk 2/4.

Mk 4 1943: Experimental. 3.7in loose liner inserted into a 4in Mk 5** gun body. Three made, project cancelled.

Mk 5 1943: Experimental. A 65-calibre 3.7in loose liner with orthodox rifling in the 4.5in Mk 2 gun body. Because of its short accuracy life, the project was abandoned in favour of the Mk 6 design. None were issued for service.

Mk 6 1943: A 65-calibre 3.7in loose liner with RD Rifling inserted into the 4.5in Mk 2 gun body.

Mk 7 1943: Mk 2 gun with simplified breech mechanism, designed to overcome a bottleneck in the production of the Mk 2 breech. Only a few experimental guns were made; by the time the design had been perfected, the bottleneck had disappeared.

Mountings:

Mk 1: Mobile, original design. Provided with Magslip data dials and with rocking-bar open sights. Gunlayers faced forward. Gun trunnioned at rear and fitted with spring balancing gear. Originally fitted with a loading tray, which was removed in 1942, but re-fitted when the Molins MFS No. 11 fuze-setter was installed.

Mk 1A: As Mk 1, but without the rocking-bar open sights.

Mk 2: Static mounting. Fitted with a counterbalancing weight instead of spring balancing gear. Magslip and rocking-bar sights, gunlayers faced the rear. Fixed to Holdfast AA Mounting No. 2 and carried on Limber Transporting 3.7in Mk 2 and 4.5in Equipments Mk 1.

Mk 2A: Mk 2 fitted with R37 remote power control.

Mk 2B: Mk 2 fitted with MFS No. 11, automatic loading gear, etc.

Mk 2C: Mk 2 with R37 RPC and MFS No. 11.

Mk 3: Wartime production, mobile, similar to Mk 1A, but with gunlayers facing rear.

Mk 3A: Mk 3 with MFS No. 11.

Mk C3: Canadian-made Mk 3; the carriage, wheels and brakes differed from British version.

Mk 4: 4.5in Mk 1 mounting modified for use with the 3.7in Mk 6 gun.

Mk 4/1: Mk 4 with MFS No. 12 and automatic loading gear.

Data 3.7in Gun Mks 1–3
Weight of gun and breech mechanism: 3,931lb.
Total length: 195.15in
Length of bore: 185.0in (50 cal).
Rifling: 28 grooves, uniform RH 1/30.
Breech mechanism: Horizontal sliding block, semi-automatic, percussion fired.
Elevation: −5° +80°.
Traverse: 360°.
Recoil system: Hydropneumatic, constant 32in on mobile mounting. Hydro-spring, constant 18in on static mounting.
Weight in action: 20,541lb mobile; 23,100lb static.
Rate of fire: Hand-loading 10rpm; auto-loading 25rpm.

Performance 3.7in Gun Mks 1–3 firing standard 28lb HE shell
Muzzle velocity: 2,600ft/sec.
Maximum horizontal range: 20,600 yards.
Maximum ceiling: 41,000ft.
Effective ceiling varied with type of fuze, predictor and method of fire control; with Predictor No. 10 and Fuze Time No. 208, it was 32,000 ft.

Ammunition (fixed, cased charge) 3.7 Gun Mks 1–3
Propelling Charge. Various charges of different propellants were authorized.
The standard charges were as follows.
Full Charge: 8lb 8oz Cordite.
Reduced Charge: 3lb 2oz Cordite, giving velocity of 1,800ft/sec.
Burst-short Charge: 12oz Cordite, giving velocity of 800ft/sec.
The last charge was used for practice against 'live' targets; the gun was given data for the actual target aircraft, but the much-reduced charge ensured that the shell could never reach the target but would burst a long way short in the interests of safety. By instrumental observation it was possible to correlate the position of the shell's burst and the position of the target aircraft and determine whether a hit would have resulted had the service full charge been in use. Reduced Charge could be used for barrage firing, but was usually used for training and for shooting in the ground role.
The cartridge case Mk 1 was of brass, necked to suit the shell, had a 5.3in rim and was 26.56in long. It was fitted with the Percussion Primer No. 11.
Shell, HE, Mk 1C. Weight 28lb with Fuze 207. This was a square-based shell with tapered nose, filled with Amatol, TNT or RDX/TNT. It was fuzed with the Fuze, Time No. 199 or 223 in the early days, later, with the mechanical Time Fuzes Nos. 207, 208 or 214. In 1944, the 'Universal Cavity' shell was introduced so that by removal of a 4½oz pellet of explosive, the proximity fuzes T98 or T149 could be fitted. With these, the MFS was cut out of operation and only the automatic-loading gear used, which increased the rate of fire to about 32rpm.
Shell, Shrapnel, Mk 2C. Issued for use against low-flying aircraft close to the gun position. Weighed

Top: 3.7in Mk 6 gun in its emplacement. **Bottom:** This 3.7in gun mounted on a 'Ram' tank chassis was a piece of Canadian inspiration. It was never put into production.

Opposite page, top: Mk 1 mounting for the 3.7in gun, photographed at the factory in 1938. The complexity of this mounting makes the production problem understandable. **Bottom, left:** 94th AA Battery (The London Scottish) using their 3.7s as field artillery, at the Gothic Line in 1944. **Bottom, right:** Ammunition for the 3.7in guns Mks 1 to 3.

28lb 1oz with a filling of 332 bullets and a Fuze Time No. 199. It was declared obsolescent in 1943 and, thereafter, used up in practice.
Shot, AP, Mk 5T. Solid steel shot weighing 28lb 1½oz and fitted with a tracer. Issued for use as an anti-tank shot for self-defence, it had a penetration of 117mm/1,000yds/30°.

Data 3.7in Gun Mk 6
Weight of gun and breech mechanism: 6,552lb.
Total length: 252.0in.
Length of bore: 240.5in (65 cal).
Rifling: 28 grooves, uniform RH 1/27, RD system.
Breech mechanism: Horizontal sliding block, semi-automatic, percussion fired.
Elevation: 0° to +80°.

Traverse: 360°.
Recoil system: Hydropneumatic, constant 18in.
Weight in action: 38,360lb.
Rate of fire: Hand-loading 8rpm; auto-loading 19rpm.

Performance 3.7in Gun Mk 6 firing standard 28lb HE
  shell
Muzzle velocity: 3,425ft/sec.
Maximum horizontal range: 25,600 yards.
Maximum ceiling: 59,300ft.
Effective ceiling with Predictor No. 10 and Fuze
  Time No. 208: 45,000ft.

Ammunition (fixed, cased charge) Gun Mk 6

Propelling Charge. Only a full charge was provided for this gun, consisting of 17lb 2oz of Cordite
in a brass case of conventional shape, 33.75in long.
A percussion Primer No. 9 was fitted. Note that this
was *not* the 4.5in AA gun case, but a special design
for the 3.7in Mk 6 gun.

Shell, HE, Mk 4C. Similar to the Mk 1C above,
but with forward centring bands and a wider driving
band. Filled 1lb 14½oz of TNT and fuzed with the
Time Fuze No. 208. Proximity fuzes were not used
during the war.

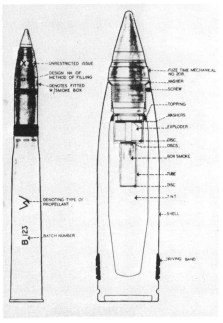

4.5in Anti-Aircraft Gun

During the 1920s and early 1930s, the War Office had been developing a heavy AA gun of 4.7in calibre, for the defence of rear areas, naval bases and similar vulnerable points. But by 1937, with the 3.7in gun having the first priority, the prospect of getting a 4.7in into production seemed slender. It was then suggested that the army adopt the Naval 4.5in gun, the ballistics of which were close to that of the projected 4.7in and which was a tried and tested equipment with facilities for production already in existence. It was further pointed out that most of the areas in which the army intended to use their heavy weapon were in close proximity to naval installations, whereby the supply of ammunition through naval sources would be assured, while the additional ammunition production resulting from army adoption of the gun could not but help the navy. The proposition was agreed to, and in 1938, the 4.5in Gun Mk 2 was approved for Land Service.

It was a conventional gun with loose liner and a short jacket, and a horizontal sliding breech block. The mounting was a static one, capable of being moved about on a special Transporting Limber. The gun had rear trunnions and was balanced by a heavy counterbalance weight on a cantilever arm behind the breech. A loading tray and hand ramming were originally used, but a Metropolitan-Vickers electric

Below: Loading a 4.5in gun during the London Blitz, 1940.

rammer was fitted in 1940, which allowed a rate of fire of 8rpm. The mounting was protected by an open-backed mild steel shield. During 1940–41, some guns were sited on the coast so as to fill a dual AA/Coast Defence role, for which they were issued with Semi-Armour-Piercing shells for seaward firing. Other than this, ground targets were never engaged except in dire emergency.

The 4.5 was largely superseded by the 5.25in gun in 1944–45, though it was not declared obsolete until 1951. There were no variant models; all other Marks of 4.5in gun were Naval except the 4.5in Medium Gun (p. 42) which was a totally different equipment. The only variant mounting was the Mark 1A which allowed more depression so that the gun could be sited on the coast and fire down to sea level.

Data 4.5 in Gun Mk 2, on Mounting Mk 1
Weight of gun and breech mechanism: 6,180lb.
Total length: 211.75in.
Length of bore: 200.25in (45 cal).
Rifling: 32 grooves, uniform RH 1/25.
Breech mechanism: Horizontal sliding block, semi-automatic, percussion fired.
Elevation: 0° to +80° (Mk 1A: −9½° +80°).
Traverse: 360°.
Weight in action: 14.75 tons.
Rate of fire: 8rpm.

Performance firing standard 54lb HE shell
Muzzle velocity: 2,400ft/sec.
Maximum horizontal range: 22,800 yards.
Maximum ceiling: 44,000ft.
Effective ceiling with Predictor No. 10 and Fuze No. 208: 34,500ft.

Ammunition fixed, case charge.
Propelling Charge. Various types were approved. A typical design was 13lb 10oz Cordite NQ/S for full charge, together with a sheet of lead foil, in the brass cartridge case Mark 6, 27.42in long. A reduced Charge of 5lb 10oz Cordite WO57 gave a velocity of 1,850 ft/sec. and was used for training. A Burst-short Charge of 1lb 6oz Cordite WT gave a velocity of 800ft/sec. and was used for training.
Shell, HE, 4.5in QF Gun Mk 1C. A square-based, taper-nosed shell weighing 54lb 7oz when filled with 4lb ½oz TNT and fuzed Time No. 207 or 209. An alternative filling was RDX/TNT, and the Fuze No. 208 eventually replaced the 207 and 209.
Shell, SAP, 4.5in QF Gun Mk 4C. This was a piercing shell fitted with a ballistic cap and filled with a 2lb 3oz charge of TNT/Beeswax. A base percussion fuze No. 501 or 502 was fitted. Total weight was 55lb.
NB. 'Semi-Armour Piercing' denoted a fairly large percentage of filling in comparison with an AP shell, and the ability to penetrate less than its own calibre

of homogeneous plate at some specified proof velocity.

Shell, SAP/NT, Mk 2 or Mk 3. These were Naval shells, supplied in 1940 to guns sited in the AA/CD role. They resembled the army design, above, but had a tracer (NT = Night Tracer) fitted below the base fuze.

Shell, Shrapnel, 4.5in QF Gun Mk 2C. This was issued for defence against close-flying aircraft. It contained 693 bullets and was fitted with the Time Fuze No. 199. It was declared obsolete in December 1945.

Below: The 4.5in gun mounted on its Transporting Limber.

 # 5.25in Anti-Aircraft Gun

In January 1941, the War Office requested a more powerful heavy anti-aircraft gun, and of the various options offered, selected the Naval 5.25in as promising the desired ceiling, velocity and lethality. Three naval twin mountings were handed over to the army in 1942, and after some tests with these, two patterns of single gun mounting were developed for army use. The first, Mk 1A, was solely for AA use and had an open-backed mild steel shield. The second, Mk 1B, was for employment in a dual AA/Coast Defence role and was protected with an armoured turret.

These guns began replacing the 4.5in in 1944–45, their employment being principally in the London area and in defended ports and naval bases such as Plymouth, Portsmouth, the Tyne and the Humber.

Installation continued after the war, but the development of guided missiles curtailed the programme and the guns were declared obsolete in 1959.

The gun was of conventional built-up type, with a loose barrel in a short jacket and a horizontal sliding block breech with electric firing and air-blast gear. The mountings used a counterbalance weight to balance the muzzle preponderance of the gun, and were completely hydraulic powered; traversing, elevating, loading tray and chain rammer, shell supply and fuze setting were all powered from an engine room placed underground close to the mounting. Laying was by remote data-transmission to Magslip dials on the mounting, but open sights were provided for close-range aerial targets. These were certainly the most complex AA mountings ever seen

Below: The 5.25in Mounting Mk 1A.

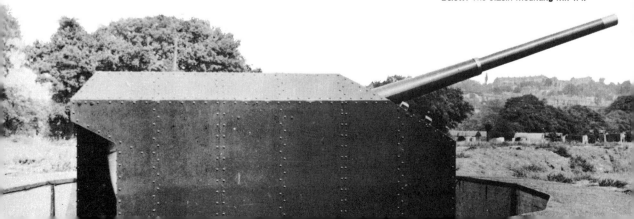

in British (or any other) service and, according to an unconfirmed report, each Mk 1B mounting, complete with engine room, underground magazine and stores, cost almost a quarter of a million pounds to install.

Variants

Many were either naval or post-war, but they are included here for the sake of completeness.

Ordnance:

Mk 1: Naval pattern, used only in the twin mounting. The breech mechanism was rather more complicated than that used later.

Mk 2: Land Service design which had a simpler breech mechanism and a heavier breech ring and block to withstand a higher chamber pressure than the naval guns.

Mk 3: Land Service design using RD Rifling (see p 109 for a description of this type of rifling as fitted to the 3.7in Mk 6 gun). Projectiles were fitted with rear driving and forward centring bands.

Opposite page, top: The 5.25in gun, without its shielding, showing the power-ramming gear beneath the counterweight; and (bottom) revealing the complex hydraulic pipework on the mounting. **This page, above:** The 5.25in single mounting Mk 1B, showing the pedestal and ammunition hoist normally concealed.

One gun was built, and trials were conducted in 1944–46, but the design was eventually cancelled in 1948.

Mk 4: Naval design.

Mk 5: Land Service design. Similar to Mk 2, but with automatic air-blast gear instead of hand operated.

Mk 5/1: As for Mk 5, but with slight dimensional changes.

All subsequent marks were for naval service.

Mountings.

Mk 1A: Land Service, AA only. As described above.

Mk 1B: Land Service dual AA/CD role. As Mk 1A, but enclosed in an armoured turret of 1in and 2in plate and provided with a power-operated shell hoist, fans and louvres for forced ventilation, and semi-automatic sights for seaward firing.

Mk 2A: Naval twin mounting. Half-inch armoured circular turret. No shell or cartridge hoists, the ammunition being handed in through the rear doors of the turret during action. Total weight 76 tons.

Data 5.25in QF Gun Mk 2, on Mounting Mk 1A or 1B

Weight of gun and breech mechanism: 9,587lb.

Total length: 275.5in.

Length of bore: 262.5in (50 cal).

Rifling: 36 grooves, uniform RH 1/30.

Breech mechanism: Horizontal sliding block, semi-automatic, electric firing.

Elevation: 0° to +70°.

Traverse: 360°.

Recoil: Hydropneumatic, constant 24in.

Mk 1A weight in action: 30tons 6cwt.

Mk 1B weight in action: 49tons 10cwt.

Rate of fire: 7–10rpm.

Performance firing standard 80lb HE shell

Muzzle velocity: 2,800ft/sec.

Maximum horizontal range: 27,000 yards.

Maximum ceiling: 55,600ft.

Effective ceiling with No. 10 Predictor and Fuze 208: 43,000ft.

Ammunition separate loading, cased charge.

Propelling Charge. All charges were contained in a brass cartridge case 30.65in long, the mouth closed with a white-metal lid. The Full Charge consisted of 24.75lb of Cordite N/P/S. The Reduced Charge was 13lb 6oz of Cordite N/S. An electric primer No. 17 was fitted in the base of the case.

Shell, 5.25in HE Mk 3C. Square-based shell filled with 5lb 6¼oz of TNT and with a Time Fuze No. 208. Total weight 79lb 15oz. It could also be fitted with a Percussion Fuze No. 117 for engagement of ground targets.

Shell, 5.25in SAP Mk 2C/NT or 4C/NT. A piercing shell with ballistic cap, filled with 3lb 3¼oz TNT/Beeswax and a Base Percussion Fuze No. 501 or 502 and tracer. Total weight 80lb. This shell was solely for use in seaward firing.

37mm Anti-Aircraft Gun

Development of an automatic 37mm gun was begun in 1920 by the Ordnance Department assisted by John M. Browning and the Colt's Patent Firearms Company. The primary requirement seems to have been for an aircraft weapon for use against both air and ground targets; secondary requirements were for a light anti-aircraft gun and an infantry-accompanying gun to replace the 37mm M1916 Trench Cannon. The first completed guns were demonstrated by John Browning himself at Aberdeen Proving Ground on 2 April 1924. Two guns were shown, one designed for a velocity of 1,300ft/sec and one for 2,000ft/sec, and, since the aircraft requirement was paramount, they were test-fired in various attitudes including upside-down. Clip-loaded, the gun was recoil-operated using a vertical sliding breech-block, and percussion firing.

After the death of John Browning in 1926, development continued and in 1927, the first 37mm gun was standardized as a 'Limited Procurement Type'. Development of a suitable carriage then lapsed and did not begin again until 1935, and the Carriage M3 was eventually standardized in 1938. Manufacture began early in 1939, and eventually some 7,278 complete equipments were built. Although outclassed by the 40mm gun, the 37mm was never completely replaced by the larger weapon during the war years. It was also used as a component of the armament of a variety of Multiple Motor Gun Carriages, sometimes by itself, but most often in the company of two 0.50 machine-guns.

The original gun was the M1; this was rifled 1/35 and was more or less a refinement of Browning's 1924 model, using 10-round clips. It was followed by the M1A1 gun, which added a charging handle to facilitate cocking and loading, and then by the M1A2 gun which was rifled 1/30, a modification adopted in order to reduce the likelihood of premature functioning of the self-destroying element in the shell.

The first carriage was the M3, a four-wheeled trailer with the wheels on detachable axles. The gun mount sat on a levelling block which allowed correction up to 10° for lack of level of the platform; unlike larger equipments, this platform had no jacking facility and hence had to be put into action on ground which was within 10° of level in all directions. The top carriage, which carried the gun, also carried a platform for the loader and seats for the two gunlayers, one for line and one for elevation. Operation of the mounting was entirely by hand, the Sighting System M2 and Control Equipment Set M1 being the standard fire-control equipments. In 1940, these were withdrawn and the British Kerrison Predictor, known in US service as the Director M5, was adopted as the standard fire-control system, with power control of the mounting by oil gears, data being transmitted electrically from the Director. The necessary alteration of the carriage to remote power control changed its nomenclature to M3A1, and shortly afterwards, a further modification, to allow firing at angles of −5°, advanced it to the M3A2.

Other 37mm Guns

For the sake of completeness, and to clear up ambiguities, all the US service and major experimental 37mm guns are listed.

M1916: This was the Puteaux Trench Cannon, adopted by the US Army from the French in 1916. It was obsolete before the outbreak of war, but numbers were retained in use as sub-calibre barrels for major artillery pieces, being then known as the M1916A1.

M1: Anti-aircraft gun (See above).

M2A1: Designed and standardized in the late 1920s, this was an improved version of the M1916 and was intended as an infantry gun. Service tests in 1932 convinced the Field Artillery and Infantry Boards that it was worthless, and it was declared obsolete.

M3: Anti-tank gun (See p 83).

M4: Aircraft gun.

M5: Tank gun.

M6: Tank gun, 3½ calibres longer than the M5.

Note: Ammunition was interchangeable between the M3, M5 and M6 guns, and between the M1 and M4 guns.

T10, T32, T33: Experimental man-pack guns developed for use in jungle warfare. Used M4 gun ammunition, it broke down into parts for distribution in the infantry squad and weighed 250lb with its tripod. 155 were made and sent to the Pacific theatre in 1944, but they were not well received and were little used.

T47: Experimental high-velocity anti-aircraft gun (3,500ft/sec) which used the chamber dimensions and cartridge of the 40mm gun to fire the 37mm shell. Project began in 1944; two pilots had been made and fired by August 1945, but the project was cancelled shortly thereafter.

Data Gun M1A2, on Carriage M3A2

Weight of gun and breech mechanism: 365lb.
Total length: 78.3in.
Length of bore: 77.98in (53.5 cal).
Rifling: 12 grooves, uniform RH 1/30.
Breech mechanism: Vertical sliding block, automatic, percussion fired.
Elevation: −5° +90°.
Traverse: 360°.
Recoil system: Hydro-spring, constant 10.75in.
Weight in action: 6,124lb.
Rate of fire: 120rpm.

Performance firing standard 1lb 5oz HE shell
Muzzle velocity: 2,600ft/sec.

Maximum horizontal range: 8,875 yards.
Maximum ceiling: 18,600ft.
Effective ceiling: 10,500ft.

Ammunition fixed, cased rounds.

Complete Round, Shell, HE, 37mm M54. Projectile weight 1.34lb; total weight of round 2.68lb. This round consisted of Cartridge Case M17 (brass) or M17B1 (steel), fitted with Shell M54 and Fuze PD M56. The shell was also fitted with a self-destroying tracer which blew up the shell after 10,500ft vertical travel. The propelling charge was 0.39lb of FNH powder, and the Percussion Primer M38A1 provided ignition.

Complete Round, Shot, AP, 37mm M59A1. Projectile weight 1.91lb; total weight of round 3.19lb. Consisted of Cartridge Case M17 or M17B1 with Shot APC M59A1, a capped steel shot carrying a 3-second tracer in its base. The propelling charge was 0.33lb of FNH powder, giving a muzzle velocity of 2,050ft/sec and a maximum range of 5,790 yards. Penetration against homogeneous plate was 1in at 500 yards; against face-hardened plate, 1.9in at the same range.

Below, top: 37mm Gun M1A2 in the firing position; and (bottom) on Carriage M3A2, prepared for travelling.

40mm Bofors Anti-Aircraft Gun

This was basically the same gun as the British Bofors (see p 97), but with modifications to suit American manufacturing methods. Its correct title was 'Gun Automatic 40mm M1 on Carriage M2 or M2A1 or M5'.

The US Navy became interested in the 40mm Bofors in 1937, but efforts to purchase specimens fell through as a result of various misunderstandings with the Bofors company. With the outbreak of war, interest revived, and it was suggested that the US Army might well look at the gun with a view to standardizing with the navy. In October 1940, the US Navy finally obtained a gun from British sources, and in December, the US Army acquired one in similar fashion. After trials and examination, the equipment was standardized as the Gun M1 on Carriage M1 by Ordnance Committee Minute 16787 of 29 May 1941, and negotiations were put in hand for obtaining a licence from Bofors and setting up manufacture in the USA.

The M1 carriage was the original Bofors design and was ill-suited to American mass-production methods. The Firestone Company redesigned it with a welded frame, simplified pivot, tubular axles, electric four-wheel brakes and other minor changes, and this was standardized in December 1941 as the Carriage M2. The M2A1 carriage followed, fitted with higher-ratio gears to give faster elevation and traverse. There were no changes in the gun design other than the alteration of dimensions and tolerances to American standards.

With the formation of airborne divisions in 1942, it became desirable to provide them with an air-portable 40mm gun, and this resulted in the development of the M5 carriage. This was the top carriage of the M2A1, slightly reduced in width so as to pass through the door of a C–47 aircraft, mounted on a simple carriage consisting of a fixed outrigger with a jack acting as a tow-bar, and a cross-axle with 7.25in x 11.50in aircraft wheels and tyres. Three more outriggers, with levelling jacks, were carried loosely on the mount and could be fixed to it by tapered wedges. Before loading into the transport aircraft, the barrel and outriggers had to be removed, and if the transport were a C–47 or C–54, the autoloader and sights also had to come off. Nevertheless,

it was a useful equipment and saw considerable use in the Pacific theatre.

Self-Propelled Equipment

As might be expected, a gun so light and fast-firing attracted a number of designers anxious to put wheels or tracks underneath it.

Gun Motor Carriage T1: Gun and Kerrison Predictor

Above: Top view of the M19, showing the arrangement of ammunition boxes around the fighting compartment.

Opposite page: 40mm gun M1 ready for action in the Pacific. **This page, below:** 40mm gun on the airborne Carriage M5.

mounted on an experimental Mack half-track with rear engine.

Gun Motor Carriage T36: Gun in cast turret fitted to chassis of the M3 Medium tank.

Multiple GMC T52: 2 x 40mm or 1 x 40mm and 2 x 0.50 machine-guns on chassis of the M4 medium tank. Work began in 1943, but stopped in favour of the T81 project.

GMC T54: Gun pedestal-mounted on an M3 half-track.

GMC T54E1: As GMC T54, but with two 0.50 machine-guns, a shield, and stabilizing outriggers added.

GMC T59: Twin 40mm on M3 half-track.

GMC T59E1: As T59, but with outriggers added.

GMC T60: 40mm and two 0.50 machine-guns; re-design of T54E1.

GMC T60E1: As T60, but with shields.

GMC T65: Twin 40mm on lengthened M5 light tank chassis, together with two 0.50 machine-guns.

GMC T65E1: Twin 40mm in barbette on M24 light tank chassis, standardized as the M19 in May 1944.

GMC T68: Twin guns, one above the other, on M3 half-track.

GMC T81: Single gun and two 0.50 MGs on M24 light tank chassis. This was projected as a form of insurance in case the T65E1 project went wrong;

when the T65E1 was standardized, the T81 was cancelled.

Gun Motor Carriage M19: Consisted of Gun, Automatic, Dual, 40mm on Twin 40mm Gun Mount M4 on a modified Light Tank M24 chassis. The guns could elevate from $-5°$ to $+85°$ and could traverse 360° in a power-operated barbette. The four-man gun crew were protected by $\frac{1}{2}$in armour shields, and 360 rounds of 40mm ammunition were carried. In addition to its planned anti-aircraft role, this weapon turned out to be a particularly useful sort of assault gun, much in demand by infantry.

Variants

No other service equipments existed, but the following experimental mountings are worth recording.

T2E1: Used air-spring suspension. Although by 1943, when the project got under way, it was unlikely to see service, it was perpetuated into the T2E2, E3, etc., as a test vehicle for various suspension ideas until the project was terminated early in 1946.

T8E1: Single-axle trailed mount which eventually became the M5.

T8E2: Modified T8E1 without various fire-control features.

T13: A lightweight airborne model intended to replace the M5. Proposed in 1944, prototypes were ready in August 1945, but the development was later terminated.

Data

Weight of gun and breech mechanism: 356lb.
Total length: 117.7in.
Length of bore: 88.5in (56 cal).
Rifling: 16 grooves, increasing RH 1/45 to 1/30.
Breech mechanism: Vertical sliding block, automatic, percussion fired.
Elevation: $-11°$ $+90°$.
Traverse: 360°.
Recoil system: Hydro-spring, constant 7.75in.
Weight in action: 5,549lb (M2A1); 4,495lb (M5).
Rate of fire: 120rpm.

Performance firing standard 2.06lb HE shell
Muzzle velocity: 2,870ft/sec.
Maximum ground range: 10,850 yards.
Maximum ceiling: 22,875ft.
Effective ceiling: 11,000ft.

Ammunition fixed, cased charge.
The ammunition originally issued for this gun was made to the standard British patterns, even to the extent of using the British Fuze No. 251. However, there were features of this round which the Americans did not like – particularly the complicated fuze – and it was later redesigned with a

different type of tracer and a much simpler fuze. Because of its origins, and because of its commonality with US naval use, the round takes on an unusual form of nomenclature.

Complete Round, Shell, QF, HE, 40mm Mk 2T/L. This is the British Mk 2 round, comprising Cartridge Case Mk 1 (M22A1 in US nomenclature), Primer Percussion No. 12, Shell HE Mk 2T, Tracer and Igniter Shell No. 12, and Fuze Percussion No. 251. When supplied complete from British sources, the propelling charge would be the current British standard (see p 100), but when assembled from components in the USA, the charge was 10.4oz of FNH powder. Projectile weight 1.93lb; total weight of round 4.69lb.

Complete Round, Shell, 40mm Mk 2 HE–T. This was the American production standard round and differed in the following particulars: the cartridge case was the M25 (brass) or M25B1 (steel) with the press-fitted Primer M23A2; the shell was of the same design, but carried the Fuze PD Mk 27 (US Navy supply) or PD M71 (US Army supply) and the Shell Destroying Tracer M3. Projectile weight 2.061lb, total weight of round 4.823lb.

Complete Round, Shot, AP, 40mm M81A1. This round comprised the M81A1 APCBC shot in the cartridge case M25, with a propelling charge of 10.4oz FNH powder. The shot, completely inert, carried a 12-second tracer. The maximum ground range was 9,375 yards, with a velocity of 2,870ft/sec and penetration was claimed to be 52mm/500yds/0° or 42mm/1,000yds/0° against homogeneous plate.

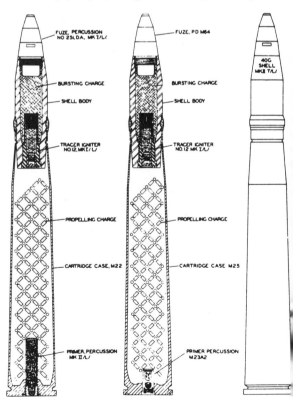

Right: Ammunition for the 40mm gun; on the left, the British round; and centre, the American.

75mm Anti-Aircraft Gun

The development of proximity fuzes for anti-aircraft guns led to the suggestion that a weapon might be designed to take advantage of the opportunity to do away with the fuze-setting step in the loading sequence, and so speed up the rate of fire. In August 1944, a formal requirement was stated for a 'Short and intermediate range AA gun to be compatible with VT Fuze'. 75mm was selected as the calibre, since this was the smallest shell which could accommodate a proximity fuze and still contain enough explosive filling to make the exercise worthwhile. Two pilot models were ordered of two types of equipment; the first, a short-term solution, was to be simply a fast-firing gun with remote power control, on towed and self-propelled mountings. The second, the long-term solution, was to have on-carriage fire control, an optical tracker and a radar set and director actually on the mounting, an interesting reversion to the pre-predictor days of AA gunnery. Again, two versions, towed and SP were to be designed, and the whole project was given the highest priority.

The gun was designed in Watervliet Arsenal and was completed by January 1945, but the mountings, being rather more involved, were not ready until the summer. An auto-loading system, using two revolving magazines behind the mounting, fed to a central rammer to give a rate of fire of 45rpm. The on-carriage model mounted an optical tracker, but the predictor/radar combination was far from ready. But when it came to test-firing, it was found that the gun could develop only 2,300ft/sec velocity, which was nowhere near the figure needed for a viable weapon, and in June 1945 the gun designers were sent back to try again, being given 3,000ft/sec as the figure at which to aim.

Eventually, and well out of our time scale, the project was completed, though the gun only ever reached 2,800ft/sec. The radar was incorporated, and the service equipment, the 75mm Gun M51, or 'Skysweeper', entered service in the early 1950s in towed form. The self-propelled equipment reached as far as an experimental model, which sat the rotating portion of the towed mounting on top of an M24 tank chassis, but no service equipment was ever developed.

Variants

Gun T22: Basic model.
Gun T22E1: As T22, but with left-handed rifling for ballistic trials in 1945.
Gun T23: As T22, but with an experimental 'Summerbell' breech mechanism.
Carriage T18: Short-term development with off-carriage fire control.
Carriage T18E1: As T18, but with components of magnesium to reduce the weight.
Carriage T19: Long-term model with on-carriage fire control.
Carriage T19E1: T19 with magnesium components.
There were several other development models during the post-war period.

Data Gun T22, on Carriage T19
Weight of gun and breech mechanism: 1,330lb.
Total length: 124.9in.
Length of bore: 118.1in (40 cal).
Rifling: 28 grooves, uniform RH 1/25.
Breech mechanism: Vertical sliding block, automatic, percussion fired.
Elevation: $-10°$ $+85°$.
Traverse: 360°.
Recoil system: Hydropneumatic, variable 24in–32in.
Weight in action: 20,625lb.

Performance firing standard 15lb HE shell
Muzzle velocity: 2,300ft/sec.
Maximum range: 14,415 yards.
Maximum ceiling: 30,000ft.

Ammunition fixed, cased charge.
The ammunition was based on the shell of the 75mm field gun and the cartridge case of the 76mm tank gun. Beyond that, few details had been worked out during the war years, and such things as charge weight and nature were constantly being changed.

Above: The 75mm Gun M51 or 'Skysweeper', which was the end result of the T22 development.

3in Anti-Aircraft Gun

The 3in gun was the oldest AA gun in American service and since, like the British 3in, many survived from the First World War until the Second World War, it is necessary to explore them in some detail. What must be grasped from the start is that there were two totally distinct groups of guns, static and mobile, and this distinction is not just in the method of mounting, but is based on the chamber dimensions and barrel lengths, and this takes one back even farther into history.

In 1915, the US Ordnance Department began designing an AA gun for static emplacement, and, as a basis, they adopted the 3in Seacoast Gun M1903, a 55-calibre gun using a cartridge case of 293 cubic inches capacity. This was eventually standardized as the AA Gun M1917. After American entry into the First World War, a mobile gun was demanded; in this application, a slightly less powerful weapon would simplify the designing of the mount, and since there were large numbers of the 3in Seacoast Gun 1898 on hand, this was taken for the purpose. This gun was 50 calibres long and used a cartridge case of 212 cubic inches capacity. Subsequent development perpetuated these basic differences, and this accounts for some otherwise inexplicable discrepancies in ballistic performance when the guns are being compared.

Development of the static series of guns followed simple lines. The M1903 was a built-up gun using an 'A' tube, jacket and locking hoops, and this construction was carried over into the M1917 gun. But it was found to be inconvenient in a gun which was liable to fire several hundred rounds in a short time and then need re-lining, and the design was therefore changed to a simple tube and loose liner. This became the M2 design. Another change was the adoption of uniform twist rifling in place of the original increasing twist. The figure first selected was 1/25, but this was changed to 1/40 in order to reduce the rotational stress on the shell and thereby simplify the designing of a new mechanical time fuze.

The M2 design was ballistically satisfactory, but it proved to be difficult to make, and the loose liner was therefore re-designed to be rather heavier and thicker so as to be more rigid and require less fine tolerances during manufacture. This was standardized as the M4 gun in 1928.

The static mounting was the M1917 and its variants (see p 125) which were all of relatively simple pedestal design. With the adoption of the M4 gun, which was heavier than the M1917, it was necessary to re-design the mount to take the greater weight, and this became the Mount M3.

The mobile gun development was rather more involved, principally because of the search for a perfect mounting. Improvements in the design of the gun followed the same pattern as that for the static weapon; indeed, the mobile equipment usually innovated and the static followed up, since the Army considered the mobile gun as the more important of the two. The rifling was changed to uniform twist 1/25 and then to 1/40 before the gun body was re-designed. The first few years of the 1920s saw several 3in gun designs come and go, since the Westervelt Board had recommended a 3in as the future 'light' gun, so there was plenty of encouragement for the designers. Eventually, in 1927, the M1 gun was standardized, 50 calibres long and with the same design of tube and liner as the M2. As with the static gun, experience showed that a heavier liner would simplify manufacture, and this led to the M3 in 1928.

The original M1918 mobile mounting was no more than a flat-bed trailer with the gun pedestal-mounted on top, and with four levelling jacks, two inclined stabilizing jacks and four outriggers. As a first approximation, it was not a bad try, but there was ample room for improvement. The design eventually perfected, after much experiment, was a relatively small pedestal surrounded by folding platforms, and stabilized by extremely long outriggers which folded in the middle, giving rise to the term 'Spider Mount' in connection with the design. Out of this came the Mount M2, carried on four pneumatic-tyred wheels and with a good deal of aluminium and welded alloy steel in its construction, in order to keep the weight down. With small subsequent modifications, this was the last 3in equipment to be approved for service.

However, in 1931, a fresh 3in project was begun, with the intention of providing a lightweight equipment on a single-axle trailed mounting. This became the Gun T8 on Mount T3. Subsequent changes resulted in the Gun T9 on Mount T4, and this version was recommended for standardization in 1938. But by that time, the 90mm gun project was under way and showed good promise, so the 3in was refused approval. Eight equipments were built, but they were never issued and were eventually taken to become the starting points for a number of tank and anti-tank gun developments. The design of the Mount T4 was, to some extent, perpetuated in the 90mm Gun Mount M1.

Except for a number of guns, both static and mobile, in the Philippine Islands and other areas of the Pacific in 1941, the 3in guns largely spent their war as training weapons, having been replaced in the field by the 90mm.

Variants

Although the 3in was virtually obsolete during the war, there were enough of them available, once the 90mm had become standard, to make them useful experimental weapons for determining fundamental questions.

Opposite page: 3in Gun M1918 on Mount M1918. **This page, top:** This M1923E static equipment was one of the many experimental models. **Bottom:** 3in Gun M3 on Mount M2A2, in travelling mode.

Above: Drill with the M3 Gun in pre-war days. **Below:** 3in Gun M4 on Mount M3, static.

Guns:

M1917: Original static model, developed from the Seacoast 3in Gun M1903. 55 calibres long, rifled 1/40.

M1917M1: Differed in construction, having a separate breech ring.

M1917MII: Modifications to breech ring.

M1917M1A2: Rifled increasing twist 1/50 to 1/25.

M1917M1A3: As M1A2, but with removable liner.

M1918: Original mobile model. 50 calibres long, increasing twist rifling.

M1918A1: Relined with uniform twist rifling 1/25.

M1918M1: Longer breech ring, reverted to increasing twist.

M1918M1A1: M1 relined with uniform twist liner.

M1: Similar to M1918, but with loose liner and uniform twist rifling 1/40.

M2: For static mounting. 55 calibres long, rifled 1/40.

M3: As for M1, but thicker liner.

M4: Similar to M1917, but of two-piece (barrel and jacket) construction. Few made.

M3A2: M3 modified to take Fisa Protectors as a preliminary standard gun for trials on the T17 series, 1944.

T15: 90-calibre 3in gun made from a 90mm barrel

forging rifled 1/30 and using pre-engraved projectiles. Intended to achieve 3,850ft/sec for super-velocity studies; the project began in July 1944 and continued after the war.

T17: High-velocity gun to use projectiles of improved design so as to achieve 3,500ft/sec.

T17E1: As T17, but with Fisa Protectors.

T17E2: As T17, but using pre-engraved projectiles, rifled with 10 grooves; later changed to 12 grooves, since the standard gauging instruments could not cope with a ten-grooved barrel. Project began September 1944 and was terminated in July 1945 without worthwhile results.

T63: A proposed 3in gun to go on the mounting of the 75mm T22 (See p 121) since the T22 development appeared likely to fail. It was to fire a 16lb shell at 3,000ft/sec at a rate of 100rpm, using a fifty-round magazine. Weight of the complete equipment was to be on a par with the 90mm Gun M1, i.e. about 20,000lb. Except for the ballistic design of the gun, all the work of design was contracted to a private company, at a reputed cost of one million dollars. The 3in calibre was selected to suit available ammunition production facilities. In the event, the ending of the war allowed the 75mm project more time to complete development, and the 3in T63 was terminated some time in 1946.

Mountings:

M1917: Original static mounting. Elevation −5° +80°.

M1917MI: Elevation improved to +85°.

M1917MII: M1917 modified to MI standard, plus changes in pedestal height and trunnion bearings.

M1918: Original mobile mounting. Solid tyres and outriggers.

M1: 'Spider Mount' standardized in 1927. Few made.

M2: Improved M1.

M2A1: M2 improved by new jacking and levelling system and new spare wheel mounts.

M2A2: M2A1 with Warner electric brakes.

M3: Static. Generally as M1917MI, but with heavier cradle and trunnions to take the M4 gun.

M3A1: Differs in using roller bearings in the trunnion seats instead of plain metal bearings.

Data

Gun M3, on Mounting M2A2 (Mobile):
Weight of gun and breech mechanism: 2,302lb.
Total length: 158.23in.
Length of bore: 151.8in (50 cal).
Rifling: 28 grooves, uniform RH 1/40.
Breech mechanism: Vertical sliding block, semi-automatic, percussion fired.
Elevation: −1° +80°.
Traverse: 360°
Recoil system: Hydropneumatic, variable 23.5in–32in.
Weight in action: 12,200lb.
Rate of fire: 25rpm.

Gun M4, on Mount M3A1 (Static):
Weight of gun and breech mechanism: 3,360lb.
Total length: 173.23in.

Length of bore: 165in (55 cal).
Rifling: 28 grooves, uniform RH 1/40.
Breech mechanism: Vertical sliding block, semi-automatic, percussion fired.
Elevation: −5° +85°.
Traverse: 360°.
Recoil system: Hydro-spring, constant 16in.
Weight in action: 15,000lb.
Rate of fire: 25rpm.

Performance Gun M3 firing standard 12.87lb HE shell
Muzzle velocity: 2,800ft/sec.
Maximum horizontal range: 14,780 yards.
Maximum ceiling: 31,500ft.
Effective ceiling: 27,900ft.

Ammunition fixed, cased charge.
The provision and supply of 3in ammunition in US service was somewhat complicated, since there was a variety of guns which fell into two groups. The first group included the M1917, M1925, M2 and M4 AA guns and the M1902M1 and M1903 coast guns, all of which had a large chamber and used a cartridge case of 293 cubic inches capacity. The AA guns M1918, M1 and M3, the anti-tank guns M5 and M6 and the Tank Gun M7 used a smaller powder chamber and a cartridge case of 212 cubic inches capacity. This accounts for some peculiar differences in ballistics between apparently identical guns firing the same shell. The basic difference lies in the cartridge case, the static guns using the Mk IM2 case, 26.7in long, 8.5lb in weight and 4.67in across the rim, while the mobile guns used the MkIIM2 case, 23in long, 6.6lb weight and 4.27in across the rim. There were also MkIM2B1 and MkIIM2B1 cases of steel, each about 8oz lighter than their brass equivalents.

Complete Round, Shell, HE, M42A1 for mobile guns M1918, M1 and M3. This round consisted of the Cartridge Case MkIIM2, a propelling charge of 4lb 14oz of NH powder, and the M42A1 high-explosive shell. This shell was filled with 0.86lb TNT and fitted with the M43A3 mechanical Time Fuze, giving it a total weight, as fired, of 12.87lb.

Complete Round, Shell, APC, M62A1 for mobile guns M1918, M1 and M3. This used the Case MkIIM2 with a propelling charge of 4.62lb of NH powder. The projectile was a capped, ballistic capped, piercing shell with a filling of 0.14lb Explosive D and a Base Fuze M66A1. The shell weighed 15.5lb as fired.

Complete Round, Shell, HE, M42A1 for Static Guns M1917, M1925, M2 and M4. This was exactly the same as the round described above except for the cartridge case; the propelling charge, shell and fuze were unchanged. Since the cartridge case was heavier, the weights of the complete rounds differed; that for the mobile gun was 24.36lb, while that for the static gun was 26.20lb.

Note: Armour-piercing ammunition was not provided for static guns.

90mm Anti-Aircraft Gun

By the middle 1930s, it was obvious that the 3in AA gun was fast becoming obsolescent, and that a replacement, capable of dealing with modern aircraft, was needed. In 1938, the Coast Artillery Board demanded a gun of greater calibre, to fire a shell of at least 21lb, the upper limit of calibre being set by the need to load the gun by hand. Preliminary ballistic studies were made, which indicated that a 90mm gun firing a 24lb shell would provide the sort of performance needed, and on 9 June 1938, the development of the 90mm Gun T2 was formally initiated, followed on 18 August by approval of the Military Characteristics of the 90mm Mounting T1. Work progressed rapidly and both gun and mounting were standardized at the M1 patterns and approved for production on 21 March 1940.

The M1 gun used a monobloc auto-frettaged tube sliding in guide rails and fitted with a vertical sliding breech block. The M1 mounting was a four-outrigger platform of unusual design, since it used a single axle with two dual wheels. One outrigger was fixed to act as a towing-bar, while the other three folded up for travelling. The top carriage was fitted with hand-operated elevation and traverse gears, and with data dials for the reception of electrically-transmitted data from the Director.

On 22 May 1941, the Mount M1A1 was standardized, together with the Gun M1A1. The mount was much the same as before, except that it now had provision for remote power control, and the cradle was fitted with the Spring Rammer M8. This was a cylinder, above the gun barrel, which contained springs and a ramming rod; as the gun recoiled the spring was compressed and the ramming rod extended. The cartridge entered the breech ring, whereupon pulling a trip lever released the spring-loaded rod and rammed the round into the breech. The Gun M1A1 was the same as the M1 except for small modifications to the breech ring to incorporate some of the spring rammer gear. In fact

the Spring Rammer M8 turned out to be mor trouble than it was ever worth and it was invariabl disconnected or removed by the gunners.

Although approved in 1941, the M1A1 equipmen actually went into production late in 1940, i advance of approval and on high priority; by th time of the North African landings in 1942, mor than 2,000 equipments had been made and issued. I became the standard field army AA gun and wa used in every theatre of war.

At the time of the introduction of the M1A1, th Coast Artillery requested a static mount capable c use as an anti-torpedo-boat gun in harbour defence or as a secondary role. As a result, the M3 mount ing was developed, a straight-forward pedestal moun fitted with a shield. Although there were mino differences, these mounts were virtually the to carriage assembly of the mobile mount M1A bolted down to a holdfast in concrete.

While the M1A1 equipment was satisfactory fron the pure AA point of view, the Chiefs of Staf decided that what was needed was an equipmen capable of more rapid response in an emergency the M1A1 took some time to get into action capable of engaging ground targets, and capable o functioning as a mobile coast defence gun. Even i the M1A1 could have been got into action mor rapidly, it was incapable of depressing below poin blank, which ruled it out as a coast defence weapon On 11 September 1942, the new project was begun and on 13 May 1943, the Gun M2 on Mount M was standardized.

The M2 gun was much the same as the M1 except for the method of attachment of the breec ring – interrupted threads instead of a continuou one. But the Mount M2 was a considerable change it was now a two-axle cruciform mount with out riggers, folding shields and folding platforms. It wa provided with hand or remote power control o elevation and traverse. The cradle incorporated th

Below: M1A1 mount deployed in an anti-tank position in Belgium, 1944

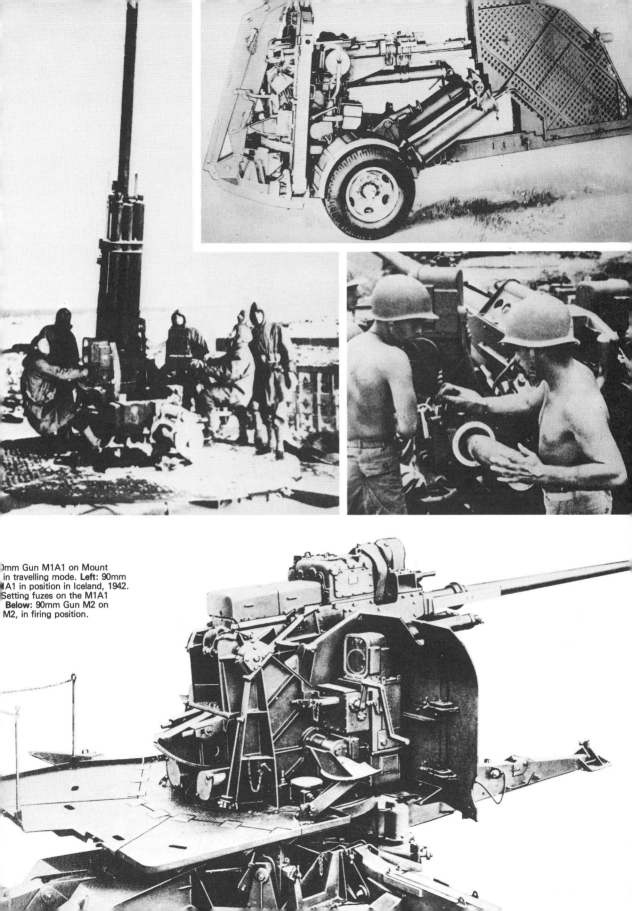

0mm Gun M1A1 on Mount
in travelling mode. **Left:** 90mm
1A1 in position in Iceland, 1942.
Setting fuzes on the M1A1
Below: 90mm Gun M2 on
M2, in firing position.

Fuze Setter and Rammer M20, driven by an electric motor above the gun; behind the breech were a set of diabolo-shaped rubber rollers which were rotated by the motor. To load, the nose of the shell was thrust between these rollers, which were rotating at low speed and drew the round forward. Between the rollers and the breech was a casing containing a set of jaws not unlike a drill chuck; as the round was drawn forward and the fuze entered this casing, the ramming rollers stopped, the jaws contracted to grip the fuze, and a set of knives then gripped the movable section of the fuze and rotated it to the current setting, as transmitted from the director. The jaws then opened sufficiently to clear the cartridge case, the ramming rollers accelerated to high speed, and the round was propelled into the gun breech; as the cartridge rim struck the extractors, this released the breech block, the block slammed shut, and the gun fired. As the round left the rollers, they retracted into the breech ring, and when the gun fired, the empty cartridge case ejected through the fuze setter casing, and past the rollers, which then moved in again and began rotating ready to accept the next round. For firing proximity or percussion fuzes, the fuze-setting function could be locked out of operation and the ramming rollers then rotated at high speed all the time, to ram the cartridge without interruption.

Like many such devices, it sounds a lot more complicated than it really was, and it certainly gave very little trouble in service, while it put the rate of fire up from 15 to 27rpm. At the minimum fuze setting, the firing cycle was 2.6 seconds. It is probable that the basic idea, the use of rollers, was inspired by the similar mechanism used in the German 10.5cm FlaK 38 AA gun, but the refinements of variable speeds and the incorporation of a fuze setter were original ideas.

Variants
In addition to the three basic service weapons described above, there were more variants of the 90mm

Above: 90mm Gun M1 on Mount M3, for coast defence.

gun than almost any other weapon used during the war, because it was a good high-velocity gun, in ample production, and thus made an excellent starting point for all sorts of research ideas:

M1A1E1: A project for liquid-injection cooling in order to prolong barrel life. 1944/45.

M1A1E2: M1A1 modified to take Fisa Protectors. 1944.

M3: Tank and self-propelled gun.

M3E2: M3 with chromium-plated bore. Eight guns with varying thicknesses of chromium, were prepared for wear trials at Aberdeen Proving Ground in November 1944.

T5: A 60-calibre gun with Probertized bore (RD Rifling – see p 108 for a description of this rifling applied to the British 3.7in AA gun) and having a projectile with driving and centring bands. To work at 42,000lb/sq in chamber pressure (the M2 worked at 38,000) and give 3,350ft/sec with a 23.67lb shell. The project began in November 1943 and was successfully completed.

T6: 60-calibre gun, as for the T5, with conventional rifling. Trial firings showed severe tearing and stripping of the shell driving bands, and scoring of the shell body. Work was stopped late in 1943.

T7: Tank development, later standardized as the M3.

T8: A modified M1 for use on the Carriage T5. (See p 90).

T14: M3 modified to use a concentric recoil system.

T15: Development to provide a gun with a better armour-penetration than the M3. To give 3,000 ft/sec with the APC Shell M82, and to be used in SP guns. (See p 91).

T16: A Hyper-velocity AA gun to give 3,500ft/sec with a 25lb shell at 42,000lb breech pressure. This was a 70-calibre gun, and the project, begun in August 1944, continued into the post-war years.

T16E1: As T16, but for Fisa Protectors.

T16E2: As T16, but with chromed bore, 10-groove rifling and pre-engraved projectiles. It was found difficult to measure a ten-groove barrel by using the standard types of bore gauge, however, and the design was later changed to 12 grooves. Continued after the war.

T18: High-velocity anti-tank gun. (See p 91).

T19: M1A1 gun fitted with a 'Crane Liner' for 64 inches of the barrel and chamber in order to decrease wear. 1944.

T20: Anti-tank gun (See p 91).

T21: Anti-tank gun. (See p 91).

T22: A 90mm gun with a 105mm chamber, proposed as a high-velocity anti-tank gun. (See p 91).

T54: Variant of the T15E2. (See p 91).

T60: A 'hotted-up' T54. (See p 91).

Mountings:

T3: Static turret mounting for dual-role AA/Coast firing. To give $-8°$ $+80°$ elevation. October 1941. With modified shielding this became the M3 mount in June 1943.

T6: Improved M3 with heavier shielding and $-10°$ depression. Development began in April 1943, but because of lessened demand for static guns, the

Below: sequence of events in the automatic fuze-setting and ramming used with the 90mm Gun M2.
1. Breech open, ramming rolls closed and rotating at low speed—fuze jaws closed.
2. Round stationary, ramming rolls stalled and fuze jaws rotating fuze ring.
3. Round jammed by ramming rolls rotating at high speed—fuze jaws open.
4. Breech closed, gun is fired—in recoil ramming rolls open.
5. Breech opened in counter-recoil, cartridge case ejected. Gun moves into battery, ramming rolls close and rotate at low speed—fuze jaws close.

Right: The standard round for the 90mm gun.

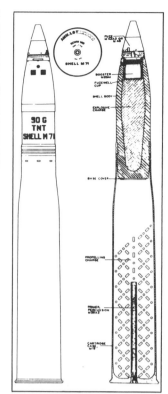

project was ended in April 1944.

Most of the development on mountings in this calibre related to anti-tank guns, and is detailed in the anti-tank section.

Data

Gun M1A1, on Mount M1A1:
Weight of gun and breech mechanism: 2,445lb.
Total length: 186.15in.
Length of bore: 181.05in (50 cal).
Rifling: 32 grooves, uniform RH 1/32.
Breech mechanism: Vertical sliding block, semi-automatic, percussion fired.
Elevation: 0° to +80°.
Traverse: 360°.
Recoil system: Hydropneumatic, variable 26in–44in.
Weight in action: 19,000lb.
Rate of fire: Hand 15rpm; power 25rpm.
Gun M2, on Mount M2 as above except:
Elevation: −10° +80°.
Recoil system: Hydropneumatic, variable 29in–45in.
Weight in action. 32,300lb.
Rate of fire: 27rpm.
Gun M1A1, on Mount M3 as for Gun M1A1 on Mount M1A1 except:
Elevation: −8° +80°.
Weight in action: 17,000lb.

Performance (identical for M1A1 or M2 guns) firing standard 23.4lb HE shell.
Muzzle velocity: 2,700ft/sec.
Maximum horizontal range: 19,500 yards.

Maximum ceiling: 39,500ft.
Effective ceiling: 33,800ft (with 30sec fuze).

Ammunition fixed, cased charges.
Propelling charge. The propelling charge varied according to the projectile in use, so as to extract the maximum velocity, and the nominal weights are noted below with each shell. The cartridge case M19 (brass) or M19B1 (steel, drawn) was used, which was 23.7in long and carried a percussion primer in its base.

Shell, HE, M58. This was the original shell for the 90mm gun, the 21lb projectile called for by the CA Board in 1938. As originally assembled, it had a velocity of 2,800ft/sec, but this turned out to be too much, since the shell was too thin in its wall section to withstand the acceleration and invariably set down beneath the driving band, giving rise to irregular ballistics if nothing worse. As a corrective measure, the charge was slightly reduced to 6.82lb of NH powder to give 2,700ft/sec and the shell was re-designed with a slightly thicker wall and given a final heat tempering treatment in manufacture to make it stronger.

The M58 contained 2.67lb of cast TNT or 2.43lb of Amatol 50/50, with the Time Fuze M43. Ammonal (2.22lb) and Trimonite (2.76lb) were also approved loadings, but it is not thought that these were employed in any number. An M58B1 shell was also approved as a manufacturing alternative, the only difference being that the bottom of the internal cavity was flat instead of hemispherical.

Shell, HE, M71. An improved shell developed during the war, this became the standard anti-aircraft projectile. It weighed 23.40lb and was filled with 2.04lb of TNT, with the Time Fuze M43. A streamlined shell, it could also be fitted with the Percussion Fuze M48 for ground firing. The propelling charge used with the M71 shell was 7.31lb in order to achieve the standard velocity with the heavier shell.

Shell, APC, M82. A piercing shell with penetrating and ballistic caps, weighing 24.06lb with a filling of 0.31lb Explosive D and a Base Fuze M68. Fired with a propelling charge of 7.31lb, it achieved a muzzle velocity of 2,670ft/sec and could penetrate 5.12in of homogeneous plate at 500 yards, or 5.5in of face-hardened plate at the same range.

Shot, AP, M77. This was the substitute standard anti-tank round which was originally produced and then rapidly replaced by the M82 above. It was rather unusual in US service, in that it was a plain steel shot with tracer and no explosive content. The propelling charge of 7.31lb gave 2,700ft/sec velocity, and the penetration into homogeneous plate was 5.6in at 500 yards.

105mm Anti-Aircraft Gun

During the early 1920s, American development of an AA gun concentrated on the 4.7in model, but it was soon felt that this was going to prove a cumbersome weapon and that something smaller than 4.7in, but larger than 3in would be welcome. Late in 1924, development of a 105mm gun got under way.[1] This resulted in the 105mm Gun M1927 on Mount M1926 which, after slight modification, was standardized as the Gun M1 on Mount M1 in 1927.[2] The principal difference between the M1927 and the M1 lay in the construction of the gun; the M1927 was a monobloc auto-frettaged gun, while the M1 used an auto-frettaged loose liner. At this time, there were considerable differences of opinion about gun construction, and a third design, using a loose liner, but non-auto-frettaged and of much heavier construction was approved as the Gun M2. After extensive comparative trials, it was determined that the loose-liner system showed no advantage in this particular gun, and in the interest of economy it was decided to revert to the monobloc design. This was standardized as the M3 in 1933; the M1 was made obsolete, and the M2 was never standardized.

After all this, no more than fourteen M3 guns were made, in 1937–38, the majority of which went to the Panama Canal Zone. In 1944/45, they were replaced by 120mm guns, and declared obsolete in February 1945, one of the few American weapons to be discarded before the war ended.

The M3 gun was a 60-calibre monobloc gun of conventional form, with · a vertical sliding block breech. It was fitted with a mechanical rammer and loading tray, supported by a cantilever arm over-hanging the breech; the rammer was operated by air, compressed in a special cylinder during recoil movement of the gun. By using this rammer, a sustained rate of fire of 20rpm could be maintained, with short bursts of 30rpm, if the shell fuzes had been pre-set. In practice, the need to set the fuzes independently, in a separate setting machine, kept the rate of fire down to about 15rpm.

The Mount M1 was a simple pedestal, anchored to a holdfast set in concrete in an emplacement. Elevation and traverse were set by hand controls according to data displayed on electrical-transmission dials.

While the 105mm M3 was, in itself, a sound enough design, the fact remained that its performance was not sufficiently better than that of the later 90mm gun to make it worthwhile perpetuating, and since the 120mm, which was concurrently developed, was offering better performance for a relatively small increase in weight, the 105mm fell between two stools and suffered accordingly.

Variants

No variant models entered service, but there were a number of interesting experimental projects.

T4: An improvement on the M3, 65 calibres long, to give 3,000ft/sec at 42,000lb/sq in chamber pressure. Development began in 1943 and continued post-war until cancelled in 1946.

T4E1: Originally a T4 with hand-operated breech, as a potential SP gun. Later used as designation for a T4 with the chamber modified for Fisa Protectors.

T4E2: T4 with left-hand twist rifling for ballistic research, 1944.

T4E3: T4 with experimental breech mechanism 1945.

T5: New design, for use in tanks. 48 calibres long, 2,800ft/sec, developed in 1944.

T5E1: T5 lengthened to 65 calibres to produce 3,000 ft/sec. Procurement of 1,152 guns authorized in August 1945, but cancelled shortly afterwards.

T5E2: Tank and heavy SP gun. Basically the T5E2 with a muzzle brake. Later became the T8.

T6: AA high-velocity design to obtain 3,500ft/sec 1944/45.

T6E1: T6 with Fisa Protectors.

T6E2: T6 with chromium-plated bore, 10 grooves and pre-engraved projectiles.

T8: Towed anti-tank gun project. (See p 92).

T18: High-velocity anti-tank gun project.

Carriage T3: A mobile carriage, similar to that of the 90mm gun, which mounted the T4 gun.

Source References
1. Ordnance Committee Minute 4389 of 15 January 1925.
2. Ordnance Committee Minute 6594 of 17 November 1927.

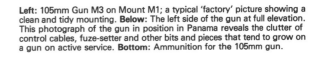

Left: 105mm Gun M3 on Mount M1; a typical 'factory' picture showing a clean and tidy mounting. **Below:** The left side of the gun at full elevation. This photograph of the gun in position in Panama reveals the clutter of control cables, fuze-setter and other bits and pieces that tend to grow on a gun on active service. **Bottom:** Ammunition for the 105mm gun.

Data Gun M3, on Mount M1
Weight of gun and breech mechanism: 6,575lb.
Total length: 259.3in.
Length of bore: 244.1in (60 calibres).
Rifling: 36 grooves, uniform RH 1/30.
Breech mechanism: Vertical sliding block, semi-automatic, percussion fired.
Elevation: −5° +80°.
Traverse: 360°.
Recoil system: Hydro-spring, constant 16in.
Weight in action: 33,538lb.
Rate of fire: 15–30rpm (See text).

Performance firing standard 32.75lb HE shell
Muzzle velocity: 2,800ft/sec.
Maximum horizontal range: 20,000 yards.
Maximum ceiling: 42,000ft.
Effective ceiling: 37,000ft.

Ammunition fixed, cased charge.
Propelling Charge. This consisted of 10.56lb of NH powder contained in the M6 brass case, 30.37in long and 6.25in across the base. A percussion primer was fitted.

Shell, HE, 105mm M38A1. A streamlined shell filled with 3.59lb of TNT, or 3.37lb of Amatol or 3.68lb of Trimonite. The original shell was the M38, fitted with the mechanical time fuze M2, but after some 18,000 had been made and issued, the M43 fuze was standardized. The M38 shell was then slightly modified, by lengthening the nose, so as to accept the M43, whereupon it became the M38A1. Weight of shell, filled and fuzed, 32.77lb. Weight of complete round, as loaded, 63.29lb.

Shell, Practice, M38A1. The same shell as above, but filled with 0.8lb of black powder in a cloth bag, together with 3.09lb of inert material to make up the weight. The powder, ignited by the fuze at the set time, was sufficient to blow the head from the shell and emit a puff of smoke for spotting.

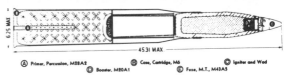

(A) Primer, Percussion, M28A2   (B) Case, Cartridge, M6   (C) Igniter and Wad
(D) Booster, M20A1   (E) Fuze, M.T., M43A5

120mm Anti-Aircraft Gun M1

The Report of the Westervelt Board specified their 'ideal' heavy AA gun as being a 4.7in with a velocity of 2,600ft/sec, semi-automatic breech, on a carriage permitting 80° elevation and 360° traverse, and firing a projectile of not less than 45lb. At that time, a 4.7in gun was already under development, reputedly as a result of the demands of 'Black Jack' Pershing himself, and work continued into the early 1920s. By 1924, the M1920E was ready for test, and was revealed as a self-propelled equipment on a mounting designed by Walter Christie, later to become famous for his high-speed tanks. The gun was a 42-calibre weapon firing a 45lb shell at 2,600ft/sec, as specified, and was fitted with a high-efficiency muzzle brake of astonishing proportions.

After this auspicious start, the usual shortage of money led to the project being shelved for several years, and it was not revived until 1938, the military characteristics being approved and design action authorized on 1 June 1939. It was finally introduced as the 4.7in Gun M1 in late 1940; the nomenclature was changed to 120mm Gun M1 on 27 January 1944. Only 550 were ever made, and except for four sent (probably in error) to Northern Ireland in 1942, and a number sent to the Canal Zone to replace the 105mm guns, they were never employed outside the Continental USA. It was considered that while the 90mm gun had adequate performance for use with field armies, the additional performance of the 120mm would be needed if aircraft were developed which were capable of overflying the USA.

The M1 gun was of conventional type and was mounted on the usual cruciform two-axle platform with outriggers. The only major mechanical innovation was a power rammer which loaded the separate shell and cartridge in one movement. The rammer used a swinging arm driven by an electric motor and operating in conjunction with a fuze setter. Shell and cartridge were placed on a loading tray and the rammer arm then supported the base of the cartridge while a fuze setter moved down to set the shell fuze. The setter then withdrew, the tray moved in line with the gun breech, and the arm then drove shell and cartridge into the breech. The pressure on the cartridge was passed to the shell by a closing plug of palmetto pulp in the case mouth. The tray and rammer then moved clear to permit ejection of the spent case on recoil.

Variant

T53: A proposal in early 1945 to produce a 120mm gun which would be interchangeable with the 105mm T5E1 in tanks, particularly the Heavy Tank T34. This development continued post-war and became the basis of the 120mm gun M58 used in the Heavy Tank M103, and also of the 120mm Gun L1A1 used on the British Conqueror tank.

Data

Weight of gun with breech mechanism: 10,675lb.
Total length: 291.0in.
Length of bore: 282.0in (60 cal.).
Rifling: 42 grooves, uniform RH 1/30.
Breech mechanism: Vertical sliding block, semi-automatic, percussion fired.
Elevation: −5° +80°.

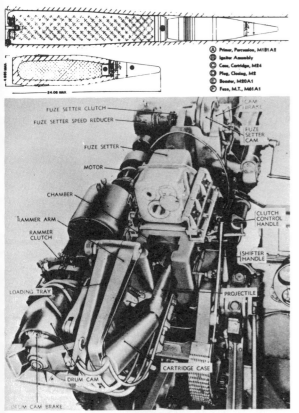

Diagram labels:
A Primer, Percussion, M1B1A2
B Igniter Assembly
C Case, Cartridge, M24
D Plug, Closing, M2
E Booster, M20A1
F Fuze, M.T., M61A1

Fuze setter clutch
Fuze setter speed reducer
Fuze setter
Motor
Chamber
Rammer arm
Rammer clutch
Loading tray
Drum cam
Drum cam brake
Cam brake
Fuze setter cam
Clutch control handle
Shifter handle
Projectile
Cartridge case

Above, top: Ammunition for the 120mm gun.
Bottom: Close-up of the fuze-setter/rammer unit on the 120mm gun mounting. The shaped tracks on the drum cam cause the rammer arm to swing down and forward and 'punch' the cartridge and shell into the chamber. For fuze setting, the whole rammer unit was rocked over to the left to bring the shell nose into line with the fuze-setter.

Traverse: 360°.
Recoil system: Hydropneumatic, variable 31in-36in.
Weight in action: 48,800lb.
Rate of fire: 12rpm.

Performance firing standard 50lb HE shell
Muzzle velocity: 3,100ft/sec.
Maximum ceiling: 57,450ft.
Effective ceiling: 47,400ft.
Maximum horizontal range: 27,600 yards.

Ammunition

Propelling Charge. The separate loading cartridge comprised the case M24 (brass) 32.8in long and 7.55in across the base. This carried a charge of 23.62lb of NH powder, a percussion primer M1B1A1 in the base and a gunpowder igniter. The mouth was closed by a cork plug M1 or 'Palmatex' palmetto pulp plug M2, which served to protect the contents and also acted as a buffer between cartridge and shell during ramming. The plug was not consumed on firing, being blown from the muzzle and landing a short distance from the gun.

Shell, HE, 120mm M73. Weighing 49.74lb, this was a streamlined shell loaded with 5.26lb of TNT and fitted with the Fuze, Mechanical Time, M61A1.

Below, top to bottom: Comparative photographs of the 120mm Gun M1. The photograph immediately below shows the gun with the fuze-setter and rammer unit added; whereas, the 120mm in the bottom picture is without it.

Opposite page: The 4.7in Gun M1920E on Christie self-propelled mounting. Note the blast deflector behind the muzzle brake.

Heavy and Super-Heavy Artillery

The Second World War was the last outing for the super-heavy guns, and even then, they only made it by default, as it were. The First World War had seen massive concentrations of very heavy artillery on all sides, largely due to the seige-like form which that war adopted. At the end of the war, the gunners had mixed feelings; they hoped that such a static war would not be repeated, and, therefore, they put their money on the development of weapons for mobile warfare. On the other hand, it might just be that this was to be the pattern of future wars, so there was some justification for hanging on to the best of the heavy artillery, greasing it, putting it in store, and bearing it in mind.

Below: 7.2in howitzer Mk 6 firing. Note the next shell on the loading tray, the bucket of water for dipping in the rammer brush in order to sponge out the chamber, and the empty ammunition boxes to allow the layer to reach the sight. As a point of interest, the gun commander was Royal Artillery, the man firing was Royal Australian Artillery, and the gunlayer on the left was Royal Canadian Artillery; all were students at the School of Artillery in 1953 when this picture was taken. (See data page 138.)

During the 1920s and 1930s, the aerial bombardment protagonists had a great deal to say about what aerial bombing could do. Trenchard, Billy Mitchell and Douhet, and several others, were never loath to step forward and say that the day of artillery was over, though, by and large, they were setting their sights on even more ambitious targets, and advocating strategic bombing rather than tactical support of field soldiers. Nevertheless, the promise was being held out that aerial bombing could deliver explosives with pinpoint accuracy to ranges which could be achieved only by the most incredible guns, if at all, and the day of super-heavy artillery was long gone.

As a result of all this, the development of heavy guns came to a halt; the designers were obliged to the air enthusiasts, because their enthusiasm and certainty allowed the gun designers to concentrate on more important aspects, such as field guns and anti-aircraft weapons. When anyone asked why they were not working on super-heavy guns, they could, with a clear conscience, point to the latest statement from the 'Blue Sky School'.

This may sound a little contrived; but the shortages of those days must be borne in mind.

When, in 1926, the RA Committee asked for a small modification to a design, they were told that they would have to wait. The Design Department had only one man, and he was working on the drawings for a new 9.2in Coast Gun Mounting for Singapore and could not be spared. So anything which took the load off the designers' backs in those days was welcome.

The gilt fell from the gingerbread in the late 1930s when the air forces had to admit that they were not geared for tactical support of troops, that their plans for war involved long-range bombing or the defence of their bases, that they had no aircraft suitable for tactical support, and that the soldiers would have to do the best they could. This led to a sudden flurry of heavy gun designs appearing on the drawing boards in 1937–38, and it is greatly to the credit of all concerned that they managed to get the designs into production before the war ended.

In April 1938, the Chief of the Imperial General Staff's Conference in London drew up a specification for a 6.85in gun to fire a 100lb shell to 26,500 yards, and a 7.85in howitzer to replace the 8in howitzer. But none of this ever went further than the drawing board, since the demands for more urgent weapons, such as the

25pdr and the 3.7in AA gun, were absorbing most of the production facilities. In the end, except for some second-rate tinkering to produce a 7.2in howitzer, and a design of 9.2in which never got beyond a prototype, British heavy artillery had to rely on elderly equipment until American production got into its stride and managed to produce enough guns for both armies. There was a great deal of sense in this. As will be seen from the individual weapon details, much of the American heavy development was on paper by 1938, since their designers seem to have taken rather less heed of the promised aerial revolution. Given the enormous potential of American production capability, it was obviously quicker to wait for results from this, than to waste time and effort, badly needed in other spheres, in making designs in Britain which would, in any event, merely have duplicated what the Americans had already done.

6in Field Gun

The 6in gun came into field service by the back door. During the South African War, Captain Percy Scott, RN mounted a number of 4.7in and 6in naval guns on to locally-made carriages and used them as field equipments with some success, and after the war, a number of Land Service guns were placed on carriages of more formal design.

The 6in went to France in 1915 and appeared to have its uses, but the gun (a Mark 7 coast artillery piece) was ill-served by the carriage, which allowed only 22° of elevation and, at 26 tons, was impossibly cumbersome. A new design was demanded and the easiest solution was to design a completely new gun which could be dropped straight into the carriage of the 8in howitzer, then in full production. This was duly done, the result becoming the Mark 19 gun. In truth, it was no more than a Mark 7 with a new jacket, but the greater elevation available improved the range, and the old guns and carriages were scrapped.

Just over a hundred were built for British service, plus a similar number which were supplied to the US Army in 1917–18. The Americans had got rid of theirs by 1939, but some still remained in the British Army and were used in France in 1939–40 and, to a lesser degree, in the Middle East. They were replaced by the 5.5in gun in 1942, after which, a handful were retained for training. They were declared obsolete in January 1944.

The 6in Gun Mk 19 was a conventional wire-wound gun with an Asbury breech mechanism. The Carriage Mk 8 was simply the 8in howitzer carriage, a two-wheeled box trail structure; the Mark 8A carriage was similar, but had small changes in design to facilitate cheaper and quicker manufacture. A firing platform of steel beams and wooden baulks was provided, but this had been developed with the mud of Flanders in mind and it was rarely seen after 1918.

Data
Weight of gun and breech mechanism: 10,248lb.
Total length: 219.22in.
Length of bore: 210.0in (35 cal).

Rifling: 36 grooves, uniform RH 1/30.
Breech mechanism: Asbury interrupted screw, percussion fired.
Elevation: 0° to +38°.
Traverse: 4° right and left.
Recoil system: Hydropneumatic, variable, 20in to 42in.
Weight in action: 22,792lb.

Performance firing standard 100lb HE shell
Muzzle velocity: 2,350ft/sec.
Maximum range: 18,750 yards.

Ammunition separate loading, bag charge.
Propelling Charge. This consisted of a single bag containing 23lb of Cordite.
Shell, HE, Mk 20B. A non-streamlined shell containing 8lb 14oz of Amatol and fitted with the Fuze Percussion No 119, 106E or 231. Weight as fired, 100lb.
*Shell, Shrapnel, Mk 18**B.* A nose-ejection shrapnel shell of standard type, filled with 874 lead/antimony bullets, each weighing just over half an ounce. The Time and Percussion Fuze No 88 was standard.

Opposite page: Starting the stockpile. An assortment of heavy guns returned from France to Aberdeen Proving Ground in 1919; the majority of them are 8in howitzers, 155mm GPG guns and 155mm Schneider howitzers. No doubt some of these equipments were still in use in 1941.

Above: The 6in Mk 19 gun, which is still on traction-engine wheels in this photograph taken in France, 1940.
Left: A might-have-been; a prototype 45-calibre 6in gun tested in the 1930s, but not adopted for service.

7.2in Howitzers

In July 1940, the grave shortage of heavy artillery led to a demand for a new weapon of about 8in calibre, with a greater range than the existing 8in howitzer, but on the same sort of carriage. In August, a series of trial firings were conducted in order to determine just how much stress the 8in howitzer carriage and recoil system would stand, and as a result, it was decided to develop a 7.2in howitzer firing a 200lb shell at a maximum muzzle velocity of 1,700ft/sec. The existing 8in howitzers were taken into workshops and the barrel liners were removed and replaced by a 7.2in liner, the breech mechanisms were altered to suit, and the resulting weapons were introduced as the 7.2in howitzer Mk 1, officially approved on 7 April 1941.

Shortly after this, a number of 8in howitzers were bought from the USA. These were similar to the British service 8in models, having been built to the British design in the USA during the First World War and adopted by the US Army. These were now converted to 7.2in howitzers in the same manner, being given various Mark numbers according to the model from which they were converted.

All these designs used two-wheeled carriages with box trails, and the force of recoil was more than the recoil systems could fully absorb; as a result, the whole carriage moved backwards on recoil. On wet ground they were quite unpredictable and extremely dangerous, the detachment having to stand well clear. To try and effect some degree of control, large wedges, called variously 'scotches' or 'quoins', were placed behind the wheels so that on recoil, the wheels ran up the slope of the wedge and then down again. Even with these, firing the 7.2 was a daunting experience, and early in 1943, it was decided that although the weapon was efficient with Charge 3, it was not sufficiently under control with Charge 4 to permit an acceptable rate of fire, and a project for a new carriage was begun.

At this time, though, the first supplies of the American 155mm Gun M1 had arrived in England. The carriage of this equipment could be adjusted to mount the American 8in howitzer, and in April 1943, it was decided to try fitting a 7.2in to the carriage in place of the 155mm gun. Trials were successfully conducted and the result was the approval of the 7.2in Howitzer Mk 5 in November 1943.

But while this had been going forward, the question was raised of the value of putting an elderly and low-powered weapon on to such a modern carriage; surely, it was asked, something more powerful could now be mounted? On examination this was seen to be obviously true, and a completely fresh design of howitzer, 33 calibres long, was prepared, proved and adopted on 21 December 1943, as the Mk 6 howitzer. As a result, it is extremely doubtful if any Mk 5 were ever built; certainly none were ever issued for service.

The Mk 6 was an excellent weapon which increased the maximum range by about two miles, and was steady and stable on firing. It became the standard equipment of Heavy Regiments, and those with the 21st Army Group fired 159,898 rounds between 'D' Day and 'VE' Day, a sufficient indication of their worth. It remained in service until replaced by the American 8in howitzer in the 1960s.

Variants
Mk 1: Converted from BL 8in Howitzer Mk 8.
Mk 1*: Mk 1, repaired by insertion of an inner 'A' tube into worn barrels.
Mk 2: Conversion of ex-USA 8in Mk 6 by removing the existing 'A' tube, shortening the jacket and inserting a 7.2in liner. Weight 3t 5cwt 2qr.
Mk 3: Conversion of ex-USA 8in Mk 7, 7* and 7** (As above). Weight 3t 11cwt.
Mk 4: Conversion of ex-USA 8in Mk 8 or 8½ (As above). Weight 3t 13cwt.
Mk 5: Conversion of Mk 1 to suit the US 155mm mounting.
Mk 5*: Conversion of Mk 1* to suit the US 155mm mounting.
Mk 6: New construction, 33 calibres long, to suit 155mm mounting.
Mk 6/1: Mk 6, repaired by having the body prepared for a shrunk-in 'A' tube.

Data
Mks 1 to 4:
Weight with breech mechanism: 3t 13cwt (Mks 1 & 1*).
Total length: 171in.
Length of bore: 161.1in (22.4 cal).
Rifling: 40 grooves, uniform RH 1/20.
Breech mechanism: Asbury interrupted screw, percussion lock 'K' and slide box 'Y'.
Elevation: 0° to +45° (loading angle 7½°).
Traverse: 4° right and left.
Recoil system: Hydropneumatic, variable, 24in to 52in.
Weight in action: 22,760lb (Mk 3).
Mk 6:
Weight of gun with breech mechanism: 11,104lb.
Total length: 248in.
Length of bore: 238.1in (33 cal).
Rifling: 40 grooves, uniform RH 1/20.
Breech Mechanism: Asbury interrupted screw, percussion lock 'K' and slide box 'Y'.
Elevation: −1°50′ +63°.
Traverse: 30° right and left.
Recoil system: Hydropneumatic, variable, .36in to 60in.
Weight in action: 14.53 tons.

Performance
Mks 1–4 firing standard 200lb HE shell:
Maximum muzzle velocity: 1,700ft/sec.

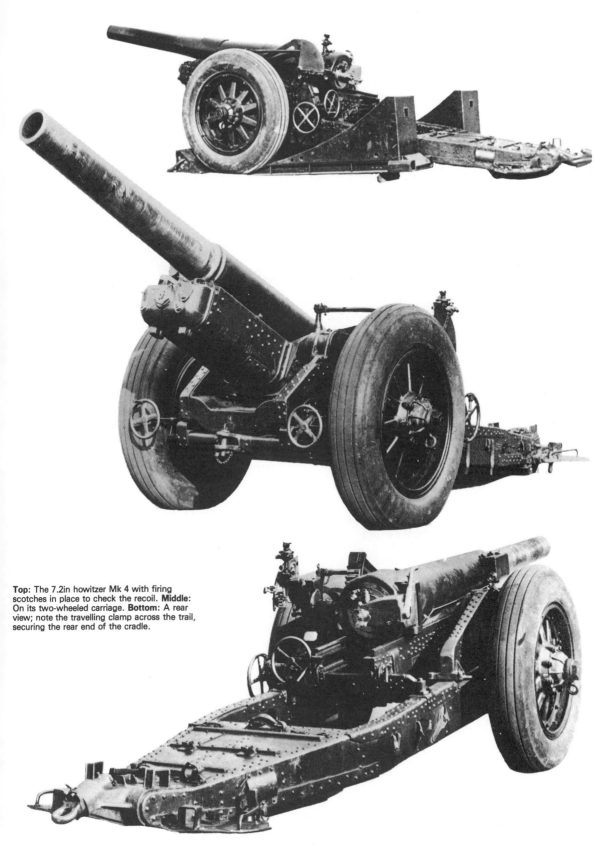

Top: The 7.2in howitzer Mk 4 with firing scotches in place to check the recoil. **Middle:** On its two-wheeled carriage. **Bottom:** A rear view; note the travelling clamp across the trail, securing the rear end of the cradle.

Maximum range: 16,900 yards.
Mk 6 firing standard 200lb HE shell:
Maximum muzzle velocity: 1,925ft/sec.
Maximum range: 19,600 yards.

Ammunition

Propelling Charge. The charge for the Mks 1–4 howitzers was a 4-part bag charge. The Charge 1 unit was shaped like a potato-masher, while the 2, 3 and 4 increments wrapped around the stem and were held there by tapes. Only the Charge 1 unit had an igniter. Performance with these charges was as follows.

Charge 1   5lb 8oz Cordite   900ft/sec   7,500 yards
Charge 2   7lb 3oz Cordite 1,050ft/sec   9,800 yards
Charge 3   17lb 0oz Cordite 1,380ft/sec   13,500 yards
Charge 4   19lb 12oz Cordite 1,700ft/sec   16,900 yards

With the introduction of the Mk 6 howitzer, a 5th charge was introduced. The earlier 4-part charge could still be fired, but for maximum performance it was discarded and the single-bag Charge Five was used. This weighed 31lb and developed the full 1,925ft/sec and 19,600 yards. It could not, of course, be used with the earlier Marks of howitzer.

Shell, HE, Mk 1D. A streamlined shell of the usual form, filled with Amatol 50/50 and fitted with a plug in the nose. This was removed before firing and a fuze was fitted, the standard fuzes being the Percussion DA No 117, Percussion DA and Graze No 119 or Percussion Graze No 231. Time or proximity fuzes were never approved for this equipment.

Above: The 7.2in howitzer Mk 6 being sight-tested.

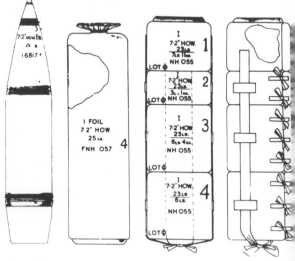

Above: Ammunition for the 7.2in howitzer.

An alternative design was the Shell HE Mk 2D, which had two driving bands, but in every other respect was the same as the 1D. The double driving band necessitated a small ballistic correction to the gun's elevation in order to achieve the same range as the Mk 1D.

No other projectiles were ever designed for the 7.2in howitzer.

8in Howitzers

The 8in Howitzer was another relic of the First World War and, by 1939, only the Mk 8 was left in service. Several were left behind in France in 1940 and, rather than perpetuate an old design, it was decided to replace it by the 7.2in howitzer. The carriages were to be used as they stood, while the breech mechanisms and any other useful bits were to be incorporated into the 7.2in design. As a result, the 8in was 'cannibalized' out of service in 1941; it was formally declared obsolete in July 1943. Except for some counter-bombardment fire in France in 1939–40 and subsequent use as a training weapon in Britain until called in for conversion, the 8in played little direct part in the war, but it was invaluable as a short-cut to the 7.2in design.

Data

Weight of gun and breech mechanism: 7,560lb.
Total length: 148.4in.
Length of bore: 138.4in (17.3 cal).
Rifling: 48 grooves, uniform RH 1/25.
Breech mechanism: Asbury interrupted screw, percussion fired.
Elevation: 0° to +45°.

Traverse: 4° right and left.
Recoil system: Hydropneumatic, variable, 24in to 52.5in.
Weight in action: 20,048lb.

Performance firing standard 200lb HE shell
Muzzle velocity: 1,500ft/sec.
Maximum range: 12,400 yards.

Ammunition separate loading, bag charge.
   Propelling charge. This consisted of a six-part charge, a total weight of 17½lb of Cordite. Performance of the charges was as follows.

Charge:	Muzzle velocity:	Range:
1	735ft/sec	4,950 yards
2	840ft/sec	6,100 yards
3	985ft/sec	7,950 yards
4	1,300ft/sec	10,750 yards
5	1,400ft/sec	11,450 yards
6	1,500ft/sec	12,400 yards

   Shell, HE, Mk 15. A nose-fuzed non-streamlined shell filled with TNT or Amatol. The Percussion Fuze 101E or 106E were used, and the weight as fired was 200lb.

Right: The 8in howitzer Mk 6 on its travelling carriage, with traction-engine wheels and a shell on the loading tray.
Below: Loading an 8in howitzer, 1940. Note the 6in Mk 19 gun in the background.

9.2in Howitzers

The number of 9.2in Howitzers in service in 1939 was small, and the first reaction was to try to increase the number by developing a new design. The existing Mk 2 had originated in 1916 and was a siege weapon of the old school, transported on three steel-tyred transport wagons drawn by traction engines. The howitzer formed Load No. 1, weight 6.55 tons; the carriage body and cradle formed Load No. 2 at 6.6 tons; and the carriage bed and earth box formed the third load, of 5.6 tons. This ponderous procession moved at little more than walking pace and took the better part of 12 hours to put together. A set of steel firing beams were laid on the ground and the carriage was built up on them, the earth box being placed on the front end of the beams, in front of the howitzer, and then filled with 11 tons of soil in order to anchor the front end during firing.

In 1939, after some debate about a possible replacement, a new design of barrel was approved, with the twist of rifling increased to 1/23, though it is doubtful if any were made. But in January 1939, a complete new equipment had been decided on and pilot models were ordered from Vickers-Armstrong and from Woolwich Arsenal. The specification demanded a split trail equipment with 50° of traverse, a range of 16,000 yards with a 315lb shell, five charges, and an equipment capable of being towed in one unit by a Scammel 10-ton tractor.

Mock-ups of both designs were ready in February 1940, and the Vickers model was selected to be built in prototype form. First proof was fired in July 1941 and was satisfactory. Handling and other trials occupied another year, and these were also passed successfully. It was found that a trained detachment could bring the new weapon into action in one hour and out again in half an hour, a vast improvement on the old design. But in October 1942, the development was shelved; the reasons for this decision are not clear, but it appears to have been the likelihood

Opposite page, top: The 9.2in howitzer Mk 1, which had a shorter barrel than the Mk 2. The earth box can be seen at the left of the picture. Middle: The experimental 9.2in howitzer on tow; and (bottom) in firing position. This page: The 9.2in howitzer being transported in three loads.

of supply from the USA of the 240mm howitzer M1 long before the new 9.2 could have been got into production. There were also doubts as to the need for a super-heavy equipment at all, doubts which seem to have been justified in view of the small number of 240mm howitzers used by the British Army.

To revert to the 9.2in Mk 2. Some were lost in France in 1940, and the remainder were patently useless in modern mobile warfare, so they were emplaced as anti-invasion defences on the south-east coast of England, to cover likely landing places. Although not formally declared obsolete until August 1945, there is little record of their having been used, even for training, after the summer of 1942.

Data
Weight of gun and breech mechanism: 9,576lb
Total length: 170.51in.
Length of bore: 159.16in.
Rifling: 56 grooves, uniform RH 1/25.
Breech mechanism: Asbury interrupted screw, percussion fired.
Elevation: +15° to +50° (firing); 0° (loading angle).
Traverse: 30° right and left.
Recoil system: Hydropneumatic variable, 20in to 44in.
Weight in action: 36,288lb, plus 11 tons of earth.

Performance firing standard 290lb HE shell
Muzzle velocity: 1,600ft/sec.
Maximum range: 13,935 yards.

Ammunition separate loading, bag charge.
Propelling charge. Two charges were provided, Normal and Super. The Normal charge was divided so as to give five charge zones, a total weight of 20¼lb of Cordite. The Super charge was a single non-divisible bag of 28¾lb of Cordite.
Shell, HE, Mk 17A. A nose-fuzed, non-streamlined shell of conventional form, filled with either Amatol or TNT. The percussion fuzes Nos. 101B, 106E, 119 or 231 were standard.

BL 12in Howitzer

This equipment was introduced in 1917, and was little more than an enlarged version of the 9.2in Mk 2, using a similar form of siege mounting. Because of its greater size, it was moved in six loads: gun, 15tons 14cwt; cradle 14tons; carriage 11tons 12cwt; rear beam 11tons 8cwt; front beam 10tons; earth box and firing beams 11tons 19cwt. Each portion was drawn by a steam traction engine or by a Holt caterpillar tractor, and it requires little imagination to understand why the troops always referred to it as the '12in Road Hog'.

One of the most interesting mechanical features of this weapon was the provision of a power rammer, probably the first ever used on a field equipment. An additional cylinder in the recoil assembly above the cradle had its piston attached to the gun breech ring. On recoil, air was compressed by the piston's stroke, and this compression acted on an hydraulic accumulator so that sufficient hydraulic pressure was available to drive a ramrod lying in an hydraulic cylinder at the rear end of the mounting.

The remaining few howitzers were deployed in anti-invasion positions in 1940, but beyond that they saw little use. In 1943, there was a proposal to form them into a Siege Train for the invasion of Europe; an anti-concrete shell was designed and approved in April 1944, but by then the 'Siege Train' idea had been discarded and the shells were not manufactured. The gun was declared obsolete in March 1945.

Data

Weight of gun and breech mechanism: 20,440lb.
Total length: 222.35in.
Length of bore: 207.6in (17.3 cal).
Rifling: 60 grooves, uniform RH 1/20.
Breech mechanism: Asbury interrupted screw, percussion fired.
Elevation: $+20°$ to $+65°$ firing; loading $+3\frac{1}{2}°$ hand, $+19\frac{1}{2}°$ hydraulic.
Traverse: 30° right and left.
Recoil system: Hydropneumatic constant, 50in.
Weight in action: $37\frac{1}{2}$tons, plus 20tons of earth.

Performance firing standard 750lb HE shell
Muzzle velocity: 1,468ft/sec.
Maximum range: 14,350 yards.

Ammunition separate loading, bag charge.
   Propelling charge. This consisted of two distinct assemblies, the 'Short Range Portion' covering Charges One to Six, and the 'Long Range Portion'

Below: 12in howitzer Mk 4 on Carriage Mk 2. Note the transport wagons in the background

covering Charges Seven to Eleven. Note that, unusually, there was no overlap of charges. Complete details of performance were as follows.

Charge:	Weight:	Muzzle velocity:	Range:
1	17lb 2½oz	810ft/sec	4,100– 6,110 yards
2	19lb 11oz	872ft/sec	4,800– 7,040 yards
3	22lb 8oz	941ft/sec	5,500– 8,030 yards
4	25lb 15oz	1,016ft/sec	6,300– 9,120 yards
5	29lb 12oz	1,100ft/sec	7,100–10,265 yards
6	33lb 4oz	1,170ft/sec	7,700–11,000 yards
7	37lb 8oz	1,250ft/sec	9,500–11,996 yards
8	40lb 2oz	1,305ft/sec	10,000–12,645 yards
9	42lb 12oz	1,360ft/sec	10,500–13,252 yards
10	45lb 6oz	1,414ft/sec	11,000–13,815 yards
11	48lb	1,468ft/sec	11,400–14,350 yards

Each portion consisted of a base charge (Charges One and Seven) with additional increments to bring the weight of cordite up to the figures given above.

Shell, HE, Mk 10. A nose-fuzed, non-streamlined shell filled with 83lb 3oz of Amatol and weighing 750lb as fired. The Percussion Fuze No. 106 or 106E was standard.

Shell, Common Pointed, Mk 1A. A non-streamlined pointed shell with a small filling of Lyddite and a Base Percussion Fuze No. 16. This shell was intended for attacking hard targets such as field fortifications, dugouts and reinforced buildings.

Above: Rear view of the 12in howitzer, showing the loading arrangements. **Below:** Ammunition for the 12in howitzer.

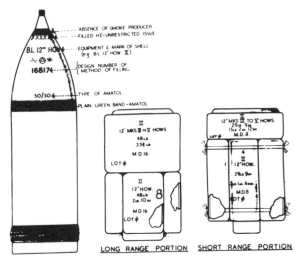

Shell, Concrete Piercing, Mk 1. This shell had a concave nose beneath a ballistic cap, since trials had indicated that such a tip shape would have less tendency to ricochet off concrete. It was filled with Lyddite and used the Base Percussion Fuze No. 270. Since the requirement lapsed, the shell never entered service.

BRITISH HEAVY AND SUPER-HEAVY ARTILLERY   145

155mm Guns

The American Army adopted the 155mm gun in 1917 when they bought 48 French Mle 1917GPF guns. (GPF stood for 'Grande Puissance, Filloux', the gun having been designed by a Captain Filloux). In ensuing years, more were built in the USA and the carriage was modified for high-speed towing. The gun was a 38-calibre weapon with a Schneider breech, while the carriage was a cumbersome split-trail two-wheel model which had a two-wheeled limber placed beneath the trail ends for travelling.

During the post-war years, the GPF was the standard heavy support weapon of the field artillery, and it was also used by coast artillery as mobile armament. A prepared concrete emplacement called the 'Panama Mount' allowed the gun to be anchored to a pivot block set in concrete. The trail ends rode on a concrete and steel racer ring whereby the gun could be traversed rapidly through large angles to permit engagement of moving targets at sea. Numbers of Panama Mounts were built in both the continental USA and in the various overseas possessions, and those in the Philippine Islands were occupied and used during the Japanese invasion.

Variants
M1917: Original French manufacture, purchased in France.
M1917A1: M1917 fitted with American-designed breech mechanism using spring-assisted closing.
M1918: As M1917, but manufactured in the USA.

Above: 155mm GPF gun in travelling mode, with the barrel pulled back and clamped to the trail. **Middle:** 155mm gun M1917 on Carriage M1917 in firing position. **Bottom:** 155mm GPF gun on the 'Panama Mount' for coast defence use.

M1918M1: M1918 with the American-designed breech mechanism.
Carriage:
M1917: Original French; solid tyres, hand-operated brakes.
M1917A1: M1917 with roller wheel bearings, solid tyres, and electric brakes.
M1918: As M1917, but of American manufacture.
M1918A1: M1918 with roller wheel bearings, etc.
M2: Introduced in 1937, this was a M1917 modified to take pneumatic tyres and air brakes.
M3: Introduced in 1937, an M1918 with pneumatic tyres and air brakes.

Data

Weight of gun and breech mechanism: 2,740lb.
Total length 234.0in.
Length of bore: 231.8in (38 cal).
Rifling: 48 grooves, uniform RH 1/25.586.
Breech mechanism: Schneider interrupted screw, percussion fired.
Elevation: 0° to +35°.
Traverse: 30° right and left.
Recoil system: Hydropneumatic variable, 43in to 71in.
Weight in action: 25,905lb.

Performance firing standard 95lb HE shell
Muzzle velocity: 2,410ft/sec.
Maximum range: 20,100 yards.

Immediately after the First World War, work began on designing an improved 155mm gun; it is difficult to say why, because the GPF was, at that time, one of the best guns of its type in the world. Two versions were built, the M1920, a built-up gun of nickel steel, and the M1920M1, a wire-wound gun. The carriage was much the same as that of the GPF,

though the gun could, if required, be removed to a separate transport wagon for movement. An elevation of 65° was possible, and a range of 25,860 yards was reached with a Super charge. Work was then shelved for some years, but in about 1929, a fresh carriage design, the T2, was begun. Shortly after this, a fresh gun design, the T4, started up, aimed at being even more powerful than the M1920. The Schneider breech was discarded in favour of an Asbury type, and in 1938, the Gun T4E2 and Carriage T2 were standardized as the Gun M1 and Carriage M1. By the time of Pearl Harbor, 65 complete equipments had been built.

The M1 gun was 45 calibres long and used an Asbury breech with spring-assisted closing gear, though it retained the agricultural 'hammer and nail' firing mechanism of the GPF. The carriage was one of the best designs ever seen, a split trail carried on a bogie unit with four dual wheels. To prepare for firing, the wheels were raised by two screw-jacks so that the bottom of the front carriage sat firmly on the ground. The trail legs were then opened and spades were placed in prepared holes in the ground, one at each trail end and one at the top end of each leg, close to the hinge. The gun was trunnioned well back and balanced by two hydropneumatic equilibrators anchored above the trunnions and pulling up on the cradle. For travelling, the gun could be disconnected from the recoil system piston rods and was then pulled back until the breech ring could be locked to the trail legs.

The original transport arrangement was the 'Limber Heavy Carriage M2', an axle with two wheels which straddled the trail ends and then lifted them up with a screw lifting jack operated by a capstan. This was considered slow, and it was replaced by the Limber Heavy Carriage M5 which, used in conjunction with the towing vehicle's winch,

Below: 155mm Gun M1 on Carriage M1.

Right: Rear view of the 155mm Gun M1, with spades dug in. **Middle:** The Limber Heavy Carriage M5 in operation. Pulling on the vehicle winch cable lifted the trail, using the sling guide as fulcrum. As the trail reached the peak of its lift, the whole axle assembly flipped over, with the sling guide going underneath and the limber lift bracket going beneath the trail ends to support them. The trail was then pinned in place. This 'flip-over' action was very dangerous and was disliked by most users. **Bottom:** 155mm Gun M1 at full elevation.

Opposite page: 155mm Gun M1 in travelling mode, with barrel pulled back and clamped to the trail. Note that the front spades were inverted and carried on the trail legs beneath the barrel.

WINCH CABLE

PRIME MOVER

LIFTING SLING

LIFTING SLING GUIDE

COUPLING PIN KEY

LIMBER LIFT BRACKET

TRAIL

TRAIL COUPLING HITCH PIN

TRAIL CLAMPING BRACKET

allowed the trail ends to be lifted or lowered in seconds. Unfortunately, the M5 was a device which demanded a fair amount of skill to use safely and efficiently, and most people preferred the slower, but more sure, M2. Both later became redundant when some unsung hero realized that by suspending the trail ends from the chain hoist in the rear of the Mack 7½ton prime mover, it was possible to tow the gun without using any limber at all. However, this adaptation was not officially sanctioned until some time after the war.

Variants
Ordnance:
M1: Original model. Used a bushing between the breech ring and the barrel.
M1A1: Breech screw threads were cut directly into the breech ring, which was screwed and shrunk directly on to the barrel without using a bushing.
M1A1E1: M1A1 with chromium-plated bore for wear trials; one made, tested in May 1944. The results 'Did not warrant the standardization of chromium-plating'.
M1A1E3: M1A1 gun with liquid-injection cooling system to combat wear. August 1944. Inconclusive results.
M2: Differed from M1A1 in having the breech ring attached to the tube in a simplified manner. Standardized in September 1944 after a 3.1% failure rate at proof of M1A1 guns.
M2E1: Proposal for a gun to fire pre-engraved projectiles, using a special 'Indexing Rammer T19' to position the driving band so as to mate with the rifling. Authorized in November 1944, tested in the summer of 1945.
T7: A 40-calibre version for mounting in the Heavy Tank T30. Used a horizontal sliding block breech with bag-charge ammunition, and a muzzle brake. Procurement of 504 guns was authorized in July 1945, but this was later rescinded when it was discovered that nobody had authorized any tanks to be built.
Carriage:
M1: Original design.
M1A1: Original test pattern T2 carriages modified to service M1 standard. Very few.

M1E1: M1 converted to high-speed tracked suspension. Used the Limber M5E1, also tracked. Developed December 1944, later abandoned.
T6: Pedestal Mount T6 for harbour defence was, in essence, the traversing part of the M1 carriage mounted in a base ring and embedded in concrete. It is doubtful if many were actually emplaced.
T6E1: The 'Kelly Mount' for coast artillery use. This was the equivalent of the 'Panama Mount' but suited to the different dimensions of the M1 carriage. It was designed in 1943 by Colonel P. E. Kelly, then Assistant Executive, Harbor Defenses of San Francisco, and was first tested at Fort Funston, after which, it was officially adopted as the 'Firing Platform M1'. It consisted of a central pivot on which the front carriage rested, and a steel track on which the trail ends ran.
T7: Low-alloy steel carriage developed in case of a steel shortage. Used unsprung 'walking-beam' bogies, screw-operated elevating and traversing gears (instead of the standard rack and pinion types), and the balancing gear used air instead of nitrogen. Development ran from 1943 until abandoned in 1945.
T8: Similar to T7, but used low-carbon steel and standard bogies. Begun in 1943, cancelled in 1945 because its excessive weight (25,600lb) did not warrant further investigation.

Data Gun M1, M1A1 or M2, on Carriage M1 or M1A1
Weight of gun and breech mechanism: 9,595lb.
Total length: 290in.
Length of bore: 274.60in (45 cal).
Rifling: 48 grooves, uniform RH 1/25.
Breech mechanism: Asbury interrupted screw, percussion fired.
Elevation: $-1°40' +63°20'$.
Traverse: 30° right and left.
Recoil system: Hydropneumatic, variable, 35.7in to 65in.
Weight in action: 30,600lb.

Performance firing standard 95lb HE shell
Muzzle velocity: 2,800ft/sec.
Maximum range: 25,395 yards.

Self-Propelled Equipments

The 155mm was an early target for the SP gun designers, a motorized carriage being produced as early as 1920, but like other projects of this period it was dropped for lack of money.

Nothing further happened until June 1941, when the Ordnance Department informed the Adjutant-General that they had completed a design study for mounting the M1917/18 gun on to a modified M3 Medium Tank chassis. Authorization to proceed with the project was given immediately and a pilot model, the Gun Motor Carriage T6, was built at Rock Island Arsenal. It was tested in February 1942, during which test (at Fort Bragg), it demonstrated its agility by firing, moving six miles, and firing again, all within 35 minutes. A towed GPF gun used as the 'control' took three hours to perform the same manoeuvre. 100 equipments were authorized and were manufactured by the Pressed Steel Car Co., being completed in 1943. The equipment was standardized as the GMC M12.

The M12 consisted of the M1917 or M1918 gun on a simple pedestal mounted in the rear of the vehicle chassis, the engine having been moved forward to give a flat working area around the gun. A bulldozer-like blade at the rear could be lowered and dug into the ground to take the firing shock off the vehicle's suspension. A driver, assistant driver, and four-man gun detachment were carried, the remainder of the detachment (8 men) being carried on the associated Cargo Carrier M30, along with the ammunition and stores.

Of the 100 M12's built, most were placed in store in October 1943, when the Army Ground Forces Command decided that there was no requirement for it. But early in 1944, when the Normandy landings were being planned, it was realized that they could be extremely useful, and 74 were taken from store and refurbished prior to being issued to various units of the US 1st and 3rd Armies, with whom they served until the end of the war.

Late in 1943, a new project began, the GMC T79, which intended mounting the M1 gun on a chassis derived from the T23 light tank. AGF disapproved of the idea – they appear to have been hostile to virtually any self-propelled gun proposition at this period – but when, in March 1944, the 'Overlord' planners demanded SP artillery for the forthcoming invasion, the T83 was begun, a design for an M1 gun on the modified and widened chassis of an M4A3E8 Medium Tank. The engine was moved forward into a compartment immediately behind the driver so as to leave a flat working space at the rear. Here the gun was mounted, using a modification of the Firing Pedestal T6 originally intended for harbour defence use. A recoil spade was fitted to the rear, and a hinged loading platform could be lowered to give the gunners more elbow-room.

Procurement of five pilot models was authorized in June 1944, and in the following month limited procurements of 304 equipments was ordered. In April 1945, the T83 was standardized as the M40,

and the procurement order increased to 600. Production, again by the Pressed Steel Car Co., actually began in January 1945, and a few equipments saw service in Europe. The M40 was adopted by the British Army for some years, and there are still a large number in use by various countries.

Below: The 155mm GMC M12 in firing position. Note the limited working space around the gun, compared with the more generous allowance for the M40 (bottom).

Ammunition separate loading, bag charge.

Propelling charge for M1 Guns. This consisted of a base and increment. The base section (Normal Charge) contained 20.35lb of NH Powder and, with the 95lb shell, developed 2,100ft/sec and ranged to 18,605 yards. The Increment section contained 10.39lb of NH Powder and could only be fired in conjunction with the Base section to give the 'Super Charge'. When used in British service, a similar combination of bags, but filled with Cordite, was provided, the weight of propellant being adjusted to give the same ballistics as the American charges.

Propelling charge for M1917/18 Guns. This consisted of similar base and increment units, but with different weights of propellant. The base unit held 18.66lb and the increment 5.70lb. The base unit Normal Charge gave 1,955ft/sec and 16,100 yards with the 95lb M101 shell.

Shell, HE, M101. The standard projectile for both M1917/18 and M1 guns, this was a streamlined shell containing 15.13lb of TNT. As supplied to the gun, it weighed 94.7lb with a ringbolt screwed into the nose. Fuzes PD M51 or TM M67 were supplied

separately and fitted at the gun position. In late 1944, a deep-cavity shell with removable supplementary charge was provided for use with the proximity fuze T76E1.

Shell, Chemical, M104. This was provided with white phosphorus (WP) smoke, titanium tetrachloride (FS) smoke, or mustard gas (HS) fillings, the latter, of course, never issued. In the WP form, the most common, it weighed 98.18lb and held 15.68lb of phosphorus. The Fuze PD M51 was standard. Fired from the GPF guns, it had a maximum range of 20,247 yards, and from the M1 gun, 25,940 yards.

Projectile, AP, M112B1. This was a piercing shell with penetrative and ballistic caps, intended for anti-ship use in the coast-defence role and also as a possible anti-concrete projectile in the field. It weighed 100lb and carried a filling of 1.44lb of Explosive D with a Base Detonating Fuze M60. Fired from the M1 gun with Super Charge, it developed 2,754ft/sec, had a maximum range of 24,075 yards and could pierce 6½in of homogeneous plate at 1,000 yards range.

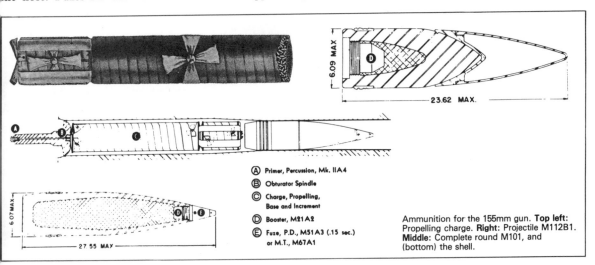

A Primer, Percussion, Mk. IIA4
B Obturator Spindle
C Charge, Propelling, Base and Increment
D Booster, M21A2
E Fuze, P.D., M51A3 (.15 sec.) or M.T., M67A1

Ammunition for the 155mm gun. **Top left:** Propelling charge. **Right:** Projectile M112B1. **Middle:** Complete round M101, and (bottom) the shell.

8in Howitzer

The US Army first adopted the 8in Howitzer in 1917, as a stopgap until the projected 240mm model came into service. The howitzer they adopted was the British 8in Mks 7 and 8; they were being built for Britain in the USA by the Midvale Steel Company of Nicetown, Pa., and as soon as the need was appreciated, a contract was placed for 80 howitzers to be built as soon as the British contract had been completed. These, the British Mk 6, were taken into US service as the American Mk 7, and the contract was extended until 195 had been built. Later, the British Army adopted their Mk 7 and the Americans promptly set the Midvale Company to

making 100 of them. After some had been built, the British design was altered in its chamber dimensions to become the 7* and the Americans adopted the modification, calling their version the Mk 8½. A number of both types was also purchased from Britain for direct supply to the AEF in France, so that at the end of the war there was a fine old jumble in US service, both Marks made in either country. The Mk 7s were declared obsolete in the 1920s, but some of the Mk 8½ survived into the Second World War and were used for training.

Immediately after the war, work began on a new 8in howitzer which it was intended to use on

Above: 8in howitzer M1 on Carriage M1. The shorter barrel on this gun eliminated the need for pulling back. **Below:** 8in howitzer in firing position, with the Limber M2 at the right of the picture.

the same carriage as the new 155mm gun, then under development. The result was the M1920 howitzer, a built-up gun on a split-trail carriage with a maximum range of 18,700 yards with a 200lb shell. Experimental self-propelled guns were also made, and an M1920M1 howitzer was produced in prototype form, a nickel-steel wire-wound gun, probably the last wire-wound gun to be developed in the USA. But in spite of some good results, the inevitable shortage of money closed the project down in 1921.

In 1927, the idea was revived and the T2 howitzer, using a centrifugally-cast barrel, was designed in 1929. The only thing overlooked by the designer appears to have been the somewhat basic fact that there was no centrifugal casting facility in the USA which could produce an 18ft five-ton casting, so the design was scrapped and the T3, using a forged and auto-frettaged barrel, was developed. As in 1920, it was designed so as to fit the carriage of the 155mm gun, and after a long period of testing and development, it was finally standardized in 1940 as the Howitzer M1 on Carriage M1.

The howitzer used an Asbury breech mechanism of the same type as that on the 155mm gun M1, and the carriage was the same as that used with the 155mm gun. However, although the two pieces were interchangeable, the change was not one which could be done by simply swapping barrels as some people seem to think. The howitzer piece was of different weight, was different in length, and had a different recoil energy from that of the gun. It was necessary, therefore, to lift off the top carriage and adjust the number of Belleville springs which supported the traversing racer under the top carriage; the nitrogen pressure in the equilibrators had to be altered; and slight alteration to the recuperator pressure was also needed. In other words, although the interchange could be made, it was not done easily or without workshop facilities.

Variants
Howitzer M1: Breech ring screwed and shrunk to the barrel.
Howitzer M2: Breech ring screwed only, and could be removed.

Self-Propelled Equipments
In 1943, a project was begun for a lightweight chassis using the running gear of the T23 medium tank and electric drive transmission, to carry the 155mm gun or the 8in howitzer, the latter model being known as the T80. However, when the characteristics were submitted to Army Ground Forces HQ in November 1943, they were not approved and the project was cancelled. The designers then turned to a less provocative specification using the power train of the M4 tank and a new 23in wide track and horizontal volute spring suspension, then under development. This became the Howitzer Motor

Carriage T84, and development of two pilot models was approved in May 1944. On second thoughts, the design was altered to use components, notably the suspension, of the heavy tank M26E1 in November 1944. The first pilot model was completed and sent for test to Aberdeen Proving Grounds in February 1945, but delays in obtaining the necessary supply of tank components held up production plans and the equipment, now standardized as the M43, did not enter service until 1946.

Data Howitzer M1 or M2, on Carriage M1
Weight of gun and breech mechanism: 10,240lb.
Total length: 209.59in.
Length of bore: 200.0in (25 cal).
Breech mechanism: Asbury interrupted screw, percussion fired.
Elevation: $-2° +65°$.
Traverse: 30° right and left.
Recoil system: Hydropneumatic variable, 32in to 63in.
Weight in action: 31,700lb.

Performance firing standard 200lb HE shell
Muzzle velocity: 1,950ft/sec.
Maximum range: 18,510 yards.

Ammunition separate loading, bag charge.
Propelling Charge. Two charges are provided, the M1 (Green Bag) for short ranges, and the M2 (White Bag) for long ranges. The M1 consisted of a base section and four increments, giving five Charge Zones, a total weight of 13.19lb of NH powder. The maximum velocity with this charge was 1,339ft/sec and the maximum range 11,170 yards. The M2 charge consisted of a base unit forming Zone 5, and two increments to give Zones 6 and 7. Total weight of the M2 charge was 28.19lb, and the powder was of a different granulation from that of the M1.
Shell, HE, 8in Mk1A1. This was actually the Shell Mk1 used with coast guns, modified to take the M51 or M67 fuzes. It weighed 200lb, carried a filling of 30.08lb of TNT, and was non-streamlined. It was standardized when the howitzer was first issued, but was later replaced by the M106
Shell, HE, 8in M106. A streamlined shell of more modern design, which replaced the Mk1A1. It weighed 200lb, had a filling of 36.98lb of TNT, and was fuzed PD M51 or TM M67. Towards the end of the war, the design was modified by adopting a universal cavity and removable supplementary charge, so as to accept the proximity fuze T76E6.

An interesting area of speculation is uncovered by the bald statement in OCM 23901 of 25 May 1944 that 'The development of a HEAT shell for the 8in howitzer has been abandoned'. Research so far, has failed to uncover what the designer had in mind, but it is probable that concrete-piercing was the aim. While the 8in howitzer was a good weapon, it takes some imagination to see it in the anti-tank role.

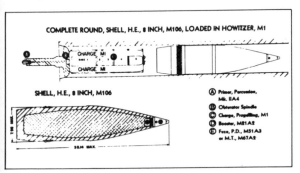

COMPLETE ROUND, SHELL, H.E, 8 INCH, M106, LOADED IN HOWITZER, M1

CHARGE M1

CHARGE M1

SHELL, H.E, 8 INCH, M106

(A) Primer, Percussion, Mk. IIA4
(B) Obturator Spindle
(C) Charge, Propelling, M1
(D) Booster, M81A2
(E) Fuze, P.D., M51A3 or M.T., M67A2

8in Gun

Probably as a result of mounting an 8in Coast gun on a railway truck (see p. 175), the US Army, in 1920, began studying the prospect of developing an 8in on a road-mobile carriage, but it was at a low priority and the project was shelved indefinitely in 1924. In 1939, the idea was revived as a possible partner piece for the 240mm howitzer then under development, and after some preliminary studies, final approval was given in June 1940 and work got under way. The design was called the 8in Gun T2, and the specification called for a range of 33,500 yards, a weapon capable of travelling in two loads, neither weighing more than 44,000lb, a road speed of 25mph, and the capability of being carried by rail without exceeding the loading gauge. Design was eased by the commonality of the carriage with that of the 240mm Howitzer M1, but the gun gave considerable trouble in development and it was not until January 1944 that it was standardized.

The principal problems were excessive bore wear and poor accuracy, leading to a large range-dispersion figure, and several possible solutions were tried. However, the M1, as standardized, was essentially the basic T2, a quite straightforward design of gun which used the same breech mechanism as the 240mm howitzer. Though admittedly unsatisfactory, it was accepted for service, since it seemed unlikely that any of the variant designs would give good results within a reasonable period of time. As a result, relatively few were built or used; for example, the 1st US Army in Europe had only 9 guns.

The carriage was the same as that of the 240mm Howitzer M1, the only changes being to the nitrogen pressures of the equilibrator and recoil system, in order to suit the greater length and weight of barrel and the more powerful recoil force. Stops were also placed on the elevating arc so as to restrict the firing elevation and avoid over-stressing the carriage, particularly at low elevations.

Variants
(It will be apparent that all the variants were designed in an endeavour to solve the bore wear problem.)
M1: Auto-frettaged monobloc barrel with shrunk-on jacket.

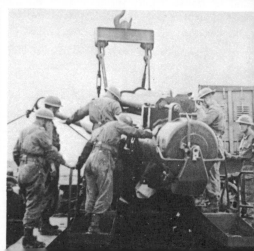

T2E1: As M1, but with British RD Rifling (see p. 108) and a two-banded projectile. Project begun in 1943; later the bore was chromium-plated.

T2E2: As M1, but rifled 1/30 to try and reduce muzzle wear. Begun in 1943, trials were finished in 1945, but they showed no significant improvement.

T2E3: M1 with the bore chromium-plated. Begun in January 1944, the project appears to have given little satisfaction and was abandoned in April 1945.

T2E4: M1 with RD rifling and chromium-plated bore to US Naval specifications. October 1944.

T2E5: M1, chromed bore, using projectiles with pre-engraved driving bands. October 1944.

Data

Weight of gun and breech mechanism: 29,800lb.
Total length: 409.5in.
Length of bore: 400.0in (50 cal).
Rifling: 64 grooves, uniform RH 1/25.
Breech mechanism: Interrupted screw, drop block, percussion fired.
Elevation: $+10°$ to $+50°$.
Traverse: $15°$ right and left (see note).
Recoil system: Hydropneumatic, constant, 50in.
Weight in action: 69,300lb.

Note: After the war, traverse was increased to $20°$ right and left.

Performance firing standard 240lb HE shell
Muzzle velocity: 2,840ft/sec.
Maximum range: 35,635 yards.
Minimum range (due to $+10°$ minimum elevation): 22,100 yards.
Note: As originally standardized, the muzzle velocity was to have been 2,950ft/sec, but this was reduced in order to counter severe erosion of the barrel.

Sequence of assembling the 8in gun. **Opposite page, left:** Lifting the carriage body from its transporter. **Right:** Lowering it over the pit. The men on the ropes prevent it from swinging and also align it accurately with the line of fire.
This page, left: Once the trail legs are opened, the spades can be fitted. **Right:** Next, the barrel is brought alongside the crane.
Opposite page, lower left: The barrel is lowered onto the mounting and (right) carefully guided into position before it is securely bolted down.
This page, lower left: At last, a perfect fit. This is the left side of the mounting, showing the line gunlayer's traversing hand-wheel, with sight bracket above. The tank at the front contained compressed nitrogen for the equilibrator, which was inside the mounting and pressed on the cradle. Note the roller under the barrel, above the nitrogen tank; this was used when assembling the equipment by means of the tractor winches. **Lower right:** Rear of the 8in Gun M1 with breech open. The breech operators stood on the platforms at each side of the breech, since the recoil pit was beneath them and prevented them standing on the ground.

Ammunition separate loading, bag charge.

Propelling charge. The charge system for the 8in gun was rather more involved than was usual, so as to provide a Reduced, a Normal, and a Super charge. By using the reduced and normal charges as much as possible, once again the wear would be reduced. Two charge systems were introduced with the gun, the M9 Green Bag and the M10 White Bag, each of which comprised a base section and an increment. Reduced charge was obtained by firing the M9 base; normal charge, by firing either the M9 base and increment or the M10 base; and super charge, by firing the M10 base and increment. Towards the end of the war, a third option was introduced, the M13 charge, which eventually superseded the other two systems. The M13 used a base and two increments; base only for reduced, base plus one for normal, base plus two for super charges. The weights and performance of the various options are best shown in tabular form.

Charge:	Bags:*	Weight:	Muzzle velocity:	Range:
Red	M9b	54.9lb	2,100ft/sec	22,775 yards
Red	M13b	58.38lb		
Normal	M9b+i	76.01lb	2,600ft/sec	30,315 yards
Normal	M10b	93.1lb	2,600ft/sec	30,315 yards
Normal	M13b+i	79.5lb	2,750ft/sec	32,500 yards
Super	M10b+i	106.1lb	2,850ft/sec	35,630 yards
Super	M13b+i+i	90.8lb	2,840ft/sec	35,635 yards

It will be appreciated that apparent discrepancies between relative weights and performance are explained by the three charges being filled with different powders. The M9 and M10 charges used different granulation, while the M13 used both different granulation and different formulation, yet another move in the constant struggle against erosion in this gun.

Shell, HE, M103. This was an unusual projectile which applied some of the theories of the French ordnance engineer Edgar Brandt, using a long false ogive (or nose) to produce a favourable ballistic shape while keeping the centre of balance in the most effective place. The shell body had a stream-lined base and a blunt nose which was threaded with the usual 2in 12tpi hole for the Fuze PD M51A2Mod3. This resembled the standard M51 type in its mechanism, but had the tapered cover removed and a long flash tube inserted, which extended through the space of the false shell ogive to the tip of the nose. Here, a fuze-head unit, comprising a firing pin, detonator and flash pellet, screwed into the top of the flash tube and formed the extreme tip of the shell. The fuze mechanism was set to 'Superquick' and, in the normal course of events, if the 'delay' setting on the fuze was wanted, it would have been necessary to remove the false ogive from the shell in order to get at the setting screw in the side of the fuze. To obviate this, an inert head unit was supplied with each shell; the live head unit was unscrewed from the flash tube

*b = base, i = increment

and the inert unit was screwed in its place. On impact, with no action from the inert unit, the delay element in the fuze body went into action to detonate the shell.

Fuze Time Mechanical M67 was also approved for this shell, and when that was needed, there was no way out of it; the false ogive had to be unscrewed from its seating on the shell shoulder, the M51 fuze removed, the M67 screwed in and set, the ogive replaced, and the inert fuze head unit screwed in so as to plug the hole in the ogive. It was a long-winded and unpopular business, invariably made worse by rust and paint causing the ogive to resist removal. If too much force were used, there was a danger of damaging the thin sheet steel ogive.

The M103 shell weighed 240lb and contained 20.9lb of TNT. Because it was supplied ready-fuzed and because of the fragility of the false ogive, it was issued in a special box for safety in transit. The inert fuze head was screwed into the ogive, and the live head was securely packed in a special compartment in the box.

Above: A self-propelled version of the 8in gun (the GMC T93) was developed, using the same chassis as that of the 240mm howitzer SP. It was never put into service. **Below:** Ammunition for the 8in gun.

240mm Howitzers

Strange as it may seem, the US 240mm howitzer can trace its line of descent back to the Siege of Port Arthur in 1904. At that affair, the Japanese deployed a number of 28cm howitzers, which did great execution, and after the war ended, the Russian Army decided that it needed a similar weapon. In conjunction with Schneider, the French gunmaker, a weapon was designed, tested in 1911, found satisfactory, and a number were built both for the Russians and, later, for the French Army during the early part of the First World War.

When the USA entered the war they sought a heavy howitzer, but considered 24cm a better calibre and they requested Schneider to scale-down the 28cm model accordingly. This was done and arrangements were made to have the gun and mounting built in the USA. American officers went to France to study the Schneider methods, and Schneider then sent technicians to the USA to assist in setting up production. No less than 2,627 howitzers and 1,214 mountings were ordered, production being scheduled for the spring of 1919. Great difficulties were encountered in making the weapons, notably in build-

ing the recoil system, and by the time the war ended, only one complete equipment had been built. The contracts were then, of course, slashed, and in the end, 330 howitzers were built, entering service as the 240mm Howitzer M1918 on Carriage M1918. In fact, it was not quite that simple; the first howitzer to be built was destroyed at its first proof shot, and it took several years of work and modification before the weapon could be called serviceable.

The M1918 was a built-up gun with the Schneider screw breech, and it was mounted on a simple siege mounting which had to be assembled on site. The equipment moved in four loads: barrel, top carriage, platform, and cradle with recoil system. Each unit was carried on a transport wagon drawn by a 10ton tractor and, on arrival, was assembled with the aid of an erecting frame and a hand crane.

In addition to its employment as a mobile siege piece, there was a modified carriage which could be emplaced in a concrete foundation for use as a

Below: The 240mm M1918 in position with (inset) the method of emplacing the mounting by means of erecting frames.

Removal of 240 mm Howitzer Carriage, M1918, Top Carriage to Top Carriage Transport Wagon, M1918, by Means of the Erecting Frame.

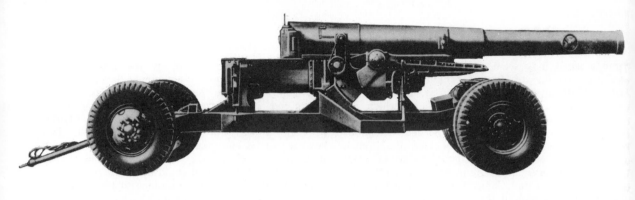

Above and below: The 240mm howitzer M1918 on its transport wagons.

coast-defence howitzer; numbers of these were emplaced in Hawaii. In spite of its age, it remained in service throughout the Second World War, though entirely as a training weapon.

Variants
Howitzer:
M1918: Basic model. 182 built at Watervliet Arsenal. Uniform twist rifling.
M1918M1: Greater barrel diameter. Nos. 183–330.
M1918A1: M1918 relined with increasing twist rifling.
M1918M1A1: M1918A1 relined with increasing twist rifling.
Carriage:
M1918: Four-unit transportable.
M1918A1: Modified for use in concrete emplacement.
M1918A2: M1918 modified for easier assembly in the field.

Data Howitzer M1918M1A1 on Carriage M1918A2
Weight of gun and breech mechanism: 10,700lb.
Total length: 204in.
Length of bore: 177in (18.75 cal).
Rifling: 84 grooves, increasing RH 1/40 to 1/20.
Breech mechanism: Schneider interrupted screw,

percussion fired.
Elevation: $-1°$ $+60°$.
Traverse: 10° right and left; 360° on A1 carriage.
Recoil system: Hydropneumatic, constant 45in.
Weight in action: 41,300lb.

Performance firing standard 345lb HE shell
Muzzle velocity: 1,700ft/sec.
Maximum range: 16,400 yards.

Ammunition separate loading, bag charge.
Propelling Charge. This consisted of six bags of NH powder, a total weight of 35.81lb. Divided, four of the bags each weighed one-fifth of the total, and the other two weighed one-tenth. It can be seen that ten different charges could then be made up by suitable combinations of bag, giving velocities from 615ft/sec to 1,700ft/sec, and maximum ranges from 3,594–16,390 yards.
Shell, Mk IIIA1. This was a streamlined shell weighing 345lb and containing 49.79lb of TNT. It could be fitted with the Fuze PD M 51 or MT M67. Earlier shells, threaded for the PD M43 and similar fuzes had been issued before the war, and were still being used up for practice, but only the MkIIIA1 was standard.

240mm Howitzer M1

The shortcomings of the M1918 howitzer were obvious enough in the 1920s, and an extensive series of tests were conducted at Fort Bragg in 1924–25 which showed that an extensive re-design was the only real solution; but with over 300 of them built, there was little hope of that, and the question of a fresh design was shelved until some future day when money might become available. In 1934, an improved carriage, suited to high-speed towing was proposed, but this, too, had to be postponed.

Better days arrived late in 1939, when the improvement proposals were brought out and reconsidered, and in April 1940, the development of a completely new weapon was begun. The first model was designated the Howitzer T1 and it was to be carried separated from its mounting on a Howitzer Transport Wagon T2. The mounting was an ingenious design of split-trail unit with the front end 'kicked up' so as to take a fifth-wheel connector; for transporting, the trail legs were closed and a four-wheeled trolley, the Heavy Carriage Limber T4, was attached to support the trail leg ends. The front end was then coupled, via the fifth wheel,

to a special Tractor T22, to form an articulated unit which could be driven like a truck and semi-trailer combination.

For some reason or other this design was not well received; it is possible that the cross-country performance was poor. In any event, the design was changed; the mounting remained a split-trail type, but it was now provided with a four-wheeled Carriage Transport Wagon on to which it was lifted or winched for movement. Both these first designs of transport wagon were later replaced by stronger, six-wheeled models, before the equipment was standardized. Towing was performed by the Tractor High-Speed 38-ton M6, or by various redundant tanks provided with towing attachments. The design was approved and standardized in May 1943, though production began in advance of standardization.

The M1 howitzer was a vast improvement on its predecessor in every way. It was longer and had

Below: The experimental model of the 240mm T1 with the carriage that had the front end arranged for towing as a semi-trailer.

a better performance, and the breech mechanism was a drop block interrupted screw. The carriage was a split trail with a cradle into which, the gun and its ring cradle and recoil gear could be dropped and secured by four massive bolts. Before emplacement, a pit was excavated into which the four recoil spades fitted, half-way along the trail legs, and into which the breech recoiled at high elevations. To facilitate loading, since this great pit was immediately behind the breech, a curved rail ran between the trail legs and supported the rear end of a 'spanning tray', the front end of which rested in the open breech. Shell and charge were then hand-rammed across this tray.

Whenever possible the howitzer was accompanied by a 20-ton Loraine Crane M2, which could dig the gunpit by means of a clamshell bucket attachment and then lift the mounting and gun into place and assemble them. In this way, the howitzer could be brought into action in about two hours. In the absence of a crane, it was necessary to dig the pit by hand; the equipment could then be emplaced by using the winches on the M6 tractors. The carriage was dragged from its wagon and across the pit; the trail legs were partly opened until they formed parallel ramps, up which the cannon transport wagon was winched and chained in place so that the barrel could be winched off the wagon and into the carriage cradle. The cannon wagon was then removed and the trail legs were fully opened. Emplacement in this fashion could take anything from eight hours upwards, depending on how quickly the pit could be dug, and how easily the units could be winched about. It was damned hard work.

The 240mm was an excellent weapon and saw extensive use, particularly in the Italian campaign. It remained in both British and US service after the war until the late 1950s, being finally retired when the ammunition stock which had been built up during the war was exhausted.

Variants

Carriage M1E2 An M1 carriage redesigned in September 1945 in order to speed up the time into action when using the winch. Doubtful if any were made.

Matériel T16 and T17. A collective term to cover the development of Cannon (T16) and Carriage (T17) transport wagons, with free-rolling tracked suspension for use on difficult terrain. The T16 used two complete medium tank suspensions, one at each end. The T17 used two, lighter, tracked bogie units. The T16E1 and T17E1 were similar, but incorporated modifications to facilitate assembly by winch. One set of the E1 equipment was issued to a Field Artillery Batallion for service in the Pacific early in 1945, but I have been unable to find reports on its serviceability or otherwise.

Gun 240mm T1, on Carriage T2

Development of this equipment was initiated in October 1944 with the idea of providing a mobile super-heavy gun with a maximum range of 45,000 yards. It was proposed that the split trail carriage should have tracked suspension, and that for short moves, the barrel would be pulled back in its cradle and locked to the trails. For longer moves, the barrel and top carriage would be removed and carried between two transport wagons, while the bottom carriage would be towed along on its tracks. The gun was to be 70 calibres long, and it was suggested that two tractors, each supporting one end of the gun, might be a better and more manoeuvrable idea.

At the same time, plans for a partner piece, a 280mm howitzer on the same carriage, were drawn up, but after the war, the whole idea was re-examined and eventually abandoned. Instead, the 280mm M65 'Atomic Cannon' was developed.

Howitzer Motor Carriage T92

This was a self-propelled equipment, development of which began in January 1944. The chassis used the basic components of the Heavy Tank T26E3, with a special top carriage assembly to take the normal howitzer tube and recoil system. Performance was the same as that of the towed weapon, though the maximum elevation was slightly less. The design was

approved and classified as 'Limited Procurement' in March 1945, 115 being authorized. In the following month, the order was increased to 144, but only five equipments were built before the war ended, and the contracts were immediately terminated.

Data Howitzer M1, on Carriage M1
Weight of gun and breech mechanism: 25,261lb.

Total length: 331.0in.
Rifling: 68 grooves, uniform RH 1/25.
Breech mechanism: Interrupted screw, drop block, percussion fired.
Elevation: $+15°$ to $+65°$.
Traverse: $22\frac{1}{2}°$ right and left.
Recoil system: Hydropneumatic, constant, 56in.
Weight in action: 64,700lb.

Top: Carriage Transport Wagon M3 with the Carriage M1 loaded. **Middle:** 240mm howitzer M1 in firing position. **Bottom:** Howitzer Motor Carriage T92, on display in 1945.

Opposite page: The barrel of the T1 howitzer on its semi-trailed transport chassis, which was of similar pattern to the proposed method of moving the carriage.

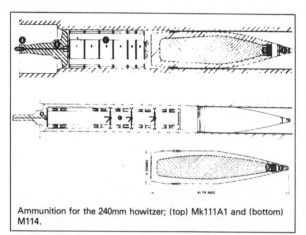

Performance firing standard 360lb HE Shell.
Muzzle velocity: 2,300ft/sec.
Maximum range: 25,225 yards.

Ammunition separate loading, bag charge.
Propelling Charge. This was a four-unit charge consisting of a base section and three increments, a total weight of 78.75lb. The four charges gave from 1,500–2,300ft/sec and from 15,175–25,225 yards range.
Shell, HE, M114. Weighing 360lb, this was a streamlined shell with a more tapered nose than that of the MkIIIA1. It contained 54.05lb of TNT, and could be fitted with the PD M51 or MT M67 fuzes. Later issues had the 'Universal Cavity' which allowed fitting of the Proximity fuze T76E6.

Ammunition for the 240mm howitzer; (top) Mk111A1 and (bottom) M114.

 914mm Mortar 'Little David'

Development of this remarkable weapon began in March 1944, and it gives every appearance of being the exception that proves the rule that outlandish ideas got short shrift on the Allied side; few weapons were as outlandish as this one.

The idea came from the 'Bomb Testing Device T1'. In order to test aircraft bombs, and in particular, armour- or concrete-piercing bombs, it is necessary to deliver them on to a suitable target, but to do this by dropping them from an aircraft at an operational altitude, which might be 20,000 feet or more, is impracticable, since even the legendary Norden bombsight could not guarantee a fair hit on the desired spot. So the practice grew up of firing them at the target from howitzers, calculating a charge and elevation which would bring the bomb on to the target at the correct velocity and attitude – a range of two or three hundred yards was enough, and at this sort of range it was difficult to miss. Various elderly weapons were pressed into service for this job, both Britain and the US employing, for example, redundant 9.2in and 12in howitzers. But as bombs grew bigger it became necessary to develop bigger howitzers for the task, and so the US engineers developed a 36in calibre mortar.

In March 1944, somebody had the idea of converting this proof-ground tool into a service weapon, the excuse being the probable strength and extent of Japanese fortifications in Japan and the closer islands. A mounting was developed and a suitable projectile was designed; in October 1944, firing tests began at Aberdeen Proving Ground. In April 1945, the equipment was considered complete and discussions began abouts its possible employment. Operation 'Olympic', the invasion of Japan, was scheduled for November 1945, and the Coast Artillery Board agreed to give the weapon its service acceptance test in September so that it could be shipped to the Pacific theatre in good time. But

the Army Ground Forces, concerned about the poor accuracy figures shown in the firing test reports, recommended postponing the acceptance until the ballistics had been investigated and the accuracy possibly improved. While this was being discussed, the war came to an end and, in October 1945, further work was suspended for twelve months and the equipment was put into store at Aberdeen. At the end of the twelve months, the project was reviewed and then cancelled. 'Little David' is still at Aberdeen, part of the museum display.

The mortar was a rifled muzzle-loader with percussion firing and with the elevating arc attached to the breech end. For transportation, it was lifted from its mounting and towed behind an M26 Tank Transporter Tractor, the elevating arc being attached to the tractor and the muzzle riding on an eight-wheeled trolley.

The mounting was simply a steel box, 18ft long, 11ft wide and 10ft deep, sunk into a pit. Inside this box was the elevating gear, traversing gear, and six hydraulic jacks which were used for mounting and dismounting the barrel. The box was towed by another M26 Tractor, being fitted with wheels for travelling. On arrival on site, the pit was carved out by a bulldozer and the box was winched down a ramp. Its wheels were then removed and the excavated earth was pushed back and packed around the box walls as a support. The barrel was then towed across the top on a steel runway and lifted by the jacks from its trolley and lowered into place. The whole performance of assembly took about 12 hours. Loading was done by a special crane; the charge was inserted into the muzzle and rammed into the chamber. The shell was then presented to the muzzle and the pre-engraved driving band was engaged in the rifling. The shell was rammed into the bore for a few inches and the mortar was then elevated so that the loading was completed by

gravity as the shell slid down the bore to the chamber
– which took about 25 seconds. A percussion primer
was then inserted into the vent, and the mortar was
fired by lanyard.

Data

Weight of barrel and elevating arc: 40 tons.
Length of barrel with elevating arc: 336in.
Length of bore: 280.44in (7.79 cal).
Rifling: Uniform RH 1/30.
Elevation: $+45°$ to $+65°$.
Traverse: 13° right and left.
Recoil system: Concentric hydraulic buffer; no
 recuperator, the mortar barrel being pumped back
 into battery after each shot.
Weight in action: $81\frac{1}{2}$ tons.

Performance firing standard 3,700lb shell
Maximum range: 9,500 yards.

Ammunition separate loading, bag charge.
Little detailed information is available. The propelling charge weighed 352lb and was in two 136lb
portions and two 40lb portions. The shell was of
peculiar shape, with a hemispherical base and long
ballistic cap, the taper of which was angular rather
than the usual ogival shape. Its weight was 3,700lb
and it was filled with 1,600lb of Picratol explosive.

Right: 'Little David' in the firing position. **Below:** Barrel of the 914mm
mortar on the move, suspended behind a modified tank transporter
tractor. **Bottom:** 'Little David' today, on display at the Aberdeen Proving
Ground Museum. At the right of the photograph is the weapon's oddly-
shaped projectile.

Railway Artillery

So far as the Western Alliance was concerned, railway artillery played no significant part in the Second World War. The railway gun is, above all, the weapon of the continental power; it is a highly efficient means of moving massive fire-power capability at high speed from one country to another. It has a secondary use, which the British, French and Americans discovered. When warfare is at a standstill, heavy guns can be brought up behind the lines and later redeployed rapidly to another sector without clogging up the roads. But during the Second World War, neither of these applications were of use to Britain or America. Some British railway guns went to France in 1939, since it was generally assumed that we were about to take up where we had left off in 1918, but the helter-skelter back to Dunkirk in 1940 left them far behind. The small number of equipments remaining in England were used as anti-invasion defences in 1940–41, being positioned some distance from the coast so as to be able to command a stretch of coastline, or be readily available to rush to any threatened area. Once the danger had passed, there was little use for them and they were retired. In 1943, there was a movement to equip a railway-gun regiment for the assault on Germany, but Allied air superiority allowed the tactical airforce to perform the task which otherwise would have fallen to the guns, and the idea was abandoned.

The United States Army had discovered a third use for railway artillery, as a mobile coast artillery reserve. In 1917–18, the German Army had deployed a number of railway guns on the Belgian coast, and had fitted most of them to concrete bases which permitted all-round traverse. This caught the fancy of the Americans who were always conscious of their massive coastline and limited number of guns. They therefore spent the 1920s in perfecting techniques for using railway guns in coast-defence applications, anchoring them to prepared bases at selected points. The theory was that the bases could be cheaply and easily built during peacetime at almost every point on the coast worth attacking, and then, when war was declared, the guns could trundle out to central positions to await the onslaught. When an attack threatened, guns could be quickly sent to the area and settled in on the prepared bases, becoming instant coast artillery for as long as they were needed.

There was a great deal to be said for this idea, but, like so many other good ideas, it was hamstrung for want of money. Even those job-inventing agencies of the New Deal, the WPA and the CCC, never got around to making railway gun emplacements (though they did some excellent work in camouflaging some coast artillery permanent installations under the guise of 'forestry'). Even when the war arrived, many of the old schemes for deployment of railway guns were given second place, since there appeared to be more urgent demands on the available men and finance. In the end, few of the guns were put into their active service positions, and none of them saw action. Like their British equivalents, most of their action was performed in front of cameras, for the comfort of the Home Front.

Below: HMG 'Boche-Buster' in France, 1918. This mounting was used with the 18in howitzer. The gun shown here is the 14in, which was externally identical with the 18in howitzer. (See data page 172.)

9.2in Railway Gun

The 9.2in gun was first placed on a railway truck mounting during the First World War, and most of the early patterns were scrapped in the 1920s. A small number of the latest and best types were retained in service, but most of these appear to have been dismantled and put into store in the late 1920s. They were brought out and reassembled in 1940, in order to provide a mobile heavy reserve to defend the east and south coasts of England. Several were deployed in Kent, between Dover and Canterbury.

The rail-mounted guns were the Mk 10 series, basically the same as the coast defence guns, but fitted with trunnions, and the Mk 13, specially designed for railway mounting. The mountings were all relatively simple types of bogie flat wagon with the gun on a revolving pedestal which also carried a loading platform. Four outriggers could be positioned so as to brace the truck against the shock of firing, and a screw-jack mechanism lifted the bogie frames so as to relieve the travelling springs of any strain. The guns were mounted on a top carriage which was a modified 'Vavasseur' barbette carriage; the gun was trunnioned into two side plates which carried rollers on their bottom edges. These ran on two inclined planes which formed the top surface of the rotating mounting. This top carriage also carried two hydraulic buffer cylinders, the piston rods of which, were attached to the bottom ends of the inclined planes.

When the gun was fired, it recoiled, drawing the top carriage back up the inclined planes and pulling the cylinders away from the pistons. The combination of the uphill movement and the hydraulic resistance caused recoil to stop as the top carriage reached the top end of the sloping planes, and the whole assembly then slid back into the firing position under the action of gravity. This system had been superseded in coast mountings since it involved a large movement of the gun and was slow in action, but in a railway gun, where speed was less important, it had the great advantage of soaking up a very great deal of the firing shock, and transmitting less strain to the mounting.

Variants
Ordnance:
Mk 10RT: Mk 10 coast gun converted by shrinking on a trunnion hoop and fitting a counterweight.
Mk 10VRT: Mk 10V converted, as above.
Mk 10*RT: Mk 10* converted as above.
Mk 13: 35-calibre gun built so as to have a preponderance of weight at the breech end, and the trunnions set well back. This made the design more compact and allowed greater elevation without the breech striking the mounting during recoil.
Mk 13*: Wartime (1940) manufactured Mk 13 with slight differences in order to speed up production. Probably very few made.
Mk 13A: Similar to Mk 13*, but used a loose liner; slightly heavier. Doubtful if any were made.

Data Gun Mk 10, on Mounting Mk 3, on Truck Mk 2
Weight of gun and breech mechanism· 64,412lb.
Total length: 442.35in.
Length of bore: 429.33in (46.6 cal).
Rifling: 46 grooves, uniform RH 1/30.
Breech mechanism: Interrupted screw, percussion or electric fired.
Elevation: 0° to +30°.
Traverse: 360°.
Recoil mechanism: Vavasseur, hydraulic buffer with gravity return. 34in stroke.
Weight in action: 202,944lb.

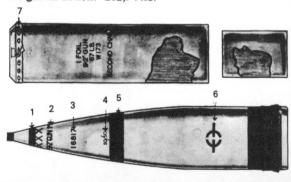

Data Gun Mk 13, on Mounting Mk 4, on Truck Mk 2.

Weight of gun and breech mechanism: 54,264lb
Total length: 335.025in.
Length of bore: 322.0in (35 cal).
Rifling: 46 grooves, uniform RH 1/30.
Breech mechanism: Interrupted screw, percussion fired.
Elevation: 0° to +40°.
Traverse: 360°.
Recoil mechanism: Vavasseur, hydraulic buffer with gravity return. 34in stroke.

Weight in action: 194,824lb.

Performance firing standard 380lb shell
Gun Mk 10, on Mounting Mk 3, on Truck Mk 2:
Muzzle velocity: 2,700ft/sec.
Maximum range: 21,000 yards.
Gun Mk 13, on Mounting Mk 4, on Truck Mk 2:
Muzzle velocity: 2,100ft/sec.
Maximum range: 22,600 yards.

Ammunition
As for coast defence Mk 10 gun (See p 198).

Opposite page, above: Ammunition for the 9.2in railway gun.
1. Absence of smoke producer;
2. Equipment and mark of shell (i.e. 9.2in gun XVIII C); 3. Design number of method of filling; 4. Type of Amatol; 5. Plain green band—Amatol; 6. Centre of gravity mark (in three places); 7. Igniter cover.
Below: 9.2in Gun Mk 13 on Mounting, Railway Truck, Mk 4 on Truck, Railway Mk 2, leaving the Elswick Ordnance Company works.

This page, right: A Mk 13 being fired in Britain in 1940; and (below) in action in France in 1918, showing the method of handing-up the ammunition. This photograph also reveals the British soldier's touching faith in the camouflage net as a 'cloak of invisibility', irrespective of what the surrounding countryside may look like.

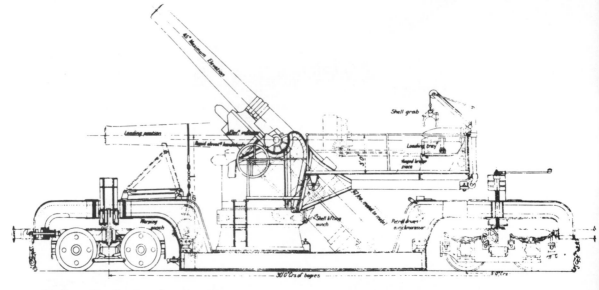

12in Railway Howitzer

The 12in Railway Howitzer was another First World War innovation, three different models having been produced. Two, the Mks 3 and 5, survived the war, were stored, and reappeared in 1939. A Mk 6 was then approved for manufacture as a replacement, but it is doubtful if any were made.

The Mk 3 howitzer was 17.3 calibres long, and was carried on a drop-bed (or well) wagon which had two four-wheel bogies. To put the equipment into action, screw jacks lowered the wagon body until side girders of the dropped section rested on the ends of the track sleepers, thus relieving the bogies of all weight and firing shock. The mounting was then anchored by steel cables and pickets to prevent it sliding when fired. While this was a simple system, it gave no sideways bracing and, therefore, the howitzer could be fired only within 20° of the track centre-line, which meant that a curved track was necessary to give a reasonable zone of fire.

In action, this firing restriction was a nuisance and the Army asked the Elswick Ordnance Works to think up a new design which could be fired at any angle to the track. This appeared in July 1917 as the Mk 5 howitzer. The howitzer was ballistically the same as the Mk 3, but externally altered so as to fit a new design of recoil system and cradle. The mounting was higher and incorporated a loading platform. Four removable girder outriggers were provided for stabilizing the mounting when firing across the track, though this could also be done by the earlier arrangement of steel cables laid to ground anchors.

A number of these equipments went to France in 1939 and were left there in 1940. They were assimilated into the German Vocabulary as the 'Haubitze Eisenbahn 633(e)' and '634(e)', but there is no record of them ever having been used by the German Army. Those which remained in England were, like other railway equipments, deployed in possible invasion areas as mobile reserves and beach bombardment batteries. They were declared obsolete in August 1945.

Variants

Ordnance:

Mk 3: Elswick Ordnance Co. design. Continuous-motion breech mechanism. Breech end built up to counterbalance the barrel weight and allow trunnions to be set well back.

Mk 3A: Approved 1940 as a replacement for Mk 3. Similar design, but with a loose liner. Doubtful if any were built.

Mk 5: Elswick design, similar to Mk 3, but with less weight at the breech end.

Mk 5A: Approved 1940, as replacement for Mk 5. Loose liner.

Mk 6: Approved 1940, as replacement for Mk 3A. Simpler construction and lighter in weight.

Mountings:

Mk 2: Two-bogie rail truck with barbette mounting. Fired between 40° and 60° elevation only. All-round traverse, but only fired at angles between 20° right and left. Loading angle 3½°.

Mk 3: Same rail truck, but higher mounting with loading platform. Fired between 0° and 45°, reduced charge being used up to 20°. Loading angle 0°. Two-speed elevating gear.

Data

12in How Mk 3, on Mounting Mk 2, on Truck, Railway, Mk 2:
Weight of gun and breech mechanism: 25,221lb.
Total length: 225.3in.
Length of bore: 207.6in (17.3 cal).
Rifling: 60 grooves, uniform RH 1/15.
Breech mechanism: Interrupted screw, continuous motion, percussion fired.
Elevation: 0° to +65°. Loading angle 3°, minimum firing angle 40°.
Traverse: 360°, but only to be fired within 20° right and left of centre-line.
Recoil system: Hydropneumatic, constant 30in.
Weight in action: 136,080lb.

12in How Mk 5, on Mounting Mk 3, on Truck, Railway, Mk 3:
Weight of gun and breech mechanism: 23,646lb.
Total length: 225.3in.
Length of bore: 207.6in (17.3 cal).
Rifling: 60 grooves, uniform RH 1/20.
Breech mechanism: Interrupted screw, continuous motion, percussion fired.
Elevation: 0° to +45°. Minimum firing angle 20°.
Traverse: 120° right and left.
Recoil system: Hydropneumatic, constant 60in.
Weight in action: 170,143lb.

Performance firing standard 750lb HE shell
Muzzle velocity: 1,468ft/sec.
Maximum range: 14,350 yards.

Ammunition
As for 12in Road Howitzers (See p 144).

Opposite page, top left: A Mk 3 howitzer being inspected by the Maharajah of Patiala in France, 1918. **Top right:** 12in Mk 3 railway howitzer in France, 1939. **Middle:** 12in Mk 5 howitzer at Elswick works, 1918. **Bottom:** Handbook diagram of the 12in Mk 5 howitzer.

13.5in Railway Gun

The 13.5in railway gun was a wartime extemporization which sprang from the marriage of an obsolete mounting with an obsolescent gun, dreamed up as an emergency measure in the dark days of 1940.

At that time, the army's heaviest weapon was the 18in howitzer; below that, came the 12in and 9.2in howitzers, and the 9.2in railway gun. By the end of the First World War, there had been 12in and 14in railway guns, but these had been scrapped after the war, and so there was no long-range heavy gun in existence.

In June 1940, the Admiralty had begun the installation of two 14in guns at Dover (See p 200). Not to be outdone, the War Office began searching round to see what might be found in odd corners, and called on Lieutenant-Colonel S. M. Cleeve, RA, who had commanded a battery of railway artillery in France in 1918, and who was one of the few remaining railway-gun experts. Colonel Cleeve knew that a number of railway mountings designed for the 14in gun/18in howitzer were still in existence. He also discovered some 13.5in guns in the Ordnance Depot at Ruddington, near Nottingham; these guns had been removed from the old *Iron Duke* class battleships. The dimensions of the 13.5in gun were sufficiently close to those of the obsolete 14in to allow them to be fitted into the 14in mountings. Work went ahead, and the first 13.5in gun was delivered on 20 September 1940. Another two followed, and all three had been completed by May 1941.

Guns, though, are not enough; it is necessary to provide men to operate them, and this the War Office were unable to do. However, the Royal Marines, who were already operating the two 14in guns in the Dover area, had men to spare, and took over the three 13.5in guns. The three equipments were all given names which, in fact, were the names that had originally graced the mountings when they were used with the 14in guns in France in 1917–18. All were sited in the Dover area, the locations being as follows:
His Majesty's Gun 'Scene Shifter'; Lydden, on the Dover–Canterbury railway line; HMG 'Gladiator' at Martin Mill on the Dover–Deal line; HMG 'Piecemaker' at Guston Tunnel, also on the Dover–Deal line.

Their objectives were twofold; in these positions they could cover most of the possible landing areas in Kent, while with a 1,250lb shell and a supercharge, they could just reach across the Channel and bombard German positions in the Calais area. In fact, because of their limited traverse and the need to push them along the railway until a convenient curve allowed them to bear in the right direction, they were not used very often. But they were certainly at war; on 10 December 1940, a German 28cm shell fell within feet of 'Piecemaker', damaging one bogie and mortally wounding a Marine gunner.

In November 1943, the Royal Marines decided that they had better things to do than look after three railway guns, and they handed them over to the army. The guns were removed from the Dover area and were used to form a 'Super Heavy Railway Regiment RA' which went into training for the coming invasion of Europe. In the end, though, their services were not required. Overwhelming Allied air superiority allowed tactical aircraft to do all the jobs the railway guns might have been called upon to perform, and by the summer of 1944, there was a general absence of intact railway bridges in France. The guns were declared obsolete in 1945 and were subsequently scrapped.

The 13.5in Mk 5 gun was a wire-wound gun which had entered service in 1912. The mounting was a simple box with trunnion mounts on the side girders which supported the cradle; the gun was locked into this by means of thrust rings. The whole of the mounting structure was carried on two bogie sets; two four-axle bogies at the front end, and one four- and one three-axle bogie at the rear. In order to allow some degree of precision in pointing the gun, the front end of the mounting could be moved sideways across the top of the bogie bolster, sufficient to allow 2° of training on either side of centre. The movement was achieved by 'warping winches', set at the trackside, from which cables ran to the mounting so that by pulling on one winch and paying out on the other, the mounting was dragged across.

It might as well be pointed out that, on firing, the mounting did not move. Stories of it recoiling up the track and into a convenient tunnel to hide are not true; nor, unfortunately, is the story that the gun at Martin Mill used to recoil all the way to Dover and bring up the rations and post on the run-out.

Data Gun Mk 5, on Mounting, Railway, 14in Mk 1
Weight of gun and breech mechanism: 170,520lb.
Total length: 625.90in.
Length of bore: 607.50in (45 cal).
Rifling: 68 grooves, uniform RH 1/30.
Breech mechanism: Interrupted screw, electric or percussion fired.
Elevation: 0° to +40°.
Traverse: 2° right and left.
Recoil system: Hydropneumatic, constant 34in.
Weight in action: 539,224lb (240 tons).

Performance firing standard 1,250lb shell
Muzzle velocity: 2,550ft/sec.
Maximum range: 40,000 yards.

Ammunition separate loading, bag charge
Propelling Charge. A bagged charge of 293lb of Cordite, divided into six sections for convenience in handling.
Shell, HE, Mk 0. A base fuzed AP shell of standard naval pattern, carrying a filling of Lyddite or Shellite and a Base Fuze No. 501.

Below: 13.5in gun manned by Royal Marines, firing from the Dover area in March, 1943.

18in Railway Howitzer

This was first mooted in 1917 to go as a 'partner piece' to the 14in gun on the same mounting. Since there was no existing 18in weapon suitable (the only one in existence being an elderly experimental gun), there was no way of 'appropriating' an existing barrel, as had been done for every other railway gun design, and the 18in had to be designed from scratch. It was designed to have the same exterior contours and dimensions as the 14in gun so as to be immediately interchangeable in the mounting without adaptors; this was possible in spite of the four-inch difference in calibre, because howitzers are less highly stressed than guns and so the barrel walls could be thinner. The design was completed in 1918 and two barrels were made, but they were not ready until after the war; they were mounted and proved in turn, after which, they were removed to store.

In 1926, the 14in guns were declared obsolete and scrapped, but the mountings were retained and one 18in barrel was mounted on HMG 'Boche-Buster'. It was taken to Salisbury Plain and fired twice during the inter-war years, once from Druid's Lodge, the end of the military railway which left the main line at Amesbury and curved away through Larkhill Camp, and once from Bulford Sidings. It was said, in those days, that the Battery Commander was the only man in the Gunners who carried a Range Table in one pocket and a copy of Bradshaw's *Railway Guide* in the other.

In 1940, Boche-Buster was sent down to the Dover area to become part of the invasion defences, and was stationed at Bekesbourne, on the Dover–Canterbury line. It was frequently photographed in aggressive poses, and was billed as a fearsome cross-Channel monster, but the truth of the matter was that, being a howitzer, it had barely enough range to command the Kent coast, and had no hope of putting a shell even half-way across the Channel. It never fired in anger, and it is doubtful if it fired very much in training either. In 1943, it found its way back to Salisbury Plain to fire trials of a new anti-concrete shell, and this seems to be the last time it ever did fire. Late in 1943, it was sent to join the 13.5in guns in the Super-Heavy Railway Regiment, but the idea of using this in the invasion was dropped, and the regiment was disbanded. The 18in howitzer was declared obsolete in April 1947 and was subsequently scrapped.

Two common beliefs might as well be cleared up here. First, there was never an 18in railway *gun*, of any description. In 1918, a gun was designed with a view to railway mounting, but when the war ended, the idea was dropped; the designs were passed to the Royal Navy and became the starting-point for a Naval 18in which eventually saw service.

Second, it has been said in the past (by me among others) that the 18in howitzer still exists, on a railway proof mounting, in the Proof and Experimental

Establishment at Shoeburyness. I have since had the opportunity to examine this equipment closely and compare it with the data on the 18in howitzer, and it definitely is not the same weapon. It is shorter, has trunnions, and has an old type of three-motion breech. According to an unconfirmed report, there was an 18in experimental gun mounted at Landguard Fort, Harwich, in 1909; as yet, no documentary proof of this has been found, but if true, it seems likely that this is the Shoeburyness weapon.

The 18in howitzer Mk 1 was a straight-forward pattern of wire-wound gun, with a continuous-motion breech and no unusual features other than its size. The mounting was that designed for the 14in gun and is more fully described in the section covering the 13.5in gun (See p 170).

Data

Weight of gun and breech mechanism: 191,968lb (85 tons).
Total length: 648.4in.
Length of bore: 624.6in (35 cal).
Rifling: 72 grooves, uniform RH 1/20.
Breech mechanism: Interrupted screw, continuous motion, electric and percussion fired.
Elevation: 0° to +40°
Traverse: 2° right and left.
Recoil system: Hydropneumatic, constant 34in.
Weight in action: 560,935lb (250 tons).

Performance firing standard 2,500lb HE shell
Muzzle velocity: 1,880ft/sec.
Maximum range: 22,300 yards.

Ammunition separate loading, bag charge.
Propelling Charge. The charge was divided so as to provide a seven-charge option in two portions, the Long Range and the Short Range. The Short Range Portion comprised a Charge 1 unit, plus incremental sections to produce Charges 2, 3 and 4, giving a total weight of 182lb of Cordite. The Long Range Portion had a base unit acting as Charge 5, plus two increments to give Charges 6 and 7, and the total weight was 282lb of Cordite.
Shell, HE, Mk 2D. A Streamlined nose-fuzed shell weighing 2,500lb, filled with either TNT or Amatol, and fitted with the Percussion Fuze No. 231. Overall length was 66.985in.
Shell, CP, BC, S/L Mk 1D. A common pointed shell with a ballistic cap and streamlined base. It was filled with Shellite and carried the Base Percussion Fuze No. 270. Weight 2,500lb.
Shell, Anti-Concrete, S/L Mk 1D. Approved in 1944, this was an advanced design which had a concave head under a ballistic cap, this shape of head being considered the best way of combatting possible ricochets from hard surfaces. It was filled with Shellite and fuzed with the Base Percussion Fuze No.

270. Total weight 2,731lb. It is doubtful if any other than those required for testing were ever made, since the requirement lapsed when the projected invasion siege-train idea was abandoned. An amusing point is that in spite of being intended for punching through reinforced concrete and weighing rather more than a ton, these shells were stencilled "FRAGILE" on their sides in large letters, because they resembled the CPBC shell externally, but the ballistic cap was one-third the length of the shell and largely unsupported, and therefore liable to damage if roughly handled in transit.

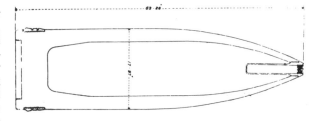

Above: The high-explosive shell for the 18in howitzer.

Left: 18in howitzer on railway mounting; the metal frames beneath the muzzle are for 'bulking out' the tarpaulin cover so as to disguise the equipment from aerial view when on the move. **Below:** The 18in howitzer firing from its battle position near Dover, 1941.

Left: 8in M1888 gun prepared for firing across the track.

Below, left: Diagram from the Railway Artillery Operating Manual showing basic dimensions of the M1888 gun. **Right:** Dimension diagram of the Mk VI Mod3A2 gun.

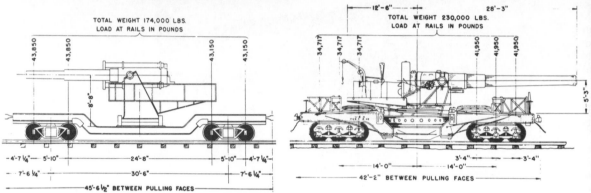

TOTAL WEIGHT 174,000 LBS.
LOAD AT RAILS IN POUNDS

43,850 · 43,850 · 43,150 · 43,150

8'-8"

-4'-7¼"· 5'-10"· 24'-8" · 5'-10"· 4'-7¼"-

-7'-6¼"· 30'-6" · 7'-6¼"-

45'-6½" BETWEEN PULLING FACES

12'-6" · 28'-3"

TOTAL WEIGHT 230,000 LBS.
LOAD AT RAILS IN POUNDS

34,717 · 34,717 · 34,717 · 41,950 · 41,950 · 41,950

5'-3"

-14'-0" · 3'-4"· 3'-4"-
14'-0" ·

42'-2" BETWEEN PULLING FACES

Above: 8in Gun Mk VI Mod3A2 on Mount M1A1; and (left) in firing position.

8in Railway Gun

Gun 8in M1888 on Mounting Barbette M1918 on Carriage Railway M1918

In 1917, the United States Army began the provision of railway guns for use by the AEF in France, and one of the first to be designed was the 8in, using the M1888 guns, numbers of which were available from coast defences and in reserve stocks. In addition, a number of Navy 8in guns were available, giving a total of 96 barrels. In order to have a reserve of barrels it was decided to build 47 equipments; the first was tested in May 1918, and by the end of the war, 24 had been completed. Eventually, 37 were built, the contracts then being terminated.

The guns were a curious mixture; Army M1888, M1888MI and M1888MII and Navy Mks I, II, III and IV. The Army guns were 32 calibres long and differed only in details of their construction; the Navy guns were from 30 calibres to 45 calibres long and had four different types of breech mechanism. The mountings were relatively simple, rotating barbettes on drop-bed flatcars on two Pennsylvania Railroad 70-ton four-wheel trucks. The cars were fitted with hand and air brakes and with outriggers and floats which extended in four directions to stabilize the car when firing. Provision was made in the design for adapting the car to either standard (4ft 8½in) or narrow-gauge track. The light railways behind the lines in France were all of 60cm gauge, and each gun car was provided with a spare set of 60cm trucks. By jacking up the car, the standard-gauge trucks could be run out and the narrow-gauge set run into place.

It might be noted that although all the official texts and drawings show this equipment on four-wheel trucks, photographs have been seen of two guns in Hawaii mounted on six-wheel trucks. It is possible that, for some reason, the guns were mounted on the cars usually provided for the 12in mortar, but no explanation has yet been discovered for this anomaly.

Another unusual feature of this equipment was the fitting of European-style spring buffers; originally, when prepared for service in France, they were given European chain-couplings and buffers. When the war ended and they were returned to the USA, the chain-couplers were replaced by the standard American MCB-Gould coupler, but the buffers were left in place.

During the 1920s, the Navy guns were withdrawn and scrapped, leaving only the M1888 models in service, and some of these were dismantled, the guns and barbette mountings being anchored in concrete to become fixed coast defences once again. One such battery was at Black Point, east of Diamond Head on Oahu Island, TH.

In 1941–42, most of the M1888 were replaced by newer models, but a number were deployed in readiness for attack. In Hawaii, where a complete regiment was stationed, all the guns were removed from their cars and put into fixed emplacements at various points on the island of Oahu. Four guns were positioned at Fort Story, Virginia, on a railway track parallel with the beach; and several were sent to Canada to form part of the defences of Vancouver until such time as permanent installations of British 6in and 9.2in guns could be made. Later in 1941, a number were earmarked for the Philippines, intended for permanent emplacement; so far as can be determined, only one gun was delivered, and this was installed in Fort Mills, on Corregidor Island, but its ancillary fire-control equipment never reached Corregidor, and the gun was never used during the siege.

Variant

Mounting M1918M1; similar to the M1918, but with a slightly larger cradle so as to accommodate the Navy guns.

Data

Weight of gun and breech mechanism: 32,218lb.
Total length: 278.5in.
Length of bore: 256.0in (32 cal).
Rifling: 48 grooves, increasing RH 1/50 to 1/25.
Breech mechanism: Rotating Tray M1888; electric and friction fired.
Elevation: 0° to +42°.
Traverse: 360°.
Recoil system: Hydro-spring, constant 488in.
Weight in action: 157,700lb.

Performance firing standard 260lb AP shell
Muzzle velocity: 2,600ft/sec.
Maximum range: 23,900 yards.

Gun 8in Mark VI Mod3A2, on Mount, Railway M1A1

In 1918, the AEF asked for a more powerful 8in gun, and plans were prepared for a new design of 50 calibre gun and a suitable mounting. At the end of the war, the idea was dropped, but in 1923, after the Washington Conference on Naval Limitation, the US Navy declared a number of 8in 45-calibre guns surplus to their requirements. The army, recalling the 50-calibre idea, took the guns and began developing a new mounting. In order to economize, the existing 12in Mortar railway mount was taken as the starting-point and, suitably modified, became the 8in Mounting M1925E. A specimen was built and tested and more modification followed, but in 1933, the usual shortage of funds led to the project being cancelled. It was revived by the Coast Artillery Board in 1938, and standardized as the Mounting M1 in 1939; only one was ever made and it was retained at Aberdeen Proving Ground for test firing. Slight manufacturing changes were made in the design, changing it to the M1A1 pattern, and all production was to this design, standardized in June 1941.

The gun was of built-up construction, of nickel steel, and the breech ring incorporated a heavy counterweight which allowed the trunnions to be set well back and thus allow the gun to reach its full elevation without danger of the breech striking the mounting on recoil, and without the added complication of balancing gear. The breech block, of Naval design, was hinged to drop open.

The mounting was a top carriage rotating on a base ring set on a drop-body flat car riding on two six-wheel Pullman trucks. A ring cradle supported the gun, and a loading platform extended behind the breech and carried a loading table. A folding 'spanning tray' could be extended from this table to enter the breech opening, and the shell was rammed from the loading table, across the spanning tray and into the gun; a downward slope of 5° of the table and tray gave gravity assistance to the men on the rammer. Two derricks for lifting ammunition were provided at the rear corners of the platform. Eight tubular steel outriggers supported the mount and car during firing, and four hydraulic jacks allowed the car to be lifted so that eight firing supports could be interposed between the track bed and the body of the car.

Twenty-nine of these equipments were built in 1941/2. A number were emplaced on the Pacific coast, notably in the Puget Sound area and at Santa Monica, California. Not all were issued, some remaining in store until after the war. So far as is known, the only remaining specimen is in a public park in Tampa, Florida, devoid of its railway car.

Data
Weight of gun and breech mechanism: 42,000lb.
Total length: 369.0in.
Length of bore: 360.0in (45 cal).

Rifling: 64 grooves, uniform RH 1/25.
Breech mechanism: Interrupted screw, drop block, electric and percussion fired.
Elevation: $-5°\ +45°$.
Traverse: 360°.
Recoil mechanism: Hydropneumatic, constant, 27in.
Weight in action: 230,000lb.

Performance
Firing standard 240lb HE shell:
Muzzle velocity: 2,840ft/sec.
Maximum range: 35,300 yards.
Firing 260lb piercing shell:
Muzzle velocity: 2,750ft/sec.
Maximum range: 32,980 yards.

Ammunition
Propelling Charge. Each gun had a distinctive propelling charge. That for the M1888 gun was in two bags, a total weight of 85.6lb of NH powder, while that for the Mk VI gun was a base-and-increment type giving a normal charge of 74.25lb and a Super charge of 108lb. The M1888 was of the 'stacked' type, in which the individual grains of propellant were carefully stacked parallel to the length of the bag, and the bag tightly laced down the sides so as to give it rigidity for ease in handling. The Mk VI charge was loosely poured into the bag, though the bag was also side-laced to give some degree of rigidity.

Projectile, AP, Mk XX. This was a Naval design of piercing shell with penetrative and ballistic caps. It carried a bursting charge of 3.4lb of Explosive D, and a Base Fuze Mk X. It could be fired from either gun. Weight filled and fuzed, 260lb.

Shell, HE, Mk 1. This was a standard type of nose-fuzed shell carrying a charge of 29.6lb of TNT and fitted with the PD Fuze M46 (superquick) or M47 (delay).

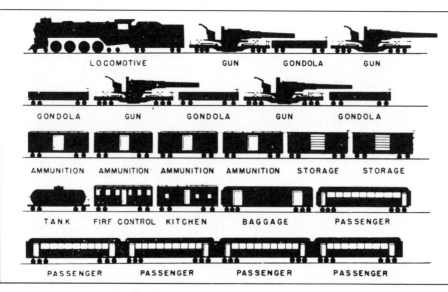

Left: Train composition for a battery of 8in Mk VI guns. Note the gondola cars, which allowed for the overhang of the gun barrels on curved track.

LOCOMOTIVE   GUN   GONDOLA   GUN

GONDOLA   GUN   GONDOLA   GUN   GONDOLA

AMMUNITION   AMMUNITION   AMMUNITION   AMMUNITION   STORAGE   STORAGE

TANK   FIRE CONTROL   KITCHEN   BAGGAGE   PASSENGER

PASSENGER   PASSENGER   PASSENGER   PASSENGER

12in Railway Gun

During the First World War, the US Army arranged for the production of a number of 10in and 12in railway guns on two patterns of mounting, both of French origin, the Schneider sliding mounting and the Creusot 'Batignolles' mount. A number of both calibres of gun were assembled to the sliding mounts and were used during the war. They were retained as 'siege artillery' for some years, but were scrapped in the late 1920s, since they were of little use as coast-defence guns, which was the direction towards which railway artillery was tending in those days. Of the Batignolles type, the eighteen proposed 10in guns were never built, but twelve 12in guns were completed by the Marion Steam Shovel Company of Marion, Ohio between 1919 and 1921. By 1941, they had been sentenced 'Limited Standard', and they were declared obsolete before the war ended. Apart from No 9, which was held in the Dahlgren Navy Yard for experimental firings, it is doubtful if any of them were ever brought out of reserve.

The gun can be dismissed fairly rapidly; it was the M1895 or M1895M1 coast-defence gun, described on p 216. Originally designed by the French, the Batignolles mounting consisted of a steel box structure carried on two bogie sets in the usual manner. The gun was carried in a ring cradle, with two recoil cylinders below and one recuperator cylinder above the cradle. To place the gun in action, the location was first selected and then the track was torn up and a prefabricated ground platform of steel cross- and side-girders was laid. Two such platforms were carried on special cars with each gun, so that, if necessary, both could be laid along a curved track. The gun could be shifted between them, in order to cover a greater arc of fire. When the platforms were completed, the track was relaid across them, and the gun was shunted into position. Wedges were then driven between the side girders of the ground platform and the main box-section of the gun mount, in order to take the weight from the suspension and wheels, and the mounting was then clamped securely to the platform.

The gun and cradle were carried in a top carriage which was front-pivoted and allowed a traverse of 5° each side of the centre line. This, together with the curved track and two ground platforms, was satisfactory in siege work, but for coast-defence operations, a special ground platform was devised. This used the racer ring, traversing rollers and racer of the 10in Disappearing Carriage M1896, mounted on a prepared concrete base and carrying a set of steel cross-beams. The gun was positioned across this turntable base, the trucks were removed, and the mounting girders were bolted to the cross-beams, thus giving the mounting a 360° traverse capability. One such base unit was built and tested, but no platforms were actually constructed in potential service locations.

Data

Weight of gun and breech mechanism: 114,700lb.
Total length: 442.8in.
Length of bore: 420.0in (35 cal).
Rifling: 72 grooves, increasing RH 1/50 to 1/25.
Breech mechanism: Stockett M1895, electric and friction fired.
Elevation: $-5°$ $+38°$.
Traverse: 5° right and left.
Weight in action: 322,044lb.

Below: 12in M1895 gun on Mounting M1918, complete with gun detachment.

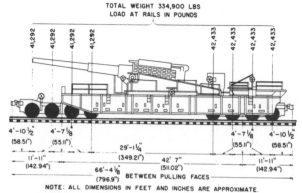

TOTAL WEIGHT 334,900 LBS
LOAD AT RAILS IN POUNDS

41,292 41,292 41,292 41,292   42,433 42,433 42,433 42,433

4'-10 ½"   4'-7 ⅛"   4'-7 ⅛"   4'-10 ½"
(58.51")   (55.11")   (55.11") (58.51")

29'-1 ¼"
(349.21")   42' 7"
ll'-ll"   (511.02")   ll'-ll"
(142.94")   (142.94")
66'-4 ⅛"
(796.9")   BETWEEN PULLING FACES

NOTE: ALL DIMENSIONS IN FEET AND INCHES ARE APPROXIMATE.

Performance
Firing standard AP shell weighing 975lb:
Muzzle velocity: 2,260ft/sec.
Maximum range: 30,100 yards.
Firing HE shell weighing 712lb:
Muzzle velocity: 2,600ft/sec.
Maximum range: 30,000 yards.

Ammunition separate loading, bagged charge.
The ammunition for this gun was as for the 12in
Coast Gun M1895, the two approved projectiles being
the AP Projectile Mk XVI and the HE Shell Mk X.
The Mk XVI was fired by a 268lb charge, and the
HE Shell by a 300lb charge. Details will be found on
p. 219.

Above: Dimension diagram of the 12in gun. **Below:** The 12in gun on the turntable mounting that was derived from spare parts of the 10in 'disappearing' gun mount.

12in Railway Howitzer

In 1917, the US Ordnance Department withdrew 150
12in M1890 mortars from Coast Defence emplacements and stores, and set about designing a railway
mounting so that they could be used as heavy
howitzers in France. A contract for 91 equipments
was given to the Morgan Engineering Co., of
Alliance, Ohio, and a special 1.7 million dollar
factory was built and stocked with machine tools
worth 1.8 million dollars. The factory was completed
in June 1918, and the first howitzer appeared on 22
August. By the time of the Armistice, the major
components for all 91 equipments had been completed, and by April 1919, 45 equipments had been
delivered. The balance of the 91 ordered were completed between 1919 and 1920.

During the inter-war years, most of the howitzers
were allocated to various defence areas of the United
States – Delaware Bay, Puget Sound, Chesapeake
Bay, etc., – and were generally placed in store at
some military post close to their service locations.
In some cases, sites were allotted and roadbed for
the necessary railway track was prepared, but the
rails were not actually laid. A small number were
retained in service, principally as instructional
weapons at the Coast Artillery School at Fort
Monroe.

In 1941, the stores were opened and the howitzers
were rolled out, dusted, and sent to their war positions, but apparently someone had second thoughts
and several of the prepared roadbeds were never

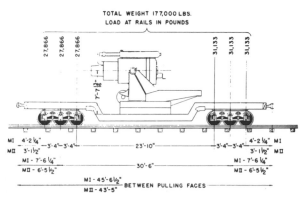

Left: Dimension diagram of the 12in howitzer carriage. **Right:** Rear view of the 12in howitzer, showing the overhead trolley used for moving ammunition from the magazine car on the left. **Below:** Front view of the 12in howitzer, with powder container on the loading table.

given their track and the howitzers never got to their allotted places. Some areas – e.g., New England – never received the number of howitzers that had been planned. In 1942, almost all were withdrawn again and sent for scrap; those few which escaped this purge were, in their turn scrapped in 1944.

The mortars were the standard seacoast M1890, a built-up 10-calibre weapon using a rotating tray breech. In seacoast service it had been fitted with a trunnion band to suit the mounting, but in the rail application, this was removed and a cast ring cradle carrying a hydropneumatic recoil system supported the mortar. This cradle was trunnioned into a top carriage which revolved on a roller race set in the floor of a railway car. The car was of the same type as that used for the 8in gun M1888, but in the 12in howitzer application, six-wheel bogies were standard. Like the 8in, the bogies could be removed very easily and replaced with narrow-gauge bogies.

Data
Weight of gun and breech mechanism: 29,000lb.
Total length: 145.25in.
Length of bore: 120.0in (10 cal).
Rifling: 72 grooves, increasing RH 1/40 to 1/20.
Breech mechanism: Interrupted screw, Rotating Tray M1888 pattern, electric and friction fired.
Elevation: $-5°$ $+65°$.
Traverse: 360°.
Recoil system: Hydropneumatic, constant 30in.
Weight in action: 176,800lb.

Performance firing standard 700lb HE shell
Muzzle velocity: 1,500ft/sec.
Maximum range: 15,290 yards.

Ammunition separate loading, bag charge.
Ammunition for this weapon was exactly the same as that for the 12in Mortar M1890 (See p 214).

14in Railway Gun

Development of this long-range gun began during the First World War, no less than four separate designs being pursued. The only one to achieve service status was a US Navy model, five of which went to France manned by US naval personnel. A total of eleven were built by the Baldwin Locomotive Works, and after the war, the last six were given to the US Army. One of the Naval equipments remains, preserved at the Dahlgren Naval Ordnance Depot, Virginia.

Since, as previously explained, the army's prime interest in railroad guns centred on their employment in coast defence, and since the naval designs were not suited to this, the six equipments were dismantled and used to build experimental weapons of various types. After tests and trials with these, the army set about developing a completely new equipment, and eventually produced the 14in Gun M1920.

The gun M1920 was a built-up 50-calibre weapon of conventional pattern. The Mounting M1920 was a girder structure carried on two two-bogie sets; the front set consisted of two four-axle bogies, and the rear set of two three-axle bogies. Hinged to the body frame was a 'top carriage' which supported the cradle, recoil system and barrel. This unit could pivot about its rear end to allow a small amount of traverse, and it could also be raised and lowered by two screw-jacks at the front end. For travelling, in order to bring the overall dimensions of the equipment within the loading gauge and allow it to pass beneath bridges, the front end of the top carriage was lowered inside the car body frame until it rested on a bolster running across the body. Before firing, the top carriage was raised by the screw-jacks (the weight so lifted was about 140 tons) until the carriage was above the body sides, after which, a 'firing beam' was run under the front end of the top carriage by a rack and pinion mechanism, and the top carriage was then lowered until its weight rested on the beam. This activity raised the gun so that the trunnions were at a height which allowed the gun to be fired at maximum elevation and still allowed the breech, at full recoil, to clear the roadbed beneath. The total lift of the top carriage was 74in; the screw-jacks were normally power operated, but hand cranks were provided for emergency use. The diagrams will make this mechanism more clear.

Firing could be done from an épi (curved track), the car body being lowered on the bogie units until the side girders rested on I-beams laid parallel with the rails. Six outriggers were installed and the equipment could be ready to fire within an hour of its arrival.

For coast-defence use, a prepared emplacement had a steel baseplate unit set in concrete and a traversing track running around this base unit. The mounting was pushed along the track until it was over the baseplate, and was then lowered until a 'Lower Pintle Plate' beneath the body centre engaged with the prepared baseplate, and the two could be bolted together. The bogie sets were now disconnected and removed, and a traversing roller unit, beneath the car body and some 16ft from the lower pintle, was lowered so as to rest on the traversing track. By operating hand cranks, the two rollers on this unit were driven round and, by friction on the traversing track, could rotate the whole 282 tons around the ball-race built into the lower pintle plate. A complete 360° rotation took about three minutes, while the complete installation in this mode could be done in about 2½ hours from arrival on the site.

Four 14in M1920 were completed, there being some small differences between the first (M1) and

the other three (M2). The first one was dispatched across the USA to Fort MacArthur, San Pedro, California, in 1927, a journey which took three months and taught everybody concerned a great deal about the operating and malfunctions of railway guns when subjected to long-distance haulage. Many of the defects which delayed progress stemmed from the running gear, and most were corrected in the M2 pattern. The second gun also went to San Pedro, while the other two were shipped to Panama in 1928, and became part of the armament of Fort Grant at the Pacific Ocean end of the Panama Canal. The San Pedro guns were fired once or twice, once from an alternative position prepared at Camp Pendleton, between Los Angeles and San Diego, in 1932. The Panama guns also fired; on one occasion, being trundled across the Isthmus via the Panama Railroad to fire from locations near Fort Randolph at the Atlantic end.

During the war, all four guns remained in these locations. The San Pedro guns were cleverly camouflaged by erecting canvas shelters, built to resemble standard army barrack buildings, over them. Several genuine barracks were built alongside and stocked with soldiers, and concealment was perfect. When required to fire, the guns were exposed by allowing the 'barrack' to split along the roof ridge, the two halves falling sideways.

In 1944, consideration was given to removing the San Pedro guns and shipping them to Europe to provide a siege-train for the US Army during the invasion of Europe. As with the similar, British idea, it was abandoned as impracticable, and the guns remained in place until they were scrapped after the war.

Variants

M1920MI: The centre-line of the breech was canted 16° to fit the recoil mechanism.
M1920MII: The breech was vertical, and the recoil mechanism was modified to suit.

Data

Weight of gun and breech mechanism: 233,782lb.
Total length: 714in.
Length of bore: 700in (50 cal).
Rifling: 126 grooves, uniform RH 1/32.
Breech mechanism: Interrupted screw, drop block hand opening pneumatic closing, electric and percussion fired.
Elevation when fired off wheels: $-70°$ $+19°$.
Elevation on emplacement: $-7°$ $+50°$.
Traverse: $3\frac{1}{2}°$ right and left on mounting.
Recoil system: Hydropneumatic, constant 35in.
Weight in action, on wheels: 730,000lb.
Weight in action, on emplacement: 631,800lb.

Performance

Firing standard 1,208lb HE shell:
Muzzle velocity: 3,000ft/sec.
Maximum range: 48,220 yards.
Firing 1,560lb piercing shell:
Muzzle velocity: 2,650ft/sec.
Maximum range: 42,285 yards.

Ammunition separate loading, bag charge
Propelling Charge. Two charges were provided, one for the HE shell and one for the AP shell. The HE shell charge was 480lb of NH powder; the AP shell charge was also 480lb, but of a differently formulated and granulated powder. Both were sub-divided into six equal parts for convenience in handling.
Projectile, HE, Mk XI M2A1. As can be deduced from the nomenclature, this was a Navy shell, pointed and base-fuzed. The Fuze BD Mk V was used, and the shell was filled with Explosive D. Weight as fired 1,208lb.
Projectile, AP, Mk VI. A piercing shell with penetrative and ballistic caps, this had a small filling of Explosive D and was fitted with the Fuze BD Mk X. Weight as fired 1,560lb.

Opposite page: 14in Gun M1920 on ground emplacement at Fort Grant, Panama. **This page, right:** Two views of the 14in gun, showing (top) the firing position and (bottom) the travelling mode.

Coast Artillery

In examining coast artillery it becomes necessary to go back much farther into the past than with other classes of ordnance, back beyond the 1920s to before the First World War and even before the South African War, although we are dealing with weapons still emplaced for active service from 1939 to 1945.

The reason for this is quite simply that once a coast gun had been put in place, it tended to stay there as long as it was capable of defeating, or even severely damaging, an enemy warship, and the reason for *that* is, equally simply, that coast guns and their mountings were expensive, and what money was available during the inter-war years could be better spent on other fields of armament. Some guns were installed in the 1920s and 1930s, it is true, but they were an infinitely small proportion of all the coast guns in service, and many of the guns which fired against the Axis powers had fired their first proof shots long before 1914.

The Washington Naval Treaty of 1922 was a peculiar catalyst in coast-defence affairs. This agreement between the USA, Britain and Japan forbade any improvement of defences over a major area of the Pacific Ocean; this effectively prevented any modernization of the defences of the Philippine Islands or Hong Kong, though the delineated area excluded Singapore. At the same time, by restricting the building of large warships it made a number of heavy guns redundant for naval purposes in both the USA and Japan, and in both cases these guns were put to use in coast defences. Moreover, since it restricted the size of warships to 35,000 tons, it led Britain to rely entirely on the 9.2in gun except for areas of the Far East where larger warships might be encountered.

The prime British concern in coast defence, at this time, was the protection of the new naval base at Singapore, and plans were first put forward for its fortification in the early 1920s. But,

not for the first time, military efficiency was sacrificed to political expediency, and very little actual construction work was done. However, planning was carried out and revised several times, so that when work eventually began, it went ahead at good speed. The armament planning had begun in about 1925, with the selection of a 15in gun as the major weapon, and a twin-barrelled 6pdr as the close-in defence against torpedo-boats. At the same time, much work went into the less glamorous aspects of fire control and range-finding, communications and observation, so that a complete fortress system was on paper in 1932 when permission was finally given to begin work. By August 1934 the first 6in and 9.2in batteries were ready, and construction of the 15in emplacements was under way. In December of that year, Japan renounced the Naval Treaty, leaving the way open for the US to install more 16in guns in Hawaii, and for Britain to overhaul the defences of Hong Kong

6in Mk 24 gun firing, Renney Battery, Plymouth. (See data page 191.)

and institute fortification programmes at Kilindini, Trincomalee and Penang.

The events of 1940 saw considerable activity around the shores of Britain, guns being installed to cover almost every possible location capable of admitting a German landing, but few of these really qualify as coast artillery. The difference is significant; coast artillery was provided with range-finding and position-finding equipment which enabled them to engage enemy warships on the move and at considerable range. But the 'Emergency Batteries' and many of the beach batteries were simply concerned with direct shooting at vessels attempting to land troops and equipment, though eventually many of them were given rudimentary fire-control systems which extended their sphere of activity a little. Actual additions to the coast defences around Britain between 1939 and 1945 were largely concerned with placing better weapons in significant positions; thus, numbers of twin 6pdr equipments were placed in the Thames Estuary in order to protect coastal shipping from possible torpedo-boat raids, and the Straits of Dover were eventually covered by a massive collection of armament in the Dover area. But in other forts there was little change, since none was really needed; the pre-war gun strength was still sufficient to deal with any likely threat, and there was no need to spend time and money on reinforcement.

In the United States, the provision of coast-defence armament appears always to have been governed by elderly precedent. The first major review of American defences was that done by the 'Endicott Board' in 1885, and for years afterwards, all activity was based on the recommendations of that Board. To quote one American authority: 'In each Annual Report, the Chief of Engineers would make a statement of the total amount which had been appropriated, the number of guns which had been mounted, and the number of emplacements provided for. This was then compared with the figures of the Endicott Board and the difference stated as being the number of guns still to be mounted, the number of emplacements to be built, the amount of money still to be appropriated . . . ' (*Notes on Seacoast Fortifications & Construction.* Engineer School US Army, 1920). After this, in 1906, came the 'Taft Board', and the same system applied. To quote the same source again: 'The War Department, in submitting its annual report to Congress, stated each year that the Endicott Board Report, as modified by the Taft Board Report, recommended a certain number of guns of each caliber, that there had been emplaced or

provided so many guns of that character, and that therefore there remained so many to be emplaced and so many to be provided . . . '

This was all very well, and at least it meant that fortifications were being built and guns provided, even slowly, but it appears to have taken little account of strategic requirements in a changing world. Another millstone around the coast artillery's neck was the Ordnance Department, who had managed to work themselves into a position in which they were the sole arbiters of ordnance design and operation, the artillerymen being simply the labourers who fired the things and cleaned them afterwards. This stranglehold was not broken until the resignation of the autocratic Major-General William Crozier, Chief of Ordnance until 1918, and it was the reason for some designs of mounting lingering in US service long after they had been discredited and discarded in other parts of the world.

One particularly interesting facet of US coast defence was their adherence to the high-angle gun or, in their (correct) parlance, the coast mortar, as this weapon had been long obsolete in Britain, it deserves some further explanation.

American employment of coast mortars had begun in the 1880s under the aegis of General Abbott, then Chief of Engineers. He proposed using mortars in blocks of sixteen, mounted on turntables so that they could command a wide arc, and concealed in pits out of view of their targets. By firing all sixteen mortars simultaneously it would be possible to deluge a vessel with a rain of projectiles, any one of which would be capable of piercing the relatively thin deck armour. This policy was accepted and several hundred mortars were eventually emplaced in the USA and its dependencies. Although called mortars, they were actually short-barrelled 12in breech-loading guns, firing at angles greater than 45°. They were emplaced behind a high concrete or earth parapet, inside which were the magazines; traverses ran from these parapets to split the mortars up into groups of four.

Improvements in fire control over the years changed the layout to some extent. With more precise control and position-finding, it was no longer necessary to fire all the mortars at once, so that the pattern of sixteen falling shells was no longer needed. Each battery of four mortars could be fired in turn, each using slightly different data, and thus keeping the enemy ship under a constant fire. One large drawback to the system was that when four mortars fired in a pit at once, the blast was fearful; light fittings were damaged, doors fell off their hinges, and the gunners all walked about bow-legged for ten minutes afterwards. The answer was to withdraw the men from the pit and then fire electrically, a process which did little to improve the rate of fire. Another problem was the mêlée in the pit when four detachments raced in to load and re-lay, a manoeuvre which called for some precise drill to avoid confusion.

At the turn of the century, the US Coast Artillery was short of men, and got into the habit of manning only two mortars in a pit for practice; to the surprise of most people, this improved the rate of fire, since there were less men milling around and getting in each other's way. So after about 1912, it became standard to build two-mortar pits.

Many of the mortars were taken for railway mounting during the First World War and never returned. Others were scrapped when it was realized that they were outranged by the guns of many warships, and, in general, they were only retained where they commanded restricted waters into which a target *had* to sail in order to threaten the area protected by the mortars. Thus there were still a large number of mortar batteries in service in 1941. Those in the Philippines were used to good effect against the Japanese advance down the Bataan Peninsula, though their worth was somewhat nullified by the lack of point-fuzed high-explosive shell for anti-personnel use. Some mortar batteries retained an active status until the end of the war, though most were scrapped in 1943–44. A battery of M1890M1 mortars is preserved in the Fort DeSoto State Park, St Petersburg, Florida, and a number are rusting away in some of the abandoned forts in Manila Bay.

The other American speciality was the disappearing carriage, another equipment which had long been obsolete in British service. Fuller descriptions will be found farther on, but in general, the idea was to mount the gun at the top of a pivoted arm so that the muzzle poked over a parapet to fire. When the gun fired, the recoil drove it back and pivoted the arm so that the gun barrel was carried back and down below the parapet, there to be held while it was loaded under cover. When ready, it was released to swing up once again and fire. In the American designs, the rearward movement was controlled by a combination of counterweight and hydraulic buffer, the counterweight providing the impulse to carry the gun back up after loading.

The British Army abandoned the disappearing carriage just before the start of the First World War because they had developed barbette carriages which gave a faster rate of fire. The US Army were slow in developing modern barbette carriages and persisted in the design of disappearing carriages into the 1920s. In subsequent years, though they doubtless would have dearly loved to have got rid of them in exchange for modern barbette mountings, the money was not available, and the disappearing guns had to remain in service. The reluctance to develop more efficient barbette carriages in the 1900s seems peculiar until one remembers that the disappearing carriage in American service was to the design of one William Crozier; rumour has it that he became a rich man on the strength of the adoption of his carriage, and his resistance to barbette designs is perhaps understandable. And in his Chief of Ordnance hat, he was well placed to make his resistance stick.

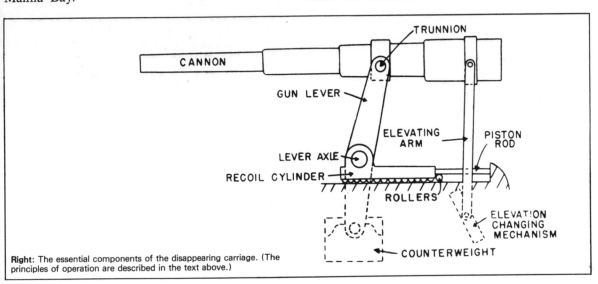

Right: The essential components of the disappearing carriage. (The principles of operation are described in the text above.)

Twin 6pdr Coast Gun

The 6pdr of 57mm calibre had been in British service since the 1880s, but by the 1920s, it was regarded solely as a practice and training device, no longer of value as a weapon. The 12pdr had supplanted it as the principal close-defence gun, since it had a more destructive shell and almost the same rate of fire.

After the First World War, however, it was apparent that the potential speed of naval attack had increased, with the widespread adoption of light fast motor-boats armed with torpedoes, and the answer seemed to be a light but fast-firing gun; the small size of the shell would be more than compensated by the multiple hits obtained by fast fire. In 1923, the Director of Artillery asked the RA Committee to consider the use of the naval 2pdr 'pom-pom' '. . . in close defence of harbour entrances etc., against fast moving surface craft and low-flying aeroplanes.' The Committee considered that the 2pdr shell would be too light, but they arranged for the loan of a gun and mounting from the Royal Navy and carried out a number of tests. This confirmed their opinion of the worth of the shell, but it also showed that the rapid-fire solution was the correct one.

After examining the problem for some time, a design for a twin-barrelled 6pdr was put forward in 1925. The mounting carried two guns side by side, controlled by layers who took their data from dials controlled by an off-mounting director and rangefinder. The guns were loaded and fired by two independent teams of gunners, and, using semi-automatic breeches, it was expected to reach a rate of 40rpm from each barrel. Laying would be continuous, and the gunners would merely have to throw the cartridge into the breech and pull the firing lever as soon as the breech closed, without having to wait for the layer. The two barrels were normally parallel, but an adjusting mechanism, controlled by the gun captain, enabled their fire to converge once a hit had been obtained with either barrel. The mounting was simply an armoured box on a pedestal, with forced ventilation to keep the fumes down, and it was installed in a pit, with a rail trolley around the rear, from which ammunition was supplied to the guns.

The guns were auto-frettaged loose-liner guns with semi-automatic sliding block breeches, similar to the later anti-tank guns. The first two guns, numbers E649 and E650, were proved in 1928; the mounting was then erected at Shoeburyness and proved in July of that year, after which, full trials of the complete equipment took place. Manufacture did not begin until about 1933, the first equipments being formally approved on 28 February 1934. They were to remain in service until 1956. Probably the most famous action in which they were engaged was the Italian torpedo-boat and human torpedo raid on Valetta, Malta, on 25/26 July 1941, when the 6pdrs sank five boats in less than two minutes.

Variants

Ordnance:

Mk 1: Basic model, as described in text.

Mk 1/1: Mk 1 modified by having the breech ring mortise radiussed to obviate the danger of cracking during sustained fire.

Mk 2: As Mk 1, but monobloc instead of loose-liner construction.

Mk 2/1: Conversion of Mk 2 by radiussing the breech ring mortise.

Note: The /1 conversion was post-war.

Mountings:

Mk 1: Basic model, described in text.

Mk 1*: Mk 1 converted to approximate to Mk 3.

Mk 2: Mk 4 altered to become semi-mobile.

Mk 3: As Mk 1*, but of new manufacture.

Mk 4: As Mk 1, but fitted with 6pdr 6cwt guns. At the end of the war there was a development programme for a 6pdr 10cwt equipment which could elevate to 80° and thus function as a dual-purpose coast/AA gun. During the war (see p 102) there was a continuing development of a 6pdr 6cwt AA gun which gradually became a dual purpose AA/coast gun. As might be expected, towards the end of the war these two became inextricably mixed, which is why a 6pdr 10cwt mounting has 6pdr 6cwt **guns on it.**

Above: The 6pdr Twin mounting on its pedestal. The pedestal and traversing ring would normally have been concealed by the emplacement pit.

Data

Weight of gun and breech mechanism: 1,060lb.

Total length: 109.72in.

Length of bore: 105.47in (47 cal).

Rifling: 24 grooves, uniform RH 1/30.

Breech mechanism: Vertical sliding block, semi-automatic, percussion fired.

Elevation: $-10°$ $+7\frac{1}{2}°$.

Traverse: 360°.

Recoil system: Hydro-spring, constant, 6in.

Weight in action: 22,132lb.
Rate of fire: 120rpm.

Performance firing standard 6.25lb HE shell
Muzzle velocity: 2,360ft/sec.
Maximum range: 5,150 yards.

Ammunition fixed, case charge.
The ammunition used in this gun was not inter-changeable with any other 6pdr gun, because of the different cartridge case. The brass case for this gun was 18.24in long and had a rim diameter of 2.79in.

Cartridge, HE, Shell, 6pdr 10cwt Mk 8. Weight of projectile 6lb 4½oz; weight of complete round 11¾lb. This cartridge comprised the Shell HE Mk 10T, Fuze Percussion No. 244, Primer Percussion No. 15 and a propelling charge of 1lb 4½oz of NQ Cordite. It was the standard service round, the fuze having a slight delay in order to permit penetration of the target before detonating. The 'T' after the Mark of shell denotes the presence of a tracer in the base of the shell.

The diagram labels read: UNRESTRICTED ISSUE; T N T; FITTED WITH TRACER; DESIGN NUMBER OF METHOD OF FILLING; NATURE OF PROPELLANT; BATCH NUMBER; NQ; B 642A.

Above: Firing the 6pdr Twin. The gunlayers (in white shirts) can be seen at their posts alongside the guns. The sergeant on the right-hand breech is just striking the firing lever as a fresh cartridge is passed under his arm, while the left-hand breech is being loaded. Note the rails on the rear wall of the pit, upon which ammunition trolleys were pushed round to replenish the ready-use trays on the mounting.

Left: Ammunition for the 6pdr Twin.

12pdr Coast Defence Gun

The 12pdr originated in 1894, as a naval gun for close-defence against fast light craft, and it was taken into coast defence in the same year for defence of harbours against torpedo-boats. With minor modification, it remained in service until 1956.

The gun was of the built-up type with a screw breech; the original cartridge was of a peculiar design with a protruding electric primer which could be replaced by an adapter of similar shape, to take an electric or percussion tube. As a result, the breech block had to be recessed to fit around this primer unit. Extraction of the fired case was performed by one of the gun numbers, who wielded a forked hook to engage the rim of the primer and pull the case from the breech. In 1935, this system was replaced by the more conventional type of extractors which engaged in the cartridge rim, but a number of the old guns still remained in service, and the hand-extraction drill was still being taught after the Second World War.

The mounting was a simple pedestal, with a shield to protect the gun detachment. Early versions had gear-driven elevation and traverse, but in later years, the traverse was changed to free-swinging, being controlled by the gunlayer hooking his arm over an arm-piece and swinging the gun about. Although virtually obsolescent by 1939, a large number were brought from store and placed in service around the British coast in 1940, in addition to those which formed part of the fixed defences.

Variants
Ordnance:
Mk 1:* Mk 1 converted for use as AA guns during the First World War and later re-converted to coast use.

*Mk 1**:* Mk 1 converted to approximate to Mk 4 by adding automatic extraction.

*Mk 1***:* Mk 1* converted to approximate to Mk 4.

Mk 4: New pattern of extractor and breech carrier to permit automatic extraction of fired cases. Introduced in 1935.

Mks 2, 3 and 5 were Naval service.

Mountings:

Mk 1: With shield and pedestal, with 18 holding-down bolts.

Mk 2: As Mk 1, but with shorter elevating arc, simpler shield and pedestal design. Weight in action 6,328lb.

Mk 3: As Mk 2, but lighter and without geared traverse. Weight in action 5,432lb.

Data
Weight of gun and breech mechanism: 1,395lb.
Total length: 123.6in.
Length of bore: 120.0in. (40 cal).
Rifling: Originally increasing RH from 1/120 at breech to 1/28 at muzzle. It was then changed to straight grooves to 85.035in from the muzzle, thereafter increasing to 1/30 at the muzzle. It was finally changed to uniform RH 1/30. As guns went for periodic re-furbishing, they were brought up to the latest design of rifling.
Breech mechanism: Interrupted screw, single motion, electric and percussion fired.
Recoil system: Hydro-spring, 12in.
Elevation: −15° +20°.
Traverse: 360°.

Below: The 12pdr in action.

Weight in action: 9,240lb.
Rate of fire: 15rpm.

Performance firing standard 12lb 8oz HE shell
Muzzle velocity: 2,257ft/sec.
Maximum range: 10,100 yards.

Ammunition

Ammunition was of the separate-loading type, the shell being loaded first and rammed into place by the loading of the cartridge behind it, the cartridge case having a white-metal lid to take the strain. The cartridge case was 15.36in from base to mouth, rim diameter 4.12in. As might be expected with a gun in service for sixty years, the number of different designs of shell and cartridge was considerable, and only representative designs will be given here.

Cartridge, QF, 12pdr 12cwt Mk 3. This consisted of a brass case filled with a charge of 1lb 15oz Cordite size 15, and a gunpowder igniter at the base end. An adapter Mk 8 was screwed into the

base of the case and into this was fitted a Tube Vent Electric 0.4in for normal firing. In the event of a failure of the electric firing circuit, this tube could be removed and replaced by the Tube Percussion 0.4in. The original electric primer used in these cartridges was obsolete long before 1939, and only the tube and adapter combination was in use.

Shell, QF, 12pdr HE Mk 5. Weight 12lb 8oz. This was a forged steel shell fitted with Fuze Percussion DA No 44 or 45 and filled with TNT, Lyddite or Amatol.

Shell, QF, 12pdr CP Mk 5. Weight 12lb 8oz. This was a pointed shell filled with 1lb 2oz of large grain gunpowder and with a Fuze Base No 12F Special. It was to be used when penetration of light structures was desired, as, for example, the upperworks of destroyers.

Shot, QF, 12pdr Practice Mk 3. Weight 12lb 8oz. This was a plain steel shot weighing the same as the standard shell and simulating the common pointed shell for practice firing against targets.

4.7in Coast Gun

The 4.7in first appeared as a Naval gun in 1887 and was adopted into Land Service in the 1890s. In subsequent years there was a bewildering variety of variant models using different breech mechanisms, different construction and so forth, leading to some very confusing nomenclature. Basically, there were four types of 4.7in; the 'A' guns, which used the old three-motion breech; the 'B' guns, which used a single-motion breech; the 'C' guns, which were for percussion firing only; and the 'D' guns, which had a peculiar solenoid-operated electro-mechanical firing

gear. Thus an 'A' Mk 1 gun is not the same as a 'B' Mk 1.

Fortunately, time washed away most of this, and by 1939, very little remained; in practice, though, the matter was further complicated by the hasty resurrection of several odd Marks which had been made obsolete in 1936, but which had escaped scrapping and were hurriedly re-introduced into service in 1940.

The surviving Marks, 3, 3*, 4 and 4* were all 40-calibre guns which differed only in minor details. The 3 and 3* were steel built-up guns dating from 1891, while the Mks 4 and 4* were steel and wire and dated from 1892. The breech mechanisms were conical, interrupted-screw blocks operated by a

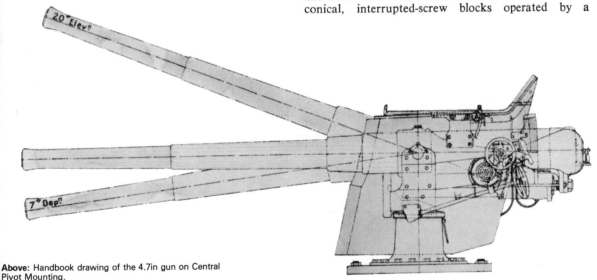

Above: Handbook drawing of the 4.7in gun on Central Pivot Mounting.

single-motion lever which extended across the rear face of the breech.

The mountings were all of the central pivot type, differing only in small details. The most significant change was in the Mk 3, which was designed to be fired from behind a high parapet.

Variants
Ordnance:
B Mk 3: Standard (see below for data).
B Mk 3:* Six guns (Nos. 804, 806–10) issued in 1901 with a non-standard breech mechanism. They were subsequently altered to B Mk 3 standard, but retained their original nomenclature.
B Mk 4: Steel and wire, 1892.
B Mk 4:* Slight difference in construction.
Mountings:
Mk 1: Central pivot − 10° + 20°. Trunnions 45.625in above the emplacement floor.
Mk 1:* Mk 1 altered by fitting pistol grip to replace electric firing gear. Sight illuminating gear added.
*Mk 1**:* Converted Naval Mk 2 to approximate to Mk 1*.
Mk 2: Similar to Mk 1, but trunnions 41.75in above floor.
Mk 3: Similar to Mk 1, but on an extra-high pedestal which also carried the traversing rack. The trunnions were 8ft 9.625in above the floor.
Mk 3:* Mk 3 mounting with a Mk 4 cradle.
Mk 4: Generally similar to Mk 2, but − 7° to + 20°, and changes in the cradle, using a larger buffer cylinder. Trunnions were 41.25in high.
Mk 5:* The Mounting Mk 5 was for the Gun Mk 5 and was declared obsolete with the gun in 1929. Some of these carriages, which had longer cradles, but were otherwise as Mk 4, had the cradles altered to take the Mk 4 gun, whereupon, their nomenclature was advanced to Mk 5*.

Data Gun Mks 3 to 4*, on Mounting Mks 1 to 4
Weight of gun and breech mechanism: 4,592lb.
Total length: 194.1in.
Length of bore: 189.0in (40 cal).
Rifling: 20 grooves, straight to 142.685in from muzzle, then increasing to 1/30 at muzzle.
Breech mechanism: Interrupted screw, electric and percussion fired.
Elevation: − 10° + 20° (Mks 1–3) − 7° (Mk 4).
Traverse: 360°.
Recoil system: Hydro-spring, constant, 8in.
Weight in action: approx 6 tons, with shield.

Performance firing standard 45lb Semi-AP shell
Muzzle velocity: 2,150ft/sec.
Maximum range: 11,800 yards.

Ammunition cased charge, separate loading.
Propelling Charge. This consisted of 6lb 4oz of Cordite in a straight-taper brass case 15.9in long. Instead of the usual type of primer in the base, it was fitted with a protruding adapter into which, a 0.4in Electric or Percussion Tube could be fitted. An electric tube was normal, but should the electric firing circuit fail, the tube could be removed from the adapter and a percussion tube substituted. Because of the protruding adapter, the breech-block was formed with a central recess; the general pattern was similar to that of the 12pdr gun. The case was closed at its mouth by a white-metal lid, which was left in place when loading and, being an alloy, melted and was vaporised in the explosion of the charge.

Shell, SAP, Mk 3. A pointed shell fitted with Base Percussion Fuze No. 501 and a filling of TNT. It took the term 'Semi-AP' because it was incapable of defeating its own calibre of plate at any fighting range, but it was quite well-suited to the attack of lightly armoured craft. Weight of shell 45lb.

 # 6in Coast Gun

The 6in gun had been a principal armament in coast defence since its introduction as the '80pdr' in 1882, when it was the first gun with an interrupted-screw breech to enter British service. Since that time, an incredible number of variants, in both bag-charge and cased-charge forms, have been employed, but the number of Marks employed by Coast Artillery during the Second World War was small, because by that time its task had been reduced to close defence and Examination Batteries. These latter were permanently-manned guns in defended ports, under the muzzles of which any ship brought in by the Royal Navy for examination – e.g., a neutral suspected of smuggling contraband – would be moored, the battery having carte blanche to shoot if the detainee performed any suspicious manoeuvre.

During the war, a small number of Naval 6in of advanced pattern were taken into coast-defence

service, on mountings which admitted of 45° elevation, so as to allow firing at extreme ranges. These were emplaced on the east and southeast coasts of England, and were allied with coast-watching radar sets so as to permit long-range engagement of enemy shipping in the English Channel, as well as their normal defence role. Notable among these were the Fan Bay and Lydden Spout Batteries near Dover.

Ordnance, BL, 6in Wire Mk 7, on Carriage, Garrison, BL, 6in Central Pivot Mk 2
This combination was introduced in 1898 and a number remained in service until 1956, though the nomenclature was changed from 'carriage' to 'Mounting' in 1933.

The gun was a wire-wound 45 calibre, with an interrupted screw breech using the first Welin screw to see service. The 'pure couple' breech mechanism

Above: 6in Mk 7 on Central Pivot Mk 2; and (right) a rear view.

was operated by a hand lever which lay across the rear of the breech, and incorporated a shot guide, which swung into place as the breech was opened so as to protect the breech aperture from damage by the shot during loading. During its life, several different styles of rifling were approved for this gun, but it is doubtful if any of the early increasing-twist patterns were still in service by 1939.

The mounting was of the usual type; a pedestal, bolted down to a holdfast in the emplacement and carrying the 'carriage body' in a ball-bearing pivot in its top. A platform and shield revolved with the carriage, and the gun slid in a ring cradle controlled by a hydraulic recoil buffer and two spring recuperators. The mounting was surrounded by a concrete emplacement, the floor level of which, was the same as that of the revolving platform on the carriage. The gun detachment, except for the gunlayers, operated on the emplacement floor, the gun platform accommodating the gunlayers only.

Variants

Ordnance:

Mk 7: Original model of 1898. Price on introduction, £1,796!

Mk 7*: Mk 7 relined with new inner 'A' tube of 45-ton steel, 1939.

Mk 7V: Similar to Mk 7, but differed in construction. Vickers Armstrong design of which only 12 were made, in 1900.

Mk 7V*: Mk 7V relined as for Mk 7*.

Mountings:

Mk 2: As described above. Cost on introduction in 1898, £890.

Mk 2A: Conversion of QF 6in mountings by changing cradle, etc.

Mk 4*: Mk 4 mounting (with automatic sights and larger platform) fitted with a short Mk 2 cradle.

Other marks of mounting were either obsolete by 1939 or not used with Mk 7 guns.

Data Mk 7 gun on Mk 2 mounting

Weight of gun and breech mechanism: 16,575lb.

Total length: 279.228in.

Length of bore: 269.5in (45 cal).

Rifling: 36 grooves; Straight to 211.06in from muzzle, then increasing to 1/30 at muzzle.

Breech mechanism: Welin interrupted screw, electric and percussion fired.

Elevation: −10° +16° with shield, +20° without.

Traverse: 360°.

Recoil system: Hydro-spring, constant, 18in.

Weight in action: 35,896lb.

Performance firing standard 100lb piercing shell

Muzzle velocity: 2,538ft/sec.

Maximum range: 14,000 yards.

Ordnance, BL, 6in Mk 24, on Mounting, 6in Mks 5 or 6

This was an updated version of the Mk 7, of the same dimensions and performance, but built-up, with an auto-frettaged loose barrel and jacket. The breech mechanism was the same Asbury pattern as used with the 4.5in medium field gun, though with an electric and percussion firing lock.

In similar manner, the Mounting Mk 5 was an updated Central Pivot Mk 2 insofar as its basic features went, the principal visible change being the all-enveloping gun-house type of shield. The greatest innovation was the ability to elevate to 45° so as to extract the maximum performance from the gun, and as a result, these were sometimes called the 'long range mountings'. The Mk 6 mounting was exactly the same as the Mk 5, but its cradle was of cast steel instead of being built up from a number of forgings.

Data
Weight of gun and breech mechanism: 16,740lb.
Total length: 279.228in.
Length of bore: 269.5in (45 cal).
Rifling: 36 grooves, uniform RH 1/30.
Breech mechanism: Asbury interrupted screw, electric and percussion fired.
Elevation: −10° +45°.
Traverse: 360°.
Recoil system: Hydropneumatic, constant, 19.4in.

Performance firing standard 102lb shell with HV charge
Muzzle velocity: 2,825ft/sec.
Maximum range: 24,500 yards.

It should be noted that there is evidence that other patterns of 6in gun were employed during the war; models either officially obsolete or never officially introduced, and on mountings of similarly dubious parentage. The Mk 21 gun, a 50-calibre weapon introduced in 1919, was apparently not as successful as had been hoped and was declared obsolescent in 1927; nevertheless, it remained 'on the books' until 1959, though official Coast Artillery School lists of service equipment do not recognize it. Similarly, it has been reported that a Mk 29 gun on Mk 6 mounting was seen during the latter part of the war, yet there is no record of a Mk 29 gun ever entering service. In the absence of positive confirmation, however, we can only confine our attention to authorized armament.

Ammunition separate loading, bag charge.
As can be readily imagined, a vast collection of ammunition was approved during the seventy-odd years of the 6in. gun's service, though the basic types were few, and the changes in pattern were of minor details rather than vital functions. The only significant change throughout the period was the gradual lengthening of the shell nose taper. We will confine out attention here to the commonest of those on general issue during the war years.

Above: A 6in Mk 24 of the Dover defences, 1940; and (left) a Mk 24 with shields removed to show details of the mounting.

Right: A 6in gun mounted on the Arrol-Withers Mobile Platform. This was first used by the Royal Navy's 'Mobile Naval Base Defence Organisation' and was adopted by the Army in 1942. By using this mounting, guns could be carried on tank transporters and placed in action in captured ports. Several were used in North Africa and Italy.

Propelling Charge. The standard propelling charge was a silk-cloth bag containing 22.25lb of Cordite, and this was used with all Marks of gun and mountings. In addition, a 'High Velocity' (HV) Charge was available for the Mk 24 gun on Mk 6 mountings; this contained 31lb of Cordite and was only used for extreme-range firing.

Shell, APC, Mk 7. This was a piercing shell with penetrative and ballistic caps, a small filling of either Lyddite or Shellite, and the Percussion Base Fuze No. 16. Weighing 102lb, it was the standard projectile for attacking ships and was capable of perforating 6in of Krupp Cemented Plate (a standard criterion of piercing ability) at 3,000 yards range.

Shell, CPBC, Mk 36B. This 'Common Pointed, Ballistic Capped' shell resembled the APC in appearance, but did not have a penetrating cap. The shell body was thinner in the wall, leaving room for more explosive, which was TNT desensitized with Beeswax. This shell weighed 102lb and was intended for attacking lightly armoured or unprotected ships.

Shell, HE, Mk 29B. A conventional nose-fuzed HE shell for attacking unarmoured ships, and for landwards firing.

The Emergency Batteries

In the summer of 1940, with invasion expected hourly, it became imperative to mount guns at every possible landing area on the east and south coasts of England. What field artillery could be spared was sent – notably the 75mm guns received from the USA – and the Royal Navy opened their storehouses and unearthed a collection of guns removed from scrapped warships in the 1920s and 1930s and loaned these to the army. The whole business was handled with the minimum of paperwork and fuss, and not until October 1940 was a roll-call held, and the transfers regularized. The full list of naval equipment handed over was as follows.

6in guns, various, on 8 types of mounting	143
5.5in guns	20
4.7in guns	30
4in guns on static mountings	196
4in guns on mobile mountings	49
12pdr and 3in guns	48
3pdrs	24
Total	510

The mountings were invariably shipboard pedestal types and a prefabricated steel-plate holdfast was devized which could be adapted to any pedestal and anchored in quick-setting concrete. Shields were fabricated locally, though in places where no facilities were available a pattern was made and the shield was constructed in the nearest Royal Ordnance Factory. The 4in mobile equipments were standard pedestals bolted down into suitable motor trucks and held as mobile reserves.

It would be impossible to try and produce data for every combination of weapon and mounting, but the salient points are as follows.

6in guns:

Mk 7: As described on p 190.

Mk 11: 50 calibres long, velocity 2,920ft/sec. Maximum range 22,100 yards.

Mk 11*: As Mk 11, but of differing construction.

Mk 12: 45 calibres; generally similar to Mk 7, but lighter.

Mk 12A: As Mk 12, but with a longer chamber.

Mk 12B: As Mk 12, but having a bore diameter of 5.985in.

Mk 13: 50 calibres long, originally for HMS *Agincourt*; muzzle velocity 2,750ft/sec. Maximum range 21,100 yards.

Mk 16: 50 calibres, originally for HMS *Erin*; muzzle velocity 2,980ft/sec. Maximum range 22,400 yards.

5.5in Gun Mk 1: Bears no relationship to the Land Service gun, having originated from the Coventry Ordnance Works in 1915. 55 calibres long, fired an 82lb shell, muzzle velocity 2,725ft/sec. Maximum range 20,200 yards.

4.7in Gun Mk 5*: 45 calibres, 50lb shell, 2,350ft/sec 16,500 yards.

4in BL Gun Mk 7: 1908 design of 50-calibre gun firing a 31lb shell at 2,820ft/sec to a range of 17,000 yards.

4in BL Gun Mk 9: 1915 design of 45-calibre gun firing a 31lb shell at 2,600ft/sec to 14,300 yards.

4in QF Gun Mk 4: 1913 design of 40-calibre gun firing a 31lb shell at 2,200ft/sec to 13,000 yards. Separate-loading cased ammunition.

12pdr: (See p 188).

3in: The Naval records say merely '3in QF Mks 1 and 4', but neglect to specify which 3in gun they mean, and there were a great variety. The probability is that they were 3in 20cwt AA guns (See p 104 for details) even though the Mk 4 should have been scrapped in 1926.

3pdr: The 3pdr Hotchkiss originated in 1885 as a

Above: The use of ex-Naval guns was not confined to Britain in 1940; this 4.5in Mk 1 gun was one of several emplaced around the Australian coast at that time. **Below:** Action stations; a QF 4in Mk 4 gun in a typical Emergency Beach Battery position. The Naval mounting is bolted down to a platform constructed of piling timber and concrete.

close-defence gun. It was identical, except for size, with the 6pdr Hotchkiss, using a sliding block breech. By the 1920s, these weapons were used only for sub-calibre practice, being clamped to the barrel of a larger gun and connected to the firing gear, so that operating the trigger of the parent gun fired the 3pdr. This allowed inexpensive practice in relatively confined spaces. It can be assumed that their use in the emergency batteries would have necessitated their being mounted on some form of pedestal. Assuming full-charge ammunition to have been available, the 3lb shell would have attained 1,860ft/sec with a maximum range of 4,000 yards.

In June 1941, the Admiralty informed the army that they had ten 9.2in Mk 11 guns in store which could be made available if wanted. These were 50-calibre guns dating from 1905 and firing the usual 380lb shell at 2,875ft/sec to 25,500 yards. The War Office acknowledged the offer, but, on investigation, it was found that the Mark 11 gun was bigger than the Mark 10 and could not be easily fitted into the standard Land Service mountings, so the offer was not taken up.

At about the same time, another offer was of twenty-seven French 138mm guns removed from the French warships *Courbet* and *Paris*. These were said to be the 1910 model, but it turned out that they were a mixture of 1910, 1918, 1923, 1924, 1925, 1927 and 1929 models, none of which was exactly the same. They were provisionally allocated the nomenclature 'Ordnance QF 138mm Mk 6 or Mk 7' depending upon the original model, an odd selection since there never was a Mk 1 to 5. In February 1942, the Director of Artillery reported that he had had the guns carefully examined at Hilsea Ordnance Depot; all were so worn as to be at the end of their useful life, one so badly that no trace of rifling remained in the bore. The offer, therefore, was declined.

The emergency batteries remained in place until mid 1944, when they began to be withdrawn. By the summer of 1946, there were none left.

8in Coast Guns

Britain first used 8in guns for coast defence in the 1880s, dispatched most of them to Singapore and Hong Kong and similar outposts, and then scrapped them in favour of 9.2in guns in 1907. But in 1940, with coast guns being demanded on all sides, a number of Naval 8in Mk 8 guns were acquired by the army. The standard naval barbette mountings were so modified that they could be emplaced in a concrete pit, and two batteries were built, each of three guns: Capel Battery and Hougham Battery, west of Dover. They remained in service from 1942 until 1952.

The guns were of 50 calibre length and of conventional design. The mountings had full power operation of elevation, traverse, breech opening and ramming. The most remarkable feature was their maximum elevation of 70°; this was incorporated in the original Naval design and was retained in the Land Service mountings. It was of no use for coast defence purposes, but the army put it to good use during air raids on the Dover area, when salvos of 256lb shells were sent up on barrage lines to discourage the enemy. It is not known whether they achieved any success in this role. As the Duke said, 'I don't know what they do to the enemy, but by God they frighten me'.

Variants
Mk 8: Wire-wound. Fitted with washout and air blast gear.
Mk 8*: As Mk 8, but without an inner 'A' tube.
Mk 8**: Built-up construction without wire. As for Mk 8, but 112lb heavier.

Data
Weight of gun and breech mechanism: 38,528lb.
Total length: 413.1in.
Length of bore: 400.0in (50 cal).
Rifling: 48 grooves, uniform RH 1/30.
Breech mechanism: Parallel screw, hand or hydraulic operation, electric fired.
Elevation: $-3°$ $+70°$.
Traverse: 80° right and left.
Recoil system: Hydropneumatic, constant, 24in.

Performance firing standard 256lb APC shell
Muzzle velocity: 2,725ft/sec.
Maximum range: 29,200 yards.

Ammunition
Propelling Charge. The standard charge was 66lb of Cordite SC in a single bag, with the usual gunpowder igniter at the base end.

Above: Hougham Battery No. 1 gun emplacement under construction. Note the pivot and traversing racer, with the ready-use ammunition store behind.

Right: Cleaning time on one of the 8in guns of Hougham Battery, Dover.

9.2in Coast Guns

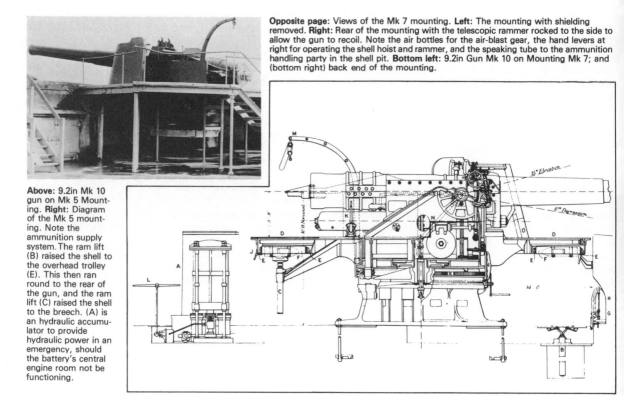

Opposite page: Views of the Mk 7 mounting. **Left:** The mounting with shielding removed. **Right:** Rear of the mounting with the telescopic rammer rocked to the side to allow the gun to recoil. Note the air bottles for the air-blast gear, the hand levers at right for operating the shell hoist and rammer, and the speaking tube to the ammunition handling party in the shell pit. **Bottom left:** 9.2in Gun Mk 10 on Mounting Mk 7; and (bottom right) back end of the mounting.

Above: 9.2in Mk 10 gun on Mk 5 Mounting. **Right:** Diagram of the Mk 5 mounting. Note the ammunition supply system. The ram lift (B) raised the shell to the overhead trolley (E). This then ran round to the rear of the gun, and the ram lift (C) raised the shell to the breech. (A) is an hydraulic accumulator to provide hydraulic power in an emergency, should the battery's central engine room not be functioning.

The 9.2in gun became the premier coast defence gun in the 1880s, and retained this position until the dissolution of Coast Defence in 1956. There were larger guns, but the 9.2in was installed in the greatest numbers and was the standard counter-bombardment gun.

There have been a vast number of variations of the 9.2in, most of which were confined to naval service, but the two in use during the Second World War were the Mks 9 and 10. The Mk 9 had appeared in 1896; in 1910 it was modernized by fitting a single-motion breech mechanism, which changed the nomenclature to 'C Mk 9'. The Mk 10, introduced in 1899, was ballistically the same, but had a slightly different breech mechanism incorporating a Welin screw block, and was capable of a slightly higher rate of fire. Both guns were wire-wound and 46 calibres long.

The mountings were all of the barbette type. The gun was emplaced in a pit so that the barrel just cleared the parapet; a working platform of steel plating surrounded the gun and formed a protective roof over the pit and the lower portion of the mounting. Beneath this 'shell-pit shield', the ammunition was brought into the pit by lifts from underground magazines and then, by means of a trolley riding on a rail suspended under the shield, was transported round to a position beneath the breech.

To load, the gun captain operated a lever which opened a trap in the shield, and then, a second lever, which actuated an hydraulic hoist to lift the shell from the trolley to the breech. The shell was then rammed; the hoist then brought up the bag charge to be loaded; the hoist went down again, the trap was closed, and the gun was ready to fire. Firing was done electrically, either from the mounting or from a fire-control centre. Traverse and elevation were hydraulic, and a 'washout' gear was fitted which squirted a jet of water into the chamber after firing and before the breech was opened, so that any smouldering residue from the charge was extinguished.

Variants
Ordnance:
Mk 9: Basic design, as described in text. Obsolete July 1941.
C Mk 9: Mk 9 converted to single-motion breech mechanism and with small exterior changes to suit the Mk 5A mounting.
Mk 10: Differed from Mk 9 only in the breech mechanism.
Mk 10V: Two guns, Nos. 240 and 241, designed by Vickers instead of the Royal Gun Factory, Woolwich (as were the Mk 10) and which thus differed in minor constructional details.

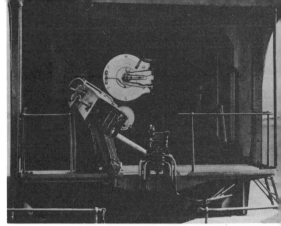

Mk 10*: Differed from Mk 10 in having the inner 'A' tube tapered to facilitate withdrawal.

Mk 15: Approved in April 1940, this was the same as Mk 10, but with an Asbury breech mechanism, and was a built-up gun. It was completely interchangeable with the Mks 9 and 10.

Mountings:

Mk 5: As described in text; elevation $-10°$ $+15°$. Hand-operated traverse and elevation. Maximum range of guns on this mounting was 21,000 yards.

Mk 5A: Mk 5 modified to use the C Mk 9 gun; the change included special arrangements for securing the gun in the cradle, new loading tray, etc. Installed in Rock Battery, Gibraltar and New Needles Battery, Isle of Wight, and probably nowhere else.

Mk 5B: Similar to Mk 5A, but with some changes in the loading arrangements to suit improved projectiles introduced between 1911 and 1913.

Mk 5C: A Mk 5 mounting installed on a non-standard pedestal (No. 4 instead of the correct No. 7) as a wartime measure. Used only in South Foreland Battery, Dover, which was installed in 1941.

Mk 6: Generally as for Mk 5, but with the maximum elevation increased to 30° and with the shields increased in height, and made of armour steel. Instead of an overhead trolley under the shell-pit

shield, a railway track was laid on the emplacement floor, upon which ran two trolleys. Introduced in 1916 as a wartime expedient, it remained in service until 1956.

Mk 6A: A conversion of Mk 5 to increase the elevation to 30°. Maximum range of guns on Mk 6 or 6A mountings was 29,500 yards. Hand traverse and ramming, power elevation and shell hoist.

Mk 7: Developed in the late 1920s, these were generally as for the Mk 5, but allowed $-5°$ $+35°$ elevation, had rapid-loading gear, hydraulic wash-out, hydraulic rammer, air-blast gear and powered elevation and traverse. The gun shielding was built up to form a large rectangular gun-house, and the power rammer was a conspicuous square-section box at the left side of the gun, which was rocked across into line with the breech by hydraulic power.

Mk 8: A Vickers design for a twin-gun mounting. Drawings were produced in 1940, and the design was then frozen 'to be initiated as and when opportunity offered'. No requirement arose, and the mounting was never built.

Mk 9: Developed in 1939 as a simplified version of the Mk 7, which could be manufactured more easily. The principal operating difference was the fitting of a rigid-chain rammer instead of the hydraulic telescoping type, and the use of a three-tiered ammunition hoist to carry up the shell and the two portions of the charge. It was officially approved in 1942, but it is doubtful if many were built.

Data Gun Mk 10, on Mounting Mk 7
Weight of gun and breech mechanism: 62,720lb.
Total length: 442.35in.
Length of bore: 429.33in (46.7 cal).
Rifling: 37 grooves; straight to 303.585in from the muzzle, then increasing to 1/30 at the muzzle.
Breech mechanism: Welin screw, single-motion mechanism; electric or percussion fired.
Elevation: $-5°$ $+35°$.
Traverse: 360°.
Recoil system: Hydropneumatic, constant, 40in.
Weight in action: approx 125 tons.
Rate of fire: 2–3rpm.

Performance firing standard 380lb HE shell
Muzzle velocity: 2,700ft/sec.
Maximum range: 36,700 yards.

Ammunition Separate loading, bag charge.
At the height of the Second World War there were 26 'approved' models of shell, evidence of the slow turnover of coast defence ammunition. Only representative types are shown here.
Propelling Charge. A typical charge was made up of two half-charge bags each containing 53½lb of Cordite tied in a bundle and enclosed in a silk-cloth bag with a gunpowder igniter at the rear end. Two such units made up the full charge; one half-charge could be fired alone as a practice charge.
Shell, HE, Mk 19B. A conventional nose-fuzed shell with a Lyddite filling. It was fitted with the Percussion Fuze No. 45P and was intended for use against the upperworks of warships or as an anti-personnel shell for landwards firing.
Shell, APC, Mk 15B. A capped piercing shell with a filling of TNT/Beeswax and with the Percussion Base Fuze No. 346. This was the standard projectile for attacking armoured ships and was expected to

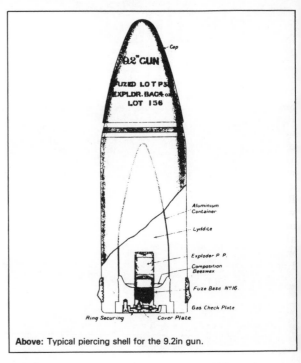

Above: Typical piercing shell for the 9.2in gun.

be able to penetrate 6in plate at 14,000 yards range and be capable of bursting on the inner side of the plate.
Shell, CPC, Mk 9A. A capped piercing shell of lesser penetrative ability and filled with gunpowder. It used the Base Percussion Fuze No. 15 and was intended for attacking lightly-protected vessels.
Shell, Shrapnel, Mk 10A. This was a hangover from the days when heavy coast guns were expected to have to deal with troop transports trying to land men in their vicinity. The shell carried a filling of about 2,500 lead/antimony balls, each weighing about half an ounce, a 2lb gunpowder expelling charge, and a Time and Percussion Fuze No. 88. They were generally used up in practice and were declared obsolete during the war.

13.5/8in Hypervelocity Gun

Some time in March 1940, before the coast of France had been occupied by the German Army, the Ordnance Board enquired of the Director of Artillery whether he had any intention of developing a super-long-range gun. He replied ". . . No such requirement has been put to us, nor do we intend to suggest the idea. Even if it should be possible to build a gun of reasonable life and sufficient accuracy . . . the limitations imposed on the size and capacity of the projectiles raise considerable doubts as to whether the labour involved would produce results comparable with aircraft bombing . . ."

And that, you might think, was that; the army were not particularly interested in super-guns, regarding them as a liability rather than an asset. But they have their uses, particularly as research tools, and early in 1942 the Director of Naval Ordnance raised the question anew, proposing an 8in 140-calibre gun to fire a 256lb shell at 5,500 ft/sec. This meant a barrel 93ft 4in long, and since there was no gun lathe in the country capable of handling such a length, it was suggested that the barrel be made in two pieces and screwed together in the middle. The idea did not appeal to the Ordnance Board and was abandoned. In its place came a suggestion for an 8in 90-calibre gun liner to be inserted into the body of a bored-out 13.5in gun, the excess length protruding from the 13.5's muzzle. This gave a length of 60ft which was the same as the 16in Naval gun and could thus be manufactured on existing machinery.

Two guns were built by Vickers-Armstrong, Nos. SE170 and SE171. SE170 was assembled at Yantlet Battery on the Isle of Grain late in 1942, and fired northwards so that the fall of shot could be spotted by the observation posts of the Shoeburyness Proof and Experimental Establishment. Much useful data was obtained, and SE171 was then installed in an emplacement forming part of the Royal Marine Siege Battery near St. Margaret's at Cliffe, Kent. Trials were first fired on 30 and 31 March 1943, the line of fire being south-west, over Beachy Head, which allowed the fall of shot to be spotted. The gun was christened 'Bruce' after Admiral Sir Bruce Fraser, then Controller of the Navy, and it continued

Above: 'Bruce' being built in the Vickers assembly shop.

to fire occasional trials until late 1944. There is some doubt as to whether it was ever fired across the Channel; legend says it was, but no official confirmation can be found. What *was* discovered was that after about 30 shots, the rifling had become so badly eroded that the ribbed shells could no longer engage properly; this resulted from the abnormally high chamber pressure, the equally abnormal high ratio of charge-weight to calibre, and the high calorific value of the propellant, which literally dissolved the steel of the gun. Experiments were discontinued and later thoughts on long-range artillery revolved around the use of discarding sabot projectiles, though none were ever produced. SE170 was dismantled in 1943; 'Bruce' survived until the end of the war and was dismantled together with the rest of the RM Siege Battery in 1946. The equipments were sent to Shoeburyness, where I saw one barrel in 1956. They were later scrapped.

The mounting was a Naval 13.5in Barbette Mounting Mk 2*, No. 27, which was modified by the Great Western Railway workshops at Swindon, the modifications largely concerning the balancing arrangements to compensate the excess barrel length. Powered elevation and traverse were provided, and loading was done by a chain rammer. The breech mechanism of the gun, originally power operated, was modified to hand operation.

Data
Weight of gun and breech mechanism: 85.6 tons.
Total length: 740.3in.
Length of bore: 721.0in (90 cal).
Rifling: 16 deep grooves; uniform RH 1/25.
Breech mechanism: Interrupted screw, continuous motion, a modified 13.5in Mk 5. Electric fired.
Elevation: $+7°$ to $+50°$.
Traverse: 70° right and left.
Recoil system: Hydropneumatic, constant, 22in.
Weight in action: approx. 200 tons.

Performance firing standard 256lb HE shell
Muzzle velocity: 4,600ft/sec.
Maximum range: 110,000 yards.
(The theoretical maximum range was calculated to be 121,522 yards, but this was never reached.)

Ammunition separate loading, bag charge.
The ammunition was specially made and, like the gun, was never officially brought into service. There were, therefore, no identifying Mark numbers.
Propelling Charge. This consisted of 247lb of Cordite; probably in two bags, though this has not been confirmed.
Projectile. The shell was flat-based, and had 16 ribs formed on the body to conform with the 16 grooves of the gun's rifling. It carried a filling of 25lb of TNT, and was fitted with either the Percussion Fuze No. 241 or the Time Fuze No. 215. These were both nose fuzes and were concealed beneath a ballistic cap. Length, with cap, 69.6in. Weight 256lb.

'Winnie' and 'Pooh'

'Winnie' and 'Pooh' were two 14in guns sited close to Dover and manned by Royal Marine gunners. In June 1940, at the instigation of Mr. Winston Churchill, Rear-Admiral Sir Bruce Fraser, then Third Sea Lord, conferred with Vickers-Armstrong Ltd. about the possibility of taking two of the 14in guns belonging to the reserve stock for the *King George V* class battleships and placing them on land mountings. With suitable modification, the standard naval barbette mountings (generally miscalled 'turrets') could be pivoted into a concrete foundation, and Vickers agreed to install two guns as quickly as possible. A site just inland of St.

Margaret's Bay was selected and work began in the following month. By 3 August 1940, the first gun had been emplaced, a task which necessitated laying special railway track to allow Britain's largest railway crane to get to the site and lift the barrel into its mounting. On that day, Mr. Churchill visited the gun position to inspect, and the Marines responded by christening the gun 'Winnie'. On 22 August, the first rounds were fired at targets on French soil.

The second gun was installed in February 1941 and forthwith christened 'Pooh' for fairly obvious reasons. During the war years, both guns were

Left: 'Pooh' photographed in March 1941. Note the absence of a gun house; it appears that 'Pooh' never had one. Below: 'Winnie' firing across the English Channel. Opposite page: Ready to fire; note the closed breech with the electric firing lead connected. The next shell is being brought on to the loading platform.

frequently engaged in counter-bombardment tasks, attempting to silence the multitude of German batteries on the French coast. Their final task was to engage Batterie Todt, four 38cm guns on Cap Gris Nez, observation being provided by an Auster aircraft of the 2nd Canadian Corps; 189 rounds were fired and a number of direct hits were recorded. On 30 September 1944, the Canadian Army swept through the Cap Gris Nez area and on to Calais, and Winnie and Pooh fell silent. They were dismantled at the end of the war, and except for two

small store buildings now used as sheep pens, no trace of the battery now remains.

Data Ordnance, BL, 14in Mk 7
Weight of gun and breech mechanism: 178,276lb.
Total length: 650.85in.
Length of bore: 630.0in (45 cal).
Rifling: 72 grooves, uniform RH 1/30.
Breech mechanism: Interrupted screw, hydraulic operation, electric fired.
Elevation: $0°$ to $+55°$.
Traverse: $65°$ right and left.
Recoil system: Hydropneumatic, constant.

Performance firing standard 1,586lb shell
Muzzle velocity: 2,450ft/sec.
Maximum range: 47,250 yards.

Ammunition
Ammunition was provided from naval stocks; full details are not known.
Propelling Charge. The standard full charge for the 14in gun was 313lb of Cordite MD, divided into four quarter-charge bags of 78lb 4oz each. Alternative propellants were also authorized.
Projectile. The projectile for cross-Channel bombardment was a base-fuzed common pointed shell weighing 1,586lb and having a filling of 154lb of TNT.

 # 15in Coast Gun

The 15in gun was originally designed for naval use in 1915. During the 1920s, the armament of the new fortress at Singapore was under discussion and, since the Japanese Navy was known to possess long-range guns in their warships, the 15in was selected as the primary armament to deal with a potential attack before it got close enough to damage the dockyard. As with all coast guns, it was quite possible to reach out to considerable ranges, but the question of fire control placed a practical limit on engagement ranges. A new and highly efficient fire-control system formed part of the Singapore plans, but even with this, a range of 22 miles was as much as could be handled. The gun was therefore adopted, being formally introduced for Land Service in February 1936, though in fact, the plans and designs were completed before 1930.

The 15in Mk 1 was a wire-wound 42-calibre gun of conventional pattern. The Mounting Mk I, introduced in 1937, was of barbette type, much like an enlarged 9.2in mounting, with full power operation. Ammunition was supplied from underground magazines and lifted to the gun by hydraulic power. Five guns and mountings were approved for the Singapore Fortress, three in Johore Battery and two in Buona Vista Battery, and these had all been mounted by 1938. Two more were approved for

Mount Imbeah Battery, Penang, but they were never installed. In 1940, it was decided to mount these two guns at Dover so as to control the straits, and Wanstone Battery was completed in September 1942. The Singapore guns were disabled at the time of the surrender and were subsequently cut up for scrap. The Dover guns remained in place until declared obsolete in 1959.

Data
Weight of gun and breech mechanism: 100 tons.
Total length: 650.4in.
Length of bore: 635.8in (42.4 cal).
Rifling: 76 grooves, uniform RH 1/30.
Breech mechanism: Asbury interrupted screw, electric and percussion fired.
Elevation: $-2°$ $+45°$.
Traverse: $240°$.
Recoil system: Hydropneumatic, constant, 45in.
Total weight in action: 373 tons.
Rate of fire: 2rpm.

Performance firing standard 1,938lb APC shell
Muzzle velocity, normal charge: 2,400ft/sec.
Muzzle velocity, super charge: 2,680ft/sec.
Maximum range, normal charge: 36,900 yards.
Maximum range, super charge: 42,000 yards.

Variants

Mounting Mk 2: Similar to Mk 1, but used a completely enclosed turret. The Buona Vista Battery guns are believed to have used these mountings.

Mounting Mk 3: Never officially introduced, this appears to have been a slightly simplified version of the Mk 2 and was used for the guns of Wanstone Battery, Dover.

Ammunition

Propelling Charge. The normal charge consisted of 432lb of Cordite SC in quarter-charge bags. Super Charge (used only by the Dover guns in order to reach across the Channel) was 490lb of Cordite SC, also in quarter-charge bags.

Shell, APC, Mk 17B. This was of naval origin and was the only piercing projectile used in Land Service; the earlier models were never seen. It was a capped piercing shell weighing 1,938lb and contained a filling of Shellite and a Base Percussion Fuze No. 159.

Shell, HE, BNF, Mk 7B. This was a streamlined bombardment shell weighing 1,920lb and fitted with both nose and base fuzes. (BNF = Base and Nose Fuzed.) The idea was that for instantaneous detonation at the target, the nose fuze (Percussion No. 117) would function first. When penetration into light cover (brick buildings, etc.) was wanted, a steel cap was placed over the striker of the nose fuze, rendering it innocuous, and thus the initiation of the shell was transferred to the base fuze (Percussion No. 159) which, like all base fuzes, functioned after a brief delay. It was not a particularly successful design, since most of the targets for the Dover guns were German defence works against which, the penetrative capacity of the BNF shell was poor, and much of the cross-Channel shelling was done with APC shell in order to defeat German concrete.

Left: A front view of Wanstone Battery No. 2 gun. **Below:** Wanstone Battery No. 1 demonstrating the system of ammunition supply by trolleys from the magazines. The shells used in this display are dummies.

3in Seacoast Gun

GUN, 3in (15pdr) DRIGGS-SEABURY, RAPID FIRE, M1898

GUN, 3in M1902M1, on MOUNT BARBETTE M1902

GUN, 3in M1903, on MOUNT BARBETTE M1903

The 3in 15pdr gun was adopted by the US Coast Artillery in 1898 for the close-in defence of harbours, particularly against motor torpedo boats; in this respect, it filled the same sort of role as the British 12pdr. The original model of 1898, produced by the Driggs-Seabury Ordnance Company, was later replaced by the M1902, designed by the US Army Ordnance Department, and then by the M1903, from the same stable. The M1903 was an improvement over the earlier versions by being 55 calibres long instead of 50, and using a larger cartridge, which improved the velocity and range figures. The guns were usually mounted upon very simple pedestal mounts, in shallow concrete pits, though some 1898s were placed on Balanced Pillar Mountings.

By 1941, the 3in was classified as Limited Standard. Although numbers of 1903s remained in service, they were principally employed as training and practice batteries and their combat role was no longer considered vital. Such defences as required small-calibre armament were scheduled to receive 90mm guns, more powerful and with more modern fire-control systems. So far as is known, the only 3in guns to fire in anger during the Second World War were those of Batteries 'James', 'Cushing', 'Hanna' and 'Maxwell Keys', all forming part of Fort Mills, Corregidor.

Below: 3in Gun M1903 on pedestal mounting. This gun, now an exhibit at Fort Casey State Park, Washington, is without its breech block and sights.

Data Gun, 3in M1903, on Mount, Barbette, M1903
Weight of gun and breech mechanism: 2,690lb.
Total length: 175in.
Length of bore: 165in (55 cal).
Rifling: 28 grooves, increasing RH twist, 1/50 to 1/25.
Breech mechanism: Interrupted screw, percussion fired.
Recoil system: Hydro-spring, 9in.
Elevation: $-10° +16°$.
Traverse: 360°.
Weight in action: 9,290lb.
Rate of fire: 12rpm.

Performance firing standard 15lb HE shell
Muzzle velocity: 2,800ft/sec.
Maximum range: 11,325 yards.

Ammunition fixed rounds, cased cartridge.
This gun used the same cartridge case as the AA Gun M4.

Shell, Fixed, HE, M1915. Weight of Projectile 15.0lb. This was a common steel shell with a blunt point and filled with 0.48lb Explosive D and fitted with Base Fuze Mk V. The Cartridge Case MkIAI carried a 5lb propelling charge and a percussion primer. This shell was the standard anti-ship projectile, pointed so as to pierce the upperworks, and fuzed so as to burst after entering the ship.

Shell, Fixed, HE, M42 or M42A1. These were the same high-explosive rounds as used with the 3in AA gun M4, and they were issued to the seacoast guns for use against vulnerable targets such as submarines, minesweepers and invasion craft. In this role, they were fitted with the PD M48 fuze.

6in Seacoast Guns

In 1939, the 6in guns in the various US Coast Defences were a mixed bag of weapons of varying vintages, mounted on an equally wide assortment of carriages and mountings, and it would be possible to ring the variations on each to produce a bewildering assortment of possible combinations. It has not been possible to arrive at an accurate list of what was actually installed, so the only guide to what was in use must be the data tabulated in the various Technical Manuals and Army Regulations which were in force in 1940. These list the following equipments.

Gun, 6in M1897M1, on Carriage, Disappearing, M1898.
Gun, 6in M1900, on Carriage, Barbette, M1900.
Gun, 6in M1900, on Carriage, Disappearing, M1903.
Gun, 6in M1903, on Carriage, Disappearing, M1903.
Gun, 6in M1903, on Carriage, Disappearing, M1905, 1905M1 or 1905M2.
Gun, 6in M1905, on Carriage, Disappearing, M1903.
Gun, 6in M1905, on Carriage, Disappearing, M1905, 1905M1 or 1905M2.
Gun, 6in M1908 or 1908M1, on Mounting, Casemate, M1910 or Mounting, Barbette, M1910.
Gun, 6in M1908, on Carriage, Disappearing, M1905, 1905M1 or 1905M2.
Gun, 6in M1905, on Carriage, Barbette, M1 (T2).
Gun, 6in M1903A2, on Carriage, Barbette, M1 or M2.

Gun, 6in M1905A2, on Carriage, Barbette, M1 or M2.
Gun, 6in M1, on Carriage, Barbette, M3 or M4.

The guns were basically similar, but differed in construction, length, and the pattern of breech mechanism. The M1897M1 was a built-up gun of 45 calibres length, with an interrupted-screw mechanism of the 'single pull' type, having a breech-operating lever lying across the back of the breech, in similar fashion to the British 'single motion' mechanism of the same period. This gun developed 2,600ft/sec with a 108lb piercing shell, and had a maximum range of about 15,000 yards.

The M1900 was lengthened to 50 calibres, but was otherwise the same, and produced 2,750ft/sec to reach 16,500 yards; one point of interest – it cost $7,527 in 1902.

The M1903 differed only in its method of construction, being slightly heavier, but the muzzle velocity was dropped to 2,600ft/sec in an attempt to reduce the erosion which had been found to wear the M1900 very rapidly.

The M1905 was another change of construction without change of performance.

The M1908 saw a considerable change. It was a wire-wound gun, which almost halved the weight, was 45 calibres long, delivered 2,600ft/sec and had a maximum range of 16,500 yards, depending upon the mounting.

Left: Section through the 6in Barbette Carriage M4, showing shield construction and connections for the Remote Power Control system through the pivot.

The M1903A2 was introduced in the late 1930s and was an M1903 with the addition of air-blast gear. This was found necessary when the gun was installed in a heavily-shielded mounting, in order to blow the gasses of combustion from the bore before the breech was opened.

The M1905A2 was a similar conversion of the M1905 by adding air-blast gear.

The M1 was developed during the war and was completely new, a built-up gun with a removable barrel liner. The breech mechanism was of the Asbury pattern, based on the design used with the 155mm Gun M1, and it was fired by a US Navy Combination Electric and Percussion Lock Mk 1; all previous designs of 6in had used the Army Seacoast Combination Electric and Friction Lock M1903. The M1 gun had a muzzle velocity of 2,800ft/sec with a 105lb shell, and a maximum range of 27,150 yards. It was a considerable advance on previous models, but seems to have fallen short in some respects; in August 1946, the Seacoast Service Test Section reported that the gun did not meet the Military Characteristics laid down, and that standardization was not recommended. Before anything further could be done, the whole future of Seacoast Artillery came under review and the gun, so far as is known, never did achieve respectability.

Mountings

Disappearing Carriages. The DC M1898 was of the basic Buffington-Crozier type, using a counterweight and hydraulic buffers which allowed a stroke of 36in. Elevation from −5° to +15° was possible, and the traverse was limited to 170°. This was not as a result of any mechanical restriction on the carriage, but simply because of the requirement for parapet protection for the equipment and the gunners.

The DC M1903 was more or less the same, except that the buffer stroke was increased to 40in in order to accept the greater recoil force of the M1900 gun. The counterweight on this model was considerably heavier, and various improvements to the retracting gear and sighting apparatus were incorporated.

The DC M1905 made some considerable changes in the layout; the counterweight was now placed at the pivot point of the carriage, and was suspended in a well, the rear end moving round to give 85° of traverse. The hydraulic buffer was removed from the carriage and built into the counterweight, the buffer piston rod being firmly anchored to the floor of the counterweight well, so that the upward movement of the weight on recoil drew the buffer cylinder from its piston.

There were further improvements to the disappearing carriage, but they were never applied to the 6in models; by 1905, the army had decided to concentrate on primary armament with heavier guns, and all available finance and research went into this.

Barbette Carriages. These carriages replaced the disappearing carriage once it was realised that a 6in gun presented an impossible target to a warship, whether or not it bobbed up and down. With the mounting in a shallow pit, with only the barrel above the parapet, and a shield around the gunners, the area presented was only a few square feet.

Data on 6in guns	Model:	length of gun:	length of bore:	rifling:	velocity (ft/sec):	weight (lb):
	M1897M1	282in	270in	inc RH 1/50–1/25	2,600	15,600
	M1900	311in	300in	,,	2,750	19,968
	M1903	310in	300in	,,	2,600	20,000
	M1905	310in	300in	unif RH 1/25	2,800	22,000
	M1908	282in	270in	inc RH 1/50–1/25	2,600	12,300
	M1	310in	300in	unif RH 1/25	2,800	20,550

Model:	Elevation:		Traverse:	Weight (lb):	Max range (yards):*	Data on 6in mountings
DC M1898	−5°	+15°	170°	64,800	11,800 (1897M1)	
DC M1903	−5°	+15°	170°	97,500	13,075 (1900)	
DC M1905	−5°	+15°	170°	113,100	16,500 (1900)	
BC M1900	−5°	+20°	360°	25,600	16,500 (1900)	
BC M1910	−3°	+15°	360°	29,991	16,500 (1908)	
BC M1	−5°	+47°	360°	137,000	27,500 (1905)	
BC M2	−5°	+47°	360°	138,300	27,150 (1903)	
BC M3	−5°	+47°	360°	138,000	27,150 (M1)	
BC M4	−5°	+47°	360°	138,000	27,150 (M1)	
CM M1910	−3°	+12°	60°	29,991†	14,790 (1908)	

*Gun mounted. †Without shield.

The M1900 BC was a simple, conical pedestal, carrying a ring cradle through which the gun barrel passed. A hydro-spring recoil system gave a constant recoil length of 15in, so that within a second or two of having fired, the gun was ready to fire again. This doubled the rate of fire, and since the gunlayer actually saw the target, and could correct his aim while loading continued and could correlate his sight with the gun's firing better than had been possible with the disappearing carriage, accuracy was greatly improved.

The BC M1910 was a peculiar affair; it resembled the M1900 in general features, but it was actually a barbette variation of the Casemate Carriage M1910 (See below) and, so far as existing records show, was extemporized simply as a means of using up two casemate mountings which had become surplus. Only these two existed, and they formed Battery 'Morgan' of Fort De Lesseps in the city of Colon, in the Panama Canal zone.

When the war clouds gathered in 1939, the provision of 6in guns to protect minor naval bases and harbours became imperative. There were a large number of M1903 and M1905 guns in store, but no available mountings, and so the Barbette Carriage M1 was developed. (It had been hoped to utilize the 155mm Gun M1 in this role, but it was found to be not entirely suited to coast defence and, in any case, production was fully committed to the field army.) The Military Characteristics were approved on 5 July 1940, and standardization was approved on 5 February 1942. The BC M1 used a racer ring

instead of a pedestal, largely because it had to carry a considerable weight. The gun was carried in a ring cradle trunnioned into two sideplates, and Waterbury Hydraulic Power was provided for elevation and traverse. An all-enveloping shield of 6in cast plate surrounded the mounting and protected the gun crew. This design was soon augmented by the BC M2, which was identical except that the power drive for the mounting was by Atlantic Elevator Co., electric motors and the mount carried remote power control equipment to permit the pointing to be controlled from the Fire-Control Centre. The design was modified in 1944 to produce the M3 and M4 BCs; these were the same as the M1 and M2 respectively, except that the cradle was of smaller internal diameter in order to accommodate the M1 gun.

Mounting, Casemate, M1910. This was a specialized design of Barbette Carriage developed for the secondary armament of Fort Drum, the 'Concrete Battleship' in Manila Bay. Two 6in guns were mounted on each side of the fort; the pair on the northern side formed Battery 'Tully B. McCrea', while the southern guns formed Battery 'Benjamin K. Roberts'. The guns were in semi-circular armoured sponsons projecting from the side of the fort, one gun above the other, and the principal change in mechanical design was the incorporation of a semi-circular armoured steel shield into the mounting, which traversed with the gun and thus sealed the casemate port and prevented enemy fire from entering. One gun of Battery Roberts was removed by the Japanese during their occupation of the fort; the others remained in place after the war, though

Below: Phantom view of the 6in Barbette Carriage M1.

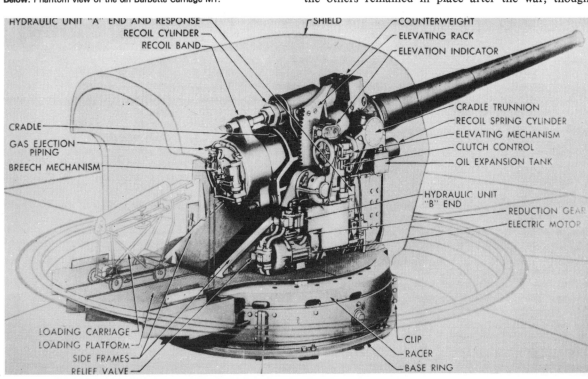

recent information indicates the likelihood of their having been stolen for scrap metal in recent years.

Ammunition Separate loading, bag charge.
Propelling Charges. Cartridges for all models of 6in gun were interchangeable, and were single bags of powder with the usual gunpowder igniter attached at the rear end. Four different charges were available: a 26lb Reduced Charge for use with the High Explosive shell; a 29lb charge used as a Full Charge with HE and as a Reduced Charge with the 108lb AP shell and shot; a 32lb Full Charge for the 108lb AP shell and shot; and a 37lb Full charge for the 105lb AP Projectile. The 32lb charge was later approved for use as a Reduced Charge with the 105lb projectile and, towards the end of the war, a new base-and-increment charge (32lb base and 5.5lb increment) was approved for use, but it is doubtful if many of these were issued.
Shell, HE 6in Mk IIA2. Weight 89.53lb. This was a conventional nose fuzed shell filled with 13.98lb of TNT and fitted with the Point Detonating Fuze M51A3. An earlier model, still in use, was the Mark II, weighing 90.3lb with PD Fuze Mk IV*, which incorporated a slight delay. The M51A3 fuze was a selective superquick or delay fuze.
Projectile, AP, 6in Mk XXXIII. Weight 105lb. This was the usual type of piercing shell fitted with penetrative and ballistic caps, and with a filling of 2.17lb of Explosive 'D'. It was fitted with the Base Detonating Fuze M60.
Shell, AP, 6in M1911 and Shot, AP, 6in M1911. These two projectiles both weighed 108lb and were obsolescent by 1940, though large numbers remained in magazines and were perfectly serviceable. Both were capped, base fuzed shell, the difference between them being in the amount of high-explosive filling. The shot had more metal and less explosive, about 1lb of Explosive 'D', while the shell had a larger internal cavity and carried about 2lb of Explosive 'D'. Shot was "for the attack of vertical armor of capital ships at ranges where perforation can be expected", while shell was for use "at those ranges where perforation of the vertical armor cannot be realised but where perforation of the lighter armor of the superstructure and upperworks can be expected". (Technical Manual 4–205, *Coast Artillery Ammunition*, 1940.)

 # 8in Seacoast Guns

The 8in gun as a coast-defence armament had a curiously parallel career in both British and American service. It was adopted fairly early in the breech-loading era, rapidly re-assessed and dropped in favour of heavier calibres, and then made a sudden comeback during the Second World War. This fall and rise occurred because in the early days, the 8in fell between two stools; it was too heavy for close-in defence but insufficiently powerful for employment as primary armament. Its original adoption took place at a time when it seemed to be heavy enough, but it was rapidly outpaced by contemporary naval armament. Nevertheless, like so much American coast-defence equipment, once emplaced, it was retained until something better could be afforded, and as a result, a handful lasted into the 1940s. The resurgence of the 8in came with the pressure to provide armament for US Naval bases in the 1940s; the 8in being selected for this task as being the optimum balance between bulk and power.

The first 8in equipments were the 8in Gun M1888 on Carriage Disappearing M1896LF, and the Gun M1896 on Carriage Disappearing M1897LF. The majority of them were installed between 1898 and 1904, to cover secondary harbours; typical installations were those of Fort Ward on Puget Sound, and Fort Dade, Florida. In 1918, most of these batteries were dismantled to provide guns for railway mounting (See p 175) and they were either left disarmed or re-armed with something else. It seems, though, that some must have remained in service somewhere, since they were still officially listed as being 'Limited Standard' in June 1943, though the Ordnance School Instructional texts of December 1942 do not mention them. No data is available. Still in service, though in extremely small numbers, was the 8in Gun M1888 on Carriage Barbette M1892, the very first 8in breech-loader to enter US service. This was a built-up gun using the M1888 rotating tray breech mechanism, a cumbersome design which assisted in keeping the rate of fire down to an official 1½rpm. It was mounted on a barbette carriage in which the gun recoiled up an inclined ramp, damped by hydraulic buffers, and then ran back into battery by gravity. This gave a four-foot recoil movement, another feature not conducive to rapid fire. Indeed, it was the slowness of operation of this type of carriage which, among other things, led to the widespread adoption, in American service, of the disappearing carriage which was capable of a faster rate of fire.

In 1940, came a need for medium-calibre artillery to be installed in various locations, and since a number of 8in guns had been obtained for railway mounting (See p 175) it seemed logical to take some of them and produce a suitable barbette mounting. These became the 8in Guns Mk VI Mod 3A2 on Carriage Barbette M1, standardized in 1943. The gun is dealt with in greater detail under its rail application (p 175); the mounting was, in effect, an enlargement of the 6in BC M1, using the same design of side plates supporting a ring cradle, in which the gun recoiled. A loading platform was attached, and this carried a loading table, which was the same as that on the rail mounting. This table sloped forward at 5° and had a folding 'spanning tray' attached to its front end. To load, the gun was depressed to 5°, the breech was opened, and the spanning tray unfolded so that its tip rested in the gun breech. The shell was now rammed from the table across the tray. The 5° downward slope reduced the effort required and allowed the shell to reach a good speed before it engaged with the rifling, and thus to seat itself firmly. Operation of elevation and traverse was by hand, while firing was done electrically from a storage battery. It can be seen that these equipments were ideal for rapid installation since they required no power facilities.

Data 8in Gun M1888, on Carriage, Barbette, M1892
Weight of gun and breech mechanism: 32,218lb.
Total length: 278.5in.
Length of bore: 256in (32 cal).
Rifling: 48 grooves, increasing RH 1/50 to 1/25.
Breech mechanism: Rotating Tray M1888; combined electric and friction fired.
Recoil system: Hydraulic buffer, gravity return, 48in.
Elevation: −7° +18°.
Traverse: 360°.
Weight in action: 88,518lb.
Rate of fire: 1½rpm.

Performance firing standard 323lb AP HE Shell
Muzzle velocity: 2,200ft/sec.
Maximum range: 16,286 yards.

Ammunition (M1888 Gun) separate loading, bag charge.
Cartridge, 8in M1888. A bag charge in two sections, weighing 85.62lb and with a gunpowder igniter at the rear end of the base section.
Shot, AP, M1911. Projectile weight 323lb. Although known as 'shot' in US terminology, this is a piercing shell carrying a 5.1lb charge of Explosive D, and a Base Fuze Mk V.
Shell, HE, Mk I. Projectile weight 200lb. This was a conventional nose-fuzed HE shell for use in situations not requiring perforative performance. It carried a bursting charge of 29.6lb of TNT, and was fitted with the nose fuze PDM46 or M47. This shell delivered a muzzle velocity of 2,600ft/sec and had a maximum range of 21,300 yards.

Data 8in Gun Mk VI Mod3A2, on Carriage, Barbette, M1
Weight of gun and breech mechanism: 42,000lb.
Total length: 369in.
Length of bore: 360in (45 cal).
Rifling: 64 groove, uniform RH 1/25.
Breech mechanism: Interrupted screw, drop block. Combined Electric and Percussion Navy Firing Lock Mk 1.
Recoil system: Hydropneumatic; 27in.
Elevation: −5° +42°.
Traverse: 360°.
Weight in action: 158,000lb.
Rate of fire: 2rpm.

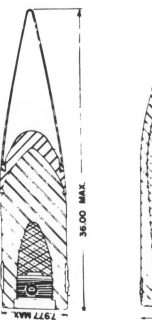

Performance
Firing standard 262lb APHE Shell:
Muzzle velocity: 2,750ft/sec.
Maximum range: 32,980 yards.
Firing 240lb HE shell:
Muzzle velocity: 2,750ft/sec.
Maximum range: 35,635 yards.

Ammunition (Mk VI Mod3A2 Gun) separate loading, bag charge.
Cartridge, 8in Complete Round Mk XX. A Base-and-increment combination of two bags, the base containing 74.25lb and a gunpowder igniter at the rear end, the increment section containing 33.75lb. The base section could be fired by itself, giving 2,100ft/sec and 22,100 yards range with the Mk XX projectile, and 2,150ft/sec and 23,200 yards with the HE Shell M103. The increment could be fired only in company with the base section.
Projectile, AP, 8in Mk XX Mod 1. Projectile weight 261.8lb; length 36.00in. As can be seen from the nomenclature, this originated as a US Navy design. It was provided with ballistic and piercing caps, and was base fuzed with the Fuze BD Mk X. It was loaded with a bursting charge of 3.4lb of Explosive D. Upon standardization of this shell, it was made available for the M1888 guns as well, the M1911 Shot being declared 'Limited Standard'.
Shell, HE, 8in M103. Projectile weight 240lb. For applications not requiring penetration, the M103 was provided. This was the same shell as that used with the 8in Gun M1 (See p 154), having a ballistic cap and nose fuze. Loaded with 20.9lb of cast TNT, it could be fuzed PD M51 or MT M67, the ballistic cap having to be removed in order to change fuzes.

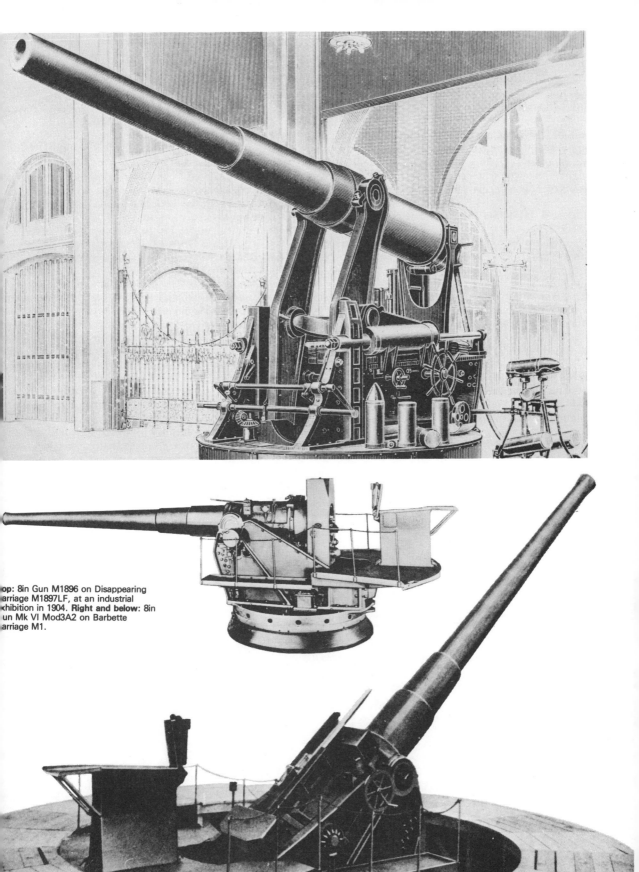

Top: 8in Gun M1896 on Disappearing Carriage M1897LF, at an industrial Exhibition in 1904. **Right and below:** 8in Gun Mk VI Mod3A2 on Barbette Carriage M1.

10in Seacoast Guns

The 10in were among the first major calibre coast guns in American service, the first of them being built at Watervliet Arsenal in 1891. They were installed on a number of different mountings, but were gradually replaced as primary armament by 12in and 14in guns. Quite a number were still in service in 1941, though sentenced 'Limited Standard', and some saw action in the Philippines.

Gun, 10in M1888MI or MII, on Carriage, Barbette, M1893

This was the original 10in design, first issues being made in 1892. It was more or less an enlargement of the 8in M1888, a built-up gun using the rotating tray breech mechanism. In the same fashion, the carriage was a scale-up of the 8in pattern, using the same combination of hydraulic buffer and gravity return. It was obsolete by 1939, but some remained in store, and six complete equipments were lent to the Canadian Army in 1940. Two were emplaced at Fort McNutt, Shelburne Defences; two at Fort Prevel, Gaspe Defences; and two at Philip's Bay, Botwood, Newfoundland. They were all removed in 1944. The guns and carriages were scrapped and the ammunition was dumped into the Atlantic Ocean.

Data

Weight of gun and breech mechanism: 67,200lb.
Total length: 367.0in.
Length of bore: 340in (34 cal).
Rifling: 60 grooves, increasing RH 1/50 to 1/25.
Breech mechanism: M1888 rotating tray; Combined

Seacoast E and F Firing lock M1903.
Recoil system: Hydraulic Buffer, gravity return, 50in.
Elevation: $-7°$ $+15°$.
Traverse: 160°.
Weight in action: 144,600lb.
Rate of fire: 1rpm.

Performance firing standard 617lb APHE shell
Muzzle velocity: 2,250ft/sec.
Maximum range: 16,290 yards.

Gun, 10in M1888MI or MII, on Carriage, Disappearing, M1894M1 LF

Although approved for introduction in 1885, it took some time to iron the wrinkles out of this design, and manufacture did not begin until 1894. The gun is the same as that detailed above, while the carriage was an early pattern of Buffington-Crozier built by the Pond Machine Tool Company of Plainfield, New Jersey. It was of unusual design, with the counterweight suspended beneath the front pivot point, and with an auxiliary base section carrying the rear end of the mounting and supporting it through the limited amount of traverse. The 'LF' at the end of the nomenclature means 'Limited Fire' and indicates an amount of traverse substantially less than 360°. This system of construction proved to be unnecessarily complicated and undesirable in practice, and the design was discontinued after relatively few had been built. However, some remained in service into the Second World War, and two were sent to Canada

Below: 10in Gun M1900 on Carriage, Disappearing M1901LF at Fort Casey, Washington.

in 1940 to be installed at Fort Cape Spear, St. Johns, Newfoundland. They were removed in 1944 and scrapped.

Data

As for Gun M1888MI, on BC M1893 except the following.
Recoil system: Hydraulic buffer and counterweight; 54in.
Elevation: $-5° +12°$.
Traverse: 70° right and left of centre.
Weight in action: 270,000lb.
Rate of fire: 1½rpm.

Performance firing standard 617lb APHE Shell
Muzzle velocity: 2,250ft/sec.
Maximum range: 15,000 yards.

Gun, 10in M1895MI, on Carriage, Disappearing, M1896LF or M1896ARF

This was an improvement on earlier designs; the gun was slightly longer and had an improved breech mechanism, while the carriage was stronger and was produced in LF (Limited Fire) and ARF (All-Round Fire) versions. The pivot was now central, and the counterweight was hung in a circular well surrounding the carriage racer. These carriages were made by the Niles Tool Works of Hamilton, Ohio.

Data

Weight of gun and breech mechanism: 66,700lb.
Total length: 369.15in.
Length of bore: 350in (35 cal).
Rifling: Increasing RH twist, 1/50 to 1/25.
Breech mechanism: Stockett M1895. E & F Seacoast Firing mechanism M1903.
Recoil system: Hydraulic buffer and counterweight; 54in (LF) or 67in (ARF).
Elevation: $-5° +12°$.
Traverse: 140° (LF) or 360° (ARF).
Weight in action: 270,000lb (LF); 268,000lb (ARF).
Rate of fire: 2rpm.

Performance firing standard 617lb APHE Shell
Muzzle velocity: 2,250ft/sec.
Maximum range: 15,000 yards.

Gun, 10in M1900, on Carriage, Disappearing M1901 LF

This final design set out to cure all the minor deficiencies of the earlier models. The gun was lengthened by 5 calibres for a slight gain in performance (and now cost $23,424). The carriage design was completely overhauled to give more strength and stiffness; a sighting platform on each side; the addition of a direct sighting telescope, and gunlayer firing; the addition of electric motors for elevating and traversing, controlled from either the sighting or working platforms; electric firing and lighting apparatus; and counter-recoil buffers and a heavier counterweight so as to lift the gun to the firing position in seven seconds. This was one of the best Buffington-Crozier designs so far, and it formed the model for carriages in other calibres. They were widely installed, and the guns illustrated here were originally part of the armament of Battery 'Warwick', Fort Wint, Subic Bay, Philippines. They were removed from there in the 1950s and brought to their present location at Fort Casey, Puget Sound.

Data

Weight of gun and breech mechanism: 76,500lb.
Total length: 420in.
Length of bore: 400in (40 cal).
Rifling: Increasing RH twist, 1/50 to 1/25. First guns had 60 grooves, later guns had 90.
Breech mechanism: Stockett M1895; Seacoast 1903 Electric & Friction fired.
Recoil system: Hydraulic buffer and counterweight. 67in.
Elevation: $-5° +12°$.
Traverse: Total of 170° for guns on flanks of batteries, and 120° for guns on battery fronts, the restriction being due to parapet requirements.
Weight in action: 398,000lb (177.7 tons).
Rate of fire: 2rpm.

Performance firing standard 617lb APHE Shell
Muzzle velocity: 2,250ft/sec.
Maximum range: 16,290 yards.

Ammunition separate loading, bagged charge.
Cartridge, 10in M1888. Comprised 176lb of smokeless powder divided into four 44lb sections, individually bagged. Each section was issued with a black powder igniter attached by a safety pin, but only one igniter was used for the complete propelling charge. This was stitched to the rearmost bag during the preparation of ammunition before firing, and the other three igniters were removed and destroyed.
Shell, AP, 10in MkIII. Weight 617lb. A capped piercing projectile of conventional type, with a small (approx 10lb) charge of Explosive D and a Base Fuze Mk V. It was later replaced by the *Shot AP M1911* which was of the same type, but with a smaller explosive content (approx 5lb) and consequently a thicker penetrating head.
Shell, HE, 10in Mk IV. A nose-fuzed shell weighing 510lb, for use against lightly-defended targets. It carried about 30lb of TNT, and was fitted with the Fuze PD M46, or Delay M47.

Gun, Dummy, 10in M1911

This was issued 'For use in armories for the instruction of State Militia, Coast Artillery Reserves' and exactly duplicated the M1895M1 gun, with the same dimensions and a working breech mechanism, except that it was made of commercial wrought-iron tube, with iron castings for the breech, trunnions and muzzle. It is extremely doubtful if any remained by 1939, but they deserve mention as being one of the only two cases (the 12in mortar being the other) where a complete dummy weapon was officially provided for training purposes.

12in Seacoast Mortars

The evolution of, and philosophy behind, US mortars in seacoast defence has been covered in the introduction to this section. The first 12in mortars were the M1886, but these were scrapped immediately after the First World War and need not be further considered.

Mortar, 12in M1890, on Carriage, Mortar, M1896

This mortar was an improvement on the M1885 design insofar as it was made entirely of steel, instead of having a cast-iron liner with steel hoops. The carriage was based on a design originated and patented by Colonel Moncrieff, a Scottish officer who had invented the first practical disappearing carriage in the 1860s. The mortar carriage consisted of a pair of heavy steel arms supported by hydraulic cylinders and powerful springs, so that on recoil, the mortar moved back and down, pivoting the arms and compressing the springs, while the hydraulic buffers assisted in absorbing the recoil. The springs then forced the arms up, returning the mortar to the firing position.

The whole carriage was mounted on a turntable, open in the centre, so that the recoiling mortar could pass through into a shallow pit beneath. It was a sound design, but it was slow in action because it was necessary to manually depress the mortar to point-blank for loading and then elevate it again to the firing angle when loading was completed. A report of firings in 1894 recorded a time of 11.4 minutes between shots. The first of these carriages was built by the Builder's Iron Foundry of Providence, Rhode Island; later models were built by Watervliet Arsenal.

Data

Weight of mortar and breech mechanism: 29,000lb.
Total length: 145.25in.
Length of bore: 120in (10 cal).
Rifling: 72 grooves, increasing RH twist, 1/40 to 1/20.
Breech mechanism: Rotating Tray M1890. Seacoast M1903 firing mechanism.
Recoil system: Hydro-spring, 23in.
Elevation: 0° loading; +65° to +75° firing.
Traverse: 360°.
Weight in action: 157,000lb.
Note: Variant model Mortar M1890M1 differed in the arrangement of hoops and weighed 29,120lb. Variant model Carriages M1896 MI, MII and MIII were similar to M1896, but with greater range of elevation for firing, from 45° to 70°, and slight changes in construction.

Performance firing standard 1,046lb Deck-Piercing shell

Muzzle velocity: from 550ft/sec (Zone 1) to 1,050 ft/sec (Zone 7).
Maximum range: 12,019 yards (65° Zone 7).
Minimum range: 2,210 yards (75° Zone 1).

Mortar, 12in M1908, on Carriage, Mortar, M1908

This was an improvement on the previous model only in the matter of construction; it was wire-wound, which reduced the weight without impairing the strength, and it used an improved breech mechanism, but it was of the same dimensions as the M1890 and gave the same performance.

The carriage, though, was a considerable step forward. The mortar tube was trunnioned into a 'sleigh' which could slide rearwards on recoil in guides inside the cradle. The cradle was trunnioned to the side frames of the carriage and carried the

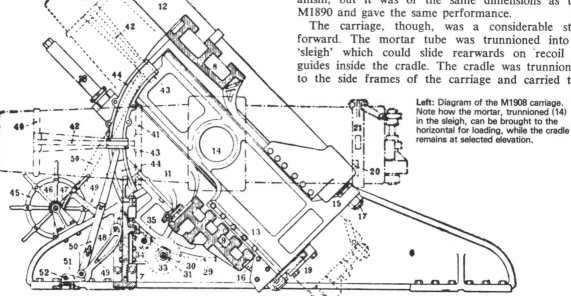

Left: Diagram of the M1908 carriage. Note how the mortar, trunnioned (14) in the sleigh, can be brought to the horizontal for loading, while the cradle remains at selected elevation.

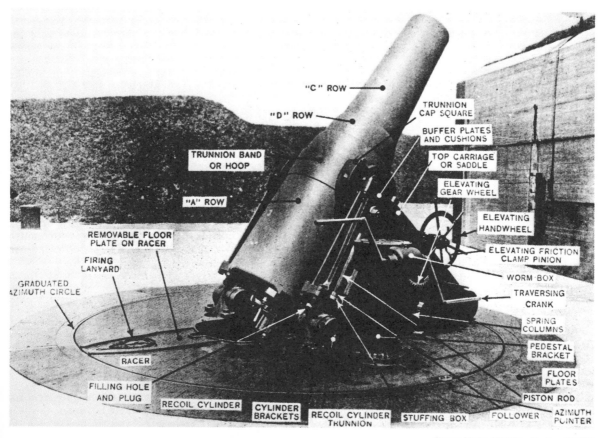

"C" ROW
"D" ROW
TRUNNION CAP SQUARE
BUFFER PLATES AND CUSHIONS
TOP CARRIAGE OR SADDLE
ELEVATING GEAR WHEEL
ELEVATING HANDWHEEL
ELEVATING FRICTION CLAMP PINION
WORM BOX
TRAVERSING CRANK
SPRING COLUMNS
PEDESTAL BRACKET
FLOOR PLATES
PISTON ROD
AZIMUTH POINTER
FOLLOWER
STUFFING BOX
RECOIL CYLINDER TRUNNION
CYLINDER BRACKETS
RECOIL CYLINDER
FILLING HOLE AND PLUG
RACER
GRADUATED AZIMUTH CIRCLE
FIRING LANYARD
REMOVABLE FLOOR PLATE ON RACER
"A" ROW
TRUNNION BAND OR HOOP

Above: Mortar M1890 on Carriage M1896.

recoil and recuperator cylinders, the piston rods of which were connected to the sleigh. It can thus be seen that the actual tube was capable of movement in the vertical plane, pivoting about its trunnions in the sleigh, without the rest of the cradle-sleigh unit moving, and it was possible to lock the tube to the sleigh or free it. The sleigh and cradle could thus be kept at the firing elevation angle at all times, and laying the weapon could continue without interruption while the barrel was unlocked, swung down to a horizontal position, and loaded. After loading, it could be swung back into alignment with the cradle, and bolted to the sleigh, whereupon it was ready to fire. This device is comparable with the 'quick-loading gear' used in some British medium field guns – e.g. the 5.5in (See p 46) and it gave this mortar a much better rate of fire. However, after this carriage had been standardized, the mortar battery construction programme suddenly slowed down and no more than about 40 of these equipments were ever installed.

Data
Weight of mortar and breech mechanism: 18,200lb.
Total length: 145in.
Length of bore: 120in (10 cal).
Rifling: 108 grooves, uniform RH 1/20.
Breech mechanism: Stockett M1908. Seacoast M1903 firing.

Recoil system: Hydro-spring, 24in.
Elevation: 0° to +65°.
Traverse: 360°.
Weight in action: 144,200lb.

Performance firing standard 1,046lb Deck-Piercing shell
Maximum muzzle velocity: 1,000ft/sec.
Maximum range: 9,200 yards.
Minimum range: 2,400 yards.

Mortar, 12in M1912, on Carriage, Mortar, M1896MIII
This mortar improved the ballistic performance by an increase in barrel length, but otherwise, was the same as the M1908 design, a wire-wound barrel with Stockett breech. The carriage was a reversion to the earlier type, abandoning the quick-loading device, the only difference between this and the earlier M1896 being the method of attachment of the mortar to the gun arms and the different range of elevations available. The reversion to this simpler pattern of carriage was justified by changes in the tactical handling of mortars, which accepted the slightly lesser rate of fire, but compensated for it in other ways. The M1912 mortars were widely installed in Panama and on the Pacific islands, as well as in locations on the west coast of the United States.

Data
Weight of mortar and breech mechanism: 33,854lb.
Total length: 201in.
Length of bore: 180in (15 cal).
Rifling: 108 grooves, increasing RH 1/40 to 1/20.
Breech mechanism: Stockett M1908; Seacoast M1903 firing.
Recoil system: Hydro-spring, 23in.
Elevation: 0° loading; +45° to +65° firing.
Traverse: 360°.
Weight in action: 165,300lb.

Performance firing standard 1,046lb Deck-Piercing shell
Maximum muzzle velocity: 1,200ft/sec.
Maximum range: 11,754 yards.
Minimum range: 2,150 yards.

Ammunition separate loading, bagged charges.
Charge, Propelling, 12in Mortar. Precise details of propelling charges are almost impossible to come by, since the inter-relation between elevation, range and charge meant that the precise weight of powder in any Zone and with a specific shell could vary depending upon the location of the mortar and its assumed fighting range. In general, the complete charges weighed 47, 58, 60, 63 or 89lb, depending upon which shell was being used, and these complete charges were divided up into 7, 8 or 10 Zones, again depending upon the mortar type and shell in use. It can thus be seen that the possible permutations and combinations of charge, elevation and shell are endless.
Shell, Deck-Piercing, Mk XXVIII. Weight 1,046lb. A piercing projectile fitted with the peculiar small cap known as the 'Johnson' after its designer, the rights to which were acquired by the US Govern-ment in 1896. This projectile carried a very small bursting charge of Explosive D, was fitted with the Base Fuze Mk X, and could pierce 6in of homogeneous armour at 10,000 yards range.
Shell, Deck-Piercing, M1898. Weight 824lb. Similar in design to the heavier projectile, this was provided in order to increase the range of the mortar, but with a somewhat lesser penetrative performance. Maximum range of the M1908 mortar with this shell was 12,019 yards.
Shell, Deck-Piercing, M1911A. Weight 700lb. A further reduction in weight and performance in order to provide a third range option. This allowed a maximum range of 14,610 yards to be reached.
Shells, HE, 12in Mortar Mk XI and Mk VIII. These were provided for tasks where penetrative ability was not needed. The Mk VIII was a common pointed shell with Base Fuze Mk V, while the Mk XI shell was nose fuzed, using the PD M46 or M47. Since these shells were considered as being for a secondary role, they were held in lesser numbers than the DP types; nevertheless, they were found to be extremely valuable in 1942, when they were fired by the various mortar batteries in Manila Bay against Japanese locations in the Bataan Peninsula. The Mk XI weighed 712lb, the Mk VIII 700lb.

Mortar, Dummy, 12in M1911.
The second dummy equipment to be provided for drill and training of the State Militia forces, this was constructed of steel plates and iron castings to resemble the Mortar M1890M1. The breech mechanism was fully functional, but with the working parts made of cast iron or a cheap grade of steel. As with the 10in Dummy Gun, it is doubtful if any remained by 1939.

Below: Four M1890 mortars in a typical pit.

12in Seacoast Guns

The 12in gun became the primary seacoast weapon during the late 1890s when the art of gunmaking was being improved, and the ballistics of smokeless powder were coming to be better understood. Although it was later supplanted by larger calibres, it was to remain the backbone of coast defences until and throughout the Second World War. Its only defect was the alarming rate of erosive wear caused by hot propellants and working the gun at the upper limits of its tolerance in search of high velocity and long-range penetrative power, but this was ameliorated, to some extent, as powder chemistry improved during the early years of the present century.

Gun, 12in M1888, M1888MI or MII, on Carriage, Barbette, M1892 and M1892 AGL

This was a built-up 34 calibre gun of conventional form. The MI and MII variations differed only in the matter of construction and the arrangement of hoops; there was no change in dimensions or ballistics.

The carriage was generally similar to the 8in and 10in models, though, of course, larger and heavier. The gun was mounted in a top carriage running on 18 recoil rollers which were contained in the 4° slope of the upper surface of the 'chassis' or lower carriage. This, in turn, was centrally pivoted, and rotated on 24 traversing rollers around a racer path firmly anchored into the emplacement. The chassis carried a loading platform at its rear end, and this supported a derrick for hoisting the ammunition. On firing, the gun recoiled up the slope of the chassis, the movement being controlled and gradually stopped by hydraulic buffer cylinders attached to the top carriage, the pistons being bolted to the front end of the chassis. At the end of recoil, the movement was reversed, the gun running back into battery by gravity. Retracting gear was provided, so that the gun could be manually hauled back, from time to time, in order to exercise the recoil mechanism.

While a sound enough design from the engineering point of view, it was slow in action. The long recoil, the cumbersome system of hand-hoisting ammunition, and the slow action of the rotating tray breech mechanism all added up to a rate of fire of slightly better than one shot per minute. It was this which enabled the disappearing carriage, with its better rate of fire, to continue in service after it had been discarded in other countries.

The M1892AGL carriage was slightly different from the M1892 and was more in the nature of a salvage operation than a design exercise. In about 1890, a design for a 'Gun Lift Carriage' was prepared, in which two 12in guns on barbette carriages were mounted at the ends of an enormous see-saw beam. Operated by a steam engine, the beam could be brought to the horizontal, when both guns were concealed behind a parapet. When ready to fire, the beam was tilted so that one gun was raised above the mask; after it had fired, the beam was swung so that the first gun descended behind cover and the second gun was raised into the firing position. One such installation was actually built at Fort Hancock, New Jersey, but it was soon seen to be a mechanical monstrosity and the idea was terminated. Several carriages for these projected mountings had been begun, and these were completed, with the necessary modifications, to approximate to the M1892 pattern. They were then called the M1892AGL (Altered Gun Lift). Their characteristics were slightly different, as noted below.

Variants

Ordnance:

M188: Built-up gun with six 'C' hoops.

M1888M1: Built-up, five 'C' hoops; only a few made.

M1888MI½: Built-up, three 'C' hoops. Length 442.56in, 35 calibre.

M1888MII: Built-up, two 'C' hoops.

M1892(1896): Originally called the M1892, this had a breech mechanism similar to that on the M1888, but was then fitted with one of the first Stockett type mechanisms, as used later on the M1895 gun; the mechanism differed in having the operating crank above the tray instead of below. After this alteration it became the M1896. Only one was made, and it remained in Sandy Hook Proving Ground for test purposes.

Data

Gun, 12in M1888, M1888MI, MI½ or MII, on Carriage, Barbette, M1892:

Weight of gun and breech mechanism: 117,127lb.

Length of gun: 439.9in

Length of bore: 408.0in (34 cal).

Rifling: 72 grooves, increasing RH 1/50 to 1/25.

Breech mechanism: Rotating Tray, electric & friction fired.

Elevation: −7° +15°.

Traverse: 360°.

Recoil system: Hydraulic buffer, gravity recuperation, constant length, 48in.

Weight in action: 229,000lb.

On Carriage, Barbette, M1892 AGL: as above except for the following:

Elevation: −7° +12°.

Recoil length: 60in.

Weight in action: 221,313lb.

Performance

On Carriage M1892, firing 1,070lb AP shell:

Muzzle velocity: 2,235ft/sec.

Maximum range: 17,342 yards.

On Carriage M1892, firing 975lb AP shell:

Muzzle velocity: 2,235ft/sec.

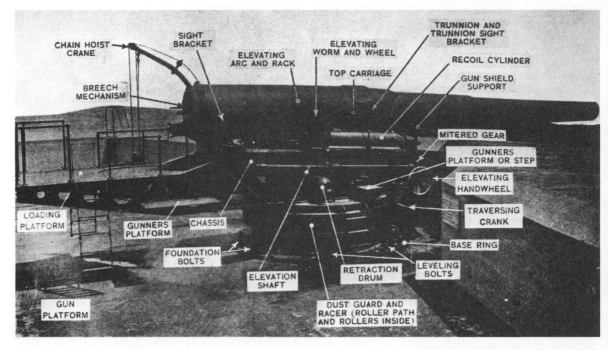

CHAIN HOIST CRANE · SIGHT BRACKET · ELEVATING ARC AND RACK · ELEVATING WORM AND WHEEL · TRUNNION AND TRUNNION SIGHT BRACKET · RECOIL CYLINDER · BREECH MECHANISM · TOP CARRIAGE · GUN SHIELD SUPPORT · MITERED GEAR · GUNNERS PLATFORM OR STEP · ELEVATING HANDWHEEL · TRAVERSING CRANK · LOADING PLATFORM · GUNNERS PLATFORM · CHASSIS · FOUNDATION BOLTS · BASE RING · ELEVATION SHAFT · RETRACTION DRUM · LEVELING BOLTS · GUN PLATFORM · DUST GUARD AND RACER (ROLLER PATH AND ROLLERS INSIDE)

Maximum range: 18,400 yards.
On Carriage M1892 AGL, firing 1,070lb AP shell:
Muzzle velocity: 2,235ft/sec.
Maximum range: 11,636 yards.

Gun, 12in M1895 or M1895MI, on Carriage, Barbette, M1917

This became known as the 'Long Range 12 inch' because of its improved carriage. The gun itself was a 35 calibre, a slight improvement on the M1888; the MI version had a slightly greater chamber volume but was otherwise identical. The mounting, though, was a vast improvement and was the first major-calibre axial-recoil type to see service, yet it came about almost by accident.

During the early years of the First World War, the US Army realized that the armament of their coast defences had largely been surpassed by that of modern battleships; some of these carried guns capable of ranging to 25,000 yards or more, while the principal US coast guns could barely reach 15,000 yards. It was decided, therefore, to institute a major re-armament programme and install 16in guns and howitzers in the ten most important locations. But since this would take time – because neither gun, howitzer nor mountings had yet been designed – an immediate improvement was sought by taking 36 spare 12in gun barrels and producing a modern carriage which would allow more of the gun's power to be used.

This mounting used sideplates to carry a ring cradle, above which were two recoil buffers and below which were two spring recuperators. A working platform surrounded the gun, below which was the sub-structure, revolving on a roller race and protected by a pit. The working platform was thus at ground level and service of the gun was quicker. Elevation was by electric power, with hand operation as a stand-by, and traversing by hand, both being operated from below the platform in accordance with data transmitted electrically from the Fire-Control Room. The gun could elevate to 35°, a figure generally accepted as sufficient in those days, although the range reached was a good deal less than the theoretical maximum; but extending the range would have given little advantage, since at 35° elevation, the shell was landing at just about the limit of optical spotting. There was little virtue in having a longer range if the fall of shot could not be observed and corrected.

The 'Long Range 12 inch' installations were begun in 1917 and completed, so far as finance allowed, by 1922. Some of the planned sites were not occupied, and many of the batteries were not provided with the complete outfit of fire-control systems and communications. The locations were as follows.

Fort Pickens, Pensacola, Florida 1 battery (2 guns)
Fort Levett, Portland, Maine   1 battery
Fort Rodman, New Bedford,
  Mass.   1 battery
Fort Hancock, Sandy Hook, NJ 2 batteries
Fort Nahant, Boston, Mass.   1 battery
Fort Salisbury, Delaware Bay   2 batteries
Fort Crockett, Galveston, Texas 1 battery
Fort Travis, Galveston, Texas 1 battery
Fort Barry, San Francisco   1 battery
Fort Sherman, Panama   2 batteries
Fort Kamehameha, Oahu, TH   1 battery
Fort Mills, Corregidor, PI   1 battery

In addition to these, in 1940 a further 2-gun battery was installed at San Juan, Puerto Rico, using

Opposite page: 12in Gun M1898M2 on Barbette Carriage M1892.

Below: 12in Gun M1900 on Disappearing Carriage M1901LF, in the 'down' position for loading; and (bottom) in the 'up' position for firing.

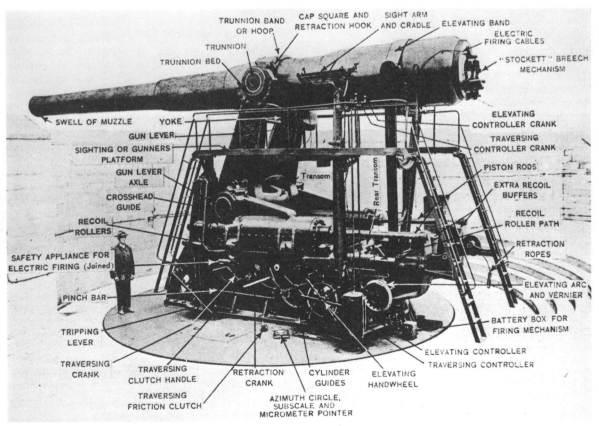

barrels and carriages already stocked as spares, while one battery from Fort Salisbury was removed and re-sited in a fresh location on Delaware Bay, and one battery, from Fort Travis as re-sited near Charleston, SC. Battery 'Smith' of Fort Mills was awkwardly sited, because of the lie of the land, and was later re-organized as two separate batteries; the right-hand gun retained the name 'Smith' while the left-hand gun became Battery 'Hearn'. (Originally, the two guns were known throughout the coast artillery as 'The Smith Brothers', a jocular reference to two bearded gentlemen whose name and portraits appeared on a tin of cough lozenges popular in the 1920s.) These two guns are, in fact, the only two Long Range 12in still in existence.

Data

Weight of gun and breech mechanism: 114,700lb.
Total length: 442.8in.
Length of bore: 420in (35 cal).
Rifling: 72 grooves, increasing RH 1/50 to 1/25.
Breech mechanism: Stockett M1895; Seacoast 1903 firing mechanism.
Recoil system: Hydro-spring, 30in.
Elevation: 0° to +35°.
Traverse: 360°.
Weight in action: 416,700lb (186.02 tons).
Rate of fire: 2rpm.

Performance

Firing standard 1,070lb APHE shell:
Muzzle velocity 2,250ft/sec.
Maximum range: 27,600 yards.
Firing 975lb APHE shell:
Muzzle velocity: 2,260ft/sec.
Maximum range: 30,100 yards.
Firing 900lb APHE shell:
Muzzle velocity: 2,325ft/sec.
Maximum range: 29,200 yards.
Firing 712lb HE shell:
Muzzle velocity: 2,600ft/sec.
Maximum range: 30,000 yards.

Gun, 12in M1895, on Carriage, Disappearing, M1897LF or M1897AGL

This was the same gun as previously discussed, but on a Buffington-Crozier disappearing carriage of the usual type. A slight mystery surrounds the AGL carriage, mentioned in an obscure American training text; it would appear from this that some components of the Gun Lift Carriages became, by some transmutation, disappearing carriages, but this is hard to swallow. A more likely explanation is that the term was applied to distinguish those later models of the M1895 carriage (numbers 12 and onwards) which were modified and improved with new sighting arrangements, new counterweights, electrical retraction gear, etc., to approximate to the M1901LF carriage, in the process of which modification, they acquired an additional 2° of elevation.

Data

Gun data as for M1895 above.
Recoil system: Hydraulic buffer and counterweight, 67in stroke.
Elevation: −5° +10° (+12° on AGL).
Traverse: 170°.
Weight in action: 601,700lb (268.6 tons).
Rate of fire: 2rpm.

Performance firing standard 1,070lb APHE Shell
Muzzle velocity: 2,250ft/sec.
Maximum range: 12,700 yards.

Gun, 12in M1895, on Carriage, Disappearing, M1901LF

This was the same gun mounted on an improved carriage which allowed 15° of elevation and hence a greater range of 17,400 yards with the 1,070lb shell.

Gun, 12in M1900, on Carriage, Disappearing, M1901LF

An improved, longer gun on the same mounting, as above. It is understood that relatively few were made, since the 14in soon replaced it as primary

Below: 242nd Coast Artillery Regiment (Connecticut National Guard) firing a 12in gun at Fort H.G. Wright, New York, in the 1920s.

armament. According to one American textbook, some of these guns were earmarked for mounting on the M1917 Barbette Carriage, but there is no confirmation of this ever having been done. Although the carriage was still listed as Limited Standard in June 1943, it is doubtful if any were still in service at that date. I believe that the only equipments installed were the three batteries, 'Cheyney', 'Crockett' and 'Wheeler, of Fort Mills, Corregidor, some of which are still there.

Data
Weight of gun and breech mechanism: 131,400lb.
Total length: 504.3in.
Length of bore: 480in (40 cal).
Rifling: 72 grooves, increasing RH 1/50 to 1/25.
Breech mechanism: Stockett M1895; seacoast M1903 firing.
Recoil system: Counterweight and hydraulic buffer, 67in.
Elevation: −5° +15°.
Traverse: 175°.
Weight in action: 673,400lb (300.6 tons).
Rate of fire: 2rpm.

Performance firing standard 1,070lb APHE shell
Muzzle velocity: 2,250ft/sec.
Note: Velocity was originally 2,550ft/sec with a 325lb charge of Pyro Powder, but it was reduced to 2,250 in order to reduce erosive wear.
Maximum range: 17,342 yards.
Penetration: 17.8in of Krupp Cemented Plate at 1,000 yards.

Barbette Carriage T1
In 1942, the US Navy Bureau of Ordnance gave sixty-two 12in 45 calibre guns to the US Army. A few similar guns had been given to the army in 1922 and some desultory work on designing a new carriage had been done during the 1920s. This was the Barbette Carriage T1, and it was revived in 1942 with the intention of mounting the ex-navy guns and installing them in Brazil. Eventually, the whole idea was cancelled, but four complete equipments were certainly built, as evidenced by Ordnance Committee Minute 26820 of 1 March 1945. What happened to them is not known, but they were certainly not installed anywhere.

Ammunition separate loading, bagged charges.
Propelling Charges. The charges were enclosed in the usual silk-cloth bags, but there was a variety of types using various grades and weights of propellant still in fortress magazines at the outbreak of war. The older designs were soon disposed of and only two types were retained as standard. The first, for use with piercing projectiles, came in two weights, one for use with the M1900 gun, the other for use with the M1888 and M1895 guns. The second type was for use only in the M1895 gun and with the nose-fuzed shell HE Mk X; it was, in fact, originally developed as a component of the bombardment round

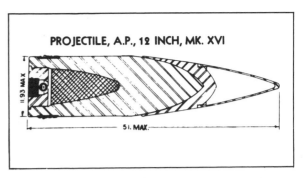

PROJECTILE, A.P., 12 INCH, MK. XVI

used with the railway gun in the siege role, but this round was later incorporated into the ammunition of the M1895 coast gun for landwards firing.

The M1900 gun AP charge consisted of .334lb of NH powder in four bags, the powder grains being stacked in the bags to give the charge rigidity. The M1888 and M1895 AP charges were of 268lb of NH powder, also stacked, and also in four bags. In each case, one bag was provided with tying tapes so that the separate gunpowder igniter could be attached just before loading took place.

The HE shell charge consisted of a base section weighing 225lb in one bag, and an increment weighing 75lb in a second bag, the increment being attached by tapes. Both bags were puttee-wrapped with wide tape in order to stiffen them and make them rather easier to manipulate, and the base section had a gunpowder igniter permanently attached.

Projectile, Armor-Piercing, Mk XVI. This was the standard piercing projectile for all models of 12in gun, and superseded a variety of shells dating from the 1890s. The Mk XVI was a naval design weighing 975lb. It was fitted with penetrating and ballistic caps, carried a filling of 22.2lb of Explosive D, and was fitted with the Base Fuze Mk X.

Shell, HE, Mk X. This was the landwards-firing anti-personnel projectile, a conventional nose-fuzed high-explosive shell, but with a short ballistic cap over the nose fuze so as to approximate to the same shape as the AP Projectile and thus achieve similar ballistic performance. It weighed 712lb and was filled with 118.28lb of TNT with a nose fuze PD M46 or M47.

Shell, Armor-Piercing, M1912A. This was an old design, the standard to which the guns were originally matched, but it was sentenced 'Limited Standard' by 1941. A capped, ballistic capped shell with Base Fuze Mk X and approximately 30lb of Explosive D, it was much the same as the Mk XVI above except that it was larger and heavier. Weight as fired was 1,070lb.

Shell, Armor-Piercing, Mk I. This shell weighed 900lb and was the original lightweight shell intended to permit a long range in exchange for a slight diminution of penetrative performance. The design was exactly as for the M1912A, but for the weight and size. It was Limited Standard by 1941, and had been replaced by the Mk XVI.

14in Seacoast Guns

In 1905, the 'Taft Board' reviewed the coast defences of the USA and made various recommendations to improve the efficiency of existing works. At the same time, it was confronted with the task of fortifying various posessions which had come into American ownership as a result of the Spanish–American War. Among the recommendations of the Board was the adoption of a new and powerful 14in gun, a weapon so powerful, and commanding such an arc of sea, that it would be feasible to install single-gun batteries. Another, and less publicized reason for adopting the 14in was that the current 12in guns were being worked almost to their limit in order to achieve a satisfactory penetrating performance, and the erosion, caused by the high velocities and hot powders, was wearing the guns out at a rapid rate. By changing to 14in calibre, the heavier shell would permit achieving the same penetrative performance at a lower velocity, thus reducing the erosion problem and prolonging the life of the guns.

Gun, 14in M1907 or M1907M1, on Carriage, Disappearing, M1907 or M1907M1LF

The M1907 was the first design to appear, a wire-wound gun of 34 calibres length, and it was immediately replaced by the M1907M1, a built-up gun of the same dimensions. Since the specification demanded a 'powerful' gun, 34 calibres seems a delicate way of approaching the target, but the reason behind this dimension was very simple; the new 14in gun had to be built to fit a set of emplacements awaiting arming on Naos Island, Panama, and these emplacements had been built for the 12in M1900 gun. Anything longer than 34 calibres in 14in would have failed to clear the parapet during the recoil stroke of the disappearing carriage, and this basic demand fixed the length of the guns. After four guns had been built to arm Battery 'Buell' and Battery 'Burnside' of Fort Grant, with a single spare barrel between them, the design was dropped in favour of a 40-calibre model.

The mounting was of the improved Buffington-Crozier type with the recoil buffer cylinder fitted vertically into the counterweight, and it appears to have been the first of this type to enter service. It was also the first disappearing carriage to achieve more than 15° of elevation.

Below: 14in Gun M1910 on Disappearing Carriage M1907M1. Note the massive gun arms and pivots. **Right:** 14in Gun M1910 in the 1920s demonstrating its firing ability at Aberdeen Proving Ground.

Data

Weight of gun and breech mechanism: 111,900lb (M1907). 118,700lb (M1907M1).
Total length: 495in.
Length of bore: 476in (34 cal).
Rifling: 126 grooves, increasing RH 1/50 to 1/25.
Breech mechanism: Stockett M1907; Seacoast M1903 Electric & Friction fired.
Recoil system: Hydraulic buffer and counterweight, 73in.
Elevation: −5° to +20°.
Traverse: 170°.
Weight in action: 619,100lb (276.4 tons).
Rate of fire: 1 round in 1½ minutes.

Performance firing standard 1,660lb APHE shell
Muzzle velocity: 2,350ft/sec.
Maximum range: 22,800 yards.

Gun, 14in M1909, in Mounting, Turret, M1909

These guns, and their special mountings, were made for installation in the two turrets of Fort Drum, Manila Bay. The guns were wire-wound, and of 40 calibres length, and the right and left guns of the turret pairs had right- and left-handed breech mechanisms. The mountings actually formed part of the turret structure, being ring cradles on girder sideplates. All operation within the turret was by electric or hydraulic power, and the turrets were generally based on naval practice, with a barbette shaft beneath, which contained the training machinery and ammunition hoists. Apart from this, though, they were of army design and used a much greater thickness of armour than would have been found on naval turrets of the day. The forward turret was Battery 'William L. Marshall', the rear turret, 'Battery John M. Wilson', and both turrets remained in action and firing right up to the time of surrender in 1942. The guns were then disabled and were left in place throughout the Japanese occupation, but recent information indicates that they are slowly being cut up by local scrap scavengers.

Data

Weight of gun and breech mechanism: 139,240lb.
Total length: 579in.
Length of bore: 560in (40 cal).
Rifling: 126 grooves, increasing RH 1/50 to 1/25.
Breech mechanism: Stockett M1907; Seacoast M1903 firing mechanism.
Recoil system: Hydro-spring, 48in.
Elevation: 0° to +15°.
Traverse: 360° (limited by the fort structure).
Weight in action: 2,316,000lb (1,034 tons) including turret and two guns.
Rate of fire: 1rpm.

Performance

Firing standard 1,660lb AP HE shell:
Muzzle velocity: 2,370ft/sec.
Maximum range: 19,200 yards.
Firing 1,208lb High-Explosive shell:

Muzzle velocity: ?ft/sec.
Maximum range: 22,780 yards.

Gun, 14in M1910, on Carriage, Disappearing, M1907M1

This was virtually the same gun as the M1909, differing in the outer hoops and by having trunnions to suit the carriage. The carriage was the same as the earlier model, with minor modifications to suit the increased weight and power of the gun. These equipments formed the primary armament of Forts Hughes and Frank in Manila Bay, each fort having two single-gun batteries. They were also used in Panama. Those of Fort Frank survived the Japanese occupation and are still there.

Data

Weight of gun and breech mechanism: 137,300lb.
Total length: 579in.
Length of bore: 560in (40 cal).
Rifling: 98 grooves, uniform RH 1/25.
Breech mechanism: Stockett M1907; Seacoast M1903 firing mechanism.
Recoil system: Hydraulic buffer and counterweight, 73in.
Elevation: −5° +20°.
Traverse: 170°
Weight in action: 682,000lb (304.5 tons).
Rate of fire: 1 round in 1½ minutes.

Performance firing standard 1,660lb APHE shell
Muzzle velocity: 2,350ft/sec.
Maximum range: 22,800 yards.

Ammunition separate loading, bagged charge.
Cartridges, Propelling Charge. These varied according to the projectile. The piercing shells used base-and-increment charges, the base section weighing 332lb in all cases. The incremental section weighed 103lb with the 1,660lb shell, and 128lb for the two lighter shells. The HE shell used a 480lb charge. All charges were sub-divided into smaller portions for convenience in handling and loading.
Shell, AP, 14in M1909. Weight 1,660lb. The normal type of capped piercing projectile with a small bursting charge and Base Fuze Mark X. Fired from the M1909 or M1910 guns, this delivered a Muzzle Energy of 63,628 foot tons.
Shell, AP, 14in Mk VI. Weight 1,560lb. A naval design of piercing shell, similar to the M1909, but lighter and thus reaching a slightly longer range.
Shell, AP, 14in Mk VIII M9A1. Weight 1,400lb. As projectile design improved, it became possible to achieve the same penetration figures with lighter shells, and thus improve the range. This was another naval shell adopted by the army.
Shell, HE, 14in Mk XI M2A1. Weight 1,208lb. A naval bombardment shell furnished to coast artillery for tasks where piercing performance was not needed. It was of the common pointed type so as to penetrate ships' upperworks or unarmoured vessels, and it was fitted with the Base Fuze Mk X.

16in Seacoast Guns

As has already been indicated, 16in guns were proposed during the First World War in order to provide the coast defences with the finest possible weapon. In fact, the idea went farther back than that, the first suggestion of a 16in coming as a result of an 1888 recommendation and the first 16in gun being developed in the 1890s, but its production was considerably delayed; not only was it a difficult manufacturing proposition but, one suspects, it was an Ordnance Department idea which took some swallowing by the Coast Artillery Corps. However, it finally got into service and appears to have acted as a sort of precedent, smoothing the way for its successors. Once the idea of such a calibre had been shown to be feasible and had been accepted, plans were made for building 14 two-gun batteries in the ten most vital locations, but the financial cutback in the 1920s looked like putting an end to this programme before it had fairly begun.

The Washington Naval Treaty of 1922, however, caused the US Navy to suspend the building of several new warships, and the 16in guns already under construction for these projected ships became surplus and available for army use. Though slightly less powerful than the army design, they were gladly received since it represented a considerable saving of money, money which could then be spent on more mountings. Finance and manufacturing problems made the re-armament programme move ever slower – apart from the cost, each mounting took three years to build, and there was only one manufacturing facility – but when the Second World War

appeared in the offing, finance became more easily available, more manufacturing capacity was found, and more batteries were installed. Various small modifications and improvements suggested themselves from time to time, so that eventually there were almost as many variant models of mounting as there were batteries.

Most of the 16in batteries installed immediately before and during the Second World War were casemated so as to provide overhead protection, but the original installations dating from the 1920s, in Panama and Hawaii, were never given overhead cover so that their fullest power could be employed all round the compass; the Hawaiian guns could, in fact, cover the entire island of Oahu and a considerable distance beyond its shores.

Although the principal series of 16in guns were on barbette mountings, there were also two guns on disappearing carriages, the largest such weapons ever built. These represented the final flowering of the Buffington-Crozier design, pushed through during General Crozier's last years as Chief of Ordnance and built, one is inclined to suspect, just to prove that they were possible.

Gun, 16in M1895, on Carriage, Disappearing, M1912LF

This was the first 16in gun to enter US Army service. Although designed and approved in 1895, manufacture did not start until June 1897 and it was completed on 25 November 1902. It was then sent to Sandy Hook Proving Ground where, on a proof

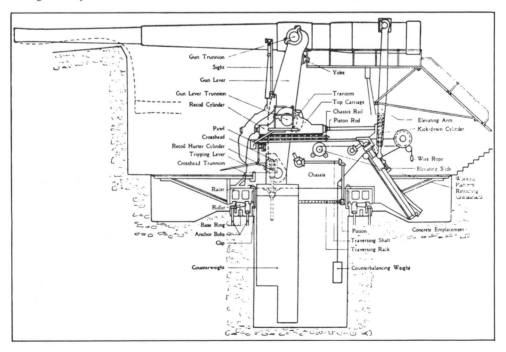

Left: Diagram of the 16in M1917 Disappearing Carriage.

mounting, it was used for test firings in connection with powder and shell development. It was returned to Watervliet Arsenal in 1917 to be refurbished. By this time a carriage had been built and in October 1917 the entire equipment was shipped to Panama where it was installed as the one-gun Battery 'Newton' of Fort Grant at the Pacific end of the Canal. It subsequently fired some 137 shots in practice prior to 1920 and was then placed on a 'care and maintenance' basis until 1936 when it fired three shots. It was then silent until 1941, after which, more practice firings took place, and finally, in October 1943, it was cut-up for scrap on site.

The gun itself was a built-up piece of conventional design, while the mounting was of the improved Buffington-Crozier pattern with a vertical recoil cylinder in the counterweight. The only thing of note was its massive size; the emplacement was 64ft across and 42ft deep to the bottom of the counterweight well, the racer ring was 24ft in diameter and the counterweight weighed 198 tons.

Data

Weight of gun and breech mechanism: 284,500lb.
Total length: 590.50in.
Length of bore: 560.0in (35 cal).
Rifling: 96 grooves, increasing RH 1/50 to 1/25.
Breech mechanism: Interrupted screw, single cut, side opening. Electric and friction firing mechanism, Seacoast M1903.
Recoil system: Hydraulic buffer and counterweight, 89in.
Elevation: $-5°$ $+20°$.
Traverse: 85° right and left.
Weight in action: 1,273,992lb (568.75 tons).

Performance firing standard 2,400lb APHE shell
Muzzle velocity: 2,250ft/sec.
Maximum range: 27,365 yards.

Gun, 16in M1919 on Carriage, Disappearing, M1917ARF

This was the first of the 'modern' design of 16in gun decided upon in 1917, and it was mounted upon the most advanced disappearing carriage ever made. The principal disadvantage of the disappearing carriage was its lack of elevation; this was a fundamental defect which was due to the geometry of the elevator arms and the gun arms at the rear which controlled elevation. Once the elevation went above 20°, the geometrical relationship began to feel the strain and, most of all, the downward thrust of the gun on recoil threw an excessive shock on to the gun arms and the elevating mechanism. The problem was solved by inserting shock absorbers or 'kickdown cylinders' into the gun arms, a form of hydraulic buffer which absorbed the worst of the downward blow. Other modifications were also incorporated, but otherwise it was simply the Buffington-Crozier design at its peak. It was even more massive than the M1912 pattern; though the basic dimensions were much the same, the traversing mass was 550 tons and the counterweight weighed 272 tons.

At the time of its adoption, this was the most powerful coast-defence gun in the world, with a muzzle energy of 125,975foot/tons. It was only to be surpassed in later years by the Japanese 40cm (15.74in) coast gun which fired a heavier shell to develop 139,682foot/tons. A fifty-calibre gun firing a shell weighing just over a ton, the M1919 could fire with accuracy to a range better than 22 miles to inflict severe, if not mortal, damage to anything afloat.

But for all its promise, only one equipment was built, installed at Fort Michie, Great Gull Island, Harbor Defenses of Long Island Sound, in the early 1920s. Its subsequent career was even less lively than that of the gun in Panama, and, like that weapon, it was scrapped in 1943.

Data
Weight of gun and breech mechanism: 340,600lb (152 tons).
Total length: 826.8in.
Length of bore: 800.0in (50 cal).
Rifling: Uniform RH 1/30.
Breech mechanism: Interrupted screw, side opening, electric & friction firing.
Recoil system: Hydraulic buffer and counterweight, 89in.
Elevation: $-5°$ $+30°$.
Traverse: 360°.
Weight in action: 1,397,760lb (624 tons).

Performance
Firing standard 2,400lb APHE shell:
Muzzle velocity: 2,750ft/sec.
Maximum range: 40,000 yards (22.7 miles).
Firing 2,340lb APHE shell:
Muzzle velocity: 2,750ft/sec.
Maximum range: 41,600 yards.

Gun, 16in M1919MII or MIII, on Carriage, Barbette, M1919

As already mentioned in the section on the 'Long Range 12in' guns, 1917 was the year in which a sudden revival of interest in coast-defence led to a proposal to install 16in guns in ten locations and, in the first flush of enthusiasm, manufacture was begun on seven disappearing carriages of the M1917 type. But the complexity of the carriage gave rise to second thoughts, and a design of barbette carriage was put forward as being a lot easier to make, simpler to maintain and, what was most vital, would give the gun as much elevation as it needed to reach its full potential. The gun was basically the same as that used on the disappearing carriage, with modifications to suit mounting in a ring cradle instead of trunnioning it to the top of a pair of elevator arms, and it also had a much improved breech mechanism. Manufacture of disappearing carriages was halted, except for the one which was finally installed, and a new design of barbette carriage was drawn up. It was deceptively simple, two side plates carrying a ring cradle with buffer and recuperator cylinders. A working platform surrounded the mounting and carried a mechanical chain rammer, loading and spanning trays, and various tables and runways for supplying the ammunition. A railway track ran around the mounting; this could be used for bringing in the necessary hoists and machinery for shifting the gun if the need arose, but its more

day-to-day use was for two ammunition trucks to move around, supplying cartridges and shells to the ammunition table on the platform. This track ran off, generally to the nearest standard gauge line, with spur tracks to magazines and store-houses, well-protected by earth and concrete overlays. The mounting was powered by electric, hydraulic and compressed-air motors to perform the various functions of elevation, traversing, ramming and breech closure.

Six of these equipments were built and installed; two in the Harbor Defenses of New York; two at Boston; and two on Oahu, Hawaii, covering the approaches to Pearl Harbor.

Data
Weight of gun and breech mechanism: 389,655lb.
Total length: 826.8in.
Length of bore: 800.0in.
Rifling: Uniform RH 1/30.
Breech mechanism: Interrupted screw, drop block, air operated. Electric & percussion firing.
Recoil system: Hydropneumatic, 40in.
Elevation: $-7°$ $+65°$.
Traverse: 360°.
Weight in action: 1,085,000lb (484 tons).

Performance firing standard 2,340lb APHE shell
Muzzle velocity: 2,700ft/sec.
Maximum range: 49,140 yards (27.92 miles).

Gun, 16in Mk IIMI, on Carriage, Barbette, M1919MI

In 1922, as a result of the restrictions on warship building made by the Washington Naval Treaty, the US Navy cancelled their project battleships Nos. 49–54 and battlecruiser Nos. 1 to 6. The 16in guns for these ships were already under construction, and 20 completed guns were passed across to the army for use in coast defences. Although of rather less power, they were otherwise very similar to the M1919 gun and, with some slight modifications to the M1919 mounting, could be used in place of the M1919 gun. Saving the expense of making guns allowed more mountings to be made and, from 1924 onwards, six equipments to this specification were built, one by one, and went to Fort Kobbe, Panama, and to Fort Barrette, Oahu, TH.

In 1938 six more two-gun batteries were approved for siting in the continental United States, and more were being mooted for the overseas possessions. Another 24 Mk II guns were transferred by the navy in the summer of 1939 to meet this demand. In 1940, with the worsening situation in Europe in mind, more installations were proposed and the navy transferred the rest of their stock to Mk II guns, 24 complete and 44 in various stages of manufacture, from unfinished castings to partly-assembled guns. But due to the time taken to manufacture and install mountings, and with the gradually improving war situation, the building programme was reconsidered and curtailed before it ever approached

The 16in Gun M1919 on Barbette Carriage M1919. **Above:** A diagram showing the simplicity of the design; and (left) one of the two 16in guns that guarded Pearl Harbor, Hawaii.

completion. By 1945, 20 batteries of two 16in Mk II guns had been put into service; six had been commenced but were incomplete or, if completed, unarmed; while another 12 projected batteries were never begun.

Data

Weight of gun and breech mechanism: 307,185lb.
Total length: 821.0in.
Length of bore: 800.0in (50 cal).
Rifling: Uniform RH 1/32.
Breech mechanism: Interrupted screw, drop block, air closure. Electric and percussion firing.
Recoil system: Hydropneumatic, 48in.
Elevation: 0° +65°.
Traverse: 360°.
Weight in action: 950,597lb (424 tons).

Performance firing standard 2,240lb APHE shell
Muzzle velocity: 2,650ft/sec.
Maximum range: 45,100 yards.

Gun, 16in Mk IIMI, on Carriage, Barbette, M2

This equipment was similar to the foregoing, except that it was modified as necessary to carry a two-inch thick armour shield. This enclosed the working area around the gun, and the whole equipment was then built into a concrete casemate to give overhead protection. The casemate restricted the maximum field of fire to 145° of traverse, and the elevation to 47°, but since the maximum range was reached at an elevation of 46°, nothing was lost. Four of these M2 equipments were built.

Gun, 16in Mk IIMI, on Carriage, Barbette, M3

As for the M2 carriage, but with improved ammunition handling equipment and rammer and stronger floor beams beneath the working platform. Two were built.

Gun, 16in Mk IIMI, on Carriage, Barbette, M4

Two were built to this specification. The principal change was the adoption of thicker (4in) armour for the shield, which restricted elevation to 46°; alterations to the carriage to permit −5° depression; improved ramming and ammunition handling arrangements; all power operation by 440 volt 3-phase electric motors; provision for remote data displays; and, as a result, an increase in weight to 1,170,000lb (522 tons or 530,703kg).

Gun, 16in Mk IIMI, on Carriage, Barbette, M5

A further improvement, this was much the same as the M4, but used more powerful motors to increase the speed of traversing and ramming, had roller bearings fitted into the trunnion seats, and made some changes in the location of compressed air tanks and piping on the mount (used for air-blast through the bore after firing). This was the last 16in design to appear; the guns of Battery Richmond P. Davis, San Francisco, activated in 1940, were of this pattern, and probably four more were built after that. The only tactical change was that the minimum angle of operation was now −3°.

Ammunition

Throughout the service of the 16in gun, there was a constantly changing variety of projectiles, the reason being that since shells of such size were produced in relatively small batches, it was possible to incorporate improvements into the next batch without having to wait for several thousand to be used up, as was the case with smaller weapons. Since, however, most of them were out of use before 1940, they are not shown here.

Propelling Charges. Details of charges for the M1895 and M1917 guns on disappearing carriages are not fully known, except that they comprised a

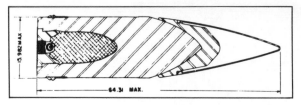

Below: A 16in Mk II gun on proof mounting at Aberdeen Proving Ground. The vast proportions of this gun can be gauged by the size of the men loading it.

reduced charge of 650lb and a full charge of 832lb.

The M1919 guns fired an 832lb charge which, at various times, was made up of 5 unequal sections, 4 equal sections, or, finally, 8 equal sections.

The Mk IIMI guns used different propelling charges which were not interchangeable with those for the M1919 guns. These were a 648lb charge for use with the 2,240lb Projectile, AP, Mk XII and a 672lb charge for use with the Shell, AP, Mk II. Both these charges were sub-divided into six equal portions, both for convenience in loading and to provide reduced charges for practice.

Projectiles. The standard projectiles for the M1895, M1917, early M1919 and early Mk IIMI guns were the Shell, AP, Mk V and the Shell, AP, Mk IX, both weighing 2,340lb. Both carried charges of about 40lb of Explosive D and were fitted with the Base Fuze Mk X. The difference between the two lay in the shape of the nose and in the type of piercing cap fitted.

A lighter shell, to permit somewhat longer ranges, was the Shell, AP, Mk IIM2 of 2,100lb which, except for weight and explosive content, was much the same as the Mk V.

At the beginning of the war, however, all these designs were sentenced 'Limited Standard', and the service projectile for all guns became the 'Projectile, AP, 16in Mk XII Mod 1'. As the nomenclature indicates, this was a US Navy design, carrying piercing and ballistic caps. Filled with 34.18lb of Explosive D and fitted with Base Fuze Mk X, it weighed 2,240lb. Nevertheless, numbers of the earlier patterns of shell remained in service throughout the war, still being quoted in performance and data tables as late as 1944.

16in Seacoast Howitzers

When, during the First World War, it was decided to make some substantial improvements in coast defence armament, one of the weapons selected was the 16in howitzer. As we have already seen, the coast mortar, or howitzer, was a major factor in American defences, and improved methods of fire control indicated that the 16in would be a formidable weapon, so the projected 16in gun batteries were each to be reinforced by a battery of howitzers. Sixty howitzers were authorized, but the end of the war, and the subsequent dearth of funds, stopped the project before it had really got under way. Only four howitzers, plus one spare barrel, were ever made. By 1922, these had been installed at Fort Story, Virginia, as Battery 'Pennington'; later, the battery was divided into two two-howitzer batteries, Pennington 'A' and 'B', and in 1941, Pennington 'B' was re-named Battery 'Walke'. They remained in active status until 1943, when they were relegated to a care and maintenance basis, and in the early 1950s they were removed and scrapped. The emplacements remain, heavily overgrown with brush, within the Military Reservation of Fort Story.

Howitzer, 16in M1920, on Carriage, Howitzer, 16in M1920

This, in fact, was a scaled-down 16in gun. The breech mechanism, cradle and carriage were almost identical with those of the 16in Gun M1919, while the barrel was exactly half as long as that of the gun. It used a barbette emplacement, the necessary concealment being achieved by siting, rather than artificially, by sinking it into a pit, as were the 12in mortars.

Data
Weight of gun and breech mechanism: 195,300lb.
Total length: 432in.
Length of bore: 400in (25 cal).
Rifling: Uniform RH 1/25.
Breech mechanism: Interrupted screw, drop block, hand opening, pneumatic closing, Navy E & P Firing Lock Mk 1.
Recoil system: Hydropneumatic, 36.5in.
Elevation: $-7°$ $+65°$.
Traverse: 360°.
Weight in action: 900,000lb (401.8 tons).
Rate of fire: 1rpm.

Performance firing standard 2,100lb APHE shell
Muzzle velocity: 1,950ft/sec.
Maximum range: 24,500 yards.

Ammunition separate loading, bagged charge.
Charge Propelling 16in Howitzer. A 296lb charge of smokeless powder divided into six sections for convenience in handling.
Projectile, Armor-Piercing, 16in Howitzer Mk HM2. Weight 2,100lb. A piercing, capped projectile of the usual type, carrying a charge of approximately 35lb of Explosive D, and fitted with Base Fuze Mk X.

Right: 16in Howitzer M1920; note that the mounting is practically identical with that of the 16in gun.

Recoilless Artillery

The idea of a gun devoid of recoil has been attracting a steady stream of inventors since the middle of the 19th century. The advantage to be gained is, quite simply, a saving in weight, first by discarding the conventional recoil system with its pistons, oil and cylinders, all of which weigh a considerable amount, and second, by making the carriage strong enough to hold the gun in the firing position, but without having to add strength and weight in order to resist the recoil shock.

Attractive as that may sound, there are some severe disadvantages. The back-blast as the flaming gas shoots from the rearward-facing jets and blows earth and stones about to form missiles is the obvious drawback, and all RCL guns have to have considerable wedge-shaped danger areas delineated behind them. This same blast destroys camouflage and immediately announces the presence of the gun, be it ever so well concealed from the enemy. It also leads to some concealment problems; you can hardly put the weapon in a pit which will trap the blast and cause it to swirl round and engulf the detachment, or position it inside a house, or in front of a wall. Less

obvious, but of vital importance in a war economy, is the RCL gun's appetite for propellant; the British 95mm RCL took 5lb of propellant to fire a 25lb shell at 1,070 ft/sec, while the conventional 95mm howitzer used 13oz to get the same performance with the same shell. Multiply this difference by several hundred rounds per day and you soon have a supply problem.

But, weighing the pros against the cons, there sometimes comes a time when the RCL shows some distinct advantage, and the most obvious case is for use by airborne troops where the saving in weight allows heavy firepower to be brought in by parachute or glider. This was where the Germans saw the need for an RCL gun and this was how they first deployed it. The same aspect was briefly explored by Britain and the USA, but since their development of airborne techniques was better than that of the Luftwaffe, they were able to land sufficiently heavy weapons without having to resort to RCLs; though there is no doubt that had some RCLs been available at Arnhem, it might have put a different complexion on the affair.

Where the Western Allies saw the advantage was in jungle warfare in the Far East and Pacific areas, where terrain conditions made it difficult, if not impossible, to get heavy weapons into positions where they could do some good. So that when the prospect of a man carrying what amounted to a 25pdr gun or a 75mm howitzer on his shoulder appeared, the opportunity was too good to miss. Such weapons, man-carried through the trees and bush, and fired at short range, could be decisive, and this was proved when the US Army managed to get some of their first weapons into action on Okinawa a scant month before the end of the war. Had the war continued for a few more weeks, British 3.45in guns would have been in use in Burma, to equally good effect.

But the development of revolutionary weapons takes time, time to solve the small problems which such programmes throw up, as well as the major ones of basic design. The Germans had begun their basic research in the early 1930s, and serious development of field weapons in 1937, with the first field employment in 1941. Neither Britain

Below: The service version of the 95mm RCL gun. (See data page 235.)

nor the USA had done any work at all in pre-war days, and serious work did not begin until 1942. So there is some credit to be taken for managing to progress from lines on paper to serviceable weapons in only three years.

Since then, of course, research and development of RCL guns has been a continuing pro-gramme, and a wide variety of RCL guns are now in service throughout the world. With the exception of the Swedes who were quietly working on RCL guns before anyone else, almost every design in use today owes its inspiration to the wartime weapons, so if they were a little late in appearing, they have made up for it since.

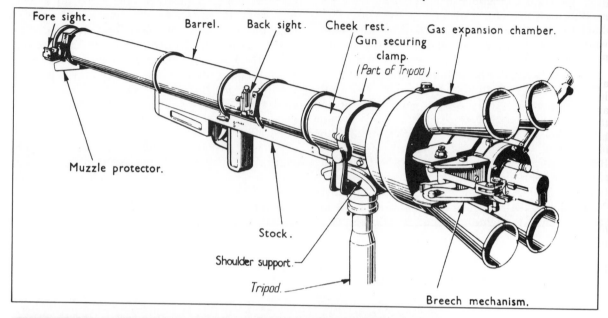

Above: A drawing of the 3.45in RCL Mk 1 taken from the Provisional Handbook. **Left:** The 3.45in Mk 1 fitted to the travelling carriage of the 3.7in RCL.

3.45in Mk 1 Recoilless Gun

The wartime development of recoilless guns in Britain was largely due to one man, Sir Dennis Burney, who fastened on to the idea early in the war, before he had any knowledge of German developments, and pursued it until he eventually managed to interest the authorities. Even then, development remained largely in his hands and it was not until late in 1944 that RCL gun development moved into the official research establishments.

Sir Dennis Burney was an outstanding engineer and inventor who, in earlier years, had been involved with airship design. How he came into the armament field is not clear; he died some years ago, the company he formed for manufacturing the guns has disappeared and no records can be traced. The information given here is distilled from Ordnance Board Proceedings, various wartime reports, and, in particular, a Provisional Handbook of RCL Guns prepared by Sir Dennis for a demonstration at Shoeburyness in June 1944.

The first 'Burney Gun' was a four-bore duck hunter's shotgun which was modified in order to prove the principle. Like the German experimenters, Sir Dennis had reasoned from the basics; during the First World War, the Davis recoilless gun had been developed, a weapon which in effect had two barrels connected to the same chamber. On firing a charge in the chamber, a projectile was discharged through the forward barrel, and an equal-weight 'countershot' through the rear-facing barrel. Since both the projectile and the countershot moved at equal velocity, each barrel reacted with the same recoil force, but, since they opposed each other, the gun, as a whole, did not recoil.

Given that equal weights and velocities cancel each other out, it can be shown that if the countershot is half the weight and moves at twice the velocity, or a quarter of the weight and moves at four times the velocity, or any other related fraction and multiple, recoillessness is still obtained, and if this line of argument be pursued to its logical conclusion, one arrives at a point where an almost weightless stream of gas, moving at several thousand feet per second, will still balance the ejected projectile.

Burney's duck gun had a rearward-facing tube attached to the chamber, a tube terminating in a convergent-divergent De Laval nozzle or venturi. When the gun was fired, a proportion of the gas generated by the explosion of the charge was piped rearward, and was given additional escape velocity by the venturi, so that it balanced the discharge of the gun. Having thus proved that the idea was workable, Sir Dennis then turned to the development of a practical military weapon.

His first was a 20mm single-shot gun, developed with a view to eventually turning it into an automatic cannon. It weighed 50lb and fired the standard Oerlikon gun shell at 3,500ft/sec, an improvement of 700ft/sec over the standard Oerlikon. But there was no requirement that the army could see, and no further work was done.

Next came a 3.45in gun capable of being fired either from a light tripod or from the shoulder; inevitably, from its calibre, it became known as the '25pdr Shoulder Gun', though in fact, the projectiles did not weigh 25lb. In its original form (known as P1) it had a single nozzle attached to the downward-opening screw breech block, and a coned cartridge case with blow-out base. In October 1942, Sir Dennis approached the Director of Artillery's Department to arrange official trials, and a brief demonstration given in the following month was, in the official word, 'promising'. During subsequent months, manufacture of 32 pilot models was begun by the Broadway Trust Company, a consortium of engineering firms organized by Sir Dennis to develop his armament inventions. In 1943, the Ministry of Supply set up their 'RCL Group' to undertake completion of Burney's designs to service standards, and the Armaments Design Department began work on a slightly different (P2) version of the 3.45in, which used Burney's other cartridge case design, a conventionally-shaped case perforated with a number of large holes in the wall, through which the gas was

Above: Exterior and interior views of the HEAT round for the 3.45in RCL, showing the original conical case with bursting disc in the base.

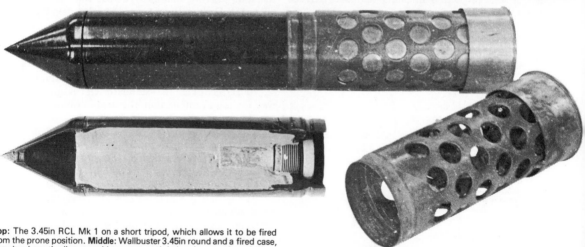

Top: The 3.45in RCL Mk 1 on a short tripod, which allows it to be fired from the prone position. **Middle:** Wallbuster 3.45in round and a fired case, showing how the liner was blown out; and, below it, a section of the Wallbuster shell. **Bottom:** Wallbuster, with the later, perforated case.
1. Nose; 2. Red ring; 3. Yellow edging; 4. Body painted camouflage green; 5. Blue band; 6. Code for HE filling; 7. Series number in ring distinguishing filled lot (stencilled on reverse). 8. Shell; 9. Driving band; 10. Tube; 11. Brass liner; 12. Batch letter and number as applicable; 13. Base; 14. Sub-batch letter as applicable; 15. Primer No. 11; 16. Primer markings.

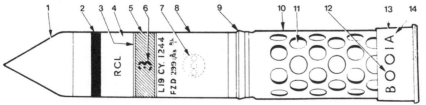

vented into an annular space around the gun chamber and then backwards through four jets arranged around the breech. In November 1944, the War Office stated a firm requirement for a number of these guns, with the intention of using them in the Far East, where heavy firepower from a portable weapon would be of great value. Unfortunately, trials showed up some problems, notably a variation between recoillessness and recoil due to erosive wear in the throats of the venturis, and before this could be cleared up and the guns put into production, the war was over. A total of 135 guns were eventually made, and most of them were issued to various units for extensive user trials in order to 'feel out' the user's reaction to such a novel weapon, but apart from this, the 3.45in RCL was never issued for general service.

Data Ordnance, RCL, 3.45in Mk 1
Weight of gun and breech mechanism: 75lb.
Total length: 68.55in.

Length of bore: 50.874in (14.75 cal).
Rifling: 16 grooves, uniform RH 1/20.
Breech mechanism: Interrupted screw, percussion fired, four venturis.
Elevation: Free.
Traverse: Free:
Weight in action: 75lb.

Performance firing standard 11lb Wallbuster shell
Muzzle velocity: 600ft/sec.
Maximum range: 1,000 yards.

Ammunition
Cartridge, RCL, 3.45in WB Shell Mk 1. This complete fixed round consisted of a cartridge case pierced with holes in the wall, and with a thin brass liner to protect the propellant, and a Wallbuster shell (see p 240). The propelling charge was 11lb 2oz Cordite. The shell was filled with Plastic Explosive and carried the Base Percussion Fuze No. 299. The weight of the complete round was 16.25lb.

3.7in Mk 1 Recoilless Gun

The next gun to be developed was a slightly heavier weapon of 3.7in calibre, mounted on a light wheeled carriage. This appears to have taken much the same development course as the 3.45in and at much the same period. The objective was to provide a weapon capable of being carried by two men, and yet capable of firing a powerful shell. Burney's original drawings show two oval jets alongside a downward-opening breech, but the design was subsequently changed to have six circular jets above and below

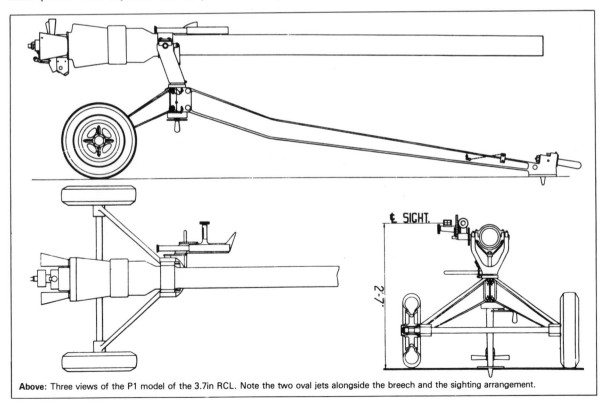

Above: Three views of the P1 model of the 3.7in RCL. Note the two oval jets alongside the breech and the sighting arrangement.

Above: A close-up of the six circular jets incorporated in the production model design of the 3.7in Mk 1. **Left:** Wallbuster round for the 3.7in RCL.

Below: The breech mechanism of the 3.7in.

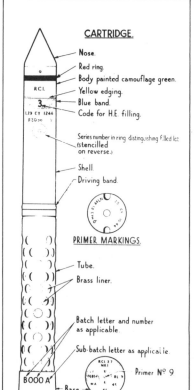

CARTRIDGE.

— Nose.
— Red ring.
— Body painted camouflage green.
— Yellow edging.
— Blue band.
— Code for H.E. filling.

Series number in ring distinguishing filled lot (stencilled on reverse.)

— Shell.
— Driving band.

PRIMER MARKINGS.

— Tube.
— Brass liner.

Batch letter and number as applicable.

Sub-batch letter as applicable.

Primer Nº 9

— Base.

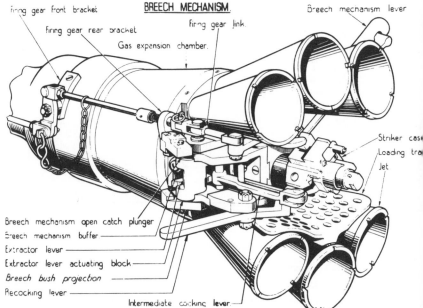

BREECH MECHANISM.

firing gear front bracket

firing gear rear bracket

Gas expansion chamber.

firing gear link

Breech mechanism lever

Striker case

Loading tra

Jet

Breech mechanism open catch plunger
Breech mechanism buffer
Extractor lever
Extractor lever actuating block
Breech bush projection
Recocking lever
Intermediate cocking lever

a side-swinging breech. In this form, the gun was accepted for trials in August 1945, was formally introduced on 4 July 1946, and declared obsolete in December 1947.

Data Ordnance, RCL, 3.7in Mk 1
Weight of gun and breech mechanism: 222lb.
Total length: 112.75in.
Length of bore: 83.717in (22.6 cal).
Rifling: 28 grooves, uniform RH 1/44.76.
Breech mechanism: Interrupted screw, percussion fired, six venturis.
Elevation: $-5° +10°$

Traverse: Free.
Weight in action: 375lb.

Performance firing standard 22½lb Wallbuster shell
Muzzle velocity: 1,000ft/sec.
Maximum range: 2,000 yards.

Ammunition
    Cartridge, RCL, 3.7in WB Shell Mk 1. This consisted of a 22½lb Wallbuster shell filled with Plastic Explosive and fuzed Base Percussion No. 295, attached to a perforated cartridge case containing 4lb 1oz of Cordite.

95mm Mk 1 Recoilless Gun

Probably the most highly regarded of the Burney designs was the 95mm field gun. Development of this was brought to official notice in April 1943 with the information that it was to use separate-loading ammunition and variable charges, an innovation which promised to give the weapon much greater flexibility than previous RCL designs had done. In September 1944, two pilot models were ready, and after examination by various committees, two more, incorporating various improvements, were begun. The two pilots were used for trials and were then sent to the School of Artillery for further tests and demonstrations, and during one of these, a premature detonation of the shell completely destroyed the gun. This set the programme back while investigations took place, but the cause of the accident was eventually found to be a faulty shell fuze, the gun design was absolved of all blame, and development picked up again.

In April 1945, a War Office meeting was held to discuss the potential of the 95mm and it was agreed to order 12 equipments, 6,000 HE shell and 1,200 Wallbuster shell. The guns were eventually built, and

in August 1946 it was stated that the 95mm was 'intended for Airborne Field Artillery', but subsequent travelling and handling trials showed weaknesses in the carriage, while the guns showed a tendency to expand their barrels when proof-fired. Most of the defects were overcome, but the equipments were never issued to service units and spent their entire lives inside experimental ranges.

The 95mm was the RCL which most closely resembled a conventional gun at first glance, if you ignored the trail which ran the wrong way. It was a large equipment (12ft 9in long, 39in high to the trunnions) with a shield and a vertical sliding breech working between the jets. On the first two pilots there were two jets, but the production models used four. The trial was a single box girder unit which ran from the axle-tree forward, beneath the barrel and, at its front end, had a towing attachment and barrel clamp. This layout reflected the lack of recoil (which is the prime reason for having a conventional gun's trail in the conventional place) and it did nothing more strenuous than support the weight of the weapon and prevent it over-balancing.

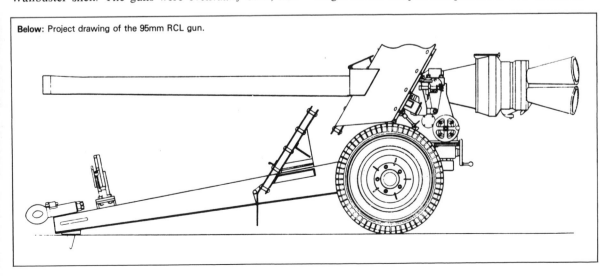

Below: Project drawing of the 95mm RCL gun.

Data Ordnance, RCL, 95mm Mk 1
Weight of gun and breech mechanism: 672lb.
Total length: 120.0in.
Length of bore: 95.5in (25.5 cal).
Rifling: 28 grooves, uniform RH 1/15.
Breech mechanism: Vertical sliding block, percussion fired, four venturis.
Elevation: $-5°$ $+35°$.
Traverse: $30°$ right and left.
Weight in action: 2,350lb.

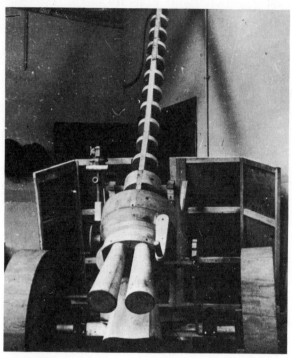

Above: Wooden mock-up of the 95mm RCL gun. Note that the disposition of the jets has changed.

Performance firing standard 25lb HE shell
Muzzle velocity: 1,600ft/sec.
Maximum range: 10,800 yards.

Ammunition separate loading, cased charge.
Propelling charge. The cartridge case was built up using the base of a 4.5in AA gun case into which, a steel sleeve was screwed to form the body of the case. This sleeve was pierced with 104 one-inch holes and lined with a plasticized paper sleeve. Three different propelling charges were provided; one variable, for use with the 25lb HE shell; one fixed weight for use with the 36lb 'Heavy HE Shell' and one fixed weight for use with the $38\frac{1}{2}$lb Wallbuster shell. Details and performance were as follows.

Shell:	Charge:	Weight:	Velocity (ft/sec):	Ranges (yards):
25lb	1	2lb 11oz	500	
25lb	2	3lb 14oz	810	
25lb	3	5lb 1oz	1,070	9,800
25lb	Super	9lb 8oz	1,600	10,800
36lb	Full	11lb 8oz	1,330	10,700
$38\frac{1}{2}$lb	Full	8lb 8oz	1,050	

Shell, HE, 25lb. This was the standard HE shell, as originally designed for use with the 95mm Tank Howitzer, filled with Amatol and with the Percussion Fuze No. 119.
Shell, Heavy, HE, 36lb. This was constructed by using two 25lb shell forgings; one had the nose cut off at the shoulder and was threaded. The other had the base cut off in front of the driving band and was also threaded. The two units were then screwed together to produce a shell 19.75in long. The filling was 5lb 3oz of Amatol, and a Fuze Percussion No. 119 was fitted.
Shell, Wallbuster, $38\frac{1}{2}$lb. This carried a filling of 6.25lb of Plastic Explosive and a Base Percussion Fuze No. 295. (For a description of the Wallbuster shell, see p 240.)

 # 7.2in P1 Recoilless Gun

The largest RCL to be considered by the army was a 7.2in weapon, resembling an enlarged 95mm, but with an interrupted screw breech, and firing bag charges. This was intended as an assault weapon for use during the invasion of Europe. The idea first appeared in March 1943, and seems to have originated in the Director of Artillery's Department rather than with the Broadway Trust. In order to assess the idea, a simulated 7.2in Wallbuster shell was fired against a reinforced concrete wall, five

Above: The 7.2in RCL on tow behind a jeep.

Above: The prototype model of the 7.2in RCL with short jets. **Right:** A detail of the longer jets used on the perfected model of the 7.2in. This gun is still in existence.

feet thick. The detonation blew fragments of concrete 60 yards beyond the wall, cut the reinforcing rods, and severely bulged the wall backwards, a result which was considered sufficiently encouraging to make development of the gun worthwhile.

In the event, though, the difficulty inherent in all recoilless guns – the back-blast – posed problems of how best to employ such a weapon in the confined conditions of an assault beach-head. Moreover, the Recoiling Spigot Mortar of the AVRE tank appeared to be able to do almost as much damage, was simpler to make, and was less of a tactical problem. The 7.2in requirement was therefore cancelled, but a number of pilot guns were built and tested. A trial in August 1944, against 6in armour plate, was most significant. Until then, Burney's 'Wallbuster' shell was considered to be just that – a device for busting walls. But at this trial, the shell blew a 117lb scab, 19 inches by 24 inches, off the back of the target plate at an estimated 600 feet a second, and this led to research into defeating armour plate which, several years later, was to lead to the squash-head shell.

Data Ordnance, RCL, 7.2in P1
Weight of gun and breech mechanism: 1,680lb.
Total length: 165.0in.
Length of bore: 132.0in (18.3 cal).
Rifling: 40 grooves, uniform RH 1/25.

Breech mechanism: Asbury interrupted screw, percussion fired, four venturis.
Elevation: $-5°$ $+15°$.
Traverse: 15° right and left.
Weight in action: 3,585lb.

Performance firing standard 120lb Wallbuster shell
Muzzle velocity: 900ft/sec.
Maximum range: 7,000 yards.

Ammunition separate loading, bag charge.
Propelling Charge. Two charges were to be provided for three projectiles:
1. 17½lb Cordite for use with the 120lb Wallbuster shell and with the 40lb hollow-charge shell.
2. 21½lb Cordite for use with the 135lb Wallbuster shell.

Both charges were simply bundles of Cordite enclosed in a silk cloth bag, with a gunpowder igniter stitched to the end, the normal bag-charge pattern.

Shell, Wallbuster, 120lb and 135lb. These shells were basically the same. The 135lb was a Burney design using a flexible mesh inner container, while the 120lb was an Armaments Research Department design without the inner container. Both were loaded with approximately 39lb of Plastic Explosive and Fuze Percussion No. 299.

Shell, HEAT, 40lb. This was an extremely unusual hollow-charge shell with a short body and abnormally long ballistic cap, to give an adequate stand-off distance. The filling, behind the cone, was 9.8lb of RDX/TNT, and a base percussion fuze designed by Broadway Trust (and never given an official number) provided the initiation at the target. It was claimed that the shell could blow a 3in hole through 6in armour, striking at 30° angle, and this seems to have been a reasonable forecast. It was designed to operate at a muzzle velocity of about 1,800ft/sec.

It is of interest to note that the 7.2 RCL was suggested by Sir Dennis Burney as a possible armament for fitting into turrets on naval landing craft, with large blast deflectors installed on the decks behind. The suggestion was not followed up.

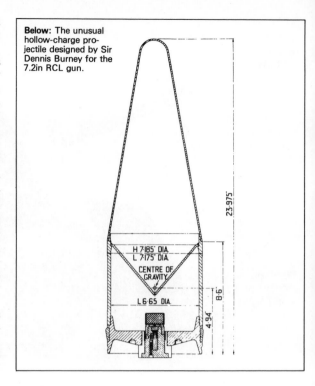

Below: The unusual hollow-charge projectile designed by Sir Dennis Burney for the 7.2in RCL gun.

Burney 8in Recoilless Gun

The last Burney design was for an 8in gun which, in the inventor's words, would combine 'The potentiality of the 7.2in Mk 6 howitzer, the American 8in Gun M1, and the British 12in 'Road Hog' howitzer. That is to say, one unit of the new design has to be approximately the same weight as the lightest of these . . . range further than the longest-ranging of the three, and fire a shell of approximately the same HE content as the heaviest shell fired by any of the three.'

Sir Dennis then explained how these conflicting demands were to be met: 'The design of the gun to fulfil these conditions would not have been possible except for the ability of an RCL gun to fire projectiles of varying weights without alteration to the recoil balance. The 8in RCL is therefore designed to fire:

1) the 200lb 8inch Howitzer shell, to compete with the 7.2in howitzer;
2) a 240lb 'Duplex' projectile to compete with the American 8inch Gun for range; and
3) a 520lb HE projectile to compete with the shell of the 12inch howitzer.'

In order to make construction as simple as possible, the 8in was designed to use existing components; the wheels and hubs from the 7.2in Howitzer, the front axle, wheels and towbar from the 40mm Bofors gun, the traversing roller bearings and racer from the 3.7in AA gun, the sights from the 25pdr, and the breech mechanism from the old 8in Howitzer.

To keep the length of the equipment as short as possible, so as to aid mobility, the cartridge chamber was divorced from the barrel and actually split into two chambers which lay at each side of the barrel, but which were connected to the rear end of the bore by a transverse passage. Each chamber had a breech mechanism at the front end and a venturi unit at the rear, while the rear end of the barrel was closed by a third breech mechanism. This arrangement brought other advantages; since the rifling began barely 18in in front of the rear breechblock, ramming the shell was easier; the outside position of the chambers aided in cooling them; and the design of the interior contours of the chambers and jets could be closer to the optimum than was generally possible with gun chambers in the conventional place. Another advantage claimed was that with three breech mechanisms, the loading of the shell and two charges would be performed simultaneously, thus improving the rate of fire; but, in fact, it was this feature which carried within it the seeds of disaster.

Work on this design continued at a low priority, and the gun was not completed until 1946. Since the army had never expressed any official enthusiasm for the gun, no acceptance trials had been arranged, but Sir Dennis was given permission to take the gun to a proof range and fire it there at his own expense. The first proof shot blew up the gun and wrecked it beyond repair. The project was abandoned forthwith but, in order to extract the utmost value from the affair, the Ordnance Board ordered the accident to be investigated. In 1958 a report finally appeared, which showed that the detonation which destroyed the gun was caused by the multiple-breech system. Each breech was provided with its own firing mechanism, but only the two chamber breeches had the locks loaded. Poor ignition of the charges by these locks had led to smouldering of the propellant, leading to a build-up in pressure of explosive gases, within the chamber and gun breech, which then detonated. The gun design was absolved of blame, but it was recommended that 'multiple firing mechanisms are not to be perpetuated in service equipments'.

Data Burney 8in RCL
Weight of gun and breech mechanism: 18,145lb.
Total length: 402.0in.
Length of bore: 382.0in (48 cal).
Breech mechanism: Three Asbury mechanisms, two venturis.
Elevation: 0° +45°.
Traverse: 35° right and left.
Weight in action: 39,200lb.

Performance
Estimated maximum ranges were as follows.
200lb shell: 26,000 yards.
240lb shell: 36,000 yards.
520lb shell: 20,000 yards.

Ammunition separate loading, bag charge.
Propelling Charge. Beyond the fact that it was of Cordite and in six equal portions, loaded three to each chamber, no details are known.

Projectiles. The 200lb shell was the service US 8in Howitzer shell. The 240lb Duplex shell was a 6.5in calibre projectile 52.6in long, fitted with two 8in discarding sabots, one at the base and one at the centre of gravity. The filling was to have been 37lb of high explosive. The 520lb 'Heavy HE' shell was a modification of two conventional 8in shell forgings, as had been done with the 95mm, mentioned above; the nose and body of one shell screwed to the base and body of another to produce a 63in long shell carrying 70lb of high explosive.

So far as is known, none of these shells (except, of course, the 200lb) was produced; the proof gun was loaded with an inert 'proof cylinder'.

A Note on the Ammunition for Burney Guns
Two questions regarding the ammunition will have arisen by now. First, what was the Wallbuster shell, and second, how did Burney expect to 'get away' with using his over-length and over-weight 'Duplex' shells? The answers to both these questions must be seen in the context of the peculiar internal ballistics of the Burney guns. (What follows is a simplified version of Sir Dennis Burney's expressed opinions and theory; it was not accepted in its entirety by the ballisticians of ARDE and other establishments, and it is noteworthy that the 120mm BAT, the eventual recoilless gun in British service, diverged from Burney's theory in several respects.)

The fundamental factor in the Burney gun was that it used a long barrel and a low chamber pressure. In this, it differed from the German RCLs which used short barrels and high chamber pressures. As a result, Burney claimed, the British gun developed a 'smoother propulsive force' because, due to the controlled escape of gas to the rear, the maximum chamber pressure was less, but the average pressure throughout shot travel was more sustained. Since the initial pressure was less, the accelerative blow to the shell was reduced, and the setback forces, which, in a normal gun, tend to crush the shell walls due to the weight of the fuze during

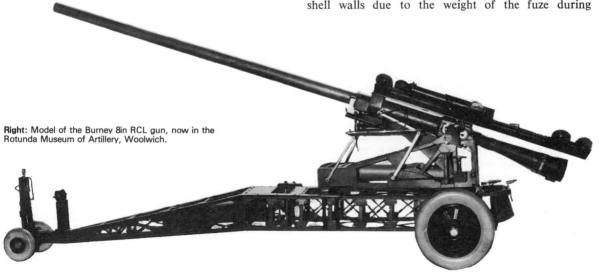

Right: Model of the Burney 8in RCL gun, now in the Rotunda Museum of Artillery, Woolwich.

acceleration, were also less. It was this theory which encouraged the development of the long Duplex and 'heavy' shells, since they could withstand the lower acceleration without collapsing. As to whether any of these were actually made and fired, we have no knowledge; all that can be said is that while numerous drawings exist, nobody appears to have ever seen a shell, or even a photograph of one.

The Wallbuster shell was based on a different premise, though the design did take advantage of the lower accelerative force. It was designed as 'An attempt to place plastic charges on either concrete or armour at a high enough velocity to enable accurate shooting to be made' and was called the Wallbuster because the original intention was the destruction of concrete fortifications. It consisted basically of a thin steel tube with a pointed head carrying a hardened 'spur' to dig into the target when striking at an angle. Inside this outer shell was an inner container made of flexible wire mesh, filled with Plastic Explosive and carrying a base fuze. This gave an unusually large explosive content – about 27% – which ensured a satisfactory result at the target. The functioning of the shell was as follows: on striking the target, the outer skin was crushed or peeled back, while the inner container continued, because of momentum, and, as a result of the flexibility of the mesh bag, squashed against the target like a poultice. During this squashing action, the base fuze was initiated by deceleration, and its delay was sufficient to allow the plastic explosive to form a pad about two inches thick before the fuze detonated it. The subsequent detonation wave had a disruptive effect within the target structure.

The Wallbuster worked well enough for it to be accepted for service in the various guns, but as soon as the war was over, all production was halted and a long and exhaustive investigation of the theory was begun. This led to extensive changes in design, notably to make it work in conventional as well as in recoilless guns, and eventually, in the early 1950s, it re-appeared as the 'HESH' or 'High Explosive, Squash Head' shell; it was later adopted by the US Army as the 'HEP' or 'HE Plastic' shell. So that although Sir Dennis laboured in vain so far as a service RCL weapon was concerned, his researches resulted in a superb tank-killing shell, and that alone was probably worth all the rest.

105mm T9 Recoilless Howitzer

American development of recoilless guns began independently in two places. In June 1943, the Infantry Section of the Research and Development Service began work on a low-pressure weapon, along much the same lines as the British Burney gun, using a perforated cartridge case. The Artillery Section began in October 1943, on a high-pressure weapon based on a captured German 105mm LG42 gun. Since this project was little more than a straight copy of the German gun, it moved quite rapidly and resulted in the 105mm Howitzer RCL T9.

The T9 was designed to use the standard 105mm Howitzer shell M1, but with the driving band pre-engraved so as to reduce the shot-start pressure. The cartridge case had a thick plastic disc in the base which, on firing, blew out through a venturi in the sliding breech block.

First firings took place in April 1944. The first test charge was 25oz of propellant, and the shell stayed in the barrel while the howitzer 'recoiled' forwards for five inches! After this entertaining start, the charge was gradually increased and subsequent firings were quite successful, though the breech block showed signs of severe erosion. However, becaue of the greater success of the design originated by the Infantry Section, the T9 project was closed down in August 1945.

Data Howitzer, 105mm, RCL, T9
Weight of gun and breech mechanism: 300lb.
Total length: 87.65in.
Length of bore: 51.25in (12.4 cal).

Rifling: Uniform RH 1/25.
Breech mechanism: Horizontal sliding block, percussion fired, single venturi.
Elevation: $-5°$ $+65°$.
Traverse: 40° right and left.
Weight in action: 800lb.

Performance firing standard 33lb HE shell
Muzzle velocity: 1,140ft/sec.
Maximum range: 7,500 yards.

Ammunition separate loading, cased charge.
Propelling charge. The charge eventually settled on was 8lb of NH powder, in a brass case with a solid plastic base disc. Details of primer location are not known.
Projectile T42. This was the standard 105mm M1 howitzer shell, modified by having the driving band pre-engraved, and with two Neoprene indexing studs attached to the shell shoulders so as to guide the driving band into the rifling.

An interesting variant development was the T9E2, which consisted of two T9s coupled together with an Automatic Feed Mechanism T23, having a magazine capacity of ten rounds. This was proposed in September 1944 for use in aircraft. Some development work was done, but the project was closed down in August 1945, though some of the results achieved were applied to the research for the T19 gun (p 244).

57mm T15 Recoilless Rifle

The developments by the Infantry Section became known as the 'Kromuskit' design, a name derived from the names of Kroger and Musser, the designers. Like the Burney guns, the Kromuskits used long light barrels, and multi-perforated cartridge cases which vented to an annular space around the chamber, and then rearwards through vents formed in the breech block. The first weapon to be designed was the 57mm RCL Rifle T15, which was first fired in November 1943. In March 1944, tests of an improved version indicated 'That the weapon is comparable in accuracy with a conventional gun'. In the following month, procurement of 100 weapons was under consideration, and by early 1945, more than 2,000 had been ordered, together with more than 600,000 rounds of HE and 200,000 rounds of HEAT ammunition.

Data 57mm RCL Rifle M18 (T15E3) on Mount, Machine Gun, M2
Weight of gun and breech mechanism: 35lb.
Total length: 61.6in.
Rifling: 24 grooves, uniform RH 1/25.
Breech mechanism: Interrupted lug. Percussion fired. 1 venturi.
Elevation: $-27°$ $+65°$.
Traverse: 360°.
Weight in action: 48.75lb.

Performance firing standard 2.7lb HE shell
Muzzle velocity: 1,217ft/sec.
Maximum range: 4,935 yards.

Ammunition fixed rounds, cased charge.
Cartridge, HE, M306. This round consisted of the Cartridge Case M30, a steel case perforated with 400 holes in the side walls, and having a gilding metal 'stop ring' near the mouth. This stop ring was to aid in engaging the pre-engraved driving band, and to positively position the round in the chamber. The case was lined with plastic to prevent the 1.0lb propelling charge from escaping through the holes. Later models of case modified the stop ring; the M301A1 had the ring formed by pressing out the case metal, while the M301A1B1 used three pressed-out 'dimples' in the case metal.

The Shell M306 was a thin-walled steel shell loaded with 0.6lb of TNT and fitted with the Point Detonating Fuze M89. A variant model was the M306A1, which contained 0.55lb of Composition B, an RDX/TNT mixture. Both shells were fitted with pre-engraved driving bands. Shell weight; 2.78lb. Complete round weight 5.46lb.

Cartridge, HEAT, M307. This round used the same cartridge case as above. The projectile was a hollow-charge shell containing 0.4lb of composition B, and fitted with the Point Initiating, Base Detonating (PIBD) Fuze M90. This fuze functioned on impact, and contained a tiny hollow-charge which fired back through a central tube in the shell to detonate a Tetryl booster charge at the base of the hollow-charge filling, thus ensuring detonation of the hollow charge filling from its rear end, for optimum effect. Shell weight 2.75lb. Complete round weight 5.43lb.

Cartridge, Canister, T25E3. An anti-personnel round using the same cartridge case as above. The projectile was a thin steel cylinder soldered to a

Above: The 57mm RCL T15 rifle on a modified machine-gun tripod; and (below) an illustration taken from the first 'tentative' instruction manual.

heavy base which carried the pre-engraved driving band. This cylinder had four slits cut into its length, and was closed with a steel disc. Inside were 133 cylindrical steel slugs. On firing, the casing split open as the projectile left the gun muzzle, and the slugs were distributed shotgun-fashion. The effective range was about 175ft, at which distance, the slugs could penetrate a 1in pine plank. Shot weight 2.75lb. Complete round weight 5.43lb.

Below: Three types of ammunition for the 57mm RCL T15 rifle. **Left to right:** HE shell, HEAT shell and canister cartridge.

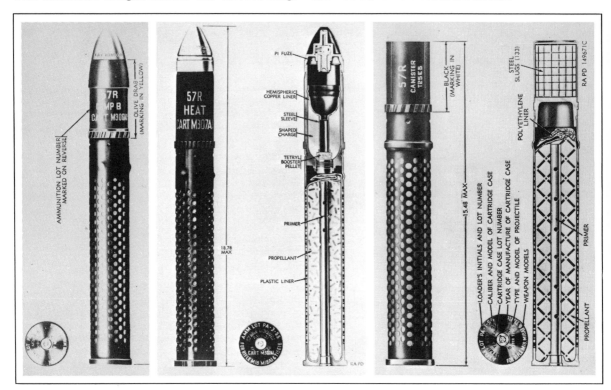

75mm M20 Recoilless Rifle

The success of the 57mm in its earliest form was enough to encourage the designers to greater things, and they rapidly developed a 75mm version which was little more than an enlargement of the 57mm, though with a somewhat better system of breech closure. Two models were developed, a 'heavy' version using the conventional 75mm gun shell, and a 'light' version using a similar projectile, but with a pre-engraved driving band. Experiments soon showed that the additional chamber pressure needed to engrave the conventional driving band led to a variety of ballistic problems, and the 'heavy' idea was dropped, effort then being concentrated on the 'light' model which became the 75mm RCL Rifle T21. After tests by the Infantry Board early in 1945, some small modifications were made, after which, it was standardized as the M20. Limited procurement of 1,000, with 30 white phosphorus, 90 HEAT and 180 HE rounds per gun, was authorized, all the projectiles being those for the 75mm Pack Howitzer, but with pre-engraved bands.

Both 57mm and 75mm weapons were issued to troops in 1945. In Europe, they were used during the last few days of the war by the 17th US Airborne Division near Essen, while in the Pacific theatre, they were first used on Okinawa on 9 June. They were extremely well received, the sole complaint being of the limited quantity of ammunition sent.

Variants

T21: Original scale-up of the 57mm.

T21E4: Breech threads cut into an inserted bushing.

T21E7: Modified so as to break into two units, barrel and chamber with breech, for easier carriage. Development continued post-war, but was eventually abandoned.

T21E13: T21E4 with rifling twist reduced to 1/30 in order to improve the performance of the HEAT shell.

T25: Since the alteration in the breech design of the T21E4 had made the components non-interchangeable with the rest of the T21 series, the nomenclature was changed to T25, and it was this model which was standardized as the M20 in June 1945.

Data 75mm RCL Rifle M20, on Mount, Machine Gun, Cal .30, M1917A1
Weight of gun and breech mechanism: 114.5lb.
Total length: 82.0in.
Length of bore:
Rifling: 28 grooves, uniform RH 1/25.
Breech mechanism: Interrupted screw, percussion fired. 1 venturi.
Elevation: $-27° +65°$.
Traverse: 360°.
Weight in action: 165.5lb.

Performance firing standard 14.4lb HE shell
Muzzle velocity: 990ft/sec.
Maximum range: 6,955 yards.

Ammunition fixed rounds, cased charge.
Cartridge, HE, M309. This round consisted of Cartridge Case M31, a necked case made of steel, and having 992 perforations. It was lined with plastic and contained a propelling charge of 3.30lb.

The projectile was basically the same as that for the 75mm field gun, but was fitted with a pre-engraved driving band. It was filled with 1.49lb of TNT and carried the Point Detonating Fuze M51A5. Shell weight 14.40lb; complete round weight 22.37lb.

Cartridge, HEAT, M310 or M310A1. This used the same cartridge case as above, but with a 3.19lb propelling charge. The shell was a hollow-charge type containing 0.99lb of Pentolite, and having a base detonation fuze. Shell M310 used the Fuze BD M62A1, while Shell M301A1 used the BD Fuze

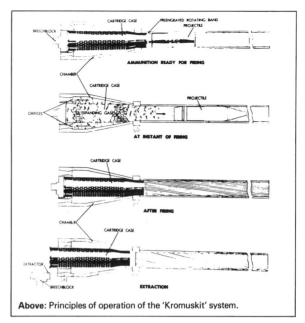

Above: Principles of operation of the 'Kromuskit' system.

M91A1, the difference being that the M91A1 was fitted with a tracer element. This shell had a muzzle velocity of 1,000ft/sec and a maximum range of 7,300 yards. Shell weight 13.19lb; complete round weight 21.06lb.

Cartridge, Smoke, M311. Basically this was the same as the high-explosive round M309, except that the shell was filled with 1.35lb of white phosphorus. The muzzle velocity was 990ft/sec and the maximum range was 7,020 yards. Shell weight 15.10lb; complete round weight 23.20lb.

Below, left: The 75mm RCL T15 rifle. Note the round of ammunition and sighting arrangement; and (right) the 75mm mounted on a modified machine-gun tripod. The box and wires are for a sight illumination system.

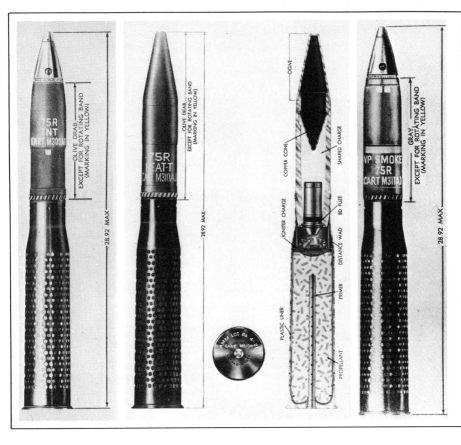

Ammunition for the 75mm RCL M20 rifle. **Left to right:** The high-explosive round, the HEAT anti-tank cartridge and the white phosphorus smoke cartridge.

T19 Recoilless Rifle

The last development of the Infantry Section was a 105mm Kromuskit, known as the RCL Rifle T19. This used the standard M1 shell from the 105mm howitzer, with a pre-engraved driving band and the usual multi-perforated cartridge case. An experimental model was made and was fired in competition with the RCL Howitzer T9. A subsequent report, published in June 1945, noted that 'The Kromuskit gave a muzzle velocity of 1,250ft/sec at 8,770psi while the T9 gave only 1,000ft/sec at 14,000psi. On the basis of the above results, and in consideration that little experience has been obtained with short, fat chambers [as on the T9] and the regularity of propellants fired from such chambers, the Ordnance Department have decided to concentrate their development on the Kromuskit . . .'

In July 1945, procurement of 5,000 guns, with ammunition, was authorized, but in October, this was cut back to 50 guns and was then postponed completely in view of a request by Army Ground Forces to develop either a breakdown design or a short-barrelled version suitable for use by airborne troops. Development work continued in the post-war years, but at low priority, and it finally appeared in service during the Korean War. It was not a success and had to be extensively re-worked.

The T9 howitzer development, as we have seen, was dropped in favour of the T19 Kromuskit, but, by that time, the Artillery Section had begun work on a 155mm RCL Howitzer T4. This also worked on the blow-out disc principle, and, it was hoped, would fire the standard 95lb 155mm shell. The project got under way late in 1944. The equipment was to be tripod mounted, with a light wheeled carriage for travelling. It was proposed to use bag-charge ammunition, and insert the plastic blow-out disc into the breech during the loading sequence, but considerable difficulties arose during the development of this idea. The principal problem was finding a plastic which could produce a disc strong enough to withstand the initial chamber pressure and yet fragment into minute pieces. The anticipated danger area behind the weapon, with large lumps of plastic being blown from the jet along with a stream of incandescent gas, was enormous. Nothing appeared during the war, and it is understood that the project was quietly interred shortly after the war had ended.

Ammunition

The following notes on the subject of ammunition may be of value to readers not familiar with artillery ammunition, and will serve as a background to the descriptions given in the entries for the guns, which have been kept brief in order to avoid repetition.

Cartridges

These fall into two groups, those which are contained in metallic (usually brass) cases, and those which are contained in cloth bags. In British service, it is possible to identify the type of cartridge used with any gun by the gun's nomenclature; e.g. 'Ordnance QF . . .' indicates a cased cartridge, while 'Ordnance BL . . .' indicates a bagged charge. No such distinction is made in American service.

Cased charges may be permanently attached to their projectile, and when this is so, the complete round is called 'fixed'. Or it may be completely separate, issued and loaded separately, when it is known as a 'separate loading' (UK) or 'separated' (US) round. Some American weapons supplied the cartridge and projectile separately, but had them joined together for loading, and these were known as 'semi-fixed' rounds. All bag charges are, obviously, separate loading, and in this connection, the term is common to both British and American usage.

Which system is used depends on the tactical use of the weapon. Where a gun requires but one charge, and is to be loaded and fired rapidly – e.g. an anti-tank or anti-aircraft gun – fixed rounds are used. But where a gun or howitzer requires to have the charge varied, either to save wear at the higher charges, or to vary the trajectory in order to pass over some intervening crest, separated or semi-fixed rounds must be used. Where such adjustment is provided, the propelling charge is sub-divided and packed into cloth bags within the case, so that the appropriate portion can be removed. These cartridges are usually provided with some form of cap or lid which protects the contents of the case prior to loading and, on loading, keeps the bags firmly in the case so that there is no danger of faulty ignition. Such caps must, of course, be of a substance which is completely consumed or destroyed when the gun is fired.

With bag charges, similar rules apply. Guns usually have one or two bags; two, where a 'reduced' practice or short-range charge is required. Howitzers may have anything up to a dozen bags so as to give the degree of selectivity required. The bags comprising the required charge are tied together with cloth tapes so as to form a compact bundle for convenience in loading.

In cased charges, ignition of the charge is performed by a 'primer'. This is a metal fitting screwed into the base (UK) or press-fitted into the base (US) of the cartridge case. Its outer end presents a percussion cap to the firing mechanism of the gun, while the inner portion carries a charge of gunpowder. When the cap is struck, the gunpowder is ignited and flashes out, from prepared channels, to ignite the propellant charge packed around it.

With bag charges, the ignition is performed by a 'tube' (UK) or 'primer' (US) which, broadly speaking, resembles a blank cartridge for a rifle; indeed, the common British tube for most of the guns in this book was the 'Tube, Percussion, Smallarm' which was no more than a 0.303 rifle cartridge case, made over. The case carries a percussion cap and a filling of gunpowder. On firing, the gunpowder explodes and flashes through a central hole ('vent') in the breech to ignite the bag charge.

While we have spoken here of initiating the firing of the gun by percussion means, there were alternative methods. Primers and tubes using electrical ignition were found in coast artillery weapons, and these used a fine incandescent wire surrounded by guncotton dust as the firing device. An electrical current passed into an insulated contact in the tube or primer (which occupied the same position as the percussion cap) flowed through the wire, ignited the guncotton and thus, the gunpowder, and started the chain of events. American coast weapons were also provided with 'friction primers' as an alternative method of firing, should the electrical system fail. These resembled the primer used with bag-charge guns, but had a rod protruding from their base in place of the percussion cap or electrical contact; the inner portion of this rod was roughened and embedded in match composition. When the rod was jerked out of the primer, the friction of the roughened portion against the match composition fired it, thus firing the gunpowder filling and the gun charge.

The propellant used in the charge was a low explosive; that is, one which burns progressively, albeit rapidly, rather than detonates. In British service, Cordite, a mixture of nitro-glycerin and nitro-cellulose, was the standard substance, but during the war years, several other propellants were introduced as alternatives, notably the American NH and FNH powders.

NH means 'Non-Hygroscopic' – i.e. not given to absorbing water – and is better described as a pious hope than as a statement of scientific fact. FNH means 'Flashless, Non-Hygroscopic', and this, too, requires some qualification. NH powder was probably less hygroscopic than some which had gone before, but in comparison with Cordite, it was very suscep-tible to damp. FNH powder might be flashless, or it might not; it depended on how the gun felt about it. Both powders were nitro-cellulose, with various additives; they were cooler-burning than Cordite, and thus developed less wear in the gun, but, by the same token, they were less powerful and, therefore, an NH charge for a given gun had to be larger than a Cordite charge. This did not bother the Americans, but it bothered the British when they bought the powder in 1940 and began to make charges from it; some guns never got an NH charge because there was not sufficient room inside the cartridge case. The question of flashlessness revolved around the combination of gun and powder, and the same powder might be flashless in one gun, but not in another. A concrete example: the FNH charge for the 75mm Gun M1897 was of exactly the same formulation as the NH charge for the 155mm Gun M1918.

High Explosive Shells
The shell, as the name implies, is a hollow container filled with high explosive, but that is only the beginning. The steel body needs to be sufficiently thick to stand up to the sudden and violent acceler-ation sustained when the charge is fired and the shell begins to move. Obviously, the better the quality of the steel, the thinner the wall need be and the more explosive the shell can contain. British shell designers worked on the assumption that high-grade steel would be needed for more important things in a war economy, and they therefore designed the shells to be made from 19-ton steel, making the walls fairly thick, and giving the shell an explosive capacity of about 8% of the overall weight. American designers, on the other hand, were less concerned with the likelihood of a steel famine, and they designed their shells to use a better grade of steel, allowing them to have thinner walls, and a capacity of 10%–15%. This gave a more satisfying bang at the target.

The shell was provided with a fuze to detonate the filling, but since the detonator in the fuze was tiny and the main filling of the shell relatively insensitive, in order to withstand travelling, loading and firing, it was necessary to provide an amplifying chain between the two. The British system was to use a substantial magazine in the fuze, which trans-ferred its detonation to an 'exploder' in the shell. This was a pellet or small bag of relatively sensitive explosive which would respond to the detonation of the fuze magazine and, in its turn, initiate the main filling of the shell. The exploder was positioned on the axis of the shell, in a recess cast or bored into the explosive filling. Despite this chain of actions, of course, the shell detonated virtually instantaneously when the fuze went into action; the various components were touching each other, and the detonating wave was travelling at some six or eight thousand feet per second.

In American practice, the fuze had a very small magazine, but was screwed into a 'booster' which contained a quite large pellet of explosive. Fuze and booster were screwed into the shell so that the bottom surface of the booster rested on the explosive filling.

Piercing Shells
These are pointed, and carry their fuzes at the base end so as to protect them while the shell is breaking its way through the armour or concrete of the target. In view of their battering function, the nose has to be extremely thick and this, in turn, means that the space left for explosive is very small. Nevertheless, there is sufficient to allow the shell to be burst once it has passed through the target, thus attacking the *target* rather than the *protection*, a point which is frequently overlooked.

Piercing shells can be sub-divided. The most potent variety were the AP (Armour Piercing) type; these had very hard tips, very thick bodies, and corres-pondingly small explosive content – as low as $1\frac{1}{2}\%$ was not unknown in large calibres. The SAP (Semi-AP) had a thinner head and more explosive – 3%–5% – and was called 'Semi' because, generally, it was not capable of piercing its own calibre in armour thickness at the mean fighting range of the gun. Finally, there was the 'Common Pointed' which, though it looked like any other piercing shell, was very thin in the head and carried 8% or 10% of explosive, and had a poor penetrative power against anything other than light masonry.

Penetrative caps had been used on piercing shells from the turn of the century, their function being to take the initial blow of impact and spread it to the shoulders of the shell rather than concentrating it on the point. Since these caps had a poor ballistic shape, it was found advantageous to place a thin metal 'ballistic cap' of tapering form on top of the piercing cap so as to improve the shell's flight and give it a better remaining velocity at any given range. British nomenclature generally indicated the presence of a cap (APC) or both (APCBC), but American terminology did not.

Carrier Shells
These are shells which act solely as vehicles, taking some active agent to the target area and there liberating it. Smoke screens are the most common

Right: High-explosive shell for the British 6in howitzer, showing (left) the method of filling, with an exploder in two sections contained inside a steel tube and with the fuze inserted into the nose; and (right) the pre-war method of marking.

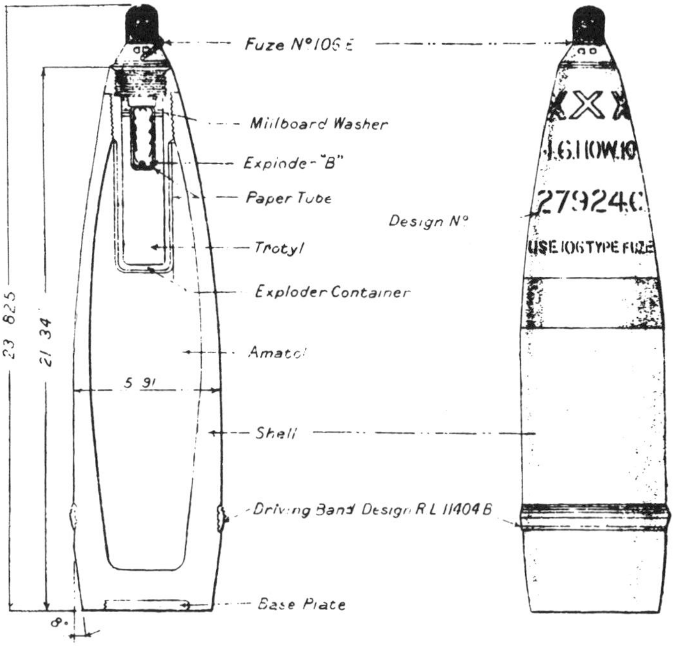

Fuze N°106 E
Millboard Washer
Exploder "B"
Paper Tube
Trotyl
Exploder Container
Design N°
Amatol
5 91
23 825
21 34
Shell
Driving Band Design R L 11404 B
Base Plate
8°
USE 106 TYPE FUZE

Below: Internal side elevation and action sequence of the American M21 Booster, which was screwed into the nose of the shell to act as a combined bore-safety device and exploder. The fuze screws into the booster and ignites the booster detonator, but only the spin of the shell will align the detonator, since it is mounted in an off-balance rotor which is locked safe by a centrifugal pin. Spin withdraws the pin and then swings the rotor to 'arm' the booster for firing.

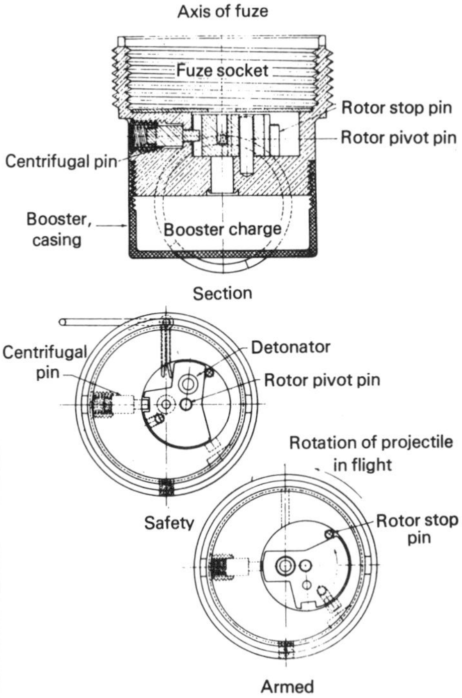

Axis of fuze
Fuze socket
Rotor stop pin
Rotor pivot pin
Centrifugal pin
Booster, casing
Booster charge
Section
Centrifugal pin
Detonator
Rotor pivot pin
Rotation of projectile in flight
Safety
Rotor stop pin
Armed

Right: The proximity fuze, because of its larger size, caused design problems. On the left is a standard British design with conventional fuze and two exploders; on the right, the 'Universal' filling with a large removable exploder.

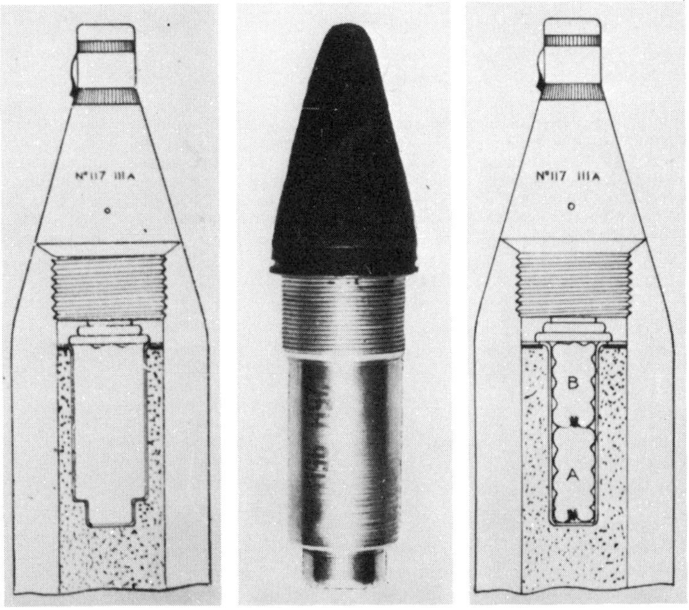

N°117 IIIA
N°117 IIIA
B
A

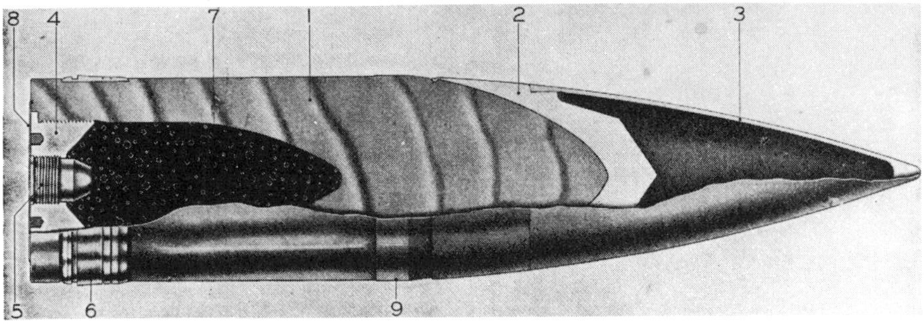

8
4
7
1
2
3
5
6
9

Left: Cutaway of a typical coast artillery piercing shell of American design.

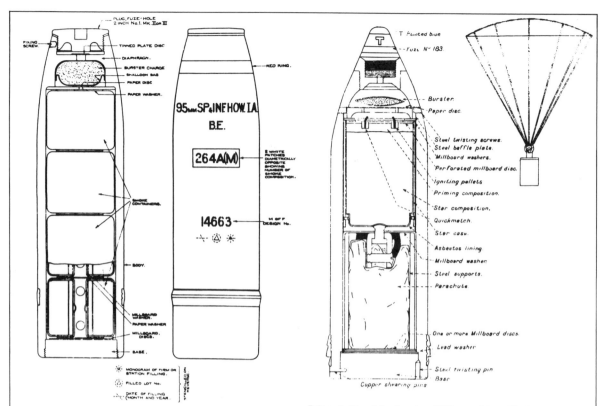

PLUG, FUZE-HOLE
2 INCH No.1. MK. II or III

FIXING
SCREW.

TINNED PLATE DISC

DIAPHRAGM.

BURSTER CHARGE

SHALLOON BAG

PAPER DISC

PAPER WASHER.

SMOKE
CONTAINERS.

BODY.

MILLBOARD
WASHER.

PAPER WASHER

MILLBOARD.
DISCS.

BASE.

MONOGRAM OF FIRM OR
STATION FILLING.

FILLED LOT No.

DATE OF FILLING
(MONTH AND YEAR.

RED RING.

95mm SP&INF HOW. I.A
B.E.

264A(M)

14663

2 WHITE
PATCHES
DIAMETRICALLY
OPPOSITE
SHOWING
NUMBER OF
SMOKE
COMPOSITION.

14 OFF
DESIGN No.

T Painted blue

Fuze No 183.

Burster.

Paper disc.

Steel twisting screws.
Steel baffle plate.
Millboard washers.
Perforated millboard disc.
Igniting pellets.
Priming composition.
Star composition.
Quickmatch.
Star case.
Asbestos lining.
Millboard washer.
Steel supports.
Parachute.

One or more Millboard discs.
Lead washer.
Steel twisting pin.
Base.

Copper shearing pins.

Above: A base-ejection smoke shell for the 95mm howitzer. The plug at the top is replaced by a time fuze before loading. This fuze ignites the gunpowder burster charge, which ignites the smoke canisters by the central channel and also builds up pressure that forces off the baseplate and ejects the canisters. **Right:** Typical design of parachute star shell, acting on the same principle of base ejection due to pressure from a small burster charge.

Below: Action of the American M48 type of fuze. The interrupter is forced out by spin, leaving the central channel clear for the flash from the detonator on impact. For delay action, the interrupter can be locked in, thus stopping the flash from the forward detonator; in this case, the delay holder assembly runs forward on impact, driving a detonator on to a fixed pin, and then the ignition burns through a 'relay' assembly to give a short delay. In either case, the flash comes out of the bottom of the fuze and initiates the booster detonator.

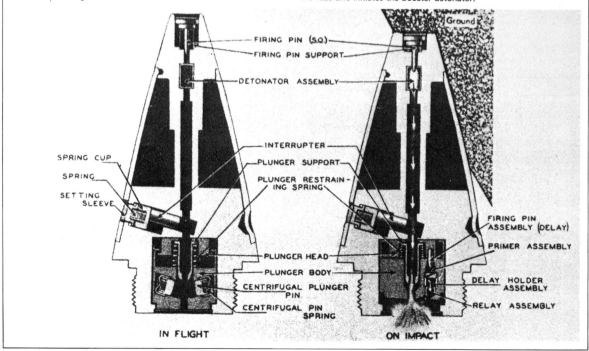

Ground

FIRING PIN (S.Q.)
FIRING PIN SUPPORT

DETONATOR ASSEMBLY

SPRING CUP

SPRING

SETTING
SLEEVE

INTERRUPTER
PLUNGER SUPPORT
PLUNGER RESTRAIN-
ING SPRING

PLUNGER HEAD
PLUNGER BODY
CENTRIFUGAL PLUNGER
PIN
CENTRIFUGAL PIN
SPRING

FIRING PIN
ASSEMBLY (DELAY)
PRIMER ASSEMBLY
DELAY HOLDER
ASSEMBLY
RELAY ASSEMBLY

IN FLIGHT

ON IMPACT

application of carrier shell, and there are two basic types of smoke shell, the 'bursting' and the 'base ejection'. The bursting smoke shell is almost the same as an HE shell, but has a central tube filled with high explosive running down the axis. Around this is the smoke agent, almost invariably white phosphorus, and an impact fuze is fitted into the head of the shell. On striking the ground, the fuze detonates the central burster, which is just sufficiently powerful to crack open the shell in a relatively mild fashion, and distribute the phosphorus in the immediate neighbourhood. Phosphorus, of course, ignites as soon as it is brought into contact with the air, and the ignition produces dense clouds of white smoke. Unfortunately, it tends to generate a great deal of heat, which causes the air in the vicinity to rise and take the smoke with it, so that phosphorus smoke exhibits a tendency to 'pillar' and leave gaps in what would be a screen.

To cure this, the base-ejection shell was developed in Britain in the middle 1930s. This used a tubular shell with a baseplate lightly screwed in. Inside the shell were three canisters loaded with a chemical composition which would emit white smoke when ignited, and do so without excessive heat. Above the canisters was a 'pusher plate', a small charge of gunpowder, and, in the head of the shell, a time fuze. When this fuze functioned, it ignited the gunpowder. The explosion of the gunpowder lit the smoke canisters and also caused a build-up of pressure which forced off the shell baseplate and allowed the canisters to leave the shell. Once out of the shell, the canisters fell to the ground, there to emit smoke. The smoke, being relatively cool, clung to the ground and formed an excellent screen, and the canisters continued to burn and produce smoke for one or two minutes. Phosphorus, on the other hand, gave off instant smoke and had to be 'stoked up' fairly rapidly.

Other carrier-shell payloads were coloured smoke, flares for night-time signalling, stars on parachutes for illuminating the battlefield, and, though never issued, poison gas. All worked on one of the two principles shown above.

Fuzes
It has been said that a fuze is a combination lock, the only key to which is firing from a rifled gun, and this fairly sums up the complexity of most fuzes. Their basic job is to set off the shell at the right time and in the right place, but to do that, they have to be so designed that transportation, loading, firing, and flight will not derange them and yet after all this, they must be ready to work. Safety is one of the most important aspects of fuze design; it was once said that the British would design a safe fuze and then spend ten years trying to make it work, while the Americans designed fuzes which worked and then spent ten years trying to make them safe.

The basic mechanical action of an impact fuze is to bring a sharp needle into violent contact with a sensitive detonator and then channel the result to the fuze magazine or booster so that the operation of the shell can begin. That much is easy. Contact can be done by simply using the impact with the target to drive the needle on to the detonator; or by using the deceleration of the fuze as it suddenly comes to a stop on impact, allowing momentum to carry the detonator on to the firing pin. But if impact can do these things, so too can the sudden acceleration as the shell is fired. The most common method of preventing premature functioning is to interpose some sort of mechanical block which is removed only by the spinning of the shell after it has begun its flight up the bore. Another system is to anchor the firing pin securely enough to resist acceleration, but not so strongly as to resist the crushing on impact.

Detonation on impact, however, is not always desirable. In some applications, it is advantageous to have the shell pass through the first obstacle; e.g., pass through the roof of a building to burst inside. This demands some form of delay mechanism to hold off the detonation for a fraction of a second after the fuze has impacted. A 'graze' fuze (British terminology) in which the deceleration of the fuze allows a detonator to run forward and strike a firing pin, will do this with no further complication, since the actual run-forward of the detonator absorbs the necessary delay time. Another method is to use the initial impact to fire the detonator, make this ignite a short channel of powder to give the delay, and then use this to fire a second detonator which initiates the shell.

The Americans were among the first to produce a fuze which incorporated both immediate and delayed action, with a selector device to allow the gunner to choose whichever he needed. A simple impact needle and detonator in the tip of the fuze flashed down a central tube to ignite a small magazine which, in turn, fired the booster. This gave 'Super-quick' action; if delay were needed, a slotted plug in the side of the fuze was turned. This locked a spin-actuated shutter so that it closed the central flash tube. The impact detonator still functioned, but the flash was prevented from actuating the fuze magazine by the shutter. Instead, a second detonator, in the body of the fuze, now ran forward, struck a needle, ignited a short delay unit and then fired the magazine, giving about 0.15sec. delay. The British percussion fuze No. 119 performed the same tasks, but took the impact element out of action by simply screwing a heavy steel cap over the tip of the fuze.

Base fuzes all work on the 'graze' principle, by virtue of their position; they cannot work by direct impact. Beyond that, there is little to say, except that fuzes for use with piercing shell usually had additional delays in order to allow the shell to pass through considerable thicknesses of armour before detonating.

The proximity fuze has been more fully described in the introductory section. It was originally developed for use with anti-aircraft guns, but its use was extended to field artillery so as to be able to burst

Above: An American proximity fuze T97 cut open. In the nose is the radio section, with a perforated plate antenna embedded in the plastic nose section. In the central section lies the battery, its stack of plates surrounding an ampoule of acid. In the rear section are the various bore-safety switches, both electrical and mechanical, ending in the fuze magazine. **Left:** The discarding sabot projectile for the 6pdr gun; (right) cut open to show the tungsten core.

shells above the ground in conditions of poor visibility, when visual correction of time fuzes was not possible; it was first used in the field application in the Battle of the Ardennes in December 1944.

Time fuzes are used where it is required to burst the shell in the air, either to shower fragments on to unprotected troops beneath, or, for example, to eject smoke canisters or propaganda leaflets over them. Two basic types exist; combustion, and mechanical. The combustion fuze relies on the burning away, at a carefully controlled rate, of a length of gunpowder. It is adjusted for length in the act of 'setting' the fuze before loading into the gun, and is ignited by the sudden acceleration of the shell causing a freely-mounted detonator to run down and strike a needle at the instant the gun fires. At the end of the set time, the gunpowder ignites the fuze magazine and causes the shell to function.

Combustion fuzes are susceptible to moisture, to shell spin, to atmospheric pressure and several other agencies, all of which means that they are reliable to about 2% of the shell's time of flight. In other words, a shell fired at a range, over which, it took 20 seconds to reach the target, might burst 0.4sec. before or after the selected point. And with the shell moving at about 1,500 feet per second, this meant that the burst might well occur anywhere in a 1,200 foot area.

Mechanical fuzes fall into two classes, the spring driven 'Krupp Mechanism', favoured by the British, and the centrifugally-driven 'Junghans Mechanism', favoured by the Americans. In either case, the firing of the shell releases the mechanism, which is then driven by the motive power and controlled by a clock-type regulator train. At the end of the set time, a firing pin is released on to a detonator. Mechanical fuzes are less susceptible to outside influences, (though they frequently have to be 'tuned' to specific guns) and are, therefore, more accurate. A 'zone' of about half of one percent is average, which brings our 1,500ft/sec. shell to a bursting zone of about 300 feet.

AMMUNITION MARKINGS

The ammunition marking system used by the British Army was put together in the 1870s. It was subsequently modified and adapted as new ammunition types came along, which put it under some strain during the First World War, and completely wrecked it during the Second. A new system, which was little more than a rationalization of the old, was put into effect in 1944, but this failed to make the grade and had to be replaced by a completely new system in 1948. Then came NATO standardization, and a fresh system appeared in the 1960s

Ignoring the post-war events, a full description of the British marking system as it stood in 1944 would take up thirty or forty pages; we cannot afford this, nor, to be honest, would such a detailed exposition be of much value. What follows, therefore, is simply a brief outline, sufficient to allow identification of a piece of ammunition with its parent weapon, and allow modellers to achieve some accuracy of detail.

The American system was far less complicated than the British, but it had grown up in a haphazard way and contained a few ambiguities, and, also in 1944, a new system was adopted which survives today and which formed the basis of the NATO system. It, too, will be covered only in outline.

The British System

Projectiles have to be painted to preserve them from rust and corrosion, and it is logical, therefore, to use different colours of body paint to distinguish between different types of projectile. The important 'Basic Body Colours' were as follows.

High-explosive shell	Buff.
Smoke shell	Light Brunswick Green.
Flare shell	White.
Star shell	White.
Incendiary shell	Dull red.
Chemical shell	Grey.

All others – shot, shrapnel, propaganda, etc. – were black.

Superimposed on this body colour came various symbols to indicate features of the shell. The most important were as follows.

Red ring near nose	Filled with explosive substance.
Green band around HE	TNT or Amatol filling.
Blue band around HE	RDX filling.
Black band around smoke	Base ejection.
Two green discs at opposite sides of shell nose	HE shell with a smoke box.
Black band in front of driving band	Gun shell, where a howitzer of the same calibre existed.
Black from rear of driving band to base	Non-standard shell (e.g. 80lb 5.5in HE shell, when 100lb was standard).
Red star on shoulder	Star shell.

Green band on chemical	Non-persistent toxic gas.
Two green bands on chemical	Persistent toxic gas.
Red band on chemical	Non-persistent irritant gas.
Two red bands on chemical	Persistent irritant gas.

It should be noted that the red ring near the nose was used on any article requiring magazine storage; even a solid steel shot bore the ring if it had a tracer in it. The normal marking was a solid red ring, but HE shells filled with explosive which tended to melt or soften in high temperatures

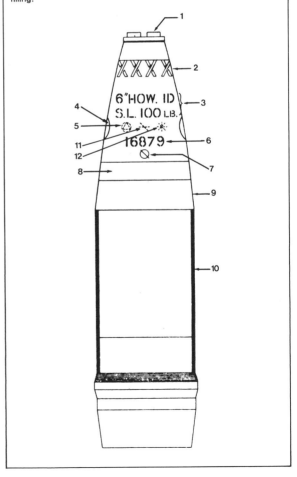

Below: Typical markings on a British high-explosive shell of the war period.
1. Top of plug to be painted blue; 2. Ring of red crosses when suitable for hot climates, otherwise a plain red ring; 3. Calibre and mark as applicable; 4. Two green discs stencilled diametrically opposite on shell fitted with smoke box. 'A' or 'B' stencilled on discs denotes type of smoke box; 5. Series number in ring distinguishing filled lot; 6. Design number of method of filling; 7. Fraction when filled other than 80/20; 8. Green band; 9. Body painted buff colour; 10. Two longitudinal black stripes, diametrically opposite, on the 4.5in howitzer shell (denoting shell is fitted with economy type driving band); 11. Date of filling (month and year); 12. Monogram of firm or station filling.

6"HOW. ID
S.L. 100 LB.

16879

were marked with a ring of red 'X's to indicate that they were not to be sent to the tropics.

Finally, plain-language lettering stencilled on the shell, gave information about the weapon for which it was intended, details of the filling, date and place of filling, and any other information which, from time to time, somebody thought it vital for the gunners to know. This could get quite recondite; at one time there was a shortage of smoke boxes to put into HE shell (to allow observers to spot the burst). The shells filled without boxes not only omitted the smoke-box marking, but had a special marking added to show that they did not have smoke boxes, which struck some of us as a bit superfluous.

Cartridges were marked by having the nature of the weapon and the weight and nature of the propellant stencilled on the side of the case or the bag. The detail about the propellant included the size of the Cordite sticks. For the 25pdr, in which a smaller size was used for Charge One than for Charges Two and Three, the side of the case was a mine of information.

The changes that took place in the system in 1944 were not such as to change the basic principles, and the information given above can be taken as correct for the entire period of the war.

The U.S. System

The pre-war American system also based the shell identification on body colours.

High-explosive shell	Yellow.
Low-explosive – e.g. shrapnel	Red.
Chemical (including smoke)	Blue-grey.
Practice & dummy	Black.

The only symbols added were from two to six small squares painted close to the shell nose to indicate whether it was of correct nominal weight (three squares) or more or less, so that the gunners could apply a correction, and various coloured bands around chemical shell to indicate the contents. These were red and green for poison gas, using the same system as outlined above for Britain (Britain adopted the American system since it was simpler than the original British method) and a yellow band for a smoke shell. Further information as to the type of gun, explosive filler, and manufacture were stencilled in plain letters on the shell. The accompanying drawing indicates these details.

Cartridges were marked simply with the nature of the weapon, the lot number of the powder, and the powder maker; other information was supplied on a printed label attached to the cartridge, or in the packing box. Cased charges for guns also had black bands around the body, or stripes on the base to indicate service or reduced charges.

In 1944, the projectile marking system was changed, insofar as the basic body colours were concerned, to the following.

High-explosive	Olive drab.
Armour-piercing shell	Olive drab.

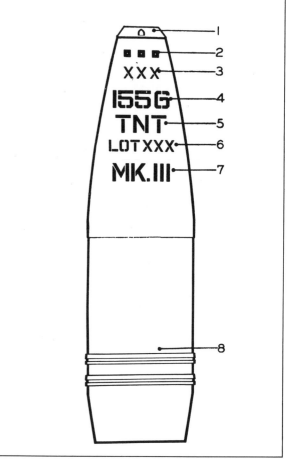

Below: Markings on an American high-explosive shell; this picture shows the system in force in 1941, when the shell was yellow with black markings. The only important changes that took place during the war were the change of colour to olive drab with yellow stencilling; the removal of item 3 (the mean weight); and the addition of an Ammunition Identification Code symbol (e.g. P1EAA) on the body of the shell above the driving band.
1. Adapter may or may not be painted; 2. Weight zone marks; 3. Mean or normal weight of shell (unfuzed) in pounds; 4. Calibre and type of cannon (G—gun; H—howitzer). GH is the authorized marking for shell interchangeable in gun or howitzer; 5. Filler. Initials indicate kind of explosive. May be as shown or AM 50-50 or AM 80-20, for Amatol loaded shell; 6. Lot number of filled shell; 7. Mark number of shell; 8. Calibre and type of cannon, mark number of shell, initials or symbol of machining plant and inspection stamps (stamped on shell under paint). Note: All stencilling is with black paint.

AP without explosive	Black.
Smoke & chemical	Grey.
Practice	Blue.
Shrapnel	Red.

The remainder of the marking system remained the same, except that the colour, in which the details were stencilled on the shell, changed so as to give the desired contrast; explosive and chemical shells had their markings in yellow, AP and practice in white, shrapnel in black. Shortly after the introduction of the system, illuminating (star) shells were introduced, and these were given white as their basic colour, with black stencilling.

Glossary

It is unavoidable, when discussing a technical subject, that obscure technical words and jargon creep in. This is not simply an attempt to blind with science, it is a recognition that certain words form a convenient short-hand of speech and save long explanations in constant use. For example, it is much easier to say 'breech ring' than to say 'the large piece of metal at the back of the gun into which the breech block closes'. Several words and phrases have been used in this book in places where an explanation is not convenient, and to save the need to make such explanations at frequent intervals, this Glossary attempts to explain all the technical jargon.

'A' Tube. Guns are rarely made of a simple lump of metal with a hole bored through. Most of the guns mentioned in this book are of 'built-up' construction (for the definition of both these terms, see below) and the innermost tube of the barrel, that one in which the rifling grooves are cut, and up which the shell travels, was known as the 'A' tube in British terminology, the various layers being lettered outwards. Having an 'A' tube meant that it was easier to re-line the gun when it became worn, since instead of having to scrap the whole mass of the barrel, the 'A' tube could be removed and a new one inserted. In large guns, an 'Inner A Tube' was used; here the 'A' tube was unrifled, but of the necessary strength to form the foundation of the gun, and the 'Inner A Tube' was a removable liner to allow repair without excessive dismantling.

Air Blast Gear. Used on heavy coast-defence guns, this was an arrangement whereby compressed air could be blown into the chamber via a port in the breech ring. It was operated immediately after firing and before the breech was opened, so that all the smoke and poisonous gases, left in the bore after the combustion of the propelling charge, were expelled from the muzzle. When the breech was opened, therefore, no fumes entered the gun-house, turret or casemate.

Asbury Breech Mechanism. An interrupted screw breech mechanism usually found on bag-charge guns, but occasionally on case-charge guns – e.g. the British 18pdr Mk 4. The essential features are (1) that the breech screw is of the Welin pattern (see below); (2) that the operating lever is vertical and on the right-hand side; (3) that there is a cam gear which automatically converts the opening rotation of the screw into a withdrawing movement, and, on closing, converts the closing movement into a rotation of the screw. The nett effect is to have a fast-acting breech mechanism which can be opened and closed very smoothly by simply pulling straight down on the handle and allowing the cam mechanism to swing it open.

Auto-Frettaged. A gun barrel is auto-frettaged when it has been pre-stressed by filling it with fluid during manufacture and then subjecting it to a hydraulic pressure substantially greater than the pressure it is expected to sustain during service. This radially expands the fibres of the metal; the inner layers expand beyond their elastic limit and take up a permanent 'set', while the outer layers are expanded below their elastic limit and, when the hydraulic pressure is released, these layers contract in an attempt to regain their former dimensions. Because of the expanded inner layers, however, they cannot do this and thus they place the inner layers in a state of permanent compression which strengthens the gun. Auto-frettage allows a certain degree of strength to be obtained in a lighter gun barrel than would be needed without such treatment, or, for the same weight of barrel, allows the gun to be stronger. In American terminology, the words 'Cold Worked' are frequently used in place of 'auto-frettaged'.

Autosight. Or Automatic Sight. Form of direct sight, used with light and medium coast artillery guns, which acts as a self-contained range-finder. If the height above sea level is precisely known (which it is, in coast artillery) this height becomes the base of a range-finding triangle, the 'side' of which is the surface of the sea, and the hypotenuse of which is the line from the sight to the target. If the angle of depression of the sight is known, the range to the target can be calculated. An autosight is fitted with a cam device, precisely ground to match the height of the sight above the sea, so that as the gun is elevated, the telescope of the sight moves in a strict relationship with the range. When the crosswire of the sight is laid on the waterline of a ship, the gun is at the exact elevation to hit that target, and no further range-finding is needed. Adjustments for tidal rise and fall are, of course, incorporated.

BL. British terminology used in gun nomenclatures, e.g. Ordnance

BL 5.5in Gun. The letters mean 'Breech Loading', but they imply rather more than that; they imply that the gun uses bag charges, and that the system of obturation (see below) is contained in the breech mechanism in the form of a resilient pad which is pressed tightly against the rear of the chamber.

Balanced Pillar Mounting. System of mounting a light coast defence gun on top of a telescoping pillar, so that when not required for action it could be lowered behind a protective parapet. Not the same as a disappearing carriage, because the gun stayed exposed throughout a period of firing and did not go into concealment after every shot. Found in some Australian forts, and used by US Coast Artillery, but extremely rare by 1939.

Barbette Mounting. System of emplacing a coast artillery gun so that the muzzle was just clear of a protective parapet, and most of the mounting was protected. From the front, all that could be seen was the gun shield and the muzzle; beneath this lay the concrete apron of the parapet, and it is from this that the expression, derived from the French word for 'bearded' is said to have come, the apron forming the 'beard' beneath the gun. Personally, I think it as far-fetched as a bucket of rice from China, but that is the official explanation.

Breech Ring. Metal reinforcing ring around the rear end of the gun barrel and into which the breech block or screw fastens when closed. It is not necessarily ring-shaped. If the breech is closed by a sliding block, the ring may be termed 'open jawed' if the rear surface of the breech block is fully visible at all times, or 'closed jawed' if the block is working in a mortise-like tube cut within the ring so that its rear surface is not fully visible at any time. Examples: the 25pdr used an open-jawed ring, the 105mm howitzer, a closed-jawed type.

Buffer. That part of the recoil system which absorbs the recoil force as the gun is moving backwards. Invariably some form of hydraulic brake.

Built-Up Gun. Method of gun construction in which tubes are shrunk over one another to place the bore layers in compression and the outer layers in tension. The amount of shrinkage is sufficient to prevent rotation of the various tubes, and the tubes are made thick enough to withstand girder stress and so prevent the muzzle from drooping excessively. Longitudinal movement is prevented by shoulders on the interior tubes contacting abutments on the exterior tubes.

Calibre. Diameter across the bore of a gun from the top of one 'land' to the bottom of the opposite groove. (The 'land' being that part of the barrel left between the grooves when the rifling is cut.) The word is also used to express the length of the bore; a fifty-calibre gun had a bore length fifty times its calibre. Thus an 8in 45-calibre gun is $8 \times 45 = 360$in long. Broadly speaking, the greater the calibre-length, the more powerful the gun may be expected to be.

Casemate. A masonry or concrete structure inside which, a coast-defence gun is mounted so that it fires through a port and is protected by the structure.

Chase. The tapered portion of the gun barrel between the muzzle and the jacket or trunnions.

Crane Liners. An American development in 1942–45, Crane Liners were hardened steel inserts which were shaped internally to the contours of the forward end of the chamber and the early part of the rifling of a particular gun. The barrel was then cut away and the liner was inserted when the original rifling had worn sufficiently to impair the accuracy of the gun. In this way, it was hoped to prolong the life of the gun in an economical manner. Similar devices were developed in Britain during the First World War, known as 'Short bore and chamber liners', but neither these nor the Crane Liner were very successful.

Equilibrators. Also known as Balancing Presses, these are the method of supporting the imperfectly balanced gun so that the gunlayer does not have to use excessive force on the handwheels in order to elevate and depress. Generally, they take the form of springs pushing upwards on the cradle, though some designs use hydropneumatic cylinders with compressed air or nitrogen as the 'spring' force. In the US 155mm Gun/8in Howitzer carriage, the equilibrators pull on the cradle, being mounted on horns above the trunnions.

Face Hardened. Type of armour plate used on tanks. As the name implies, the face of the plate is made extremely hard by carbonizing and heat treatment, while the remainder of the plate is less hard but more tough and resilient. Face hardened plate places a great strain on the tip of the shot as it strikes, and was countered by adopting capped shot.

Firing Pedestal. A form of collapsible jack which can be carried beneath the axle of a split-trail carriage, and lowered so that the weight of the gun rests on the pedestal and on the two trail ends. This gives good support, prevents the gun bouncing on its pneumatic tyres when fired, and makes the gun rather easier to swing through large angles.

Firing Segments. Similar in principle to a firing pedestal, but in the form of steel segments which swing on the axle, inside the wheels, and which can be dropped, and the gun heaved back, so that the weight is taken by the segments instead of the wheels.

Fisa Protectors. Another American device for combatting erosive wear in high-velocity guns, the Fisa Protector was a steel sleeve which surrounded the cartridge neck and mouth, and the lower part of the projectile in a round of fixed ammunition. The gun chamber was cut away so that the Protector fitted snugly into the place where the chamber mouth and commencement of rifling would normally have been. When the gun fired, the protector acted as both these and also took the erosive punishment. It was then extracted with the cartridge case. Much work was put into this idea, but it was never brought to perfection and the project was abandoned shortly after the war.

Homogeneous. Homogeneous armour plate is of the same consistency throughout, and thus offers a constant resistance to shot, unlike face-hardened plate.

Hoops. American terminology for the various layers in a built-up gun, which surround the basic tube and place it under compression.

Hydropneumatic. Any device relying on liquid and gas for its operation, but, in artillery applications, generally used to define a recoil system in which the recoil energy is absorbed by some form of hydraulic buffer, and the gun is returned to the firing position by compressed air or gas.

Hydro-Spring. Recoil system in which the recoil energy is absorbed by a hydraulic buffer and the gun is returned to the firing position by the power of springs, compressed during the recoil movement.

Hypervelocity. Generally used to identify any gun firing at a muzzle velocity of 3,000 ft/sec. or greater. The term was coined when such velocities were rare; as they became more common, towards the end of the war, the term fell largely into disuse and was only retained to identify experimental weapons with abnormal velocities.

Jacket. This is defined differently in British and American usage. In British ordnance, the jacket is the outermost tube of the barrel. In American ordnance, it is one of the inner sections, a tube which surrounds the barrel tube either wholly or partly; beneath the jacket there are tubes; above the jacket there are hoops.

Krupp Cemented Plate. An early form of face-hardened plate, in which a hardened and carburized plate was welded to the face of a toughened plate. Invented by Krupp, it was widely adopted for battleship armour and, as such, it became the criterion of coast defence armour-piercing shell performance. Frequently abbreviated to 'KC Plate'.

Limited Standard. American expression, equivalent to the British term 'obsolescent'. In effect, an article approved for service for so long as it remains acceptable or usable, in the knowledge that a better article ('standard') is available for first-line service.

Liner. The inner tube of a barrel which can be inserted and removed without having to completely dismantle the gun hoops. The word is also used to describe an inner barrel of a different calibre inserted into a 'parent' gun, e.g. the 3.7in

Mk 6 gun used a 3.7in 'liner' in the jacket of a 4.5in gun.

Lock. The firing mechanism for a bag-charge gun, attached to the outer side of the breech screw. It takes the form of a miniature breech, and is loaded with a 'tube' (British) or 'primer' (US) which resembles a blank cartridge for a rifle. When this is fired by the lock, a flash passes down the vent (a hole bored axially through the breech screw) to ignite the propelling charge inside the gun chamber.

Magslip. Form of electrical transmission system used to pass gun data from a control-room or predictor to a gun, where it is displayed in the form of dial readings.

Monobloc. Gun barrel made from a single block of metal, without tubes or hoops. Generally surrounded wholly or partly by a jacket, if only for convenience in attaching to the carriage. Generally, but not necessarily, auto-frettaged.

Obturation. The sealing of the gun breech against the unwanted escape of propelling gases when the cartridge is fired. Can be done in one of two ways; either by using a metallic cartridge case which expands against the sides of the chamber and the face of the breech block so as to form a seal; or by using a resilient pad, in the breech screw assembly, which is pressed tightly against the rear face of the gun chamber and held there by the thrust of the breech screw.

Preponderance. The degree of imbalance of a gun pivoting about its trunnions. If the gun were fitted with the trunnions at the centre of gravity there would be no preponderance, and this has sometimes been done. But in general, it is desirable to fit the trunnions closer to the breech so that the breech does not strike the ground or some part of the mounting when the gun is fired at an angle of elevation. Moving the trunnions back will lead to muzzle preponderance, and this can be countered by equilibrators so that the handwheel effort needed to elevate or depress the gun is kept within reasonable bounds. Perfect balance is neither desirable nor is it achieved; a slight muzzle preponderance is retained, so

that the elevating gears are kept under a slight load at all times, thereby taking up any backlash in the gears.

QF. British terminology; used in description of guns, e.g. Ordnance QF 25pdr Mk 1. The letters mean Quick Firing, but, like their opposite, BL, they mean more than they say. QF implies that the obturation is performed by a metallic cartridge case.

Recuperator. That part of the recoil system which returns the gun to the firing position when recoil has stopped. Usually either a spring or a cylinder of compressed air or gas, the recoil movement places additional pressure on them and thus builds up sufficient energy to return the gun. The process of building up this energy also assists the buffer in absorbing the recoil force. Recuperation can also be achieved by gravity or by counterweights.

Retracting Gear. Used with American coast barbettes (early pattern) and disappearing carriages, the retracting gear was a winch and rope by which the gun could be pulled back or down to the recoiled position. With barbette guns, this was done for purposes of repair, with disappearing guns, in order to conceal them beneath the parapet without having to fire them. With both types of carriage it was regularly used as a means of testing and exercising the recoil arrangements, heaving the guns back and then letting gravity return them to the firing position.

Substitute Standard. American terminology; a piece of equipment accepted for service on the understanding that it is second-best and that it will be replaced as soon as the better model is available.

Selsyn. An abbreviation of 'Self Synchronous' and is another term for a data transmission system using synchronous motors to position dials on the gun.

Stacked Charge. Type of bag charge used in American service, particularly with heavy coast defence guns, in which the individual grains of propellant were carefully 'stacked', layer by layer, into the bag and the bag was then tightly laced so that it was comparatively rigid and thus easier to handle and load. Stacking also improved ignition, since the internal perforations of the grains were aligned to some degree and allowed rapid flame transmission from one end of the charge to the other.

Thrust Rings. Raised rings, formed in the outer hoop or jacket of a gun, which engaged in suitable lugs in the gun cradle or some other component of the recoil system, so as to transfer the thrust of the recoiling gun to the recoil system. Used only where the gun did not have trunnions. Examples are the British 25pdr gun and 9.2in coast gun.

Travelling Lock. Clamping device to hold the elevating portions of a mobile gun while travelling, so that the elevating and traversing gears are not strained by vibration and bumping.

Washout. A water jet built in to the chamber of a heavy gun, so that water can be squirted in to extinguish any smouldering residue from the bag charge before the breech is opened. Such residue is rarely met, but if, as is generally the case with coast and naval guns, somebody is standing close behind the breech with the next round's bag charge in his arms, it only needs one flash-back to kill everybody in the turret, and the draught generated by the breech block swinging open can easily fan a smouldering remnant into a blaze which will ignite the gas-air mixture in the chamber mouth with spectacular and disastrous effects. A washout is also worth its weight in gold in the event of a misfired bag charge; this, too, could be smouldering and could explode violently as the breech is opened in order to remove it. But a squirt from the washout removes all danger.

Welin Screw. Type of breech screw which has the surface divided into a number of segments which are struck with varying radii. The number of plain segments is less than half the total number, varying from one-third to one-quarter. Thus the screw can be entered into the breech and locked by a fraction of a turn which corresponds to the number of segments; e.g., the British 6in Gun Mk 7 screw had four threaded and two plain segments, and it was locked in place with one-sixth of a turn. The advantage of the Welin screw is that, due to the additional bearing surface obtained by having the segments of different radii, the necessary strength can be obtained with a short length of screw, and this, in turn, means that the screw can be swung from the breech aperture without having to be axially withdrawn. The short screw also means a shorter breech in the gun and this, in turn, reduces the gun weight.

Wire-Wound Gun. A built-up gun in which one layer of the assembly is formed of wire strip, tightly wound. The advantages are that the whole of the wire can be tested for strength, which is impossible with a forged tube; by winding with various tensions, the tension on the gun can be adjusted layer by layer; wire has twice the tensile strength of forgings; and should the wire fail in service, the effect is local and is not likely to split along the length of the gun, as would a tube. The drawback is that wire gives no longitudinal strength to the gun, and it is necessary to enclose it completely in a full-length jacket; even with this, wire-wound guns show a distinct tendency to droop at the muzzle. About 185 miles of wire were used in winding the British 15in gun, and this was wrapped in 79 layers at the breech end, tapering to 20 layers at the muzzle.

Below: Loading a 12in Mortar M1890. (See data page 212.)

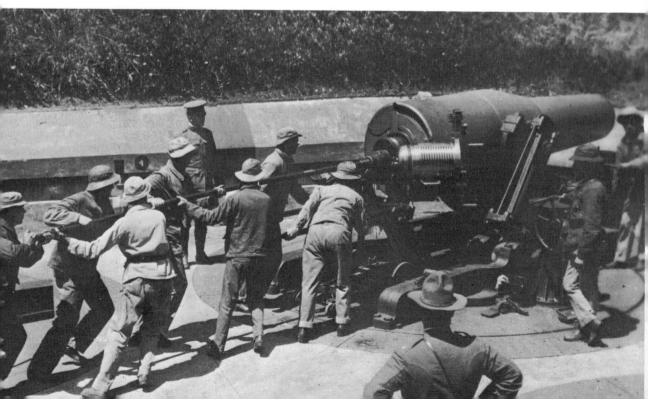